Norbert Elias

For my wife
Barbara
and for my friends
Joop and Maria Goudsblom

Norbert Elias

Civilization and the Human Self-Image

STEPHEN MENNELL

Basil Blackwell

First published 1989

Basil Blackwell Ltd
108 Cowley Road, Oxford, OX4 1JF, UK

Basil Blackwell Inc.
432 Park Avenue South, Suite 1503
New York, NY 10016, USA

British Library Cataloguing in Publication Data
Mennell, Stephen
    Norbert Elias: civilization and the human self-image.
1. Sociology. Theories of Elias, Norbert, 1897–
I. Title
301'.092'4
ISBN 0–631–15533–3

Library of Congress Cataloging in Publication Data
Mennell, Stephen.
    Norbert Elias: civilization and the human self-image /
Stephen Mennell.
    p.   cm.
    Bibliography: p.
    Includes index.
    ISBN 0–631–15533–3
    1. Elias, Norbert.   2. Civilization–Philosophy.
    3. Sociology–Europe–History–20th century.
    I. Title.
CB18.E44M46 1989   901–dc19

Set in 10 on 11½pt Ehrhardt
Disc translation by Hope Services, Abingdon
Printed in Great Britain by
Bookcraft Ltd, Bath, Avon

Contents

Contents   vii

Preface

I first met Norbert Elias in 1972. Quite by chance, I had been asked by a publisher to collaborate in the translation of his book *What is Sociology?* Until then I had known nothing of his work. Unusually among early enthusiasts for his sociology, I was never either Elias's student or his colleague.

There were inordinate delays in publication of my translation – an experience, I discovered, not uncommon for Elias's translators and publishers. This did not deter me. I was fascinated by his writings and by his approach to sociology, which seemed to me to go a long way towards solving some of the problems of sociological theory I had been struggling with since my time as a graduate student at Harvard and in my early years of teaching at Exeter. Perhaps most central of these problems was the apparently unbridgeable gulf between so-called 'microsociology', dealing with individual people in face to face groups, and 'macrosociology', dealing with large-scale social structures and processes. Eventually I plucked up courage to use his ideas in teaching, and embarked on research on the history of eating, in which they were also put to work. Courage was needed only because Elias's is still very much a minority standpoint among social scientists and historians.

I am convinced that Elias is one of the most important sociological thinkers of the twentieth century, whose work is of relevance and interest far beyond a single academic discipline. Indeed, only the most outstanding of academics achieve the distinction of having books written about them during their lifetime. In my opinion, such a book about Elias's work is overdue. For I have long been dismayed by the disjuncture between my reading of his work and the notions that some of my fellow sociologists attribute to him (now that they have begun to take cognizance of him). I have written this book to help readers to find their way around his voluminous and scattered publications in two or three languages.

Norbert Elias is a good friend of mine, and for that reason it has to be said emphatically that this book is absolutely not an 'official guide' to his work. He shares no responsibility for its contents. It is understandable that he has misgivings about such a book being published in his lifetime. For one thing, his work is not complete – he is still writing and publishing extensively. For another, there is a risk that a critical exposition of his published writings may be read *instead* of the writings themselves. I must emphasize that my book is intended not as a substitute for reading Elias's own work but as a stimulus to do so. Finally, and most importantly, Elias feels that his work speaks directly for itself. There I must partly and reluctantly disagree with him. Some of it certainly does speak directly and with great vividness; but it requires a vast amount of work, and a willingness to abandon some old-established habits of thought, to come to terms with his work as a whole. Many colleagues have told me over the years that they have never come properly to grips with Elias, not even teaching their students about him, because they found it difficult to place him intellectually and to work out how all the aspects of his work fit together.

One reason for the difficulty is that, even when the content is at its most brilliant, the architecture of some of his work is very complicated. In this book I have therefore sought to make the principal elements in his thinking more easily visible, without actually disentangling them, since their entanglement is an essential characteristic. I have tried to indicate through the references all the scattered places where he tackles a particular issue.

Since Elias's standpoint has remained remarkably consistent throughout his career – compared with, say, Max Weber or Talcott Parsons, Elias's point of view shows only minor changes of emphasis and attention, though it has greatly broadened in application – it might be thought that an exposition of his views would be quite easy. But that is counterbalanced by the complex intertwining of substantive research and theorizing which is an indispensable quality of his work. In Elias's case, one simply cannot outline the 'theory' apart from evidence from which it springs – his work is 'theoretical-empirical' at once. I have on the whole emphasized the substantive content of his work in the earlier chapters, only gradually making his vision of social science explicit.

I have tried not to clutter the exposition with too many asides to the arguments of Elias's critics. Where those criticisms clearly rest on a misreading or inattentive reading of what Elias says, I have tended to answer them tacitly in the course of exposition. Major difficulties, of course, need more direct treatment, which they receive in chapter 9 and elsewhere.

Nor have I expended much effort on a 'history of ideas' dissection of Elias's work. For one thing, my friends Hermann Korte and Artur Bogner will shortly be publishing books dealing with the milieu within which Elias's ideas took shape, and with his intellectual relations to Max Weber and the Frankfurt School. Besides, it is central to his thinking that knowledge grows and develops over many generations, through the refinement and development of earlier ideas. That is true of Elias's own work, but, as he once remarked, 'If you look back over your shoulder long enough, you get a stiff neck.' Looking at it *analytically*, it may be seen that some of his phrases, concepts and concerns are taken over from earlier writers. What I hope I have conveyed in this book, however, is the extraordinarily powerful and original *synthesis* which Elias creates. His books and articles abound in ideas and suggestions which cry out for further research, testing, elaboration, modification and extension. Rather than writing a 'history of ideas', I have tried instead to show how Elias himself has extended and developed his earlier ideas, and also how younger generations of social scientists have taken them up in a vigorous and varied research tradition hitherto little known in the English-speaking world. (A bibliography, edited by Willem Kranendonck, of the work of the Dutch sociologists influenced by Elias is in preparation for publication in English.)

This book was written as part of a wider programme of work on the 'reversibility of civilizing processes', for which the Nuffield Foundation awarded me one of its Social Science Research Fellowships in 1986–7. I spent much of that year once again enjoying the hospitality of St Antony's College, Oxford; I must especially thank my host there, Theodore Zeldin. In 1987–8, I was a Fellow-in-Residence at the Netherlands Institute for Advanced Study in the Humanities and Social Sciences (NIAS), Wassenaar, Netherlands. In these convivial surroundings I spent the happiest year of my academic career; the list of my friends from many different disciplines is too long to thank by name, though they know how much I owe them. I must especially thank my fellow NIAS-barman, Zdzisław Mach, who read most of the typescript as it neared completion.

Three people read each chapter as it was written: Joop Goudsblom, Eric Dunning and Cas Wouters. Their deep knowledge of Elias's work immeasurably improved my book, though none of them can be blamed for remaining faults: they could all have done it better! Others who read particular chapters and gave valuable advice were Godfried van Benthem van den Bergh, Nico Wilterdink, Anton Hemerijk, Mike Featherstone, Bill Jordan and Bill Forsythe. And, as always, my wife Barbara told me when I became boring, edited the text professionally, helped me type some of it and tolerated my prolonged absence. Anne Simpson, a NIAS expatriate who has not quite gone native yet, typed the rest. Bark Jonker supplied photographs of Norbert Elias, and the *Mittelalterliche Hausbuch* engravings are reproduced by permission of the Bodleian Library, Oxford. My thanks to them all.

Stephen Mennell
NIAS
Wassenaar, April 1988

PART I
Introduction

1

Norbert Elias:
a Determined Life in Uncertain Times

'It is as if Norbert Elias has always been an old man', observed a Dutch newspaper in 1984.[1] Elias, a German sociologist who was a refugee from Hitler and lived the best part of forty years in England, had to wait a long time for recognition. When it came, it was in his native land and particularly the Netherlands – not in his adopted country of citizenship – that he found himself an intellectual celebrity. By then he was in his late seventies or his eighties. In a notably vigorous old age, Elias came at last to be regarded by many social scientists 'as having one of the world's most original and penetrating sociological minds'.[2] His writings, moreover, address issues of concern and fascination to people well beyond the narrow world of professional social science.

The time fuse which so long delayed Elias's impact was set by the National Socialists' accession to power in 1933 when Elias, as Karl Mannheim's academic assistant in Frankfurt, barely had his foot on the first rung of the German academic career ladder. Eventually, he found himself in London, not even at first able to speak English, and with few prospects. He set to work for three years and produced his masterpiece, *Über den Prozess der Zivilisation*. It was published in Switzerland in 1939. That was not the most propitious year for the publication of a large, two-volume work in German, by a Jew, on, of all things, civilization. It remained largely unknown and unread among both the German- and English-speaking publics for thirty years. Elias himself remained in England, leading an insecure existence on the fringes of academic life. Only in the last eight years before reaching retirement age did he obtain a university post, at Leicester.

During the quarter century 1940–65 he published little and was little regarded, but he continued to write, research and think. With great determination and inner sense of purpose he developed, extended and refined the ideas presented in *The Civilizing Process* (as his book was later to be known in

English). That huge work was ambitious enough, tracing as it did the 'civilizing' of manners and personality in Western Europe since the late Middle Ages, and showing how this was related to the formation of states and monopolization of power within them. But Elias always saw it as more than a single thesis. It was also a paradigm to be developed as a model of a sociology which represents a radical rejection of many of the basic assumptions of conventional sociology.

Yet the scale of Elias's undertaking was revealed only in the years following his retirement. *The Established and the Outsiders* appeared, in English, in 1965. The decisive event, however, was the republication in 1969, when Elias was already over 70 years old, of the original German text of *The Civilizing Process*. Elias was more and more sought after as a visiting teacher in German and Dutch universities, and eventually returned to live on the continent. Most of his later books and essays therefore appeared first in German. The books include (under their English titles) *The Court Society, What is Sociology?, The Loneliness of the Dying, Involvement and Detachment* (collected essays on the sociology of knowledge and the sciences), *Time: An Essay, The Quest for Excitement* (collected essays, originating from English, on the sociology of sport), *Humana Conditio* (subtitled 'Observations on the Development of Mankind in the Forty Years since the Second World War'), and *The Society of Individuals* (containing essays ranging in date from 1939 to 1987). A selection of his poems, entitled *Los der Menschen*, was also published on the occasion of his ninetieth birthday in 1987. Other works, such as his study of Mozart, *The Bourgeois Artist in Court Society*, have remained incomplete or unpublished.

English translations of Elias's main works began at last to appear in the late 1970s and 1980s. Yet most English-speaking sociologists have only a partial and often superficial knowledge of his writings. Still less are they acquainted with the work – almost wholly in German or Dutch – of the many younger sociologists who, influenced by Elias, have begun through their own research to extend, test and develop Elias's ideas. My task in this book is to provide as best I can an overall view both of his work and theirs. Before turning to examine that work in detail, however, I shall say a little more about Elias's life and career, for in his own history are many clues to the development of his thought.

FROM BRESLAU TO HEIDELBERG VIA THE TRENCHES AND PHILOSOPHY

Norbert Elias was born in Breslau on 22 June 1897, the only child of Hermann and Sophie Elias, and lived there until he became a soldier in 1915. His parents were comfortably off. A dozen or so years before his birth, his father had set up a small enterprise manufacturing clothes, and led a hard-working life centred very much on his business and his family. Elias remembers his mother as 'the nicest mother I could have had . . . very cheerful, happy and affectionate'. They lived in a respectable neighbourhood, though it was certainly not in the best part of the city, and indeed there were slums and poor quarters nearby. Their apartment was spacious enough for parties; there were a cook and a nanny; in the same neighbourhood lived a grandmother and aunts, forming something of an extended family.

Breslau is today the city of Wrocław in Poland, but it was then an entirely German city of half a million, a prosperous old town at the centre of a thriving agricultural region, a cultural centre for the Silesian Catholic aristocracy, with an old-established Jesuit university which Elias was to attend. His father was probably frustrated by not having had enough money to attend university himself, and was determined that Norbert should study to be a doctor. Like the city they lived in, the Elias's were entirely German. Sophie Elias's grandparents had lived further east, in the part of Poland ruled by Russia, but her parents were German. Hermann Elias came from Posen (now Poznań) – a Polish-speaking city under German rule – but his parents and grandparents had been German and he attended a German high school there. In short, Norbert Elias remembers his father as being 'very German, very Prussian' – he even had the same style of moustache as the Kaiser – 'and nothing else'. But, of course, the family was also Jewish.

Asked during his old age whether, as a child, he felt more a member of the Jewish community or of the wider German society, Elias said that the very question reflected events that have unfolded since then. At the time, the issue did not arise. He knew as a child he was both a German and a Jew. He went to the synagogue a few times every year, on the great festival days. (After his childhood, he was never a believer in any form of religion.) But all the Breslau Jews felt they were Germans. Even so, they were alert for signs of antisemitism. Two incidents stick in Elias's memory. When he was about five and out with his nanny, some street urchins shouted 'Jew-boy, Jew-boy, Jew-boy' at him. Much later, an incident in class at the Johannesgymnasium when he was fifteen or sixteen brought home to him the situation of the Jews in Wilhelmine Germany. The school itself was exceptional in having several Jewish teachers on the staff. On this occasion, however, discussion came round to the careers the pupils wanted to follow in life, and Elias said he wanted to be a university professor. A class-mate retorted 'That career is blocked to you by birth!', a comment greeted with hilarity by the class and even by the teacher. 'And really', recalls Elias, 'it wasn't malicious – it was a shrewd observation. It stung me forcibly, because I had never realized that such a career was practically out of the question under the Kaiser.'

Yet these were isolated incidents. Again, reflecting in old age, Elias observed that from the point of view of his own theory of established-outsiders relations, 'for many people it must have been an extraordinarily annoying characteristic of Jews that they did not recognize their own inferiority.' The Jews of Breslau were full of optimism, naïvely so as it turned out. Pogroms were something that happened in barbaric Russia – they couldn't happen in Germany, under the Kaiser! They all felt very secure in Breslau.

Security was something which Elias specifically obtained from his own family and it is to this he attributes his staying power, tested when he wrote his books and no-one took any notice of them:

I put that down to the great feeling of security I had as a child . . . I have a basic feeling of great security, a feeling that in the end things will turn out for the best, and I attribute that to an enormous emotional security which my parents gave me as an only child.

I knew very early on what I wanted to do; I wanted to go to university, and I wanted to do research. I knew that from when I was young, and I have done it, even though sometimes it seemed impossible . . . I had great confidence that in the end my work would be recognized as a valuable contribution to knowledge about humanity.

Elias was fortunate in the school chosen for him by his parents. It was an outstanding humanistic Gymnasium with a distinguished staff, several of whom went on to be noted university teachers. Elias's mathematics, classics and French masters made a particular impression on him, and with another he was a member of a special group which met together to read Kant. At the Johannesgymnasium, Elias acquired the foundation of a humanistic, classical education then favoured by the German bourgeoisie. Starting with presents at his bar mitzvah, he took pride in collecting the works of the authors of the German classical era – Schiller, Goethe, Heine, Mörike, Eichendorff among others – in a uniform series. This early immersion in German literature was highly significant for his future study of human problems, even though he gradually came to realize the inadequacy of their philosophical-idealist, humanistic orientation. 'My own sociological orientation developed, so it seems to me, out of the struggle against their alienation from reality [*Wirklichkeits-fremdheit*] and its unmistakeable consequences in sociology itself' – though of course he only gradually became conscious of this.

Being deeply identified with the German cultural tradition did not make Elias a nationalist. The Kaiser was seen as a ridiculous figure, and, besides, nationalists were naturally antisemitic. When war came, his father was in favour of it, but Elias was against. 'I have never been a patriot – I was strongly anti.'

Such feelings did not keep him out of the war. He was a reluctant soldier, but had no choice; in 1915, when he reached eighteen and left school, he joined the Signals Corps, which his family thought would be safer than the infantry. He describes himself as one of the world's least apt soldiers, but also speculated that he may have owed his subsequent excellent health to military training: long marches with heavy packs made him very strong.

He was first sent to Poland, behind the Eastern front, but then to the Western front – near Péronne in northern France, where he saw dead men for the first time in his life. He lived underground in a dug-out, but does not remember ever being in the front line. His group's task was maintaining telegraph lines between the front and headquarters. It was not without danger – he remembers a comrade being shot next to him while repairing lines, and having to drag him back to safety. 'The front itself was horrible. Horrible.' He is not sure whether he suffered any form of shell-shock; perhaps recollection of it was repressed. At any rate he had no recollection of how he came to return to Breslau, and to a Germany in which only a few organizations – the officer corps, the Social Democratic Party, and the churches – remained intact. He remembers enrolling as a medical student, still in uniform, and watching a famous surgeon doing amputations, but the year 1918 and the beginnings of his university studies always remained a blur.

He registered at Breslau to read both philosophy and medicine, which was then quite possible, though it meant he had to work extremely hard. His interest in philosophy was of long standing; medicine he studied because his father wished him to, but he found himself keenly interested in that too. He completed the pre-clinical part of the medical course: that is to say, he attained the level equivalent to the first MB degree in a British university. Half way through the first clinical semester, however, he realized he could no longer ride both horses at once, and dropped medicine to concentrate on philosophy. That was not before having witnessed children being born, nor, more importantly, before receiving a solid grounding in one of the natural sciences.

His medical studies left a lasting mark on him. He had been fascinated by his work in the dissecting room, and retained an interest in the complex interconnections between muscles, bones, nerves and inner organs; the idea of complex interweaving of social interconnections into what he sometimes refers to as a social 'tissue' was to be prominent in his sociological work. He could not imagine, he said later, how a sociologist could form an adequate picture of human activities without an understanding of how the organism fits in. For instance, the communicative signalling of feelings to other humans is a primary peculiarity of the human constitution. Thanks to having himself worked in the dissecting room on the musculature of the face, Elias could never lose sight of how smiling and laughing rested on biological endowments. Still more useful was knowledge of the biological structure and functioning of the brain. That did not, of course, lead him to reduce mental activity to biology. Indeed, quite the opposite.

In fact Elias was led to compare what he had learned in the dissecting room about the working of the brain and nervous system with the neo-Kantian image of humans espoused by his philosophy teacher, Richard Hönigswald. There was nothing in the biology of the central nervous system, he realized, corresponding to the division taken for granted in philosophy between the 'external' world and the 'internal' world of 'the mind'. This notion has been a dominant strand in Western philosophy at least since the Renaissance, running through Descartes to Leibniz's 'windowless monads' and culminating in Kant: the connecting thread is a preoccupation with how the single adult individual mind, looking out from inside, is able to have knowledge of the external world. So entrenched is the conception of the mind as 'internal' and sharply demarcated from the external world that it is also taken for granted in sociology and, indeed, enters into the general mode of self-experience among people at large in modern societies. Yet, says Elias, 'This discrepancy between the philosophical-idealist and the anatomical-physiological image of man disturbed me for many years.' He gradually came to the view that this way of looking at man was an instance of the philosophical tendency to reduce observable processes over time to something timeless and unchanging – a tendency he was later to label 'process-reduction' (*Zustandsreduktion*). He did not work this out in detail until much later – not finally until teaching his introductory course in sociology at Leicester in the early 1960s – but he considers that his running battle against the *homo clausus* image of man goes back all the way to his medical studies. His views were sufficiently formed for them to cause a serious rift with Hönigswald.

Richard Hönigswald (1875–1947), who held the chair of philosophy at Breslau and later taught in Munich and New York, was one of the most original among the dominant neo-Kantian philosophers of the time. Elias remembers the impact of his sharp intellect: 'from him – and from my father – I learned to think'. In one respect at least, Elias also remembers a strong affinity with his teacher: Hönigswald, he says (in a letter quoted by Wolandt, 1977: 132), 'paid no dues to the *Zeitgeist*', which at that time meant the fashionable phenomenology, ontology and existentialism of Husserl, Heidegger and Jaspers. As was then usual, Elias interrupted his work at his own university in Breslau to spend semesters in Heidelberg and Freiburg. In Heidelberg, he studied not only with 'the venerable Rickert', but also with the much younger Jaspers, with whom he struck up a friendly acquaintance, without ever disguising the scepticism he had brought with him from Breslau about Jaspers's existential philosophy. 'And since then, perhaps strengthened by Hönigswald's stand, I have since been immune to all trends of fashion, whether Sartre, Wittgenstein, Popper, Parsons or Lévi-Strauss' (quoted by Wolandt, 1977: 132). Unfortunately, Elias's scepticism also extended to central tenets of Hönigswald's own philosophy, and Hönigswald seems to have been less tolerant of sceptical students than was Jaspers. Since, on his return to Breslau, Elias was writing his doctoral dissertation under Hönigswald's supervision, this was not a trivial matter.

Nor was the basis of disagreement trivial. It was central to Elias's thesis, which was entitled *Idee und Individuum: Ein Beitrag zur Philosophie der Geschichte* (*Idea and Individual: A Contribution to the Philosophy of History*). It also went to the heart of the whole Kantian tradition in philosophy. Elias's objection concerned Kant's contention that certain categories of thought – Newtonian space, time, causality, and some fundamental moral principles – are not derived from experience but are inherent, eternal and universal in the human mind. Much of Elias's later work is informed by the conviction that this view, though untenable, has flavoured many branches of modern thought (see chapters 7 and 8 below). In his thesis, Elias argued that ideas could not be seen as individual products; intellectual history had to be seen in terms of 'chains' of generations, anticipating his later emphasis on the need to think in terms of people in the plural, not 'the Individual' in the singular. Looking back, he thought that his experience of the First World War and of the great German inflation of 1922–3 had led him to see the relative powerlessness of the individual against social forces, and made him conscious of the 'peculiarly esoteric character of basic philosophical assumptions'. So his thesis on the place of the individual in history began his involvement with the diachronic ordering of human interdependence, and put him on the track of long-term social processes as a form of order *sui generis*. But he then had no philosophical tools for dealing with it. He eventually came to think that such long-term processes needed to be investigated from a *sociological* not a philosophical point of view. But for the moment he remained a philosopher, and in need of another, senior, philosopher's approval for his thesis. For a time there was deadlock with Hönigswald. 'We both stood by our opinion – in my case until the present day – until I had to recognize that his power-potential was greater than mine.' Elias made the necessary amendments, shortening his thesis considerably, and it was accepted for the degree of doctor of philosophy (Dr.phil.) by the University of Breslau in January 1924, the degree being awarded in philosophy and psychology, with chemistry and history of art as subsidiaries.

Elias seems never to have looked at his thus mangled philosophy thesis again, and for many years believed it was lost. In fact, fifty-six years later, a simple enquiry revealed that it was safe and sound, sitting in the archives of what is now the University of Wrocław. The thesis nevertheless marked Elias's farewell to philosophy and to Hönigswald, who was 'much too authoritarian for my taste'. Nevertheless, his dispute with Hönigswald is very relevant to why, much later, Sir Karl Popper and Talcott Parsons were to be two of Elias's principal Aunt Sallys. Both stand clearly in the Kantian stream of thought, though neither is normally described as 'neo-Kantian'.[3] The symptoms can also be seen elsewhere in modern sociology, in the work of the many and varied devotees of abstract theorizing, and in such schools as phenomenological sociology, ethnomethodology and conversation analysis.

While struggling with these philosophical problems, Elias was also struggling with the consequences of the great runaway German inflation of 1922–3. His father, who by now had retired from business, was financially very badly hit by the total collapse of the currency, and for a time he himself had to go into business to help support his parents. He became the export manager for a local foundry in Breslau, and worked there for about two years. He looks back without regret on the time he spent there. 'Perhaps my recollection is selective, but in my memory, business life was very interesting.' For the future sociologist it was valuable experience. He learned a lot of economics in a practical way. He also comments that 'My perception of capitalists is strongly influenced by the foundry-proprietor: he was a very nice man.'

After the new Reichsmark was introduced and the currency restored to stability, his parents were able once more to live comfortably on their income. In the meantime, Elias had had three or four humorous short stories (about the ancient Greeks!) accepted by the *Berliner Illustrierte*. Being paid for those made him feel a free man again, and able to return to university. If necessary, he was convinced, he could earn his bread by journalism. In practice, he had to rely once more on his tolerant father for some support in the further studies necessary to begin a German academic career. He arrived in Heidelberg in 1925 with no academic patron, and already in his late twenties. He came with a doctorate in philosophy and psychology, but intending to study a subject new to him, sociology.

IN HEIDELBERG: THE WEBER CIRCLE AND KARL MANNHEIM

In Weimar Germany, sociology enjoyed high status and many students were attracted to it, especially in Heidelberg. There had been a few chairs in the subject before the war; it had then been associated, in the persons of such figures as Max Weber and Georg Simmel, with the liberal bourgeoisie. Many others of this old guard – Tönnies, Sombart, Scheler, Oppenheimer – were still very active in the 1920s. The younger generation of German sociologists, on the other hand, were generally more to the left: sociology became associated with the rise of social democracy. Behind both stood 'the colossal figure of Karl Marx' (Elias 1984b: 22). In Heidelberg both strands came together. Max Weber had died in 1920, and was not yet so internationally famous as later. But his brother Alfred (1868–1958) occupied a chair of sociology at Heidelberg, and his widow Marianne still lived there; between them they kept alive Max Weber's memory and intellectual influence. Elias had first learnt of Weber's work from Karl Jaspers – who revered Max Weber – on a walk together during the earlier period he spent in Heidelberg; but it was only now that he read Weber, and Marx, in depth. Among the younger generation, the most notable figure was Karl Mannheim, who 'was quite brilliant, and at his best at this time'. His lectures drew crowds of students away from Alfred Weber and the old guard: 'there was a great tension between the two, though it was expressed in a very civilized manner'.

Heidelberg in the 1920s was in the grip of the student fraternities – the *farbentragende Verbindungen* – who carried on the old traditions, duelling prominent among them. There was constant conflict between them and the minority of *Freistudenten* who belonged to no fraternity at all. Elias was one of the latter, as were all of Mannheim's students. The division was one of, among other things, right and left. In any case, as a Jew, Elias could not have belonged to any of the old fraternities. There *were* Jewish fraternities imitating the others (he belonged briefly to one in Breslau) but he thinks they were objects of ridicule to the very fraternities they were aping. At any rate, all this was but one symptom of 'the extraordinary politicization of intellectual life'. There were indeed left-social-scientists and right-social-scientists. Right-wing students would not attend Mannheim's seminar. The tolerant, liberal Alfred Weber, on the other hand, balanced the ticket by having one Communist academic assistant and another who was a Nazi. The latter was Hans Freyer, who was later to play a key role in organizing sociology under Hitler, and who also tried to moderate Nazism. 'I knew him very well. He was very civilized. I was very civilized. We were all civilized people. And the very civilized Alfred Weber – I don't think he had any idea what was happening.' This experience of the politicization of social science was undoubtedly reflected later in Elias's concern with problems of involvement and detachment.

During the Heidelberg years, Elias was entirely unpaid. He was passing through the transitional phase which was then quite normal in a German university career. He had to seek a full professor prepared to sponsor him as his protégé, in order to ascend to the rank of *Privatdozent*. This process of *Habilitation* involved writing a further thesis, the *Habilitationsschrift*. Alfred Weber eventually agreed to be Elias's sponsor, but there were already several ahead of him on Weber's list, so quite a few years would have to elapse before he could expect to achieve *Habilitation*. His proposed subject met with Weber's approval, however. It was to be on the significance of Florentine society and culture in the transition from pre-scientific to scientific thinking. Undaunted by being only just about able to read Italian, Elias visited Florence. He remembers looking up documents on the young Galileo, and on the crucial experimental art of such fifteenth-century artists as Masaccio and Uccello, whose development of perspective and the representation of three dimensions in two he saw as connected with the general question of how people moved from mythical to scientific thinking.

Karl Mannheim (1893–1947) was only a few years older than Elias, but already one rung further up the ladder. As a *Privatdozent* he was entitled to give courses of lectures and to receive payment from the students who attended, though otherwise receiving no salary. But he had private means, his wife coming from a wealthy Hungarian family. Elias and Mannheim rapidly became close friends. Partly because Elias was older than most of the other students, but at the same time was able to get along with them better than Mannheim, he became a sort of intermediary between Mannheim and his students. In that way, Elias slipped unnoticed into the role of Mannheim's unofficial academic assistant. In return, Mannheim advised him about his career. It was Mannheim who secured Elias's introduction to Marianne Weber's elite salon. Marianne was a great figure; she had great influence over Alfred, and her veto was death. But the Weber circle was very enjoyable if one were in favour, and Elias remained welcome there.[4] He gave his first paper at a seminar on the balcony of her house, overlooking the garden. It was on the sociology of Gothic architecture: he spoke about the differences in the structure of French and German society in the Middle Ages and how they were reflected in the structure of cathedrals in the two countries. 'At the end there were polite applause and friendly words. A small step on the road to a university career. In the salon of Max Weber's widow I had not been rejected.'

It is not easy to say exactly what influence Alfred Weber had on Norbert Elias. As we have seen, Elias came from Breslau already groping for ways of understanding long-term processes of social development, and his reading of Marx and Max Weber confirmed his leanings. Alfred Weber in his way was also working problems of this kind. His interests were especially directed at the peculiarity of 'culture' as a vital aspect of human societies and their development. His fullest statement is his book *Kulturgeschichte als Kultursoziologie* (*Cultural History as Cultural Sociology*, 1935). He argued that culture could not be reduced to economic relationships or explained in terms of economic interests. It always had to be understood in terms of social behaviour, but its pattern of development differed from that of economics, science and technology. In these there was progress, whether of a linear or dialectical kind, together with reversals. But in art, religion and culture in general, there were no progressions and regressions: culture was rather to be seen as the self-realization of the soul of a people.

It quickly became clear to Elias that in his work on the sociology of culture, Alfred Weber was reworking and extending into a general theory an old tradition in German thought, which had found expression particularly in the antithesis between the concepts of 'culture' and 'civilization'. Broadly speaking, the two concepts had developed in relation to the clear separation in German society between the ways of life of the princely courts and of the bourgeoisie; 'civilization' had come to be used with a pejorative undertone to characterize the French-orientated fashions of the courtiers, in contrast to the native German 'culture' of the middle classes. Here Elias was on familiar ground. During his early visit to Heidelberg, Jaspers had encouraged him to write one of his first major seminar papers on the dispute between Thomas Mann and the *Zivilisationsliteraten*. During the First World War and until around 1922, Thomas Mann had been a conservative and nationalist. In *Betrachtungen eines Unpolitischen (Reflections of an Unpolitical Man*, 1918), he had taken up the old distinction between 'civilization' and 'culture' in attacking the writers he called the *Zivilizationsliteraten*. By that he meant principally his own more leftist brother Heinrich, together with a few other writers such as Kurth Hiller, who in the context of 1914–18 stood for Western rationality, humanity and parliamentary democracy and whom, moreover, Thomas Mann accused of writing in a French manner.

All this is mainly worth mentioning because, years later, Elias was to begin *The Civilizing Process* with an introductory chapter on the origins of the concepts of civilization and culture in Germany and France. Since its relevance to what follows in the book is not apparent at first glance, it has often caused puzzlement. And, because the two words were also prominently used by Alfred Weber, superficial readers have often jumped to the conclusion that the presence of the chapter is explained by the massive influence of Alfred Weber in the background. But Elias does not by any means accept Weber's distinction between 'civilization' and 'culture' as contrasting components of all historic societies. He is interested instead in how the two concepts came to be used as emblems of two competing groups and their ways of life. The chapter thus owes much more to Elias's studies of French and German social history, partly prompted by his interest in the unfraternal feelings of the brothers Mann, than it does directly to Alfred Weber. Furthermore, Elias's contention that developmental processes in a specific direction can be discerned in culture runs expressly counter to Weber's views.

Yet in several ways, Norbert Elias had more far-reaching intellectual differences with Karl Mannheim. That did not affect their friendship, nor Elias's recognition of Mannheim's brilliance. But although at that time Elias was closely associated with him, Mannheim was never simply his intellectual model. Elias, as we have seen, had already taken a strong line of his own in his disagreement with Hönigswald, and the same and related issues separated him intellectually from Mannheim. They went to the heart of the sociology of knowledge which Mannheim was then developing, notably in *Ideology and Utopia* (1929a). Like Marx, Mannheim treated the problem of 'consciousness' and 'social being' as if consciousness were not one of the continuous constitutive elements of human society. 'The dualistic thesis of consciousless being and beingless consciousness is a fiction' writes Elias (1984b: 34). This fiction is, however, central to a long and respected tradition of thought, the tradition which distinguishes between society 'outside' and the individual mind 'inside', and is preoccupied with notions of what the single, autonomous individual knows. That is, in fact, the same tradition running back through Descartes and Kant over which Elias had already entered into dispute with Hönigswald, and to which Mannheim always subscribed.

Directly out of the dualistic view of 'social being' and 'consciousness' arose Mannheim's argument that all thought is socially conditioned and distorted. But such a radically relativistic proposition throws into doubt all human knowledge (including Mannheim's own theory), and Mannheim himself shrank away from the full consequences of this position. He experimented with several ways of breaking out of relativism. One route was what he called 'relationism': if people from different class positions have different partial perspectives on the world, could it perhaps be argued that 'truth' was the sum of these partial perspectives? Another emergency exit from relativism which Mannheim tried was the idea that intellectuals were less closely linked to economic forces and therefore had a less distorted perspective on social reality than other classes.[5] Finally, Mannheim's treatment of 'utopia' can also be read as an attempt to rescue socialism from relativism; this may not have been entirely unconnected with Mannheim's need for party political patronage in securing himself a chair of sociology (Elias 1984b: 36). Be that as it may, later sociologists have not judged any of Mannheim's proposed escapes from relativism to be very successful.

Mannheim showed brilliantly how ideologies could be analysed and related to the social circumstances of their development. Perhaps his masterpiece in this respect is his essay on the social origins of conservative thought in Germany (1927). For Elias, however, that was only a beginning:

For me, the critique of ideology was only a means to an end, only one step on the way to a social theory which took account of the fact that one could observe both distorted and undistorted knowledge of reality. The doctor's knowledge of the human body, which can heal, is no ideology. Why should one not be in the position of producing non-ideological knowledge of human society?

This standpoint was to find expression again much later in Elias's discussion of involvement and detachment, in which the problem of 'objectivity' in social science is treated as an issue neither of philosophy, methodology, nor of individual motivation, but as a question of long-term social development in its own right.

Elias's differences with Mannheim were no threat to their friendship because Elias was much the junior, in rank if not in years. Mannheim did, however, have a propensity to precipitate serious rows with figures senior to himself. This happened most notably with Alfred Weber and, later, with Morris Ginsberg of the London School of Economics, the doyen of British sociology in the 1930s and 1940s. In both cases one effect was to jeopardize the prospects of Elias, as someone closely associated with Mannheim.

The rivalry between Alfred Weber and the up and coming Mannheim had been polite and unspoken and so it was astonishing when it came out in the open at the annual congress of German sociologists in Zurich in 1928. The occasion was Mannheim's presentation of his paper on 'Competition as a cultural phenomenon' (1929b), 'an intellectual firecracker' as Elias later described it. Tönnies, Sombart and several others applauded it, but Alfred Weber reacted angrily to a passing reference to himself and liberalism, and to what could be read as a relativizing of the ideal of *Wertfreiheit* (value-freedom) associated with Max Weber. As it happens, the published proceedings of the conference afford us our first glimpse in print of Elias as sociologist: they contain transcriptions of his contributions from the floor to two discussions (Elias 1929). The immediate consequence of the rift between Mannheim and Weber, however, was to make uncomfortable Elias's position as the close friend of the one and *Habilitation* candidate of the other. This helped persuade Elias, when in 1929 Mannheim was called to the chair of sociology at Frankfurt, to accept the invitation to go with him as his academic assistant – official and paid, instead of unofficial and unpaid. At the time, he was still fourth in line on Weber's list, and could not expect to become a *Privatdozent* for at least four years. Mannheim put him first on his own list and promised *Habilitation* at the end of three years' service as academic assistant.

FRANKFURT: IN THE MARXBURG

The Department of Sociology at the University of Frankfurt was housed in the ground floor of the famous Institut für Sozialforschung. The Institut, known to later social scientists as 'the Frankfurt School', was a well-endowed and independent group of Marxist scholars: its history has been vividly charted by Jay (1973). It owned the building, known jokingly as the Marxburg, and the University rented accommodation for the Department there. The Director of the Institut was Max Horkheimer, and other leading figures included Theodor Adorno, with whom Elias seems to have been particularly friendly, Friedrich Pollock, Erich Fromm, and Leo Löwenthal. In the University at large there were many other notable figures, including Paul Tillich the philosopher and theologian, Löwe the economist, Wertheimer the *Gestalt* psychologist, and S. H. Fuchs (later Foulkes) the psychoanalyst. Students of sociology were encouraged to attend lectures by all these, for sociology was not regarded as a narrow academic specialism. The Department at Frankfurt had shed the authoritarian and hierarchical character then still prevalent in many German universities. After seminars, discussions continued in cafés – one discussion with Paul Tillich lasting until one o'clock in the morning. Cafés were favoured rather than bars, because unmarried young women would have been out of place in bars. It was very definitely a mixed circle, and this was in sharp contrast with other departments where staff and students met only formally and where many students belonged to traditional male societies, meeting in *Gasthäuser* and 'apart from excursions to women of another class' mixing little in female company (Seglow 1977: 17).

There was a clear division of labour between Mannheim and Elias.

Mannheim gave the big lectures and took part in university politics. Elias attended the lectures so as to be able to reassure Mannheim, whose native tongue was Hungarian, that he never made any errors in German. Elias was responsible for dealing with student problems and was indeed, as at Heidelberg, the main link between Mannheim and the students, for Mannheim always maintained a certain distance between himself and the students. One student recalls Elias as he was in those days:

He was immensely liked . . . understanding every individual's problems . . . He was a slim man in his thirties, a sportsman, who went swimming almost every day (as he still does), and a noted skier. He was already bald, his head framed on both sides with black hair . . . There was always a friendly smile on his face . . . He spoke slowly and deliberately, earnestly and courteously, but also with much laughter. (Freund 1977: 13)

Elias's own teaching was in small seminars, and it was he who supervised the many doctoral dissertations. He encouraged students to look sociologically at something in which they were already involved, keenly interested, and knew a good deal about. Gisèle Freund was already a keen amateur photographer when she went to Frankfurt, and Elias suggested she write her doctorate on the social development of photography in the nineteenth century. Though the thesis was completed in exile and submitted to the Sorbonne (Freund 1936), she credits Elias with the beginnings of her career as an internationally known photographer and scholar of photography. Ilse Seglow's experience was as an actress before she came to study in Frankfurt. She was encouraged to embark on a study of the acting profession, and her account of how Elias advised her to go about it (Seglow 1977) shows that his approach to sociological research had taken shape long before it found expression in his own publications.

The students of the Department and the Institut were nearly all highly politicized and well aware of the dangers of fascism. Oddly enough, the radical students regarded neither Horkheimer nor Mannheim as particularly radical (Seglow 1977: 17). Elias himself avoided political commitments altogether. His interviewers on one occasion (1984d) were astonished to discover that, so far as he could recall, he had never even voted – neither in Germany nor later when he was a British citizen. To vote, his interlocutors objected, was surely the minimum level of participation in a democracy, and they could hardly credit that he did not vote at the crisis of the Weimar Republic. Elias half-admitted that it was strange: 'Well, I certainly wasn't right-wing. All my friends were on the left, and my sympathies were on the left in political arguments.' What prevented him joining a political party was his profound dislike of all political ideologies, which always involved both self-deception and distortion of social reality. 'I believe that the malaise of humanity is to be blamed on the fact that they become motivated by unrealistic ideas.' As we have seen, he differed from Mannheim (and many other sociologists since) in having much more confidence in the possibility of achieving through social science a progressively less distorted knowledge of how societies work. All political ideologies involve mythical thinking, and it was his task to unmask myths of all kinds and to help influence society by creating more realistic knowledge about it. Asked whether people did not have a need of myths, he answered

Yes, but then they must write poetry, as I have also done. I also had a need of myths and art . . . People need myths, but not to give them form in social life . . . It is now my view that people would live together better without myths. Myths always eventually exact a penalty of us.

Elias's pursuit of realistic knowledge took him on one occasion to hear Hitler speak. He wore an aristocratic disguise, with a monocle and a little Tyrolean hat, getting past the SA guards in the middle of an escort of big, Aryan-looking students.

[Hitler] was an extraordinarily good speaker, but what sticks in the memory above all was that he picked up children to bless them. That I'd never seen before! He let children come up to the podium and laid his hands on them and spoke to them.

In 1932, with the emergence of private armies on the streets, Elias came as close as he ever did to activism, again in the name of realism. He remembers addressing a trade union committee, reviewing the situation, and warning them to be prepared to take up arms. They had not thought of it. Again their ideology was unrealistic. The Social Democrats and unions felt that law was decisive – they believed in the *Rechtsstaat*, the state under the rule of law; there was no place for violence and they wanted no revolution. Elias thought it merely realistic to acknowledge that law cannot function without the ultimate prop of violence – a point which later played a much bigger part in his thinking.

When Hitler came to power in February 1933, Elias went hurriedly through all the stages of *Habilitation*, except for the *Privatdozent*'s inaugural lecture. It did him no good. He went into exile – too old to start again as a student, but too young to be a professor. His *Habilitationsschrift* was not published until thirty-six years later: it was *The Court Society*.

EXILE

Elias remained a month or two longer in Frankfurt than most of his friends, to see how the wind was blowing. That was, he said later, mainly due to his naïveté,[6] but it proved fortuitous. He had the presence of mind to go back to the now empty Marxburg and remove all copies of the membership list of the Red Student Group and other incriminating evidence. Means of disposal apparently included flushing material down the lavatory in his flat. A few days later the SS came to collect him – as administrator of the Sociology Department he had the keys to the Institut – and took him across Frankfurt in a military truck. He was able to be a bit cheeky, because he believed they would find nothing of importance. When the SS lieutenant commented on books by Marx and Marxists, he said 'That's nothing to do with me!' Subsequently he was summoned before the Nazi Commissar appointed to take over the University, for questioning about the 'military activities of the Sociology Department'. A document had been found referring to the 'Liberal Flying Group'! Elias had to explain that it referred to a series of seminars on liberalism, between which various professors circulated, and his explanation was accepted because one of the professors was a member of the NSDAP. Elias saw at first hand that the takeover of power was *both* violent *and* very rationally organized – the two things are not mutually exclusive.

He was no longer Assistant, although his salary was paid until October 1933. In April, with a girlfriend (Gret Freudentag) who had a car, he visited Basle, Zurich and Berne to see whether there was any chance of a job in a Swiss university. No success. He returned to Germany, visited his parents in Breslau, and then left for Paris. It was an obvious choice: he had felt an affinity with French culture since his schooldays, and spoke perfect, almost accentless French.

Elias lived in Paris nearly two years, in the Montparnasse area, and was quickly involved in the stimulating intellectual life of the cafés, knowing André Gide and André Malraux among others. While there, he published two articles in German emigré journals, one on 'Kitsch-style in the age of Kitsch' (1935a) and the other on the rather pointed subject of 'The expulsion of the Huguenots from France' (1935b). Although Elias was already thirty-eight, these were his first published sociological works. He established good connections with the Ecole Normale Supérieure, and particularly with the historian of science, Alexander Koyré and the sociologist Celestin Bouglé, but they had no money to employ him. His father had given him what money he could spare and, there being no prospect of an academic job, he invested it all in a small factory making wooden toys. His partners were two German working men, both Communists, one of whom he had known in Frankfurt. He remembers with relish an encounter between the German proletarian, Turek, and the 'very refined' Gide. His partners made the toys; Elias's job was to persuade stores to sell them. It did not work. The business lasted nine months, and he lost all his money. There followed the only period in his life when he actually went hungry – he remembers having to ask an acquaintance to buy him coffee and a roll. 'It was hopeless – there was no future.' Two friends from Breslau who were already in England suggested he cross the Channel. He was reluctant, particularly because he did not speak English, but in 1935 finally made his way to Britain. Before doing so, he visited Germany for the last time before the war to see his parents. With hindsight that seems dangerous, but at the time the country remained outwardly orderly, still superficially a *Rechtsstaat*.

On arrival in London, Elias had to seek the support of a committee set up to assist Jewish refugees. He told them he could only pursue his career if they gave him enough money to write a book. They said that was unrealistic – because he did not speak English he would have to write in German. So they gave him only a very small allowance – just sufficient for the rent of a bed-sitting room and enough to eat. Nevertheless, they were sympathetic to his work and extended the grant as the scale of his undertaking became apparent.

It is not absolutely clear when work on *The Civilizing Process* began. As he tells the story, on arriving in London, Elias had no clear idea what he was going to write. He spent his whole time in the library at the British Museum, reading almost randomly anything that interested him in the catalogue. Then he came across manners books and found them fascinating. What interested him was that academic psychologists of the time (though not the Freudians) thought that by measuring the attitudes and behaviour of present-day people, usually by means of questionnaires and attitude scales, they could generalize to mankind as a whole – past, present and future. Yet in the manners books

I suddenly found material which demonstrated that other standards of behaviour had been known, and how they had changed. So I began *The Civilizing Process*, fully conscious that it would be an argument against the psychological studies of attitudes and behaviour of that time . . . For me it was quite clear that this well-trodden way was no more than an effort to fit humans into the methods of the natural sciences or biology, so that the whole human process of change was pushed aside. That was how it all began.

He claims to have worked full-time on the book for just three years. Yet the origins of the book must have antedated his arrival in London. In his preface he thanks Bouglé for his help, and, more mysteriously, the preface is dated 1936.[7]

The Civilizing Process will be discussed in the following chapters, yet the almost cloak-and-dagger story of its publication belongs here. No English publisher would have been interested in such a work in German. Elias found a publisher in Breslau prepared to handle the book, and it was planned to send copies of the first volume to Prague for publication in 1937; this now exceedingly rare first version bears the imprint of the Academia bookshop in the Czech capital, but apparently no copies actually reached there. And before the second volume was finished, the Breslau publisher, himself a Jew, fled abroad without paying the printer. Elias's father had to do that, and it could be done only with the consent of the Nazi authorities, because Jews could no longer use their bank accounts. While printing was being completed in Breslau, Elias found a publisher in Switzerland, Fritz Karger, who had recently founded the Haus zum Falken firm to publish emigré works.[8] His father then had to make a case to the authorities for the printed sheets to be sent to Switzerland. Once there, they were bound, and 'Printed in Germany' was blacked out in Indian ink. Only through a remarkable oversight by the Nazi authorities and his father's diplomatic skills was the book ever published at all.

Sales were minute. By the time the book was ready, Austria and Czechoslovakia as well as Germany were under the Third Reich: there was no longer any market to speak of for books in German by Jews. Elias was in any case to receive no royalties for it, but Karger, who believed in the book, had contracted to distribute a large number of free copies for review in journals and newspapers. Even that was impeded by the war. Goudsblom (1977b) has traced such reviews as appeared. The book was especially well received in the Netherlands by the leading sociologist W. A. Bonger and the prominent critic Menno ter Braak. Foulkes made it known to an international psychoanalytic audience. In Britain, the only major review was by Franz Borkenau in *The Sociological Review*. Karger (1977) remarks that after the war, in view of the negligible sales and few reviews, it was surprising to find the book known to groups of initiates in various countries. Some references to it turn up in unexpected places. One example is *A Restatement of Liberty* (1951) by Patrick

Gordon-Walker (later British Foreign Secretary) whom Elias knew in London. Another is Harold Nicolson's *Good Behaviour* (1955), where it is quarried for quaint medieval manners with little sociological understanding; Nicolson was later taken aback to find Elias alive and kicking and present at the same reception in Leicester. Thomas Mann also apparently read the work with appreciation.[9] But the circle of people who knew the book at all was minuscule.

Norbert Elias's parents clearly played an important part in his life right up to the publication of *The Civilizing Process* in 1939. He saw them for the last time in 1938, when they visited him in London, it being then still possible. He pleaded with them not to return to Germany, but they insisted: their friends were all in Breslau, they knew no-one in London, and how would they live? Besides, said his father, 'What can they do to me? I have never done anything wrong to anyone – I've never broken a law in my life.' The last letter Elias received from his mother came via the Red Cross from a transit camp. She told him his father had died in Breslau in 1940. She herself is believed to have died in Auschwitz in 1941. This was the great trauma of Elias's life: he could never come to terms with the image of his mother in the gas chamber. The influence of his parents always remained in his character though. From his father he acquired an integrity, or stubbornness, and an unwillingness to compromise on matters of principle. His father, in retirement, had acted as a voluntary adviser helping people to make their tax returns but never condoned any kind of falsification or evasion in accounts. Something of the same attitude, and of Elias's position since childhood as a member of an outsider group, can be seen in his stubborn defence of his own sociological views and refusal to adapt to the conventional wisdom. 'I always knew the ruling things are phoney', he said, probably thinking of 'things' dominant in sociology especially since the 1950s. 'In England I could have had a much more comfortable life if I had accepted dominant ideas, but I was not disposed to compromise. That I really could not do.'

Elias had no close contact with British sociologists until after the publication of *The Civilizing Process*, when he obtained a Senior Research Fellowship at the London School of Economics. At the outbreak of war the LSE had been evacuated to Cambridge, so he spent a happy few months there, punting on the river in his spare time. This was rudely interrupted when he was packed off, along with all other Germans in Britain in 1940, into internment – first at 'Camp Huyton', an unfinished housing estate on the fringes of Liverpool, and then to the Isle of Man. Eric Wolf, later a famous American anthropologist of peasant societies but then an interned German teenager, recalls his first encounter with social science through two lectures given at Huyton by Elias on 'The network of social relationships' and 'Monopolies of power' (Wolf 1977). The picture of internees organizing their own educational programme gives too rosy an impression. Not a few refugees from Hitler, finding themselves now interned in British camps, took their own lives. For Elias, it was only an interlude, although one still recalled with signs of anguish many years later (1985a: 53–4).

In due course he returned to Cambridge. There he was very friendly with

C. P. Snow – the only member of the British establishment, perhaps, with whom he did become close – and was often his guest at high table in Christ's College. It was there that he first absorbed English culture, and for the first time began to feel really at home in England. Many of the essays which date from his years in England, on subjects ranging from the naval profession to fox hunting, reflect the wide reading through which he came to grips with the distinctive features of his adopted country.[10]

At the end of the war Elias was employed by the British security services to pick out unrepentant Nazis among prisoners of war. For almost a decade thereafter, however, he had no secure employment. He made a meagre living by giving extra-mural classes (but not as a tenured Staff Tutor), and he gave occasional guest lectures at the London School of Economics and Bedford College, where Morris Ginsberg and Barbara Wootton respectively were helpful. During these years too, Elias played a key part as one of the co-founders of the Group Analytic Society. The psychoanalyst S. H. Foulkes, whom he had known in Frankfurt, formed a group of four or five who met regularly at his house and laid the theoretical and practical foundations of group therapy.[11] On the map of psychoanalysis, Foulkes was close to Anna Freud, while the perhaps better-known group of psychoanalysts around Maxwell Jones at the Tavistock Clinic were orientated more towards Melanie Klein.[12] There was strong rivalry between the two groups. Elias remembers seeing impressive demonstrations of psychodrama at the Tavistock, but group therapy developed in a rather different direction. As the only sociologist among the founders – the others were all psychiatrists – Elias had something distinctive of his own to contribute. As we shall see, a central theme in his thinking is that the individual and society are not separate things, but only two differing perspectives. This idea, already implicit in *The Civilizing Process*, had been discussed most explicitly in a section omitted from that book and finally published decades later in *Die Gesellschaft der Individuen* (1987a); at roughly the time of his close association with group analysis, Elias developed the argument further in an essay ('Problems of self-consciousness and the image of man') eventually included in the same volume. Foulkes worked the viewpoint into his techniques of group analysis. Later, when he had taken part in one of Foulkes's training groups, Elias led therapeutic groups himself. Furthermore, after the war, Elias underwent psychoanalysis himself – interrupted by breaks when he was unable to pay for the sessions. Of course, at the time, it was not unusual for intellectuals to undergo analysis for intellectual reasons; in America, Elias's near-contemporary Talcott Parsons was training as a lay analyst. Asked whether he had any more personal reasons for seeking analysis, however, Elias replied: 'My greatest problem was that I wrote so slowly. I found it disturbing that I could not produce more, even though I had so many ideas.' Ilse Seglow, herself an analyst, also used to comment that he always had great difficulty in letting his written work ('his children'!) go.

Finally, in 1954, Elias at last received two offers of academic posts in British universities, at Leeds and Leicester. Significantly, both offers came from refugee sociologists like himself, Eugene Grebenik at Leeds and Ilya Neustadt at Leicester. Elias chose Leicester largely because it was much closer to London and the British Museum. Neustadt, more than twenty years younger than Elias, came originally from Odessa; he had worked as a librarian at the LSE and had known Elias since the war years. The two men had had similar career problems, as well as sharing a similar outlook on sociology. Neustadt was Senior Lecturer-in-charge of the Department of Sociology, and later Professor. Elias, who would never have claimed administration as his forte, was Lecturer and later Reader. It is a little startling to realize that when he set his feet on the first secure rung of the academic career ladder, he was already 57.

Sociology was new to Leicester in 1954, and indeed it was only in the late 1950s and the 1960s that the subject grew rapidly and came to be taught in most British universities. Under Ilya Neustadt and Norbert Elias, the Department at Leicester grew rapidly to become one of the largest and most influential in the country. By the early 1970s it had around twenty-five members of staff, and a large number of its graduates had become prominent sociologists in their own right (Chris Bryant, John Eldridge, Paul Hirst, Graeme Salaman and Bryan Wilson among them). Moreover an astonishing list of distinguished sociologists, whether Leicester graduates or not, taught in the Leicester department during Elias's time there. They include Martin Albrow, Sheila Allen, Joe and Olive Banks, Richard Brown, Percy Cohen, Eric Dunning, Anthony Giddens, John H. Goldthorpe, Earl Hopper, Mary McIntosh, Nicos Mouzelis, Gordon Horobin and Sami Zubaida.

While at Leicester, Elias's own work branched out in a number of new directions. In retrospect, one of the most important was the work on the sociology of sport which he undertook in collaboration with Eric Dunning. Just as in Frankfurt days, when he had encouraged Gisèle Freund to study photography and Ilse Seglow the theatre from a sociological point of view, so in Leicester Elias continued to encourage students to work on topics of which they had personal knowledge. Dunning was a keen footballer and cricketer, and in the early 1960s asked Elias somewhat diffidently whether it was acceptable to study the sociology of sport. Elias thought it a fascinating and important field and, separately and together, both of them have since written a great deal on the subject. Significantly, Dunning was one of the very rare British undergraduates who could read German, and indeed did read *The Civilizing Process* while a student.[13]

Another product of the Leicester years was the book *The Established and the Outsiders* (1965) which originated as a community study of a Leicester suburb by John L. Scotson for an MA thesis under Elias's supervision. Elias reworked it with Scotson for publication, using it as a vehicle for the theoretical elaboration of ideas which had been in his mind at least since the 1935 essay on the Huguenots, and perhaps since his childhood as a Jew in Germany. (These themes are discussed in chapter 5 below.) In the early 1960s Elias also successfully applied for a major research grant from the Department of Scientific and Industrial Research (the precursor of the national Research Councils) to investigate school leavers' adjustment to working life. The results of this 'Young Workers Project' eventually appeared in publications by colleagues at Leicester, not by Elias himself. Long after his official retirement, Elias continued to be very active in the Department at Leicester. He presented several papers at the staff seminar which were published, if at all, only years later.

Yet in spite of the apparent success of the Leicester Department, Elias came to look back with great disappointment on the years he spent there. In alliance with Ilya Neustadt, he had attempted to give the Department a distinctive outlook based on his own developmental perspective in sociology. For this purpose, he took particular pride in working out a first-year introductory course in sociology, the main theoretical ideas of which (though not all of the illustrative material) eventually found their way into *What is Sociology?*. The 1950s and 1960s were, however, an unfavourable time during which to be trying to champion a developmental approach in sociology. Up until around the middle of the century, most sociologists had been conscious of the necessity for knowledge of the past in order to understand human society. There then began a long retreat into the present, into what Johan Goudsblom (1977a) was to christen 'hodiecentrism' in sociology. Talcott Parsons and the functionalist approach were dominant. Sociologists in the main tried to explain facets of contemporary society as parts of static 'social systems', with the past relegated to a 'historical background' inessential to explaining how things are now, and 'historical sociology' regarded as a quite separate specialism in its own right, a minority taste for a small number of sociologists. All this ran exactly counter to Elias's views, and though in the late 1970s and 1980s there has been something of a revival of sociological interest in past societies there has been no general acceptance of Elias's view that developmental explanations are the very essence of all sociological theorizing.

One source of disappointment was that, with the exception of Eric Dunning and perhaps one or two others who remained at Leicester, none of those now distinguished sociologists who graduated from Leicester or taught there early in their careers has followed the direction of Elias's thought. 'Most of them viewed my way of thinking, about long-term processes, as the vision of an outsider; and they probably thought that it would lead to no career for them. In sociology it clearly was not in fashion to think about long-term processes.' Richard Brown (1987) has reminisced about Elias's years in Leicester, not concealing that relations with younger colleagues were sometimes prickly. It really does appear to be true that Elias was regarded by most colleagues and students as an eccentric, if perhaps lovable, continental. The disjuncture between him and them is poignantly caught in the unusually full notes taken by one student, Ian Wilson, of the course on sociological theory taught jointly by Elias and Percy Cohen (subsequently Professor at the London School of Economics) in 1960–2. Elias's lectures were clearly quite demanding, and a comprehensive presentation of his own long-gestated point of view. Cohen's lectures were about functionalism and especially Talcott Parsons, and read in the 1980s they seem very dated.[14] But all who were in Leicester at the time remember quite clearly that Cohen was regarded as the voice of the present and future, Elias as a voice from the past.

Although Elias says that he was always confident his work would eventually be recognized, its prolonged neglect was traumatic for him. He reports that he has had a recurrent nightmare dating from Leicester years of a voice on a telephone repeating 'Can you speak louder? I can't hear you.' It has to be remembered that until the late 1970s none of Elias's major works was available in English translation, and few anglophone sociologists read German with ease. In the early 1970s most of the staff of the Leicester department were Leicester graduates who had picked up Elias's ideas from the Leicester air, so to speak, rather than from the books. In so far as they accepted them, that seemed to them to be 'just sociology' as they knew it, rather than anything very distinctive; in so far as they rejected them, it was perhaps in part because only a garbled impression can be given without detailed study of the texts.

Yet Elias is himself partly responsible for the neglect of his work in the English-speaking sociological world. Patrick Gordon-Walker had tried to interest English publishers in *The Civilizing Process* not long after it was first completed;[15] the historian F. L. Carsten tried again soon after the war, as did Bryan Wilson in the 1950s. In the late 1950s a draft translation of the first volume was actually made, but Elias did not approve it. Again in the early 1970s Eric Dunning prepared a translation of the first volume, but again Elias did not give his approval. The difficulty then was that Elias began to rewrite the book, wishing in particular to include a new section (based on research notes not used for the original version) about masturbation.

AFRICAN INTERLUDE

Elias's long residence in Britain was coming gradually to an end in the mid-1970s. It had been interrupted once before, however, in 1962–4 when, immediately following his formal retirement from Leicester, he went to the University of Ghana as Professor of Sociology. West Africa gave him much to think about. He did a great deal of field work with his students and visited their homes. He began to buy African art and rapidly built up a large and quite outstanding collection; on his return to Leicester there was enough to mount a major exhibition at the City Art Gallery (Elias 1970c). What attracted him to African art was the same thing as had attracted him to Picasso, a 'stronger and more direct appeal to the emotions than in traditional nineteenth-century art or the art of the Renaissance'. He related that to his theory of the civilizing process, hypothesizing that the strong upsurge of the process in the Renaissance was reflected in an increasing realism in art, against which there had been a full reaction only in the late nineteenth and the twentieth centuries. Non-naturalistic art, such as that seen in African masks, was associated with much greater possibilities of emotional expression. From this, and from what he observed in the less Westernized parts of West Africa, he was led to think afresh both about Freud's theory of personality and about his own theory of the civilizing process. For many years afterwards, Elias worked intermittently on the material he had gathered on the Krobo tribe, though he has not published much of it so far. It was reflections about his experiences in Africa, however, that later made him the target of sharp criticism by anthropologists – but that story can wait until chapter 10.

THE YEARS OF RECOGNITION

Had Elias survived only the biblical allotment of three score years and ten, he would not have lived to enjoy his belated recognition. Only small numbers of social scientists and historians became acquainted with his ideas by reading the first, 1939, edition of *The Civilizing Process*. One who did, and who was to play a major part in making Elias's work well known on the continent, was Johan Goudsblom, who found the two volumes in the University of Amsterdam library when a student in the early 1950s. He first met Elias in person when Elias attended the Third World Congress of Sociology in Amsterdam in 1956, and maintained contact from then onwards.

Wider recognition had to await the reissue of *The Civilizing Process* in German in 1969, followed quickly by the first ever publication of *Die Höfische Gesellschaft* (1969a) and *Was ist Soziologie?* (1970a). For fifteen years after the war, German sociologists had (like those in the rest of Europe and much of the world) been orientated to American-style sociology, dominated by number-crunching empiricism and the conceptual schemes of Talcott Parsons. The year 1968, the year of student revolutions, marked an intellectual sea-change. *The Civilizing Process* suddenly fell on fertile ground, and became something of a cult book among German and Dutch sociology students. The expensive hardback edition was pirated on photocopiers, and Elias arranged for the Suhrkamp publishing house to bring out a cheap paperback in 1973. Somewhat incomplete and imperfect French translations also appeared in 1973–5, and Elias suddenly found himself in the Paris best-seller lists. Even earlier, he found himself much in demand as a guest lecturer in German and Dutch universities. In 1969–71 he was a visiting lecturer in Amsterdam, in both the sociology and history departments, and at the Institute of Social Studies in the Hague. He established a wide circle of contacts among Dutch academics including, in addition to Goudsblom, the political scientist Godfried van Benthem van den Bergh and the anthropologist Anton Blok. Students and young lecturers of the time recall his appearances as exciting occasions and many fell under the spell of his forceful personality. They included such names as Christien Brinkgreve, Rineke van Daalen, Bart van Heerikhuizen, Paul Kapteyn, Bram Kempers, Ellie Lissenberg, Ali de Regt, Ruud Stokvis, Bram van Stolk, Bram de Swaan, Nico Wilterdink, Cas Wouters and the historian Pieter Spierenburg, who through their own researches were to extend Elias's approach in diverse ways to a huge variety of topics. Wouters in particular contributed to an important discussion about whether or not the 'permissive society' represents a reversal of the main trend of the civilizing process. By the mid-1970s, Elias had ceased to be a merely academic celebrity in the Netherlands and, thanks to television and the press, become known to a wider public.

In Germany too, he was invited to various universities, notably Konstanz, Aachen, Bochum and Bielefeld. While he was at Konstanz, around 1971, one of the most tragi-comic episodes in his intellectual history occurred. He had written a book-length typescript on 'The balance of power between the sexes' which, as usual with his work, existed in numerous drafts, top copies, carbon copies, typescript and manuscript. He piled *all* the versions on the floor of his room in the Department at Leicester, and then left for several months in Konstanz. The cleaning lady took the opportunity to tidy his room and consigned the lot to the incinerator. That is one Elias book which will never come to press – although in 1986 he published an article on relations between the sexes in ancient Rome which represented a small part of the lost book, reconsituted from memory.

After 1975, Elias was rarely in England. For five years from 1979 he lived more or less permanently in a flat at the Zentrum für Interdisziplinäre Forschung at the University of Bielefeld. Peter Gleichmann of Hannover and Hermann Korte of Bochum universities were especially prominent among his German associates, while Michael Schröter played an important role in helping Elias to edit many of his essays for publication. In Germany too, Elias became the subject of television programmes and articles in the press. Germany as a nation also made amends for the past by conferring on him numerous honours. The first of these was the title and pension of Professor Emeritus of the University of Frankfurt: Theodor Adorno, shortly before his death in 1969, had used his influence in advising the German government that, had it not been for Hitler, Elias would undoubtedly have reached that rank in a German university. In 1977, Elias was the first recipient of the Theodor W. Adorno Prize, conferred by the City of Frankfurt in the Paulskirche (see the speeches of Elias and Wolf Lepenies 1977). The same year, a *Festschrift* (Gleichmann, Goudsblom and Korte 1977) was presented to Elias in Aachen on his eightieth birthday. Later honours included an honorary doctorate from the University of Bielefeld. In 1986 President von Weizsäcker bestowed on Elias the Grosskreuz der Bundesdienstordens, one of the highest decorations the Federal Republic can award. From France in 1987 came an honorary doctorate from the Université de Strasbourg III. His ninetieth birthday in June 1987 was marked by two academic conferences in his honour and by a special double issue of the journal *Theory, Culture and Society*. At a large gathering in the Old Lutheran Church, Amsterdam, tributes were paid by Pierre Bourdieu and other admirers from several countries and disciplines, culminating in the Dutch Minister of Education and Science, in the name of Queen Beatrix, conferring on Elias the insignia of a Commander of the Order of Orange-Nassau. On his ninety-first birthday in 1988, he was presented with the Premio Europeo Amalfi, for *Die Gesellschaft der Individuen* as the best sociology book published in Europe in 1987.

It would be wrong to give the impression that Elias, or his younger colleagues, have become a majority voice in either German or Dutch sociology. They are still minorities, but they are at least taken seriously. In Britain, the USA and the rest of the anglophone world, however, few sociologists seem to have been inclined to come to grips with his work as a whole, though his books have been widely read since their translation. Richard Sennett invited him to lecture in New York in 1979, and he also spent some weeks at the University of Indiana, Bloomington.

Neither honours nor the lack of them seem to have made much difference to Elias. He ploughed on with his work regardless, publishing more in his eighties than ever before. Although his eyesight was failing, he continued to work long hours in his flat in Bielefeld or his house in Amsterdam, with the assistance of a succession of young bilingual or trilingual German or Dutch assistants. A typical day began around noon with a swim and revision of the previous day's work before a meagre lunch. The assistant would arrive around two o'clock in the afternoon, and with only a short break for dinner Elias would then dictate until as late as eleven o'clock at night. Only after then would it be safe to call round for an hour or so of conversation over wine or Scotch. The regime is most redolent of the life of the keen young graduate student, intoxicated with ideas. Perhaps that is what Elias always remained. His work always came first – a commitment dating back, it seems, to schooldays and so strong as to conflict with other commitments which are often more important in other people's lives. He never became committed to any political standpoint, and he never married. There was certainly at least one long-term relationship with a woman in his life, and many close friendships, but it never came to marriage. 'Women', observed Elias revealingly in an interview, 'were always jealous of my work . . . I didn't want to be disturbed. The work was my task . . . Alas, alas, the women didn't want that' (1984e). One recalls the case of Kant, of whom it was said 'as he never married, he kept the habits of his studious youth to old age' (*Encyclopaedia Britannica*, quoted by Bertrand Russell, 1946: 679; Russell comments 'I wonder whether the author of this article was a bachelor or a married man').

Elias's commitment to his work is extraordinary. Over the course of a very long life full of difficulties which would have deterred many, he has worked to refine, clarify and extend insights into human society which recognizably date back in origin all the way to his student days in the 1920s. The rest of this book will therefore be concerned not with Elias the man but with his ideas, as well as with the research others have pursued under his influence.

PART II

The Civilizing Process

2
Manners

One of the ways in which modern people most like to see themselves is as 'civilized'. The word is hard to define exactly because it has a wealth of connotations. To be civilized is to be polite and good mannered and considerate towards others; clean and decent and hygienic in personal habits; humane and gentle and kind, restrained and self-controlled and even-tempered; reluctant to use violence against others save in exceptional circumstances. To be a civilized person is to have learned a great deal since childhood; after all, infants cannot even control their anal sphincters, and cannot brook the slightest delay in their feed without throwing a tearful tantrum. Well into childhood it is difficult not to lurch between aggression or tears one moment and affection the next. Above all, though, to be civilized is to live with others in an orderly, well organized, just, predictable and calculable society.

Such is the self-approbation of people who describe themselves as civilized. In the present century, some voices have been heard to say that we have become too civilized for our own good. Sigmund Freud wrote about 'civilization and its discontents' (1930), and others have suggested that civilized men and women have grown too far from 'nature' for their health and happiness. But, in the main, people who think of themselves as civilized feel considerable self-satisfaction in the description. For the notion of being civilized is useful not only for self-approbation but for the disapprobation of others. Upper-class people visiting remote villages or urban slums in their own societies have often found much in the behaviour and circumstances of life of the lower orders to describe as uncivilized. Still more have people from the industrialized countries visiting the countries of what is now called the Third World found much to shock them: from people failing to use handkerchiefs or defecating under the public gaze, to cruelty to animals, public executions, and manifold manifestations of arbitrary rule. To describe what they saw, they have often used words like 'squalor', 'coarseness' or 'barbarism'; but forced to use a single word, they would as likely as not reach for 'uncivilized' – though perhaps not using the word with such self-confidence as formerly, especially now that the governments of the Third World have a more powerful voice in world affairs.

Many modern people who feel satisfaction in being so civilized are not greatly aware that their own ancestors – even the upper classes of medieval Europe – behaved in ways which people would today regard as squalid, coarse and barbaric. If they are aware of this, it probably serves only to increase the sense of self-satisfaction in having become so civilized.

It was far from Norbert Elias's aim in writing *The Civilizing Process* to increase anyone's self-satisfaction. The value-judgements involved in the popular use of the words 'civilized' and 'uncivilized' are obvious, and he begins by showing how these connotations developed. His more basic concern, however, is with the facts to which the words relate, facts less obvious – and more interesting to a social scientist. Unfortunately, in the book, Elias does not signal clearly the point at which he stops using the word 'civilization' in its native or popular sense and begins to use it in a technical, social scientific, more detached way – the point, so to speak, when he drops the quotation marks. The distinction is always clear in context but confusion can persist because the accumulation of value connotations was also an important aspect of the civilizing process in the factual, technical sense. Yet to understand civilization in the technical sense, readers have to distance themselves from the everyday value-laden connotations of the word. Elias's intention is to show by the examination of empirical evidence how, factually, standards of behaviour and psychological make-up have changed in European society since the Middle Ages, and then to explain why this has happened. (The word in German which is usually translated into English as 'make-up' is *Habitus*. By 'social habitus', Elias means that level of personality characteristics which individuals share in common with fellow members of their social groups. Since then, Pierre Bourdieu has used the word habitus extensively in his works (e.g. 1979), the word has become current among sociologists, and Elias himself now uses it in English.)

Even while writing the book, Elias was conscious that the investigation of such long-term processes of development would be viewed with scepticism by most professional historians, who tend to specialize by period, region and topic and to regard work on larger canvasses as merely speculative. In more recent years there has been a revival of interest in very long-term processes of economic and social development: one can mention the works of William McNeill (1964), Immanuel Wallerstein (1974, 1980) and Eric Jones (1981) on how Europe and the West achieved world dominance, and McNeill's books on the role of disease (1976) and military power in human history (1982). To the idea of very long-term processes of *psychological* development, however, there is to this day very great resistance. Why?

First of all, historians and sociologists do not dispute that accepted modes of social behaviour have changed over time. Nor is there any dispute that different periods and different kinds of society have been associated with different outlooks, world-views or mentalities. For example, among historians Johan Huizinga's investigation of the world view of the late Middle Ages (1924) – with its opening chapter on 'the violent tenor of life' to which Elias refers[1] – was widely acclaimed. So too have been the studies of *mentalités* undertaken by members of the influential *Annales* school of historians under the leadership of Lucien Febvre, Marc Bloch and Fernand Braudel (see for example Febvre 1938). Nor, on the whole, is the question of correlation between social structures and the psychological make-up of people involved in them controversial among sociologists. There may be arguments about the empirical accuracy of Ferdinand Tönnies's (1887) ideas on outlooks associated with *Gemeinschaft* (community) and *Gesellschaft* (association, society), or about whether Georg Simmel (1902–3) and Louis Wirth (1938) correctly identified the 'blasé' outlook and other particular psychological traits they attributed to urbanism as a way of life – but that did not prevent their writings being a powerful influence on sociologists' research over many decades. And the 'culture and personality' school of anthropologists investigated the correlation between social organization and personality structure in many societies. A few eccentric voices, such as Anthony Giddens (1984: 241), have argued that there is no such connection, and that the relationship between the two is purely random. Of course, if one looks at human beings from a sufficiently high level of abstraction, they and their societies can all look alike. All human societies past and present, for example, have facility in the use of language and in the control of fire. Similarly, if one chooses a very low level of abstraction, the differences between human groups are so numerous that any pattern is lost in mass of detail. At a sociologically more meaningful level of investigation between these two extremes, however, most social scientists have long accepted that the connection between social character and social structure is both non-random and of great interest.

Broadly speaking, then, correlation is not the problem. What causes hackles to rise is the proposition that there is a consistent long-term *direction* or *trend* in the social behaviour and psychological make-up of European people. Had Elias been content to show the mechanisms by which some ways of behaving came almost by chance to be deemed more civilized than others – and such random elements, like one of two semantically equivalent phrases being considered civilized and the other vulgar, are common – there would be little controversy. But, through his study of empirical evidence, Elias became convinced that over and above the many random elements there was a long-term trend in the changes he was studying. In consequence he has sometimes been charged with reviving the *progress* theories of Victorian times – a period when the rising industrial classes found much appeal in the writings of people like Herbert Spencer which seemed to show them as the vanguard of a continuous process of human improvement. Today we live in less self-confident times: one of the few propositions about long-term trends in social structure and mentality still held in respect by sociologists – Max Weber's hypothesis about long-term rationalization leading mankind to entrap itself in an 'iron cage' (1904–5; 181) – is perhaps accepted because of its pessimism. Elias, on the other hand, was concerned to be neither optimistic nor pessimistic, to depict neither improvement nor deterioration, certainly not to show that any group of people was better than another. But he was led by his evidence to see a long-term trend, a civilizing process. And the existence of such a trend cannot be disproved by merely theoretical reasoning:

it is not possible to decide in a purely theoretical, speculative way whether the changes in psychical make-up observable in the course of Western history took place in a particular order and direction. Only a scrutiny of documents of historical experience can show what is correct and what is incorrect . . . That is why it is not possible here, when knowledge of this documentary material cannot be presupposed, to give a brief preliminary sketch of the structure and central ideas of the whole book. They themselves take on a firmer form only gradually, in a continuous observation of historical facts and a constant checking and revision of what has been seen previously through what entered later into the field of observation. And thus the individual parts of this study, its structure and method, will probably be completely intelligible only when they are perceived in their entirety. (1939: I, xii)

It cannot be emphasized too strongly that the two volumes form a single book, and must be read together. For English-speaking readers that has been obscured by their publication several years apart under separate titles, with only sub-titles to indicate that they are two halves of the same work.[2] Much of the originality of Elias's argument lies in precisely the connection between the two. The argument, moreover, is too complicated to be set out at once in a simple linear cause-and-effect flow chart. It proceeds in a wave-like or spiral way, which can make it seem repetitive; but usually it is found that at each repetition, new elements have been introduced, so that one moves as it were up a spiral staircase rather than in a flat circle. All in all, finding one's way around the two volumes of *The Civilizing Process* is made no easier by its eccentric organization into four huge 'chapters', each divided into many sections and subsections, and still less easy by the fact that the two volumes of the English translation are set out in two different ways. To assist in the task of navigation, I have produced a reorganized, more orthodox contents page for the whole work, and rectified some omissions in the published version.

THE CIVILIZING PROCESS:
SOCIOGENETIC AND PSYCHOGENETIC INVESTIGATIONS

Standardized Table of Contents

*Volume I: Changes in the Behaviour of the Secular Upper Classes
in the West*

Volume II: Changes in Society – Outline of a Theory of Civilization

CIVILIZATION AND CULTURE

Elias begins his book by studying the accretion of so many evaluative meanings
in the notion of 'civilization'. Under its diverse connotations, he points out, it
has come to have one single general function:

this concept expresses the self-consciousness of the West . . . It sums up everything in which Western society of the last two or three centuries believes itself superior to earlier societies or 'more primitive' contemporary ones. By this term Western society seeks to describe what constitutes its special character and what it is proud of: the level of *its* technology, the nature of *its* manners, the development of *its* scientific knowledge or view of the world, and much more. (1939: I, 3–4)

By the nineteenth century, the ways people in the West used the *word* civilization showed that they had already largely forgotten the *process* of civilization: it was for them completed and taken for granted. At this stage, confident of the superiority of their own now apparently inherent and eternal standards, they wished only to 'civilize' the natives of lands they were now colonizing and, for a time, the lower classes of their own society (1939: I, 104).

In France, the word *civilisation* began to be used with these connotations from the latter half of the eighteenth century.[3] It was the Physiocrats and other reformers, generally of bourgeois origins, who first associated it with ideas of progress and social improvement; but, significantly, they derived the term from *civilité*, the word which courtiers had used since the sixteenth century to describe their own polished manners and courtly modes of behaviour, and originally to distinguish them from the more rough and ready *courtoisie* of their medieval forbears. The French intelligentsia had taken on many of the ways and attitudes of the courtiers, attitudes which in spite of the Revolution flavour French culture to this day, and *civilisation* came to be associated with the progress and identity of the nation as a whole. That happened partly because the French court was relatively more open to outsiders than was the case in Germany.

In Germany the word *Zivilisation* took on rather different shades of meaning from its French and English equivalents. The social and political context was very different. There was no single state or political centre. Instead, there were numerous small courts, all of them in the seventeenth and eighteenth centuries French-speaking and relatively closed to outsiders. Princes and their courts regarded the German language as vulgar. So the question 'What is really German?' remained acute, and was pondered less by francophile and francophone courtiers than by a thinly scattered stratum of German-speaking and, again, mainly bourgeois intellectuals. In their hands the word *Zivilisation* – again by derivation from *civilité* and association with the polished manners of courtiers – came to mean 'something which is indeed useful, but nevertheless only a value of the second rank, comprising only the outer appearance of human beings, the surface of human existence' (1939: I, 4). In contrast, it was through the word *Kultur* that German intellectuals expressed their own pride, achievement and identity, and it came to be associated, in contrast to the *Zivilisation* of the court – the superficiality, ceremony and polite conversation – with inwardness, depth of feeling, immersion in books, development of the individual personality, with all that was natural, real and genuine. Kant, in his *Ideas on a Universal History from the Point of View of a Citizen of the World* (1784), seems to have been the first to have used the two concepts in contraposition like this. The idea of *Kultur*, it should be noted, was used by the German intelligentsia to demarcate and distinguish themselves and their achievements both from the established courtly circles 'above' them and from mass outsiders – peasants and common townspeople – 'below' them.[4] So, at first, the antithesis between *Kultur* and *Zivilisation* expressed primarily a social contrast. As the German bourgeoisie rose in power and prestige, however, they had less need to contrast themselves with French-speaking courtiers, and from about the time of the French Revolution, the idea of *Zivilisation* came to be associated more particularly with France and with the Western powers generally. In that way, the *Zivilisation/Kultur* antithesis came to play a part in German nationalism.

Valuable as is any insight into the cultural roots of nationalism (and therefore very understandable that Elias should have written about this in the 1930s), the opening part of *The Civilizing Process* is frankly now an obstacle for many readers. Especially for English-speaking readers lacking a detailed knowledge of French and German history and literature, it is a good idea to omit this section at first reading. The section is important to an understanding of the work as a whole, particularly in showing that Elias's is not a simple nineteenth-century 'progress' theory of history, but it may make more sense after reading the rest of volume I, volume II, and *The Court Society*. Better to plunge first into Elias's examination of the history of manners.

THE HISTORY OF MANNERS

In tracing changes in manners since the Middle Ages, Elias draws evidence from many sources, including literature, paintings and drawings, and historical documents depicting how people were said to have behaved. His principal sources, however, are the 'manners books' of Germany, France, England and Italy which, from the thirteenth to the nineteenth century, set out the standards of acceptable behaviour by people in society. To call them 'etiquette' books would be misleading, since that implies a concern with niceties and minutiae of precedence or who should sit where at a dinner party. The books Elias studied, particularly the earlier ones, deal with far more basic matters, questions of 'outward bodily propriety' which it would later become embarrassing to mention. They tell their readers how to handle food and conduct themselves at table; how, when, and when not to fart, burp or spit; how to blow their noses; how to behave when passing someone in the act of urinating or defecating; how to behave when sharing a bedroom, or indeed a bed, with other people at an inn, and so on. In earlier centuries such matters – discussion of which now causes embarrassment, or at least the humorous sensation of a taboo having been broken – were spoken of openly and frankly, without shame. Then gradually, from the Renaissance, a long-term trend becomes apparent towards greater demands on emotional management and more differentiated codes of behaviour, and thresholds of shame and embarrassment advance.

Elias focused particularly on the most basic, 'natural' or 'animalic' of human functions – eating, drinking, defecating, sleeping, blowing one's nose – because these are things that humans cannot biologically avoid doing, no matter what society, culture or age they live in. Moreover, infants are born in the same emotional condition everywhere, so the *lifetime* point of departure is always the same. Therefore, if change occurs in the way these functions are handled, it can be seen rather clearly. Implicitly Elias was choosing strong ground from which to fight a battle with those who see the relationship between social personality and the structure of societies as merely random.

The authors of the manners books included some who were prominent in their time. One of the earliest German texts, the thirteenth-century verse *Hofzucht* (*Courtly Manners*), is attributed to Tannhäuser, now best known as the hero of Wagner's opera, but in life one of the most celebrated of the German minstrels or *Minnesänger*. In England, the fifteenth-century courtier John Russell wrote a *Book of Nurture* for the guidance of a young nobleman in the service of a great lord, and William Caxton printed a *Book of Curtesye*. Other influential works of the sixteenth century were Giovanni della Casa's *Galateo* (1558) and Baldesar Castiglione's *Il Cortigiano* (1528). Most famous of all the authors was Erasmus of Rotterdam, who published his Latin *De civilitate morum puerilium* (*On Civility in Boys*) in 1530. His book was widely translated and imitated. Its very title was important in marking the transition from the older notion of *courtoisie* to the later one of *civilité*. In later centuries the books were even more numerous, but their authors on the whole less distinguished. Elias makes particular use of Antoine de Courtin's *Nouveau traité de civilité* (1672) and La Salle's *Les Règles de la bienséance et de la civilité chrétienne* (1729), but draws on many more besides these. Some of the books went through many editions and what is left unsaid in later editions is often as significant as what is said.

What the books say is also more significant than which individuals wrote them. These are not simply individual products – they are not expressions of a single individual's own particular view of how people ought to behave, but individual versions of a common tradition. In the medieval period particularly, there is very great overlap between the precepts in the French, English, Italian and German books. This may mean that the authors read each other, but Elias argues that any such literary connections are less important than the links with the social contexts in which they wrote; in other words, the similarities of the texts 'correspond to the unity of actual behaviour in the medieval upper class, measured against the modern period' (1939: I, 66). In the Renaissance, it is true, a more individual tone of voice can be heard in Erasmus's book, but the modes of conduct he and his less distinguished successors recommend do nevertheless correspond closely to actual behaviour – as we can determine it from other sources – in the social circles to which the books were addressed.

What were those social circles? Primarily the *secular* upper classes, as Elias makes plain in the subtitle to the first volume of the German edition, omitted from the English. Ecclesiastics had made Latin compendia of precepts of Christian behaviour long before the appearance of the first secular manners books in thirteenth-century Provence and Italy. But, as we shall see, there were other forces at work over which the Church had no control. Its teaching was

shaped by changing power relationships such as those between men and women
as much as it shaped them.

The books' audience was in the beginning specifically a courtly one; all the
early terms for 'good behaviour' – courtesy, *courtoisie*, *cortezia*, *Hofzucht* – refer
to courts, to a specific location in society. The standard seems first to have been
set in courtly circles around great lords, a group much narrower even than the
knightly class as a whole. So, whatever the modern reader may think of their
recommendations about table manners or toilet habits, these books are
definitely not addressed to peasants! Later the audience widens perceptibly –
but still not as far as the peasants. In the late seventeenth century, De Courtin's
audience seems to include provincial nobility and distinguished foreigners
visiting the royal court of France, but also probably the leading bourgeois strata
who were not yet assimilated into courtly society and who wished to know the
standards of good behaviour in the best circles (1939: I, 99). By the eighteenth
century, Elias is able to distinguish, for table manners at least, a separate
sequence of manners books more explicitly directed to the middling bourgeoisie
and often setting a lower standard more reminiscent of courtly standards a
generation or two earlier.

Finally, the books set out *adult* standards. Erasmus's *De civilitate*, it is true,
was addressed to boys and used as a school book. But the books in general
represent the (steadily increasing) corpus of what a young person needed to
learn in order to behave and feel as an adult.

THE CURVE OF THE CIVILIZING PROCESS

Elias breaks up the middle part of his first volume into sections on behaviour at
table, the 'natural functions', blowing one's nose, spitting, and behaviour in the
bedroom. Each section begins with excerpts from the manners books in
temporal sequence, so that we 'hear people of different ages speaking on
roughly the same subject' (1939: I, 99). Then Elias develops his interpretation
in comments on each section, seeming sometimes to repeat himself as a similar
trend emerges in each aspect of behaviour, but also subtly adding to his
argument at each stage. The excerpts speak for themselves with great vividness,
but for reasons of space, a brief summary of the changes observed in each area
will have to suffice for present purposes.

Table manners

Compared with later periods, there are relatively few prohibitions on behaviour
at table during the Middle Ages. One is told that one ought not to slurp soup
from one's spoon or smack one's lips noisily. Everyone takes food from a
common dish, places it on a flat trencher of bread, and eats with the fingers, but
it is bad manners to put something one has chewed back into the pot (if you
can't swallow it, throw it on the floor), or to offer a tasty morsel from one's own
mouth to a friend. One should not blow one's nose on to the table-cloth (which

is for wiping greasy fingers), nor into the hand which one uses for taking food from the common dish (do it into the other hand). Table utensils are limited generally to a common spoon for serving from the pot; apart from that, one uses one's own general purpose knife or dagger. By Caxton's time, however, there are prohibitions on the use of the knife – it is not to be passed blade first to other people, nor pointed at one's own face.

In the sixteenth century the fork makes its appearance, at first only for lifting food from the common dish, and the napkin as an optional refinement. By 1560 it is more common for each guest to have his or her own spoon. By the late seventeenth century, one no longer eats soup directly from the common dish, but uses a spoon to ladle some into one's own dish. But now, says Courtin, there are some *gens si délicats* that they would not wish to serve themselves from the soup bowl when someone else has helped himself to a second helping with a spoon that has already been in his mouth. So one must at least wipe one's spoon on one's napkin, or better still, ask for a clean one for the purpose. Only shortly before the Revolution did table manners among the French courtly upper class attain something resembling those of a modern formal dinner party, with its plethora of knives, forks and spoons for each course, and it took more than another century for this to become a more or less general standard in society as a whole.

The 'natural functions'

About urination and defecation, the medieval texts do not say very much: 'Before you sit down, make sure your seat has not been fouled' is one suggestive precept. The reticence does not spring from shame or embarrassment; from many sources it is apparent that people were then able to perform and speak about their bodily functions in the presence of others in a way that is reminiscent of what may be seen today in Africa or the East. Erasmus still discusses these functions quite openly, and 'calls things by their names', though he advises that it is bad manners to speak to someone encountered in the act of urination or defecation. People continued, even in the best circles, to be less than punctilious in performing these functions only in places set apart for the purpose. As late as 1589, the Brunswick Court Regulations decree: 'Let no-one, whoever he may be, before, at, or after meals, early or late, foul the staircases, corridors, or closets with urine or other filth, but go to suitable prescribed places for such relief.' At first, these functions and their exhibition are 'taken as much for granted as combing one's hair' (1939: I, 136), but gradually they are invested with feelings of shame and repugnance, until eventually performed only in the strictest privacy and not even spoken of without acute embarrassment.[5]

Blowing one's nose

Medieval people blew their noses with their fingers. Erasmus instructs that mucus which falls to the ground must be immediately trodden on. Handkerchiefs were known as a luxury item, not in general use. To blow one's nose on one's clothing was already 'rustic', but seemingly common enough. By the late seventeenth century, upper-class people had ample stocks of handkerchiefs and their use was obligatory. Eighteenth-century books laid down polite ways of using them, and for a person to gaze at the product or poke his or her nose was disgusting.

Spitting

In the Middle Ages, it was not only a custom but also seemingly a felt need to spit frequently. One spat freely on the floor, though not, preferably, on the table nor in the common washbasin. In the sixteenth century, it was required that sputum be trodden on, at least if it contained any purulence. Gradually the use of a handkerchief became necessary if one spat, at first in the houses of the great, then in other places kept clean, churches, and finally everywhere. By the nineteenth century, spitting was considered 'at all times a disgusting habit', though the spittoon remained an item of furniture in many places. Finally the spittoon disappeared, and so apparently did the felt need to spit, first in upper social circles and then more generally. As recently as the 1960s, most British buses had 'No Spitting' signs, but those too have now disappeared. Spitting is an interesting case: once considered as much a bodily need as urinating, defecation or nose-blowing, unlike them it has proved eliminable as near as makes no odds. Changes in diet may have played some part, but social pressures very certainly did.[6]

In the bedroom

The final area in which Elias makes use of sequentially ordered excerpts from the manners books – though by no means the last area of conduct discussed in volume I – is behaviour in the bedroom. 'The bedroom', observes Elias (1939: I, 163), 'has become one of the most "private" and "intimate" areas of human life'. In medieval society, this 'privatization' had not yet come about. People were received in bedrooms, even from the bed. It was common for many people to spend the night in the same room – in all but the upper class, these might not unusually include both men and women (cf. Flandrin 1976: 98–102; Shorter 1976: 39–44). People generally slept naked. The sight of the naked human body must have been an everyday commonplace – and not only in the bedroom. Engravings (see figure 1) show young people of both sexes unconcernedly sharing the bath-house, and in some towns it was customary for the family to undress at home and go to the baths naked or very scantily clad (1939: I, 164).

The early manners books often concern themselves with how one should behave when sharing a bed with another person (of the same sex), for example in an inn. One is told to lie still and lie straight, and to keep to one's side of the bed. Garments specifically intended to be worn in bed slowly came into use during the Renaissance, as did the fork and the handkerchief, and Erasmus instructs his readers 'When you undress, when you get up, be mindful of

FIGURE 1

Reproduced from *Das Mittelalterliche Hausbuch* (ed. Bossert and Storck, 1912)
by permission of Bodley's Librarian, Oxford.

modesty.' Something was happening to people's feelings akin to how the Bible describes events in the Garden of Eden: 'and they saw that they were naked and were ashamed'. By the eighteenth century, to have to share a bed was quite exceptional (for the upper classes). Details of how to behave if the necessity arose were left unspoken, and La Salle advised 'You ought neither to undress nor go to bed in the presence of any other person.' These feelings of embarrassment about the body and the bedroom notoriously reached a still higher peak in the nineteenth century.

A SEQUENTIAL ORDER OF DEVELOPMENT

These brief summaries are enough to suggest at least something of common pattern underlying various aspects of the history of manners. How can this pattern, this curve of development, best be characterized?

In general the medieval standards of behaviour, *in comparison with later times*, could be described as simple, naïve and undifferentiated. The impulses and inclinations are less restrained, the commands direct: Don't slurp; don't put gnawed bones back in the common dish; don't blow your nose on the tablecloth; don't urinate on the tapestries. There are, Elias says, 'fewer psychological nuances and complexities in the general stock of ideas' (1939: I, 63), and also greater variations within the common standard. But the Middle Ages are in no sense an 'absolute beginning'. Elias repeatedly emphasises that they by no means represent a bottom rung, still less a zero point in the civilizing process (1939: I, 215). Modes of acceptable behaviour are socially conditioned in societies of every kind; the civilizing process is *a process without a beginning*. What is true, however, is that the medieval standard of behaviour is a convenient starting point for a study of the process because, although never absolutely static, manners appear to have changed only very slowly during the Middle Ages. Over and over again, down the centuries, the same good and bad manners are mentioned, and yet, argues Elias, 'the social code hardened into lasting habits in people themselves only to a limited extent' (1939: I, 82).

Then, at the time of the Renaissance, change becomes perceptible. 'Now, with the structural transformation of society, with the new pattern of human relationships, a change slowly comes about: the compulsion to check one's behaviour increases. In conjunction with this the standard of behaviour is set in motion' (1939: I, 82). This is evident late in the fifteenth century, when it is captured in Caxton's *Book of Curtesye*:

> Thingis whilom used ben now leyd aside . . .
> Thingis sometyme alowed is now repruid.
>
> [Things formerly done are now put aside . . .
> Things once allowed are now reproved.]

It was still more so in the sixteenth century. Erasmus is a pivotal figure in an age of transition. One moment his attitudes seem purely medieval, the next almost modern. He shows all the old medieval unconcern in referring directly to matters later too disgusting to mention, and yet at the same time his recommendations are constantly enriched and nuanced by considerations of what other people *might* think. One vivid example: he tells boys to sit still in their seats, and not constantly shift about because that *gives the impression* of always farting or trying to fart. This tendency becomes steadily more pronounced. In 1672, De Courtin told his readers that fingers were not to be used in eating *greasy* foods, since that led to the need to lick one's fingers or wipe them on the napkin or table-cloth, all of which were 'distasteful to behold'. The rule about eating with one's hands was thus at first not absolute or very consistent, and 'not remotely so self-evident as today' (1939: I, 96). Only very gradually did the prohibition become an internalized habit, a piece of 'self-control'. A critical period of further development came towards the end of the reign of Louis XV when not only table manners but several other aspects of acceptable behaviour reached among the French upper class a stage resembling what came to be general modern usage. It was then (1774) that La Salle's book was issued in a revised edition with extensive changes:

The difference is partly discernible in what no longer needs to be said. Many chapters are shorter. Many 'bad manners' earlier discussed in detail are mentioned only briefly in passing. The same applies to many bodily functions originally dealt with at length and in great detail. The tone is generally less mild, and often incomparably harsher than in the first version [of 1729]. (1939: I, 96)

The movement towards many things no longer being spoken about ran in conjunction with a movement towards moving many of the same things *behind the scenes of social life*. This is most obvious in the case of urination and defecation being rigorously confined to places set apart for the purpose, and in the increasing privacy of the bedroom. But it is seen also in requirements for greater care and discretion in spitting or blowing one's nose in the presence of others. The hiding behind the scenes of what has become distasteful is one of the most characteristic features of the civilizing process in Europe. Today people tend to think of this as something specifically Victorian, but the trend dates from much further back than the nineteenth century.

Plainly what Elias is depicting is not just a matter of changes in surface manners, but also of changes in people's feelings – psychological changes. Speaking of the people of the Middle Ages, who ate together in the customary way, taking meat from the same dish, wine from the same goblet and so forth, Elias argues that they stood in a relationship to each other markedly different from that which modern people have, and the difference involved not only their rational consciousness but the character and structure of their emotional life. In particular,

What was lacking in this *courtois* world, or at least had not developed to the same degree, was the invisible wall of affects which seems now to arise between one human body and another, repelling and separating, the wall which is often perceptible today at the mere approach of something that has been in contact with the mouth or hands of someone else, and which manifests itself as embarrassment at the mere sight of the bodily functions of others, and often at their mere mention, or as a feeling of shame when one's own functions are exposed to the gaze of others, and by no means only then. (1939: I, 69–70)

From the Renaissance, as we have seen, the standards to which people were conditioned 'were set in motion', and the code of 'civility' required people increasingly to 'look about them' and 'check their behaviour'. Standards could be said to be 'rising', as successively more 'refined' models required ever more minute and subtle self-checking. The *'social'* dynamism, Elias argues (1939: I, 101) went hand in hand with a *psychological* dynamic with a regular and relatively autonomous pattern of its own, which he describes as *the advance of the threshold of embarrassment, shame and repugnance.*

When first forming, many of the new standards were not absolute and unambiguous but conditional upon circumstance and, especially, the company one was in. So, at any particular moment, conformity to whatever was then the very latest in refinement might require conscious effort even among adults. But in due course, children were trained by adults not only to conform in their behaviour, but to feel shame, embarrassment and disgust – feelings which arise automatically and unconsciously in circumstances which a few generations before would not have been felt at all, even among adults. This happened in many aspects of child rearing, from toilet training to table manners. Why, for instance, did people come to feel disgust at eating with sticky fingers? Because social superiors made subordinates feel inferior when eating like that, and because adults told children that such habits were disgusting, with consequences Elias describes as follows:

the displeasure towards such conduct which is thus aroused by the adult finally arises through habit, without having been induced by [the present action of] another person . . . Since the pressure or coercion of individual adults is allied to the pressure and example of the whole surrounding world, most children, as they grow up, forget or repress relatively early the fact that their feelings of shame and embarrassment, of pleasure and displeasure, are moulded into conformity with a certain standard by external pressure and compulsion. All this appears to them as highly personal, something 'inward', implanted in them by nature . . . [I]t becomes more and more an inner automatism, the imprint of society on the inner self, the super-ego, that forbids the individual to eat in any other way than with a fork. The social standard to which the individual was first made to conform by *external restraint* is finally reproduced more or less smoothly within him, through a *self-restraint* which may operate even against his conscious wishes. (1939: I, 127–8; my italics)

Such are some of the characteristics of the curve of the civilizing process: the progressive 'refinement' of outward manners, the advancing threshold of embarrassment and repugnance, the hiding of what is felt to be embarrassing behind the scenes of social life, and the psychological concomitants of these processes. But how were these changes set in motion? Several 'reasonable' explanations may suggest themselves to people looking back from the present day. Indeed, the writers of manners books themselves gave 'reasons' why new standards should be adopted. For Elias, however, an account wholly in terms of rationality and reason is neither consonant with the historical evidence nor acceptable as a social scientific explanation.

'REASONS' FOR THE CHANGES

'Material reasons'

Cannot eating with bare hands in the Middle Ages be accounted for by the poverty – in comparison with the modern world – of even the upper classes of those days? Could they simply not afford to give each guest at dinner his own knife, fork, spoon, plates and glasses? Or take the disgusting toilet habits of medieval people. Can they not be explained simply by the lack of sanitary technology, sewers and lavatories?

The answer is no – 'material reasons' do not supply simple answers. Material conditions are entangled in complex ways with other strands of social development, but they certainly do not provide any simple single-factor explanations. Changes in attitude towards the natural functions, for example, are demonstrably not a response to improvements in sanitary technology; on the contrary, says Elias (1939: I, 140), it would be possible to 'demonstrate the sociogenetic and psychogenetic bases of these inventions and discoveries when they came'. (For instance, the reputed invention of the water closet by Sir John Harington around 1590, let alone its widespread use, clearly came well after feelings of repugnance and shame towards defecation and related smells had begun to rise.)

Nor can material poverty explain the persistence of the sparse use of utensils at the tables of the medieval upper class. As Elias points out (1939: I, 67), there were changing fashions in the shaping of spoons and other utensils which it required wealth to follow, but the wealth was not used on acquiring increased quantities of spoons. And indeed the secular upper class of the Middle Ages indulged in extraordinary luxury at table, not just in quantity or elaboration of food (cf. Mennell 1985: 40–61), but also in the quality of the utensils: spoons made of gold, crystal and coral, knives with ebony handles for Lent, ivory for Easter, and inlaid for Whitsuntide. Yet none of this led to a change in the way of eating with the hands from a common dish, sharing a platter and so on. It is not the poverty of utensils that maintains the standard, it is quite simply that nothing else is needed. To eat in this fashion is taken for granted. It suits these people (1939: I, 67).

It is important to be clear that we are here speaking of the secular upper class, and they constituted only one element in a society marked by extreme contrasts of behaviour when compared with modern society. One of the ways in which these contrasts were manifested was in the consumption of meat, and one way in which the secular upper classes indulged in luxury at table was by devouring 'quantities of meat that to us seem fantastic' (1939: I, 117). On the other hand, in the monasteries, an ascetic abstention from eating meat was widespread; here abstention stemmed from self-denial justified by spiritual reasons, again not from shortage. But at the third pole of medieval society among the peasantry, a largely vegetable-based diet was determined precisely by the physical constraint of meat being in short supply for them.[7] So Elias recognizes that, of course, different forms of constraint co-existed; but the very persistence of great social disparities and the unevenness of controls – extreme indulgence alongside extreme self-denial – is one of the defining features of medieval society.

'Reasons' of health and hygiene

To the modern mind it seems even more obvious that considerations of hygiene must have played an important part in bringing about higher standards. Surely the fear of the spread of infection must have been decisive, particularly in regard to changing attitudes towards the natural functions, nose-blowing and spitting, but also in aspects of table manners such as putting a licked spoon back into the common bowl?

Elias is able to show, however, that in each case standards of restraint rose first, and only later were reasons of hygiene advanced as *a posteriori* justifications of the new standards.[8] For instance, when spitting was accepted and frequent, it was said to be unhealthy to retain sputum; only *after* spitting became socially unacceptable was it declared unhygienic. In Erasmus, medical arguments are not found very often. When they are deployed, it is almost always on the side of not restraining the natural urges: it is unhealthy to try to hold back a fart (so do it as discreetly as possible, disguising the sound with a cough). Later, especially in the nineteenth century (but even before the discovery of microbes), reasons relating to health nearly always served to justify the restraint of natural urges. That extended sometimes even to standards the breach of which, in fact, carried little risk of infection or damage to health. The supposed hazards of masturbation are possibly the most famous example. Reasons of health and of morality at this stage often overlapped and served a similar purpose:

Much of what we call 'morality' or 'moral' reasons has the same function as 'hygiene' or 'hygienic' reasons: to condition children to a certain social standard. Moulding by such means aims at making socially desirable behaviour automatic, a matter of self-control, causing it to appear in the consciousness of the individual as the result of his own free will, and in the interests of his own health or human dignity. (1939: I, 150)

There is nothing in the historical evidence to suggest that manners changed, thresholds of sensitivity and embarrassment advanced, for reasons that we can describe as 'clearly rational' and based on a demonstrable understanding of particular causal connections such as how infections are spread. At most, writes Elias, the advance of the threshold of repugnance

may be connected at some points with . . . indefinite fears and therefore rationally undefined fears and anxieties which point vaguely in the direction subsequently confirmed by clear understanding. *But 'rational understanding' is not the motor of the 'civilizing' of eating or of other behaviour.* (1939: I, 116, my italics)

In that last sentence, Elias in effect sides with Freud against Max Weber. On the more specific point, Elias's view has received strong support from Johan Goudsblom's investigations (1986a, 1979) of social reactions to leprosy in the high Middle Ages, to the plague from the late medieval period, to syphilis in the Renaissance, and to cholera in the nineteenth century. Even in the latter case, middle-class feelings of repugnance towards their inferiors' smelling and lack of cleanliness seems to have motivated a concern with sanitation even before it was clearly understood how cholera was spread.

'Reasons of respect'

But if reasons of health and hygiene came to prominence only well on in the civilizing process, what other reasons did people give for distinguishing between 'good' and 'bad' behaviour?

'Religious reasons' do not seem prominent in the secular manners books. The reason most often initially given in manners books from the sixteenth to the eighteenth century to justify new standards was that the old, relatively less restrained, behaviour showed a lack of respect for one's fellows, but *particularly towards social superiors*. One was told to turn away from a person of higher rank when blowing one's nose. One was told only to spit into a handkerchief, or not at all, when people higher ranking than oneself were present: not to do so evoked disdain and showed disrespect. An especially vivid illustration of the principle concerns states of undress: it was said to be disrespectful for a man to appear unclothed before another of superior rank, yet for the superior to do so in front of an inferior could be a sign of his benevolence and affability. (The custom of the royal couchée and levée is a well-known illustration.) This pattern – in which forms of behaviour were considered distasteful or disrespectful in social inferiors which superiors were not ashamed of in themselves, and in which reasons of respect served as the main justification for new standards – was transitional. Later, by the nineteenth century especially, shame in such matters was felt also by the superior in the presence of inferiors, and as the standard came to apply more equally to all ranks, so the controls became more automatic, 'unconscious' and 'natural' for adults. It was, again, at this stage that reasons of hygiene and morality came to the fore, retrospectively, in training children to the seemingly 'natural' standard.

It is obvious that 'reasons of respect' as I have called them are just as much retrospective justifications, and just as little instrumentally rational causal purposes as are reasons of hygiene. They are, however, highly significant as clues to the beginnings of Elias's own explanations of the dynamic of the civilizing process. For the civilizing process, in important respects, *consists* of changes in ways of showing and demanding respect. The dynamic came, he argues, from changes in the structure of social relations.

THE DYNAMIC OF SOCIAL RELATIONS

The manners books and other historical evidence show, argues Elias, that more demanding standards of control over impulses were first imposed by people of higher rank on their social inferiors or, at most, their equals. *Why* they were able to do so leads us into Elias's complex account of the connection between changes in manners and in social stratification and the social distribution of power-chances.

He argues that from the Renaissance onwards, 'feelings and affects were first transformed in the upper class, and the structure of society as a whole permitted this changed affect standard to spread slowly throughout society' (1939: I, 115). This was in marked contrast to the medieval period, when 'the social structure was far less conducive to the permeation of models developed in a specific social centre through the society as a whole' (1939: I, 117). What happened during the waning of the Middle Ages was certainly not the sudden emergence of an egalitarian, non-hierarchical society. The old ruling class of warriors was in decline, as Elias was to show in more detail in the second volume. Old social ties were, if not broken, extensively loosened and in process of transformation. Individuals of different social origins were increasingly thrown together, and the social circulation of ascending and descending groups and individuals speeded up (1939: I, 79).

Then, slowly, in the course of the sixteenth century, a more rigid social hierarchy began to establish itself once more, and a new aristocratic upper class began to form *from elements of diverse social origins*. The process started earlier in some parts of Europe than others, and almost everywhere there were reverses until well into the seventeenth century. But everywhere there was beginning to emerge a new upper class of courtiers, differing from and by no means all descended from the old warrior class. Forced to live with one another in a new way, these people were more acutely confronted with the problem of what constituted a uniform standard of good behaviour. Very gradually, in accordance with the new power ratios, the sense of what to do or not to do in order not to offend others became subtler. Their increased interdependence was associated with a greater degree of consideration of others and with an increased level of *mutual identification* – a correlation which plays a recurrent part in Elias's thinking.

In this somewhat more open and socially more competitive society, the customs, behaviour and fashions of the emerging courtly elite were continually being imitated by the strata immediately below them. Indeed, by asserting their power as definers of *savoir-vivre*, courtly circles actively promoted the adoption of their ways by their inferiors: in effect they 'colonized' the bourgeoisie, as Elias sometimes puts it. Yet, as elite manners were imitated, they inevitably lost something of their value as means of distinguishing the upper class. This compelled those above towards further refinement and development of elite behaviour.

In this overall process, there are many apparently random or arbitrary elements. Yet the fact that in origin a convention may be quite arbitrary does not make it any the less compelling. Take what Elias calls 'the modelling of speech at court' (1939: I, 108–13). 'Un de mes amis' and 'un mien ami' meant exactly the same thing, but that did not prevent the one from being defined as 'the way people speak at court' and the other as 'smelling of the bourgeois'. In this and many other examples, linguistic and non-linguistic, the usage associated with the court became the model which – in France at least – has survived as the standard usage for everyone to the present day. This process of standardization or modelling, the passage of the model from one social unit to another, and the eventual moulding of the individual person to the social model, is one of the most important elements in the whole civilizing process.

Some doubt may yet remain, however, whether this is actually a process which (abstracting from short-term fluctuations and regressions) has a long-term *direction*. Is there more to it than an account merely of how fashions are formed and adopted? In particular, are the later people who behave according to later fashion really *psychologically* any different from the earlier people who behaved according to an earlier model? Elias argues that they are, that the civilizing process does involve sequential changes in a consistent direction over the long term in the psychological make-up of European people.

This directional change is manifest in a changing pattern of controls over individual behaviour. 'Reasons of respect' indicate that restraint on urges and impulses was in the first place imposed only in the company of others, more or less consciously for social reasons. Both the kind and degree of restraint correspond to the social position of the person imposing them, relative to the position of those in whose company he is. Later, argues Elias, as the hierarchy of society becomes somewhat less rigid, and people very gradually become more equal and dependent on each other, the *social* reference of shame and embarrassment recedes from consciousness. That is because renunciation and restraint of the impulses and emotions is compelled far less by particular persons, and to a greater extent by the less visible and more impersonal compulsions of social interdependence, the division of labour, the market and competition. This kind of compulsion is experienced particularly by the ever-growing bourgeois groups who work, trade or follow a profession for their living. It is these pressures along with corresponding ways of conditioning children from an early age and explaining correct behaviour in abstract terms of morality and hygiene which make it appear that socially correct behaviour is voluntarily produced by the individual, on his own initiative, of his own free will (1939: I, 152). Not only does it, for example, become just as embarrassing for a social superior to be seen unclothed, urinating, defecating or spitting by an inferior as vice versa, but the sense of shame and embarrassment comes to operate *even when one is alone*. And the controls become much more internal, unconscious and automatic:

Precisely because the social command not to show oneself exposed or performing natural functions now operates with regard to everyone, and is imprinted in this form on the child, it seems to the adult a command of his own inner self and takes on the form of a more or less total and automatic self-restraint. (1938: I, 139)

Elias refers to this change as a tilting in the *balance* between external constraints (*Fremdzwänge*) and self-restraints (*Selbstzwänge*), towards the latter.

The second respect in which a *directional* change can be observed is in the increasing psychological distance between children and adults. The amount that the child has to learn by way of self-control to attain the adult standard has increased greatly over time. To us, the table manners and toilet habits of medieval adults resemble what we associate with the behaviour of young children, and indeed in these respects the difference between the behaviour of the medieval adult and the medieval child was much less – the child had less far to travel. Indeed the excerpts from manners books show a direction of development over many centuries in Western European society which closely resembles the development seen in the life of each *individual* child as he or she undergoes the process of 'growing up'. (One small illustration: infants are taught not to remove food from their mouths!) That is because every young person is subjected automatically from earliest childhood to an individual civilizing process which moulds the person's behaviour – to a greater or lesser degree, and with greater or lesser success – to the standards then prevalent, which themselves have developed through the *social* civilizing process. Therefore the *psycho*genesis of the adult personality make-up in our 'civilized' society cannot be understood in isolation from the *socio*genesis of our 'civilization'.

This principle constitutes what Elias calls the *sociogenetic ground-rule*, that 'the individual, in his *short* history, passes once more through some of the processes that his society has traversed in its *long* history' (1939: I, xii, my italics; cf. II, 286). This must not be misunderstood, however: Elias is not proposing that 'ontogeny reproduces phylogeny' – the charge always levelled in criticism of Victoran social evolutionists like Herbert Spencer. Elias specifically warns against the idea that each phase of a society's history is reproduced in the life-history of every individual person. 'Nothing would be more absurd than to look for an "agrarian-feudal age" or a "Renaissance" or "courtly-absolutist" period in the life of the individual. All concepts of this kind refer to the structure of whole social groups.' Nevertheless, it is important to remember that even in a society which has undergone a very long civilizing process, no human being comes into the world civilized, but that from the moment of birth every baby is subject to moulding by grown-ups who themselves have been civilized to a greater or lesser degree according to the society and period in which they live. And thus, in order to attain the standard set by grown-ups, which itself has been attained by the society in the course of its history, the individual has to pass through a personal civilizing process – but not through each of the sequential stages of the social civilizing process.

Much later, Elias (1984a: xxxiv) complained that the model of the civilizing process was often vulgarized, and represented as if its central feature were solely a continuous increase and reinforcement of self-restraint. Perhaps some incautious formulations in *The Civilizing Process* do encourage such an interpretation in terms simply of quantitatively 'more' self-restraint. Indeed shifts in that direction do occur. But this way of understanding the theory risks implying that in medieval society, or in tribal societies at a later date, self-restraint is uniformly weak or absent, and that affective or instinctual outbursts are equally strong in all areas of life. What was always in Elias's view more characteristic of people in such societies was rather the uneven, often discontinuous character of the self-restraint:

In certain life-situations it can be of an extent and severity far exceeding the level of self-control required in more developed societies. At the same time, in other situations it leaves the way open to a release of instincts or affects far more violent and spontaneous than the behaviour patterns that would be felt tolerable in more developed societies. The property of the self-control patterns of people in similar societies which is especially striking in comparison with those of people in highly developed industrial societies is their lack of uniformity. A powerful ritualization and formalization of behaviour with corresponding caution and self-restraint in some situations often goes hand in hand with an unbridled liberation of affects in others. The swings of behaviour from one extreme to the other tolerated and even encouraged by society are greater. (1984a: xxxiv–xxxv)

The strength of Elias's arguments about the directionality of changes in personality structure will become much clearer if we now turn first to three areas of behaviour and feeling not much discussed by Elias in 1939, and then to two important sections of *The Civilizing Process* we have hitherto ignored, on relations between the sexes and changes in aggressiveness.

Death, sleeping, appetite

Elias's theory has, as we shall see, been extended in many directions. Three later extensions are worth mentioning here, however, because they are so closely related to the first volume of *The Civilizing Process* – Elias's own book *The Loneliness of the Dying* (1984b), Peter Gleichmann's essay on sleep (1980), and my own work (1987a) on appetite.

Elias's concern with death seems to have been prompted by Philippe Ariès's writings (1974, 1975) on the subject. Though full of admiration for Ariès's historical erudition, he criticizes him for presenting a one-sided view. Ariès tries to document his assumption that in earlier times people died serenely and calmly. Elias points out that life then was often uncertain, brief and wild, and that dying could be full of torment, pain, agony. Death, it is true, was more openly seen and talked about. The presence of other people could sometimes be comforting and helpful to the dying, but there were other cases where 'the heirs standing around the bed mocked and taunted the dying old man'.

In modern society, where death so often takes place in a hospital ward, the physical pain of death is frequently much less, but loneliness can be an increasing problem for the dying. It is not merely that medical technique can displace psychological comforts, and relatives, from the bedside. It is also that ageing and dying are gradual processes, in the course of which increasing frailty brings with it increasing isolation from the living. At the same time, the living find it difficult to identify with the dying: 'Death is the problem of the living. Dead people have no problems.' The problem is unique to humans, because alone of all living beings they *know* they are going to die. Answers to the nature of death change in the course of social development: the supernatural systems of collective belief that could unleash passionate communal feeling in the Middle Ages have declined, surviving most strongly among groups whose existence is most precarious. In their place there is now more scope for individual fantasies of immortality, though most people know these *are* fantasies.

Modern society has witnessed the repression of death both on the level of individual consciousness and on the social plane. Like so many of the other animalic aspects of human life which Elias discussed in *The Civilizing Process*, death has been removed behind the scenes of social life. Elias uses poetry, prose and letters to show the advancing threshold of repugnance towards thoughts of death. Marvell's warning 'To His Coy Mistress' that worms would 'try her long-preserved virginity' is contrasted with a present-day German brochure advertising the services of cemetery gardeners entitled 'A Green Space in the Town' and making no explicit reference to death whatsoever.

Sleeping and appetite are two aspects of bodily functioning about which Elias said little directly in 1939, even though he wrote a good deal about the related subjects of manners in the bedroom and at table. Gleichmann outlines the changes that have taken place in the social aspects of sleep over the centuries. In the Middle Ages, the sleeping–waking cycle of individuals appears to have been relatively undisciplined. People were often depicted as sleeping in the daytime, and in any place that was convenient: under a tree, in a corner, or wherever. There were no special places to sleep; even nobles slept in their living chamber. And sleeping was public matter, sleeping space being shared with others, as we have seen. Changes in sleeping customs came with industrial work. Fatigue and sleepiness came to be understood as something to be experienced away from work, at home. Securing a private, quiet place to sleep has become surrounded by social rules: bedrooms are preferably not used for daytime purposes, members of the opposite sex normally sleep in the same room only if they are sexual partners, and so on. Sleep has become part of the economy, as in 'dormitory suburbs'; hotels and hospitals do their accounting on the basis of the number of beds. Physiological sleep studies have consistently viewed sleep as something completely individual, overlooking the increasing social disciplining of the sleeping-waking cycle: even the sleeping pill is partly to be understood in terms of the pressure to sleep at a socially appropriate time.

My own exploration of changes in the social patterning of appetite suggests a similar trend. In the Middle Ages there was an oscillating pattern of eating related to the general insecurity of life and of food supplies in particular. As well as physical shortages of food, such pressures as there were towards control of appetite from the Church, from sumptuary laws and medical opinion have the marks of external rather than self-controls. The beginnings of greater self-control over appetite can be seen in upper-class circles by the eighteenth century, when they distanced themselves from lower ranks more by the delicacy than quantity of food. The virtue of moderation was increasingly stressed by fashionable bourgeois gastronomes in the nineteenth century. The problem and the fear of fatness gradually spread down the social scale, slimming becoming a prominent popular concern in the twentieth century. The incidence of pathological eating disorders like anorexia nervosa and bulimia also appears to be related to changing standards of control over appetite.

THE BODY AND SEXUAL RELATIONS

During the half century since Elias wrote his section on 'changes in attitude towards relations between the sexes' (1939: I, 169–91), there has been an enormous amount of historical research on sexuality, marriage, and the position of women in Western European society since the Middle Ages. On the whole, Elias's pioneering remarks hold up well in the light of later evidence.

In matters of sexuality, according to Elias a similar civilizing direction of development can be discerned: a gradual removal of sexuality behind the scenes of social life, an advancing threshold of shame and embarrassment, somewhat greater mutual identification between men and women, a shift in the balance between external and self-controls, and an increasing psychological distance between childhood and adulthood.

First, the removal of sexuality behind the scenes. The sight of the naked body, at least in the proper place, was an everyday occurrence in the Middle Ages. Elias does not claim it was never quite the normal thing for men and women to *make love* under the public gaze, but copulation must not infrequently have been stumbled upon without excessively traumatic embarrassment.[9] Artists depicted it in scenes of everyday life in a matter of fact way, without heightened attention or prurience (see figure 2). There was, writes Elias (1939: I, 214), no element of the 'tendency to excite or gratify a wish-fulfilment denied in life, characteristic of everything "obscene".' Even in the sixteenth century, both Erasmus and his theologically more orthodox imitator Morisotus – in books addressed to young boys and used as school texts – talked about prostitutes and brothels as perfectly familiar and unexceptional parts of everyday life. How much more familiar must have been manifestations of ordinary 'marital' sexuality: one thinks of the custom of wedding guests 'laying together' the bride and groom in bed – in earlier times quite naked, later only symbolically, fully clothed on the bed. And it is easy to forget that, among the lower strata in Western European countries, it was quite usual until very recent times indeed for parents and children to sleep in the same room. Only gradually – though inexorably – did sexuality come to be more strongly associated with shame and embarrassment.

Secondly, what Elias had to say about marriage and the changing balance of controls and mutual identification in relations between the sexes seems consistent with later research, such as Georges Duby's *The Knight, the Lady and the Priest* (1981) based on French sources and the study of marriage in medieval Germany undertaken directly as a test of Elias's theory by Michael Schröter (1985, 1987).

Elias shows how knights in the ninth and tenth centuries, and the majority of them a good deal later, did not behave with particular delicacy towards their own wives, still less towards women of lower rank. In the greater part of feudal society, men ruled and the dependence of women was unconcealed and almost unrestricted. Nothing compelled men to constrain and control their drives, there was little talk of love: women served as means of physical pleasure, little

FIGURE 2
Reproduced from *Das Mittelalterliche Hausbuch* (ed. Bossert and Storck, 1912)
by permission of Bodley's Librarian, Oxford.

else. They were subject to abrupt, sometimes violent, sexual advances.[10] There are many accounts of nobles and kings, let alone lower orders, beating their wives, frequently punching them on the nose (1939: II, 78–84). Duby (1981: 220) remarks that 'there was a good deal of rape in noble households'. As for mere peasant women, a knight would certainly feel free to dispense with preliminaries.

Duby's and Schröter's works bear out the strong contrasts, the diversity and the relative discontinuity of controls which mark the medieval period in matters of sexuality as in other aspects of behaviour. Until the thirteenth or fourteenth century in Germany, and perhaps a century earlier than that in France (these are matters of gradual transition, so there is no purpose in trying to give precise starting and finishing points), marriages were established and supported principally by families and neighbours or by land-owning and courtly circles. Marriages were initiated not just by agreement but quite commonly by abduction of women. Incestuous liaisons within the Church's then rather extensive definition of the prohibited degrees were tolerated. So, quite openly, was concubinage. Given the importance of the inheritance of land and titles for the knightly stratum, it was necessary that the choice of partners remained more or less detached from individual sexual attraction. That was consistent with the Church's long-standing deprecation of excessive love within marriage.[11] More generally, the Church's teaching put a high value on asceticism and abstinence practised to extremes by only small minorities in cloisters while applying it with much tolerance and adaptation to the world as it actually was. Neither Church nor state played a large role in matters of marriage, and 'the demands of the Church cannot be taken as a measure of the real standards of secular society' (1939: I, 183).[12]

Only as land-owning families lost their function as largely autonomous survival units as part of the state-formation process to be discussed in chapter 3 did the Church and state come to play the part in the control of marriage that we take for granted today, or did until quite recent years. Though the autonomy of feudal lords and knights declined, the problem of legitimacy – that is, really a problem of legitimate *inheritance* – remained. By the twelfth century, according to Duby (1981: 196), great respect was paid in the highest circles in France to legal forms, though the Church applied the rules very flexibly in practice. According to Schröter, only in the sixteeenth century did Church control of marriage become predominant in Germany.

Even after this, it long remained quite normal for a husband's bastard children to be accorded an honourable place and raised with his legitimate offspring. Extramarital relationships on the part of the socially 'weaker sex' were, however, regarded as reprehensible – an asymmetry directly reflecting the very unequal power balance between the sexes. The pressures on the libidinal life of women have, with rare exceptions, been greater throughout Western history than on men of equal birth. In warrior society, women in high positions always found it easier to control, refine and fruitfully transform their affects than did men of the same rank, probably in consequence of the conditioning of females from early in life (1939: II, 82). Later, in aristocratic court society, the social power of the sexes was *relatively* rather more equal than before – women played an important part in forming social opinion, and were subjected to fewer external controls (Elias 1969a: 49–51; cf. Lee 1975). But greater self-constraint was expected of them; Elias cites Mme Lafayette's novel *La Princesse de Clèves*, in which the heroine's husband, knowing her to be in love with another man, remarks, 'I shall trust only in you . . . With a temperament like yours, *by leaving you your liberty, I set you narrower limits than I could enforce*' (1939: I, 184; cf. II, 307). Forms of bourgeois marriage typical of the nineteenth century took this line of development further still. While not fully exploring the intriguing question of 'why the occupational work that became a general way of life with the rise of the bourgeoisie should necessitate particularly strict disciplining of sexuality' (1939: I, 184), Elias does make the interesting suggestion that under this way of life,

the renunciation and restraint of impulses are compelled far less by particular persons . . . it is now, more directly than before, the less visible and more impersonal compulsions of social interdependence – the division of labour, the market, and competition – that impose restraint and control on the impulses and emotions. (1939: I, 152)

It is these pressures, transmitted through the corresponding mode of training children within the family from an early age – now at this period with a strong emphasis on absolute dictates of 'morality' rather than the more conditional 'reasons of respect' – that make it appear as if 'socially desirable behaviour is voluntarily produced by the individual himself, on his own initiative'.

Which brings us back, thirdly, to the increasing psychological distance between childhood and adulthood. The phrase risks misunderstanding. Elias does not mean the same thing as *social* distance between children and adults. In earlier centuries, children might well be far more subservient to and socially dependent on adults than was typical later; and yet, at the same time, they 'lived very early in the same social sphere as adults', a sphere in which 'adults did not impose on themselves either in action or in words the same restraint with regard to sexual life as later' (1939: I, 175). The gradual concealment of sexuality behind the scenes of social life was not merely spatial. It also involved 'the gradual formation of the peculiar segregated area in which people came to spend the first twelve, fifteen and now almost twenty years of their lives'.[13]

This development had important psychological consequences. It helped to make problems of 'growing up' progressively more severe. The increasing sense of shame surrounding sexual relations led eventually to adults experiencing great difficulty in talking about sexual matters to children and 'today this difficulty appears almost natural. It seems to be explained almost by biological reasons alone that a child knows nothing of the relations of the sexes, and that it is an extremely difficult task to enlighten growing girls and boys about themselves and what goes on around them' (1939: I, 169). By the nineteenth century, the problem of 'sex education' (as it would be called still later) had become acute. But there was nothing 'natural' about it. In other times, the problem had scarcely existed – as when Erasmus and Morisotus were able to assume that boys equally 'naturally' knew all about brothels and prostitutes. Yet by the nineteenth century, 'a thick wall of secrecy' had been erected around the adolescent. At least one book explicitly recommended that girls be told as little as possible, and the general concern was to instil 'modesty' – meaning the feelings of shame, fear, embarrassment and guilt necessary for conformity to the same social standards of instinctual controls as adults. It was above all, Elias emphasized, the personality structure of adults themselves, with its very highly developed pattern of self-constraints, which made it so difficult for them to speak of these things (1939: I, 179–81).

The reader may well wonder at this point (if the thought has not arisen before) whether the walls of which Elias speaks have not already been breached, in the course of the manifold developments known popularly in the later twentieth century as 'the permissive society'. Elias himself, writing in the 1930s, noted the relaxation of many taboos after the First World War, and asked whether this represented a decisive reversal of the civilizing process or merely one of the many temporary turnabouts seen before in history (1939: I, 186ff). He also wondered whether some *specific* relaxations were possible only against the background of still higher *general* standards of self-constraint. But this is to raise a major question, much researched and debated in recent decades, which will be pursued in more detail in chapter 10.

AGGRESSIVENESS, VIOLENCE, CRUELTY

Elias also seeks to show that the same curve of the civilizing process seen in many other aspects of behaviour can be traced through changes in aggressiveness and cruelty over the centuries.

In the early Middle Ages, Elias points out, the majority of the secular ruling class were leaders of armed bands. For them, war was a normal state of society; they had little other social function but to wage it; they loved battle. It is difficult for the modern mind to grasp the joy and exultation they felt in the clash of arms, but still less easy to come to terms with the sheer pleasure warriors then derived from cruelty, from the destruction and torment of other human beings. Already, suggests Elias, 'the release of the affects in battle in the Middle Ages was no longer, perhaps, quite so uninhibited as in the early period of the Great Migrations, but it was open and uninhibited enough compared with the standard of modern times' (1939: I, 192). Long into the Middle Ages, for example, the mutilation of prisoners was practised with evident relish.[14] So were rape and pillage in victory. Very gradually over the centuries, these military pleasures were subjected to increasingly strong social control anchored in the state organization. Indeed, tighter discipline and control over the impulses came more and more to be conditions of success in the changing circumstances of military conflict.

Yet the pleasure taken in cruelty, torment and killing was by no means confined to a military context. It is even more difficult for people today to understand the pleasurable excitement their ancestors experienced in the spectacle of burning heretics, public torture and executions, well-known and abundantly documented as that is. Just as incomprehensible is cruelty to animals as a source of pleasure: Elias mentions the custom in sixteenth-century Paris of celebrating Midsummer's Day by releasing a few dozen cats from a net into a bonfire below, for the amusement of the spectators (often including the King and Queen) at the shrieks of the burning animals (1939: 1, 203).[15]

Of course, writes Elias, medieval people did not always go around 'with fierce looks, drawn brows, and martial countenances as the clearly visible symbols of their warlike prowess'. Rather, what was more characteristic of their temperament was their volatility, their propensity to switch suddenly from mood to mood – from merriment, via sudden offence at a joke taken too far for example, to violent brawling. This temperament was as typical of townspeople and peasants as of the warrior class itself.[16]

Elias argues that aggressiveness and impulses towards cruelty and ready resort to violence underwent a long-term process of moulding and taming together with the other changes to facets of behaviour already discussed. They, too, come to be impeded by shame and repugnance, and they, too, come normally to find expression in only 'refined' and indirect forms. Even among soldiers, who are expected to have the temperamental as well as technical abilities to kill and maim, the venting of aggression comes to be highly disciplined and circumscribed. (Elias remarks, however, that cruelty and pleasure in the torment of others can still break out more directly and uninhibitedly (1939: 1, 192). Colonial history, periods of revolution, and of course the Nazi concentration camps furnish ready instances of this.)

One prominent component of this transformation of the impulses of aggressiveness and cruelty identified by Elias is the transfer of emotions from direct action to spectating (1939: 1, 202–3). Boxing matches and certain other forms of sport represent a late stage in this shift towards visual pleasures; the rise and decline of public executions are phases in the same process. Pieter Spierenburg argues in his important book *The Spectacle of Suffering* (1984: 202) that executions and other punishments carried out under the public gaze, which became institutionalized in the course of the later Middle Ages, 'first served to seal the transfer of vengeance from private persons to the state'. In the emerging states of Western Europe, authorities were preoccupied until well into the sixteenth century with maintaining a highly unstable and geographically limited monopoly of violence. Displays of physical punishment were still considered indispensable to the bolstering of authority into the early modern period. The pleasurable excitement spectators experienced witnessing executions and tortures may become more comprehensible when it is realized that such events were directly linked to people being forced to relinquish direct action for vengeance through the vendetta or the lynch-mob.

Spierenburg's book contraposes Elias's theory to that of Michel Foucault. In his well-known book *Discipline and Punish* (1975), Foucault depicted the transition from public executions in the eighteenth century to incarceration in the nineteenth as rather abrupt. This picture was derived more from the assumptions of structuralist philosophy than from archival sources. Spierenburg, in contrast, demonstrates from the archives that the process was far more gradual.

Some mitigation of the more extreme, mutilating punishments can be detected from the early seventeenth century. In most Western European countries executions were removed within prison walls during the nineteenth century, and abolished in the twentieth. But over the whole of that period there is clear evidence of a gradual but eventually accelerating increase in sensibility towards the suffering of the victim: 'the spectacle of punishment, even if it was inflicted upon the guilty, was . . . becoming unbearable. By the end of the eighteenth century some of the audience could feel the pain of delinquents on the scaffold. . . . [I]nter-human identification had increased' (Spierenburg 1984: 184). Echoing Elias, Spierenburg (1984: 204) argues that psychological controls were largely confined to the context of a person's own group. During the early modern period, the mutual dependence between social groups increased, and in consequence the context of psychological controls widened and an increase in mutual identification took place.

This seems to have been extended in part even to identification with other animals. It is striking that not only are cats no longer publicly burned for popular entertainment, but slaughterhouses have been removed well behind the scenes of social life, and there has been some tendency away from serving food at table too strongly reminiscent of the animals from which it came (1939: I, 118–22).[17]

In short, much of what earlier aroused pleasure came to arouse displeasure instead. How this comes about, Elias explains, is that 'socially undesirable expressions of instinct and pleasure are threatened and punished with measures that generate and reinforce displeasure and anxiety' (1939: I, 204), which through constant recurrence come to be associated with behaviour that in itself may be pleasurable. Thus 'socially aroused displeasure and anxiety fight with hidden desires'. As in the case of sexuality and other behaviour, parents are the main (not sole) agents through which disapproval and punishment of socially undesirable behaviour is transmitted, but they are in a sense only intermediaries. The taming of aggressiveness especially is the consequence of a much broader change in the structure of society. Medieval society had lacked any central power strong enough to compel people to restrain their impulses towards violence; but '*if in this or that region, the power of central authority grows, if over a larger or smaller area people are forced to live at peace with one another, the moulding of affects and the standards of the economy of instincts are very gradually changed as well*' (1939: I, 201).

CONCLUSION

That quotation contains in a nutshell the connection between social structure and personality structure. It also points to why Elias, after depicting the curve of the civilizing of behaviour so fully in the first volume, found it necessary to devote the bulk of the second volume of *The Civilizing Process* to the superficially very different subject of the dynamics of the formation of states.

For, in a sense, the first volume only hints at an explanation of the changes in manners and personality it describes, and to read that volume in isolation (as it so often has been) is misleading. Certainly *some* layers of explanation are offered in the first volume: changing modes of conditioning children within the family, and their consequences for personality structure are described. This is linked in a complex web of explanation to the removal of many activities behind the scenes of social life, to an increasing division between public and private spheres, and to the changing balance between external and self-constraints. Furthermore, the first volume begins to link all that, as we have seen, to changes in the structure of the secular ruling classes in Western Europe from the Renaissance onwards, the emergence of a new aristocracy, the rise of absolutist courts, social competition and emulation. Elias is in effect arguing that the changes in people's psychology and social behaviour were enforced by the necessity of adapting to new forms of social life:

The question why men's behaviour and emotions change is really the same question why their forms of life change. In medieval society certain forms of life had been developed, and the individual was bound to live within them, as knight, craftsman, or bondsman. In more recent society, different opportunities, different forms of life were prescribed, to which the individual had to adapt. If he was of the nobility, he could lead the life of a courtier. But he could no longer, even if he so desired (and many did) lead the less constrained life of the knight. From a particular time on, this function, this way of life, was no longer present in the structure of society. Other functions, such as those of the guild craftsman or priest, which played an extraordinary part in the medieval phase, largely lost their significance in the total structure of social relations. *Why do these functions and forms of life to which the individual must adapt himself as to more or less fixed moulds, change in the course of history?* (1939: I, 205; my italics)

In other words, the first volume was concerned with the behavioural and psychological consequences of a changing social structure; but Elias then felt the need to dig even deeper, to uncover the dynamics of the structured processes of change in the social structures themselves. A second volume was necessary.

3

States and Courts

In his investigation of how personality and standards of behaviour are linked to the broader structure of society, Elias is led in the second volume of *The Civilizing Process* far back in time beyond even the earliest of his manners books. He turns to the very beginning of the Middle Ages in the centuries which saw the end of the Western Roman Empire and the great 'migrations of peoples' into Europe.

Elias sought the dynamics of structured processes of change in the patterns of social interdependence and competition between the major interests in society. The first words of the second volume assert that:

The struggles between the nobility, the Church, and the princes for their shares in the control and the produce of the land run through the entire Middle Ages. In the course of the twelfth and thirteenth centuries, a further group emerges as a partner in this play of forces: the privileged town dwellers, the 'bourgeoisie'. (1939: II, 3)

But within this broad continuity, the intensity and consequences of the struggle fluctuated markedly.

Like Marc Bloch, who was writing his great study *Feudal Society* (1939–40) at roughly the same time, Elias distinguishes between two broad epochs in the Middle Ages. During the 'first feudal age' (Bloch's phrase for the period roughly AD 850–1050), *centrifugal* forces were dominant: the central authority of kings and emperors became progressively weaker and effective rule was fragmented among numerous lords, each controlling a small local territory. The dominant process was one of *feudalization*. This period reached its nadir at different dates in different parts of the continent but the eleventh century is roughly the hinge between it and the 'second feudal age'. During the twelfth century, notably in the region which was to become France, the first signs are evident that *centripetal* forces are once more gradually becoming dominant. There are many fluctuations, but the long-term trend becomes one towards growth in the power of kings and their central authority *vis-à-vis* the local magnates. Uncertainly at first, but continuing over the centuries with what becomes a more and more compelling force, a process of *state-formation* sets in.

Elias's major enterprise in the second volume of *The Civilizing Process* is in fact a sociological theory of state-formation processes. Max Weber, in what is little more than an aside, defined the state as an organization which successfully upholds a claim to binding rule-making over a territory, by virtue of commanding a monopoly of the legitimate use of violence (Weber, 1922a: I, 54). Elias set out to demonstrate the *process* through which that monopoly was established and extended; also, more than Weber, Elias emphasizes that it is a question of a *twin* monopoly of violence *and taxation*.

Later in his career, as we shall see in chapter 9, Elias stressed that he saw the European state-formation process (and indeed the European civilizing process in general) as only one phase in a much longer-term integration process for humanity as a whole. In this *very* long-term perspective, centripetal, integrating forces have dominated. Nevertheless there have been many fluctuations, and Elias begins his second volume by studying the centrifugal, disintegrating forces at work in the first feudal age.

CENTRIFUGAL FORCES DOMINANT: ANTIQUITY TO FEUDALISM

Louis VI (the Fat), who reigned from 1108 to 1139, though nominally king of a much larger region, was effectively ruler only of his own family domain, the Duchy of Francia centred on Paris and Orléans (Elias 1939: II, 93 ff). Indeed he scarcely set foot outside it. The whole map of the region which today is France was divided up into similar small dominions, and Francia was not even the largest among them.

Nor was Louis even entirely secure in his own domain. He spent most of his reign in the saddle, fighting to secure control of his own territory not only against the incursions of such neighbours as the Dukes of Normandy but against the challenge of rival families within his own lands. One of these held a fortress at Montlhéry, commanding the route between Paris and Orléans, and thus between the two major parts of Louis's lands; the family were descended from a royal official who a century earlier had been granted land at Montlhéry by Louis VI's great-grandfather. Louis mounted a series of major military expeditions against the fortress, and the struggle lasted most of his reign before he finally captured it. *Montlhéry is fifteen miles from Paris.*

How could this decentralization and fragmentation of rule, this extreme weakness of 'central' rulers, have come about? For Louis VI was, after all, one of the Capetians who had succeeded the Carolingian line as kings of the West Franks.[1] Nominally he was lord of a territory defined by the Treaty of Verdun in 843 and including most of what is modern France, stretching from the Pyrenees to a boundary not quite so far east as now. The Treaty of Verdun had cut into three the much larger empire of Charlemagne (768–814), which had spread across what is today Germany, Italy, the Low Countries and France into parts of Spain. Before that, and of course before the 'Dark Ages', the Roman Empire – to which Charlemagne looked back when he assumed the title of Holy Roman Emperor – had encompassed a far greater territory still. So, to return to our question, how had it come about that Louis VI, and numerous other rulers of his time, had retained only such puny power over such limited dominions?

Towards the end of the Roman period population had fallen, the markets had emptied, the chains between the producers and consumers of commodities had shortened, the use of money declined, and there had been a shift from an urban to an agrarian way of life with more people leading a more or less self-sufficient or autarkic existence through the local production of rural communities.[2]

Then, with successive waves of migrating tribes – especially at this time Teutons, notably the Franks – Europe gradually filled up again, and these trends were to some extent reversed. A period of belligerent, expansionist central lords reached its apogee in the vast empire of Charlemagne. Yet even under Charlemagne, the centrifugal forces towards disintegration were extremely strong. A mainly barter economy did not yield taxes adequate to support a central administrative machine or a standing army capable of defending and maintaining order within a territory of that size. Even the Emperor himself and his central officials lived essentially off the produce of his own family lands, moving from one estate to another. For the rest of the territory, the state of economic, military and transport arrangements made inevitable the delegation to local officials of comprehensive military, administrative and judicial powers. And the only way of securing their services and enabling them to carry out the duties of their office was to attach to the office sufficient land to support them. Charlemagne's dukes and counts were in effect farmers with military functions. The risk of placing in the hands of officials both the means of violence – to repel external aggression and maintain internal order – and the land to support them is obvious. The officials repeatedly seized any opportunity to use their military resources to assert their own independence of the centre and, whenever possible, to make their office hereditary in their own family. Centrifugal forces constantly reasserted themselves, and the long-term trend was towards weaker central rulers and the effective autonomy of local lords. 'The strength of the centrifugal tendencies towards local *political autarky* within societies based predominantly on a barter economy corresponds to the degree of local *economic autarky*' (Elias 1939: II, 28).

The familiar text-book image of the 'feudal system' involves the exchange of pledges between great hereditary lords and lesser hereditary lords, and between lords and husbandmen – pledges of protection by the more powerful in return for pledges of service, military or agrarian, by the less powerful. The image is misleading. For when centrifugal forces had run their fullest course, society had assumed a largely *cellular* structure of self-sufficient units. The webs of interdependence bonding together the people of different territories were weak. Oaths of fealty meant little if a local ruler had no need of the protection of his nominal overlord, and if the overlord lacked the power to exact dues and services from his nominal vassal. Louis VI had several nominal vassals (most obviously the Dukes of Normandy, who were also Kings of England) whose lands, and in consequence military power, were at least equal to his own.

The dilemma throughout the period was that a central ruler's only means of securing services was to grant land to subordinates, yet giving away his own land only weakened his own power. This centrifugal tendency could be offset as long as kings and emperors were still conquering new land, still acquiring lands of their own (that applied to both the Carolingian Empire and the Roman Empire before it). But as conquest of land externally became more difficult, centrifugal forces gained dominance. Inside the Western Frankish Empire too, from the ninth century onwards, there was no longer very much usable land – usable in terms of the agricultural technology of the time – that had not been pre-empted. 'Land, the most important means of production, the epitome of property and wealth in this society, became scarce' (1939: II, 38). It had been filled up not merely by the great migration of peoples, but by the rise in population which followed it. The increase in population was not the 'first cause' of the ensuing socio-economic-political changes; it was only one of several elements intertwining in a complex pattern of cause and effect (Elias 1939: II, 32). He is not a 'demographic determinist'. His argument is that *in this particular period*, because land was by far the most important means of production and source of power, and because the low division of labour afforded relatively few alternative means of livelihood, increasing population had a simpler and more direct effect on the struggle for land than in a more complex society.

There emerged the peculiarity of a surplus population not just of the labouring classes but also of the upper classes – a 'reserve army' (only too literally) of landless knights, often younger sons of enfeoffed knights – desperate to acquire a fief of their own. This, argues Elias, helps to explain 'the sociogenesis of the crusades' (1939: II, 38ff). Norman knights conquered Sicily and England in the eleventh century, the early crusades established feudal kingdoms in the Holy Land, and the Teutonic Knights pushed eastwards into Slavic territory. Many others strove to acquire land in Europe.

The competition for land eventually ran into the buffers. By the twelfth century, expansion had come to an end. It became increasingly difficult for warriors who did not already have land to obtain any, or for families with small possessions to enlarge them. 'Property relations were ossified. It grew more and more difficult to rise in society. And accordingly class differences between warriors were hardened. A hierarchy within the nobility corresponding to the magnitude of land ownership emerged more and more clearly' (1939: II, 58).[3] This process of closure brought the text-book image of a neat hierarchy – albeit one beset periodically by violent conflicts a little closer to reality. Somewhere around AD 1100,[4] the scene was set for centripetal forces gradually to regain dominance.

In fact, even while the process of feudalization and the extreme fragmentation of effective power had been proceeding, some contrary forces had been at work. In the ninth to eleventh centuries, towns, trade and the use of money had also grown, weaving a mesh of social interdependences – however small at first – as a counterpoint to the main theme. As early as the Carolingian period, inland transport – and with it the use of money – was developing in Europe, perhaps partly (as Henri Pirenne (1937) famously proposed) in consequence of the decline of the Mediterranean, the prime thoroughfare of the ancient world, following the Arab conquests. Towns, the division of labour, trade and the use of money all began to grow. Apart from the 'surplus' of landless warriors just mentioned, population growth also produced a surplus of landless people from the labouring classes; unable to conquer territory, they formed a growing artisan class in the towns which were expanding noticeably in the eleventh century. And not only expanding in size but still more changing in function. Such agglomerations of people as there had been in the ninth century were scarcely 'towns'; little more than extensions of the fortress and administrative centre of a lord, they had had no really independent economic life, with very limited trade and division of labour. These proto-towns had simply formed part of the cellular structure of society at large; in them, as on a manor, commodities were largely produced and consumed in the same place. All this began to change. With the exchange of products down longer chains – longer both geographically and in terms of the specialization of labour – and with larger markets, there was also a greater need for the use of money as a unified standard of exchange. Elias emphasises that there is little point in debates about whether the revival of money (more exactly, he says, a slow long-term shift in the *balance* between the barter and monetary sectors of the economy) was cause or effect of change. The essential point is to examine 'the actual social processes which, after the slow ebb of money traffic in declining antiquity, once again brought forth the new human relationships, the new forms of integration and interdependence, which caused the need for money to increase again' (1939: II, 47). The cellular structure of society began to differentiate and larger numbers of people began once more to be bonded together in longer chains and more entangled webs of interdependence.

A comment is called for on the prominence of economic matters – trade, towns, transport, markets, money, land and labour – in Elias's accounts both of feudalization and state-formation. Although he always speaks with great respect of Marx's own pioneering contribution to understanding processes of social development, Elias is highly critical of the one-sided causal weight which Marxists often attribute to narrowly economic forces. Where the bonds of interdependence between people are so undifferentiated, at once social, economic and political, it seems to Elias irrelevant and misleading to attempt to prove a one-sided primacy of 'economic' causality. Elias says that political autarky *corresponds* to economic autarky, not that it is determined by it. The connection is a two-way one through time, economic fragmentation being conditioned by political fragmentation as well as the other way round, just as later he argues that economic integration is conditioned by political integration as well as vice versa. Recent Marxist theorists, Louis Althusser, Etienne Balibar, Nicos Poulantzas among them, have been prepared to recognize the part played by 'political' and 'ideological' forces in perpetuating or reproducing the *dominance* of a given 'mode of production'. But they have still hoped to distinguish dominance from *determination*, reserving that latter 'in the last resort' for economic forces.[5] Elias, like Marx himself, is always looking for the *immanent dynamic* of real social relations between people – relations including unequal, exploitative interdependence, and the internal tensions which cause change – and why development went one way rather than another. The notion of 'mode of production' does not always seem helpful in this task, tending to focus attention on how the apparently fixed shape of a building is determined by the foundations on which it is erected. This seems true even of Perry Anderson's stimulating study *Passages from Antiquity to Feudalism* (1974a) which, although Anderson had not read Elias, covers the same period as the part of Elias's book that we have just been discussing. Anderson's basic explanation of feudalism is that 'The catastrophic collision of two dissolving anterior modes of production – primitive and ancient – eventually produce the feudal order which spread throughout medieval Europe' (1974a: 128), and the variants of feudalism in different parts of Europe are explained essentially in terms of the differing percentages of the two ingredients – the ancient Roman and the primitive Germanic (Anderson 1974a: 154ff).[6] For all that, Anderson's excellent study, paying attention as it does to varieties of feudalism in both Eastern and Western Europe, can usefully be read alongside Elias.

CENTRIPETAL FORCES DOMINANT: STATE-FORMATION PROCESSES

Louis VI concentrated throughout his reign on consolidating his own possessions and establishing the supremacy of his family over all other rivals *within* the Duchy of Francia. After him, the military endeavours of his successors were directed more outwards, to the struggle with the similar princely rulers of neighbouring dominions for supremacy within a wider area. By similar means, other families were establishing themselves as the 'central' houses of the other dozen or score dominions in the former west Frankish Empire. As they made effective their feudal overlordship of the minor warrior houses in each territory, the free competition for land came to operate within a more confined circle: only the emergent 'central' houses now competed directly with each other. The first stirrings of the long process of state-formation were happening in the region. And, even if the process started earlier or later in Germany, Italy or England, even if it were accelerated or retarded, and no matter how the details varied, Elias argues that the main components of the process can be discerned there too.

There are three principal elements in Elias's complex discussion of state-formation processes. First, the *monopoly mechanism*. This term refers to two intimately related processes: the gradual concentration of the means of violence and taxation (the two principal means of ruling) in the hands of a single ruler and administration in each territory; and the enlargement of the territory through competition with and elimination of neighbouring rulers. Second, the *royal mechanism*, which refers to the internal balance of social forces *within* the developing state. And third, the *transformation of 'private' into 'public' monopolies*. For purposes of schematic outline, I will deal with each of the three in turn.

However it is misleading to think of them as successive stages, since the beginnings of the latter two processes are evident and intertwine with the process of monopolization while it is still in train. Moreover, other strands – the growth of towns, of the money economy, of intermediate 'bourgeois' strata – are also spliced into the overall process of development.

The monopoly mechanism

Elias defines the monopoly mechanism in the following proposition:

if, in a major social unit, a large number of the smaller units which, through their interdependence, constitute the larger one, are of roughly equal social power and are thus able to compete freely – unhampered by pre-existing monopolies – for the means to social power, i.e. primarily the means of subsistence and production, the probability is high that some will be victorious and others vanquished, and that gradually, as a result, fewer and fewer will control more and more opportunities, and more and more units will be eliminated from the competition, becoming directly or indirectly dependent on an ever-decreasing number. (1939: II, 106)

The proposition is phrased in strikingly general terms. As Elias makes quite explicit (1939: II, 95, 149), there is an exact analogy between the monopoly mechanism as it applies to state-formation and the competition of firms in markets. Economists' models of competition begin with a multiplicity of freely competing small firms but, except in truly perfect markets (which are rare in the real world), the process of competition generally leads to the domination of markets by a smaller number of larger firms, represented in its varying degrees by economists' models of imperfect or monopolistic competition, oligopoly, duopoly and outright monopoly. Marx, of course, had discussed the emergence of monopoly capitalism, and his writings must have been in Elias's mind as he formed his own theory in the 1930s. But so also were certainly Mannheim's brilliant essay on competition as a general social process (1929b: see p. 14 above), to which Elias gives a footnote, and probably the discussions among economists of the time about competition in imperfect markets, triggered particularly by the books of Joan Robinson (1933) and E. H. Chamberlin (1933).

Elias's main purpose, though, was to show the part played by the monopoly mechanism in processes of state-formation. In 'modern' societies, the central authority of the state has achieved a high level (again, as always, Elias refrains from speaking in absolutes) of monopolization over the means of violence and of taxation. That is to say, it has control especially over the armed services and police: if it has not, we speak of the state as being weak or unstable. The free use of military weapons is denied to the individual.[7] That is not to say that weapons are never used by individuals against each other, but an offence is committed when they are, and if the forces of the state – army, police, courts, prisons – are unable to keep infringements within reasonable control, then we think something is going seriously wrong with the state. In the same way, the central authority of a modern state reserves to itself the right to tax the property or income of individuals. The two monopolies are related: the financial resources flowing into the central authority enable it to maintain its monopoly of military force, and that in turn maintains the monopoly of taxation. 'Neither has in any sense precedence over the other; they are two sides of the same monopoly' (1939: II, 104). A protection racket operated by gangsters would be an example of a crime which infringed both the related monopolies at once; such rackets are far from unknown in the modern world, but if the police do not succeed sooner rather than later in eliminating them, then we again think something is wrong with the state. From another angle, the state itself may be seen as a kind of monopolized protection racket; it is important not to see only the beneficent aspects of modern states, which are Janus-headed.

Yet these twin monopolies of violence and taxation have not always existed. A relatively advanced division of labour (or 'social division of functions', as Elias often phrases it to broaden it beyond the narrowly economic) is required before an enduring, specialized organizational apparatus for administering the monopoly can emerge. Only when such a complex apparatus has evolved does control over army and taxation take on its full monopoly character. And it is only with the emergence of the specialized apparatus for ruling and of a continuing monopoly, argues Elias (1939: II, 105), that dominions can be said to have taken on the character of 'states'. From then on, social conflicts are generally concerned not with challenging the existence of monopoly rule, but only with questions of who shall control it, from whom they are to be recruited, and how the burdens and benefits of the monopoly are to be distributed.

In the ninth to eleventh centuries, this monopoly structure was only weakly developed in Western Europe. We have seen how centrifugal forces reduced the map of what is today France to dozens of tiny territorial units. The acquisition of land, and with it 'governmental' functions, was left to the 'private enterprise' of numerous local warriors, competing by military means. Much of the second volume of *The Civilizing Process* is taken up with a detailed study of how this competition led through a long series of 'elimination contests', to the emergence of a single powerful central state, France, in the region of the former west Frankish Empire.

The initial differences between the score or so of competing dominions in the region at the time of Louis VI were slight. Of course, the 'market' in which they were competing was not perfect, and the territories did not start absolutely equal in the struggle. There were some basic geographical advantages and dis- advantages – size, topography, fertility and resources, lines of communication. Some lords, generally the bigger ones, found towns growing around their fortresses. They were slow at first to recognize the advantages, and in the eleventh and twelfth centuries struggled to retain feudal rights over the people of the towns. As towns gradually won charters of emancipation, however, the benefits to the lords on whose lands they stood became apparent. Towns created trade; trade brought increasing use of money and could be taxed; money taxes could be used to finance larger armies and larger administrative machines. In this way, towns, trade and money helped tilt the balance in favour of larger territorial magnates at the expense of the smaller (1939: II, 66ff, 184). (The process worked the other way as well: the emergence of stronger lords facilitated the wider use of money, the growth of towns and of burgher groups.)

Still, to start with, the differences between the various dominions in the west Frankish area were not very great, and it was by no means a foregone conclusion that it would be the Paris kings, the Capetian Dukes of Francia, who would emerge as victors from the competitive struggle. The support of the Church and their traditional prestige as possessors of the crown were advantages to some extent, but the final outcome was very long in doubt. There remained rival centres of monopolization, most notably the Duchy of Burgundy and the 'English' domains in 'France'. Both 'France' and 'England' were being formed as state-societies through this integration process and elimination contest. The Norman Conquest of England in 1066 greatly disturbed the equilibrium of the competing Frankish dominions, by giving the Dukes of Normandy and their Angevin successors vastly greater lands than any of their competitors. The struggle for supremacy between the Paris and London kings, each entangled in shifting alliances with second-rank magnates, is one of the great themes of the Middle Ages. The advantage swung first one way, then the other. Only the Hundred Years War finally settled the issue in favour of the Paris kings. Even then some territorial consolidation remained to be achieved. Although by the fifteenth century the Valois were by far the most powerful house, centrifugal forces had undergone a resurgence as members of this very family, having been granted great domains to govern as apanages,[8] attempted to assert their autonomy. Burgundy and Brittany were the last two great duchies to be absorbed into Valois territory, as much by political marriages as conquest, and from the early sixteenth century France began to expand eastwards towards something resembling its present boundaries.

So brief a summary unduly emphasizes one side of the monopoly mechanism: the progressive reduction in the number of competing territorial units as, through military conflict, the smaller and weaker units are eliminated from the competition and absorbed into the larger and stronger, which thus become territorially even larger. But the other side of the coin is at least as important: the concomitant process of *internal pacification*. The gathering of the control of the means of violence into fewer and fewer hands – eventually into the single monopoly apparatus of each state – means that over time fewer and fewer warriors can set about acquiring land by the 'private enterprise' means of using military resources under their own control. Gradually their military activities are subordinated to those of the central ruler, just as other acts of violence in time come under the jurisdiction of the royal courts. The process is very gradual all the same, and for a long time the kings' monopoly over the means of violence is partial, fluctuating and uncertain; by the same token, the risk of violent death or injury for people in general – one of many sources of the insecurity of life in medieval and early modern Europe – declined only slowly, and indeed internal pacification can hardly be said to be complete or absolute even today. But in long-term perspective, the trend is clear: conflicts between individuals or groups within a given territory came to be conducted less and less with violence, and, if violence were used, conflicting parties had to contend with the use of the monopoly forces on one side or the other.

Throughout his exposition of historical details, Elias returns time and again to general implications for our understanding of processes of state-formation (and indeed other long-term processes of social development).

Although the theory of the monopoly mechanism in state-formation is explicitly analogous to the formation of economic monopolies, Elias is emphatic that the monopolization of the means of violence and of taxation is not *reducible* to an economic process. Both are examples of processes of monopolization of a power resource, but it is anachronistic to think of the 'economic' and the 'military-political' as separable entities in medieval Europe. Today we are accustomed to thinking of 'economics' and 'politics' as two distinct spheres of society, each with its own distinct functions. We think of 'economic' activities and institutions as all those serving the creation and acquisition of the means of consumption and production. We also take it for granted that the production and above all the acquisition of these means normally takes place without threat or use of physical or military violence. Nothing is less self-evident (1939: II, 149). In the early stages of state-formation the competition for land – the principal means of production – is at once economic and political: to attempt to divide the process into separate 'spheres', and then to seek 'causal' relations between these spheres, is simply futile and misleading. What *is* true is that state-formation, the division of labour and lengthening chains of social interdependence, the growth of towns, trade and money all intertwine and reinforce each other. Towns and trade and the growing use of money generated taxes which helped support military machines which conquered more territory. An elaborate social division of labour and an adequate supply of money were necessary for the support of complex and permanent administrative apparatuses. But at the same time, the internal pacification and increasingly orderly administration of larger and larger territories were necessary conditions of economic growth. This is not an abstract matter: it comes down to questions such as how much long distance trade could develop when merchants were in constant risk of their lives on the road, and how big towns could grow if food supplies had to come from farmers a few miles away in territory controlled by a rival lord with whom one's local lord was constantly at battle. So the various elements in the process interweave and support each other. Any attempt to separate out one strand as the 'first cause', or to represent history as a sequence of static 'stages', distorts the essentially processual character of social reality.

A second issue to which Elias constantly returns is how far the working of the monopoly mechanism is 'inevitable'. He rejects the view that such processes must be regarded either as completely 'inevitable' or completely adventitious and unstructured – that is one of the many 'false polarities' to which he objects.[9] Elias's definition of the 'mechanism' quoted above (p. 67), it must be noted, is framed in terms of high probability, not of certainty or inevitability.[10]

A distinction needs to be made between the relatively high compellingness of the overall process and the relative indeterminacy of any particular outcome within it. To grasp the point, reflect that at the beginning of the Wimbledon Tennis Championships one can be quite certain that there will be one winner from the final two weeks later, but much less sure which player it will be. Even so, there are differences between the elimination contests involved in state-formation and in tennis tournaments! A tennis competition has formal rules which decree there shall be one winner; the state-formation contest is impelled solely by its structure, not by formal rules. Unlike in tennis, there may arise a permanent stalemate, or *all* the contending parties may be destroyed.[11] All the same, given the initial condition of a society with numerous power and property units of relatively equal size, there is a very high probability that under strong competitive pressures, the tendency will be towards the enlargement of a few units and finally towards monopoly (1939: II, 99). The competitive pressure is generated by the particular way in which warrior lords are socially interdependent with each other. The constant violent conflicts over land were in no way simply the 'result' of people's aggressive motivation. On the contrary, the feudal magnate *had* to fight with neighbours to extend his territory. In some abstract philosophical sense a magnate with, for the time, an unusually pacific outlook was 'free' to choose merely to try to hold on to his existing domains and avoid conflict with his neighbours. But the consequences of such a course of action were perfectly plain: anyone who declined to compete, merely conserving his property while others strove to increase theirs, necessarily ended up 'smaller' and weaker than the others, and was in ever-increasing danger of succumbing to them (1939: II, 43). Each knew that if his neighbour acquired more land – even if from a third party rather than from himself – the increased economic and military resources it brought meant inevitably that the balance of power between him and his neighbour was tilted to his own disadvantage, and it was extremely probable that sooner or later his domains would be invaded, his army defeated, his lands absorbed by the more powerful neighbour, and he and his family killed.

Yet, as Elias repeatedly stresses, that does not mean that a high probability was attached to any *particular* outcome of the struggle. It was highly likely that a large state would emerge somewhere in the general region of modern France, but there was nothing at all certain about its eventual boundaries (the regional diversity between the north and south, between *langue d'oc* and *langue d'oeil* among other things, might well have resulted in separate northern and southern states emerging). Above all, the whole weight of Elias's narrative goes to show how it long remained uncertain that the Capetians, the Paris kings, would emerge as final victors and monopolists. Whenever one looks at a historical process *a posteriori*, knowing what was the final outcome, it is difficult to perceive the uncertainties at each stage, the range of different outcomes which might have been. And the *a posteriori* perspective also leads one far too easily to imagine that the participants at each stage foresaw the outcome, that they had a long-term strategy or plan, which, in the end, they succeeded in implementing. Nothing could be further from the truth. Early French kings *may*, for all we know, have occasionally entertained daydreams of restoring their rule over the old west Frankish region (their successors eventually expanded beyond the Treaty of Verdun boundaries), but if so it was nothing so abstract which guided their military endeavours against their rivals: they just fought the next battle. There was no grand plan; instead, writes Elias: 'To some extent the

same is true of the French kings and their representatives as was once said of
the American pioneer: "He didn't want all the land; he just wanted the land
next to his"' (1939: II, 160). He continues:

This simple and precise formulation expresses well how from the interweaving of
countless individual interests and intentions – whether tending in the same direction or
in divergent and hostile directions – something comes into being that was planned and
intended by none of these individuals, yet has emerged nevertheless from their
intentions and actions. And really this is the whole secret of social figurations, their
compelling dynamics, their structural regularities, their process character and their
development; *this is the secret of their sociogenesis and relational dynamics.* (1939: II, 160; my
italics)

One of the most difficult aspects to grasp of such 'relational dynamics' (later
Elias would say '*figurational* dynamics') is that the rather high compellingness of
the overall trend is quite compatible with recognizing that 'accidents' may
simultaneously have a powerful effect on the shape of the final outcome. In the
elimination contest through which the monopoly mechanism unfolds, *which*
territory triumphs, rises and grows is often crucially affected by who wins a
battle, by the outstanding abilities of an individual leader, by one man's
longevity or a ruling house's lack of male heirs (1939: II, 99). Such 'accidents',
however, tend to have greater impact earlier in the process than later, when the
greater complexity of state apparatuses makes them relatively more autonomous
from individual events and personalities. The compellingness increases as the
process continues: it is not a constant.

Elias traces the operation of the monopoly mechanism in greatest detail
through the example of France, because it was there that it took its course most
undeviatingly, and because, partly as a result, France was for long the foremost
power in Europe and set the example for other states (1939: II, 116). The same
mechanism can however be seen at work elsewhere, he argues (1939: II,
96–104), though taking rather different paths according to circumstance. The
so-called 'Holy Roman Empire', including as it did initially most of modern
Germany, Austria, Italy, Switzerland and the Low Countries, contained too
large an area and too great a diversity of interests for the monopoly mechanism
to work to the benefit of the nominal central ruler, the Emperor. At first,
centrifugal forces worked there rather more slowly than in the west Frankish
region; in the eleventh and even twelfth centuries the writ of the Emperor still
ran a good deal more widely than that of Louis VI of Francia. But a succession
of families exhausted their resources – still essentially their family lands – in
trying to assert the imperial hegemony. Each imperial defeat at the hands of
alliances of diverse interests of regional magnates and towns (alliances usually
under the banner of the papacy) further consolidated decentralization. The
centrifugal tendency continued to sap the emperors long after centripetal forces
gained dominance in France. In Germany – where, as in France, it was the
consequence of the competitive interdependence of numerous small territories
– the monopoly mechanism worked to the benefit not of the emperors but of
middle-rank magnates, especially on the peripheries of the imperial territory.

Families like the Habsburgs and the Hohenzollerns eventually created independent empires of their own partly outside the old Imperial territory. It was only in the mid-nineteenth century that Austria and Prussia attained a duopolistic position in Germany, and the war of 1866 resulted in the former's expulsion from the German Confederation and the consolidation of an (admittedly still federal) single German state under the dominance of the latter. The pattern in Germany (and in Italy) was for centralized monopolies to be consolidated in fragments of the former imperial territory; only much later than in France did one of them absorb the rest to form states with their modern boundaries.

The opposite was the case in England (1939: II, 102), a much smaller territory than either France or the Empire. The Norman Conquest, and William I's careful distribution of feudal holdings in such a way as to minimize the risks of lords acquiring consolidated territorial power bases, meant that for several centuries the English monarchy was unusually strong and centralized in comparison with its continental counterparts. That did not prevent frequent bouts of baronial battling whenever the monarchy happened to be relatively weak – when a king like Stephen or John had little land of his own, or a weak claim to the throne; or, like Henry III and Edward II, lacked as an individual the political and military skills of kingship. Nevertheless, in England, struggles came relatively early to be about who should control the monopoly rather than about its existence. And, unlike in Germany, the territory under monopoly control tended to expand, into Wales in the first instance.

Even to talk about 'France', 'Germany', 'England' and 'Italy' in this way is to risk distortion by implying that state-formation processes each unfolded within pre-defined boundaries, cut off from what was happening within another set of boundaries. Elias specifically argues to the contrary, drawing attention to the constant linkage between inter-state and intra-state tensions. Throughout the later Middle Ages, England and the various territories which were to constitute France formed a single system of tensions. The final expulsion of England from the system permitted the further consolidation of the French kings' hold over the mainland part of the former more extensive system. But the emergence of a more centralized French state in turn facilitated its further expansion eastward, creating a new and wider system of tensions with the Valois (later Bourbons) and Habsburgs as the principal poles. By the time of the Thirty Years War in the seventeenth century, the system of tensions had spread to involve all the states of Europe; by 1914–18 it involved most of the world. Elias was to return to the question of inter-state tensions and their linkage with the balance of forces within states in writings such as *Humana Conditio* (1985a) nearly half a century later. For the moment, it is the internal balances of forces which will lead us more directly back to the moulding of behaviour and the overall theory of civilizing processes.

The royal mechanism

The establishment of secure monopoly apparatuses meant a steady accretion of power to the crown, culminating in the 'absolutist' monarchies of the later seventeenth and the eighteenth centuries. These arose in many of the states of Europe, but again the archetype is France, where the personal dominance of the monarch was summed up in Louis XIV's celebrated (if apocryphal) claim that '*L'état, c'est moi*'. Such a boast is more paradoxical and thought-provoking than it may seem at first glance. How could one man so dominate what was now such a huge territory, differentiated society and complex administrative machine?[12] For, unlike his ancestors of five hundred or more years earlier, Louis XIV could scarcely oversee personally every detail of his rule. Elias poses the paradox thus: 'the more [monopoly power] is accumulated by an individual, the less easily can it be supervised by this individual, and the more surely he becomes by his very monopoly dependent on increasing numbers of others, the more he becomes dependent on his dependants' (1939: II, 108). Like any other particular individual in the face of pressure from a whole network of interdependent people, the king would always be powerless if his whole society, or even a considerable part of it stood together against him (1939: II, 173). Yet 'absolutist' monarchies did arise and survive for a long time.

One possible resolution of the paradox, associated with Marxist thinking, is that 'absolutist' kings ruled, and used their control of the military forces to dominate society, in the interests and with the support of one class, the nobility. Perry Anderson, for instance, in his book *Lineages of the Absolutist State* (1974b), interprets absolutism as essentially a royal defence of the declining feudal class. While by no means denying that control of military forces remained an important instrument of rule, Elias denies that in a more differentiated society with an advanced division of labour, a money economy and a diversity of social classes, the connection between landholding, military strength and political domination is so simple and direct as it was around the end of the first millennium AD. His own solution of the paradox of 'absolutist' rule is more subtle, and I think in the end it fits more of the facts more convincingly.

Elias states his main proposition as follows:

the hour of the strong central authority within a highly differentiated society strikes when the ambivalence of interests of the most important functional groups grows so large, and power is distributed so evenly between them, that there can be neither a decisive compromise nor a decisive conflict between them. (1939: II, 171)

It is when these circumstances arise that the 'royal mechanism' functions effectively.[13]

The reason why, in such a figuration, the major social groups – the nobility and bourgeoisie and their various divisions, the Church, peasants and artisans – do not make common cause against the monarchy is that 'they tie each other's hands' (1939: II, 170). They do that because, with the advancing division of social functions, human relationships acquire a special quality of 'open or latent *ambivalence*':

In the relations between individuals, as well as in those between different functional strata, a specific *duality or even multiplicity of interests* manifests itself more strongly, the broader and denser the network of interdependence becomes. Here all people, all groups, estates or classes, are in some way dependent on one another; they are potential friends, allies or partners; and they are at the same time potential opponents, competitors or enemies. (1939: II, 167)

The idea resembles what political sociologists were later to call 'cross-pressures' and to see as contributing to the stability of pluralist democracy in countries like the USA and Great Britain in the twentieth century.[14] Elias dates its significance from long before anything reasonably called 'democracy', showing how it contributed to the rise of 'absolute' monarchy. The processes of economic, social and political development we have been describing had steadily woven all social strata into denser webs and long chains of functional interdependence. Of course there were conflicts of interest and feelings of enmity, but not unmixed with nor unmoderated by the awareness that 'more and more perceptibly, every action taken against an opponent also threatens the social existence of its perpetrator; it disturbs the whole mechanism of chains of action of which each is a part' (1939: II, 168). That is, according to Elias, one of the chief forces moulding civilized conduct, but we shall return to that. For the moment, Elias's argument is that in early modern Europe the process had already produced a relatively even balance of power and a large ambivalence of interest between the most important functional groups – the various elements of nobility and bourgeoisie. There was, in the current jargon, a 'stand-off'. And in those circumstances, *the dependence of each of the major interests on the central co-ordinating monopoly power is increased*. Within such a figuration, argues Elias, the interests of the central ruler are never *quite* identical with those of any other class or group (1939: II, 172). In saying that, he is contradicting that strand of Marxist thinking which stems from the famous remark of Marx and Engels (speaking of a later stage of development) that 'The executive of the modern state is but a committee for managing the common affairs of the whole bourgeoisie' (1848: 37). Elias does not deny that a ruler's interests may converge with those of one class, but if he elevates one class decisively above the rest, he weakens his own position. That is because, if one class is unequivocally superior in power to the others, the dependence of the whole system of internal tensions on the ruler is diminished. This view does have something in common with another, more sophisticated idea of Marx's – his explanation in *The Eighteenth Brumaire* (1852) of 'Bonapartism'. (Again, Marx was writing of a later period, France under the Second Republic (1848–52) and Second Empire (1852–70).)

Elias illuminates the principle by comparing it to a tug-of-war between two very evenly balanced sides. Both sides heave with all their might, but neither can dislodge the other from its position. Great forces are at work, but they are locked up, so to speak, in the tremendous tension in the rope. In this situation, a single person who is able to interpose his own strength first on one side, then on the other, can control the whole contest. He need not be very strong in himself: probably he could not withstand the pull of one of the sides alone, certainly not both pulling together. Yet the forces arranged as they are form a 'machine' which magnifies the effect of his smallest effort. On the other hand he has to take great care not to allow the tension itself to be relaxed, nor permit either side to gain a clear advantage; real tugs-of-war usually end up in collapse. So 'an extremely cautious manipulation of this apparatus is called for if it is to function for any length of time without disruption' (1939: II, 174), and that means that the person manipulating it is subject to its regularities and compulsions as much as everyone else involved. He has greater scope for decision than the rest, but is equally dependent upon the structure of the apparatus. His power – the power of the 'absolutist' king – is thus anything but absolute.

Elias is well aware that the actual structure of social tensions was not bi-polar, like a simple tug-of-war, but much more complex and multi-polar. And that serves only to differentiate his interpretation still further from a Marxist view like Anderson's. Elias's theory of the 'royal mechanism' seems to me to fit more subtly the facts of fluctuations in royal policy, both the short-term shifting of the royal weight from one foot to another to maintain an oscillating balance between competing interests, and also a longer-term trend apparent over many reigns. The theory makes obvious why, for example, kings so often allied themselves with whatever was for the time being the *second* most powerful social group rather than with the most powerful. Thus, in France and England (though not so much in Germany), kings gave powerful positions at court and in the royal administration to men of bourgeois origin during the Renaissance period, precisely during an important stage in the royal struggle to tame the old warrior class and to deprive it of its independent military capacity. Later, as the power of the nobility in general declined, French kings (in England the outcome was very different) switched some of their own weight back from bourgeois towards noble elements. What actually happened was much more complicated in detail, as Elias discusses at greater length in *The Court Society* (1969a: 146–213). In brief, under royal sponsorship in the sixteenth century there was formed, from among a *minority* of the old warrior nobility families and some families of bourgeois origin, a new court nobility increasingly distinct from the old landed nobility. Equally under royal sponsorship, mainly in the seventeenth century a new and separate hereditary elite of magistrates and officials, the *noblesse de robe* drawn wholly from families of bourgeois origin, rose in power. Both groups entered into the multi-polar tug-of-war, against each other and against older groups, to royal advantage. The process was not smooth: it was punctuated by the last spasms of noble military power – the Wars of Religion in the late sixteenth century, localized rebellions like Montmorency's of 1632, and finally the Fronde (1648–53) in the seventeenth. Yet although the process did not happen at a stroke, nor by the design of one particular king, the long-term trend is clear: the social institution of the monarchy reached its greatest power just when the nobility was forced to compete in many ways with the bourgeoisie, and – the other side of the coin – when the bourgeoisie had become strong enough to compete.

The hypothesis of the royal mechanism also seems to fit rather well the facts of the role of parliaments or estate assemblies in early modern Europe. Such assemblies existed in most countries in the later Middle Ages. Generally their assent was required before the monarch could levy taxes. In most countries there were struggles between kings and assemblies, with varying outcomes. Where 'absolutist' monarchies developed, assemblies tended to be abolished, or at least stripped of power. In France, the Estates-General simply were not summoned after 1614 – until 1787, on the eve of the Revolution.[15] Many of the symptoms of the emergence of an absolutist monarchy were also evident in England under the Tudors and the early Stuarts, but there Parliament had always been a rather strong institution compared with most of the continental assemblies. Charles I did attempt for twelve years to govern without Parliament, but was eventually forced to call it again, setting in train the events leading to his defeat in the Civil Wars. In England, unlike France, a successful alliance between land-owning nobility and gentry on the one hand and urban interests on the other was too strong for the king, and of course such an alliance upsets the balanced tension of forces, the necessary initial condition in Elias's model for the operation of the royal mechanism. Nor was that necessary condition restored when the monarchy itself was restored in 1660 – the outcome of the struggle brought about irreversible shifts in the balance of forces. Struggles between monarchs and their estate assemblies elsewhere in Europe had various outcomes between the two polar exemplars of those in England and France. H. G. Koenigsberger (1977) examined cases from Portugal to Poland and from Sweden to Sicily, asking how far the model of the royal mechanism applied to each. Broadly his conclusion was that the model helped to explain a great deal. But its operation was distorted in many countries by foreign intervention in internal struggles (Elias himself pointed to the interlinkage of inter-state and intra-state struggles). And in some instances (like Poland), the lack of economic and social differentiation prevented the emergence of the complex of balanced tensions which, again, is the precondition for the operation of the royal mechanism.

One may conclude that the particular figuration of power which is the starting point for the royal mechanism did not arise quite so widely in medieval and early modern Europe as did the figuration which favours the operation of the monopoly mechanism. Nevertheless, the idea encapsulated in the image of the tug-of-war is a powerful one and, bearing in mind Elias's contention that the interests of the central ruler are never *quite* identical with those of any other class or group, it can be used with advantage in understanding the functioning of powerful regimes long after the 'Age of Absolutism'. In an appendix to *The Court Society* (1969a: 276–83), Elias examines the distribution of power in Hitler's Germany. He shows how misleading can be the modern concept of 'totalitarianism' and the notion of the dictator as monolithic, brooking no arguments. In fact Hitler appears not merely to have tolerated but preserved and cultivated rivalries between various competing groups in the Nazi state machine. Some historians have seen this as evidence of a surprising hesitancy and indecision on his part. Elias's interpretation is very different: for all the vast differences between the regimes, Louis XIV and Hitler both acted as if they knew that a diminution of tension between competing groups would also diminish their own power. More generally, Elias disputes the notion that there can be a state without structural conflicts, whether 'democracy' or 'dictatorship'.

From private to public monopolies

Elias defines this as

the phase in which control over the centralized and monopolized resources tends to pass from the hands of individuals to those of ever-greater numbers, and finally to become a function of the interdependent human web as a whole, the phase in which a relatively 'private' monopoly becomes a 'public' one. (1939: II, 115)

Although he speaks of the French Revolution as being a decisive event in this phase, the origins of the process lie much further back in time. They are a continuation of the depersonalization and institutionalization of the exercise of power which began as soon as the growth of territory under the control of one prince, and the increasing complexity and specialization of society, made it impossible for one man to exercise all the functions of rule personally. The process is thus, once again, a product of the longer chains and denser webs of interdependence binding people together within society. As the central administrative apparatus grows, so it gradually comes under the control of broader strata. Nevertheless, even the immense and complex apparatus at the apex of which stood Loùis XIV remained in important ways 'private'. It was still essentially an extension of the royal household, an administration of the sort especially familiar to sociologists through Max Weber's discussion of 'patrimonial' bureaucracy (1922a: II, 1006–69).[16] Even as late as that, there remained no distinction between the public and private revenues and expenditures of the king. Only when, at the Revolution, the balance on which the king's power depended tilted sharply in favour of the bourgeoisie – establishing eventually a new social balance with new axes of tension – did personal monopolies begin to become public monopolies in an institutional sense (Elias 1939: II, 201).

At this point, an aside is in order about the word 'bourgeoisie'. Elias often uses the term as shorthand, but he is conscious of the risk (associated with some Marxist historical writing) of introducing anachronistic nineteenth-century definitions of class into earlier periods (Elias 1969a: 218). We need to be historically specific about the interests of social groups at different periods. Plainly the 'bourgeois' townspeople of the eleventh century are not the same as the 'bourgeois' capitalists of the nineteenth, nor were their interests identical, even if an historical lineage can be traced between them. That is obvious. Less obvious, however, is the difference between, on the one hand, the commercial bourgeoisie, whose emergence disrupted the balance of tensions in France and who were to be eventual beneficiaries of the Revolution, and, on the other hand, the traditional 'bourgeois' groups who had done much to maintain the stable balance of tensions to royal advantage under the Ancien Régime. For three centuries or so before 1789, the 'bourgeoisie' had not been trying to destroy the nobility but to join it – and with some success. Most obvious among them were the *noblesse de robe*. It is crucial to understanding Elias's interpretation of the balance of tensions in France under absolutism that he sees the *robins* not as members of the nobility proper but as an intermediate stratum having risen from and retaining many interests in common with the bourgeoisie (1939: II, 176ff; 1969a: 61–2, 169–71, 208, 270ff). Their interests were not identical with the lower bourgeois but they served in effect as their spokesmen; *all* were dependent on maintaining their privileges under the crown – that was as true of tax farmers or merchants buying monopolies and guildsmen holding on to their ancient privileges as it was of the high *robins* and those who had purchased offices of profit at more lowly levels. Moreover, even from their behaviour it is apparent that motivation in pursuit of rank, honour and prestige was more important to them than motivation by economic interests (1969a: 64–5). So these older 'estate-bourgeois' groups were bound up with the maintenance of the old equilibrium: their rivalry with the great nobility was deeply *ambivalent*. Only with the emergence of bourgeois forms *not* dependent on privileges derived from the crown did this cease to be true – and then the old middle class was swept away along with the monarch and the nobility.[17]

Even so, it is important to be clear that Elias does not see the outcome as one in which the state is the executive committee of the bourgeoisie. He argues that 'in the long run the subordination of the quest for the optimal functioning of the overall network of interdependencies to the optimation of sectional interests invariably defeats its own end' (1939: II, 115). Why that should be so – why such plans tend to have unintended and unforeseen consequences which render them void – is discussed further in chapter 11.

It is also a mistake to see the overall process of state-formation as one in which fewer and fewer people become 'free' and more and more become 'unfree', although at certain phases of monopoly formation it can appear that way. No, the process as a whole tends to increase the two-way interdependence of people and social groups on each other. Interdependence does not mean *equal* interdependence: those who are less dependent on others than others are on them remain more powerful. But the web of interdependence increasingly constrains all – the more powerful and the less powerful. And this has long-term effects on their feelings and behaviour. Elias writes:

If relatively independent social functions are increasingly replaced by dependent ones in society – for example, free knights by courtly knights and finally courtiers, or relatively independent merchants by dependent merchants and employees – the moulding of affects, the structure of drives and consciousness, in short the whole social personality structure and attitudes of people are necessarily changed at the same time. (1939: II, 107)

That takes us back to the first volume of *The Civilizing Process* and forward to *The Court Society*.

COURTS, CIVILIZATION AND CULTURE

The noble courts of a past age may at first glance seem of little significance in understanding the modern world. Yet they are; for they were at the centre of what Elias considers one of the most decisive transitions within every major civilizing process, the *transformation of warriors into courtiers*. In this process of *courtization*,[18] a warrior nobility was replaced step by step by a tamed nobility with more muted affects, a court nobility. More than any other Western group, the people of court society were specialists in the elaboration and moulding of social conduct. It was among them that a basic stock of models was formed which – though modified and fused with others in the course of diffusion to other groups and strata – are, together with the cultural legacy of court society, still a key component in present-day society. The sociogenesis of courts was an indispensable precondition for all subsequent spurts and counter-spurts in the civilizing process (1939: II, 258–9).

Why 'counter-spurts' as well as 'spurts'? Because the process of pacification of warriors did not follow a smooth course. Not all knights underwent the process at once or at the same rate. Benjo Maso (1982) has gone further than that, and contended that the development of the aggressiveness of medieval warriors took a different path from what one might expect on the basis of a simple straight-line interpretation of the civilizing process. He produced evidence to show that fighting spirit among knights became not weaker but stronger in the course of the Middle Ages. Knightly virtues like pugnacity, courage and impetuosity, he argued, became more pronounced in the face of the threatened position of the warrior class. The explanation he offered for this seeming anomaly was that for the nobles of about 1050 war was primarily a means to increase or maintain their possessions, whereas for the knights of three hundred years later it had become a calling, a means of legitimating their weakened but still privileged positions. Consequently, they were more or less obliged to give evidence of the supposedly innate qualities that distinguished them from the common soldiers and in accordance with their honour. But though Maso's work represents just the sort of detailed research needed to refine the theory, it does not refute it. For Elias always emphasizes that only a minority of the warrior knights became directly caught up in the life of courts: the rest suffered instead a slow attrition of their social positions. By the end of the Middle Ages, the minority of courtly knights was larger than before, but *'the bulk of the knights . . .* still lived in much the same way as they had in the ninth or tenth century'; they were 'wild, cruel, prone to violent outbreaks and abandoned to the joy of the moment' (1939: II, 72; my italics). Maso may well be right that some of them at least were more, not less, prone to such affective outbursts of aggression and, paradoxically, the process of courtization of some warriors may have helped to produce the opposite trend – at least for a period – among those excluded from it.

Nor does Elias argue that courts were the sole sources of the civilizing of behaviour. It has been suggested that *The Civilizing Process* – explicitly concerned with the *secular* upper classes – greatly underestimated the significance of the Church and monasteries as centres of lordly power in the shaping of conduct. Mayke de Jong (1982) described the active conflict-regulating role of monks in eleventh-century Flanders, and Bram Kempers (1982) the civilizing campaigns of the clergy in Italy. Mart Bax (1987) has extended Elias's arguments by contending that in addition to their parts considered separately in the civilizing process the competition *between* the clerical and secular authorities gave a further impetus to civilizing pressures.[19] Nevertheless, the courtly life grew up around magnates – some of them clerical – whose military and economic power was particularly great, and whose courts were therefore likely to be correspondingly powerful as civilizing forces.

'Nothing is more fruitless when dealing with long-term social processes', writes Elias (1969a: 232), 'than to attempt to locate an absolute beginning.' Courts, like the bourgeoisie, seem always to have been rising. What the term signifies – even ignoring its legal and other derivative senses – changes gradually in the course of social development, and it is always possible to trump the claim to have found the 'first' court. Sombart (1913) saw the papal court at Avignon in the fourteenth century as the first 'modern' court, in the sense that it was no longer simply the base of a feudal warrior nobility but a centre which attracted a cultured and leisured elite with some expertise in the arts of consumption. It was followed by the splendours of the courts of Renaissance Italy, before the royal court of France attained undisputed leadership of Europe in matters courtly during the seventeenth and eighteenth centuries. Elias argues, however, that the French court of the age of absolutism was linked through a continuous line of development to the courts of the Capetians, notably Louis IX (St Louis, 1226–70), and that 'The survival of the court tradition in France from the thirteenth to the eighteenth centuries, despite fundamental changes in the social structure, was one of the most important preconditions for the refinement of court culture in France and for the formation of a specifically "French" tradition' (1969a: 158).

Early forms of court culture, not only at the royal court of France but at the courts of major territorial lords throughout France, Germany and Italy, can be seen as early as the twelfth century. In the age of the troubadours and *Minnesänger* can be heard a faint pre-echo of the courtly attitudes and behaviour of centuries later. By reason of their wealth, the great feudal courts had far greater cultural significance than the towns (Elias, 1939: ii, 75ff). They became the first secular centres of literate culture, attracting scribes for administration but also minstrels to sing the praises of their lord. In their small way, poets and singers played their part in the competition between feuding, feudal lords. Like Sombart, however, Elias emphasizes the role of women in the formation of this early court culture. Within the very limited circle of the court, encouraged especially by the presence of a lady, more peaceful forms of conduct became obligatory. In the literature of the troubadours of Provence and the *Minnesänger* of Germany can be detected a very partial modification of the affects. The themes of gentle devotion to a noble lady, the expression of unattainable love are reflections, suggests Elias (1939: ii, 77), of the dependent status of the singers: many of them were drawn from the surplus population of the upper class, landless younger sons of knights. The sentiments they express are very much at odds with the general knightly mentality of the time. (Of that, the blood and gore of the *chansons de geste* are probably more typical.[20]) Nevertheless, it was in the limited circle of these early courts that – as the word implies – the *courtois* code of behaviour took shape and spread through the later Middle Ages.

'Primitive' and unrestrained as the *courtois* standards, described in chapter 2, may seem to modern eyes, they nevertheless represented a small advance in refinement over still earlier patterns (Elias 1939: II, 86).

Even so, the crucial phases in the formation of the courtly culture of the age of absolutism did not lie quite so remotely in the distant past. In France, decisive developments took place in the reign of François I (1515–47), who broke the hitherto rather rigid connection between land-holding and rank by conferring titles of nobility, especially for military achievement, on men of non-noble origin. It was at this period that there began the reconstruction of the upper class. The royal court grew in size, with many of the nobles resident there for much of their time, and the distinction between those families which 'belonged to the court' and those which did not became increasingly important. Its significance grew in proportion as the traditional military functions of the vassal and knight declined. The line passed *through* the old nobility, with the provincial nobility ceasing – after the final spasm of the Wars of Religion – to be effectively part of the power elite of France. Economically, they were undermined by inflation: their revenues tended to be fixed in money terms. Perhaps their poverty has been exaggerated; their economic decline was relative to the costs of maintaining the style of life expected at court.[21] Why that style of life was so necessary and so extravagant for courtiers is one of the main things Elias seeks to explain in *The Court Society*.

In the time of François I, the 'arteries connecting provincial life with the court, rural life with the town, were not as constricted as they became later' (1969a: 162). Especially under Henri IV (1589–1610), it became more difficult for non-court strata to gain membership of court circles. In the final stage, under Louis XIV (1643–1715), the royal court became concentrated on Versailles, capable for the first time of housing both the ministries of government and the high nobility in a single centre on a more or less permanent basis. Slowly, during the seventeenth century, the royal court was transformed into a relatively closed social formation, a court society 'whose customs, including the way of speaking, dressing and even moving the body when walking and in conversation, differed markedly from those of all non-court formations' (1969a: 186). In *The Court Society* Elias sets out to show how this social formation functioned as a means both of preserving and controlling the nobility, how it moulded their personality, and what were its cultural consequences.[22]

Elias begins in characteristically indirect fashion, by examining the physical structure and appearance of the dwellings of the various grades of the nobility and high bourgeoisie in France under the *ancien régime*. Both in their external appearance and internal layout, the houses betray an acute consciousness of rank; even the words used for them were graded according to the owner's status – the *palais* of a prince, the *hôtel* of a nobleman, the *maison* of a bourgeois. Size varied with rank, and so did ornamentation according to a well understood code. The pediment of the house of a duke would be more modest than that of a prince, but grander than that of a mere archbishop, marshal or count. And so on. Internally, too, the layout was geared to considerations of rank. The suites of rooms – one or more antechambers, the bedchamber, the inner *cabinet* – occupied by the master and, separately, the mistress of such a formal house functioned as a micrometer for measuring the relative rank of host and guest. The further the host advanced through the succession of rooms to meet the guest, and the further inwards through the suite the guest was conducted, the greater was the deference denoted to the visitor.[23] Furthermore, Elias emphasizes, these noble houses show how relatively undeveloped (in comparison with later bourgeois industrial society) was the distinction between the 'private' and 'public' spheres of life. This was a *non-working* upper class: its members had no separate occupation. For them, social life was not only a source of relaxation, amusement and conversation, as is our 'private life'. It was at the same time the functional equivalent of what the occupational sphere is for most people in modern society, in that it was the direct instrument of their career, the medium of their rise or fall, and subject to social demands and duties (1969a: 53). Rank must be expressed. Their social identity depended on it: *noblesse oblige.*

The sense of rank meant that one must not too obviously outshine those of higher rank than oneself: boundaries must be respected. More to the point, however, one must oneself keep up the style of house expected of one's own rank and certainly not be outshone by lower ranks. What went for house went for many other aspects of the style of life: numbers of servants, clothes, furniture, food, carriages, hospitality, entertainment, and much else that could be described as 'luxury' but was to them necessity. A nobleman's rank determined expenditure in accordance with it. Unfortunately rank did not also determine his income. Many families were ruined in a characteristic cycle of indebtedness. Their expenditure being fixed, they sold land to raise money, but that then reduced future income. Their other means of increasing income were limited. They could hope for rich marriages, inheritance, or favours from the king (although positions at court, in the army, the Church or the diplomatic service also involved obligations to appropriate social display). On the other hand they could not increase their income by working or entering trade, which carried the risk of 'derogation' or loss of noble rank.[24] Many simply took ever greater loans; there were many noble bankruptcies and would have been more had the king not averted them by paying off favourites' debts.

To the later observer, most of this noble expenditure appears mere 'luxury' and 'extravagance'. From the standpoint of bourgeois economic rationality, it seems *irrational* spending on non-essentials and trivialities. They seem trivial because, although perhaps pleasurable, they are aspects of what today would be 'private life'; a modern businessman, for example, finds his social identity principally in his work, and in private life 'cuts his suit to fit his cloth'. Looking at a nobleman in eighteenth-century France, he asks 'if he were running into debt, why did he not reduce his expenses?' Yet to see such behaviour as merely irrational is highly misleading.

Sociologists are familiar with the problem particularly from Thorstein Veblen's mordantly witty picture of 'conspicuous consumption' among the plutocrats of late nineteenth-century America in his celebrated book *The Theory of the Leisure Class* (1899). Unfortunately, Veblen's indignation was itself based on an uncritical acceptance of bourgeois economic values, and this blocked his way to a clear understanding of the social compulsions underlying prestige consumption (Elias 1969a: 67). Nor did Sombart advance the problem very far when he defined luxury as 'any expenditure in excess of the necessary' (1913: 59), for, as he added immediately, 'obviously this is a relative definition which becomes intelligible only when we know what constitutes "the necessary"'. Max Weber came nearer the point when he wrote that 'luxury' was to an aristocratic ruling class 'not something "superfluous" but one of the means of its social self-assertion' (1922a: II, 1106). Elias takes the argument further, showing more persuasively than Veblen or Sombart and in more detail than Weber that expenditure on consumption of many kinds was a necessary expression of the seigneurial ethos of rank, and how that ethos both grew out of the structure and activity of court society and was necessary for its continuation. It was a compelling necessity, not 'freely chosen'.

Elias in fact argues that the conspicuous consumption of court society represented a specific form of rationality under a specific form of social compulsion, a 'court-rationality' very different from bourgeois or 'economic' rationality. Both require rational foresight and calculation. (Both therefore require restraint of short-term affects for the sake of certain vital interests – a point to which we shall return in chapter 4 when discussing the connection between civilizing processes and processes of rationalization.) But what is being calculated and made calculable is very different:

Bourgeois-industrial rationality is generated by the compulsion of the economic mesh; by it power-opportunities founded on private or public capital are made calculable. Court rationality is generated by the compulsion of the elite social mesh; *by it people and prestige are made calculable as instruments of power.* (1969a: 111; my italics)

The exact calculation of ornamentation appropriate to a house is one instance of court rationality in action, but Elias studies it in more detail in the life of the court itself and especially in the role played there by etiquette.

Drawing on the famous diaries of the Duc de Saint Simon and many other accounts of daily life at Versailles, Elias examines the elaborate ritual and etiquette of the court. The daily rituals of the king's bedchamber, the *levée* when he rose and dressed in the morning and the *couchée* when he undressed and went to bed, are a prime example. To attend them was both a privilege and a duty for the most prominent nobles. In the morning there were six entrées to the bedchamber – that is, six groups of people who in succession had the right to enter, each carrying a different connotation of prestige and royal favour, and nobles vied with each other for these rights. Once inside, the ritual itself gave rise to other moments of distinction and favour: who would have the privilege of handing the king his shirt, or of briefly holding a lantern (in an already well-lit room!)? It sounds absurd, and most of the ritual had no utilitarian justification at all; it was principally an affirmation of the participants' common membership of the court, distinguishing them from non-members (1969a: 103). But every element in it had a precisely graded meaning and prestige-value. Prestige-value, argues Elias (1969a: 87–7, 111), fulfilled a role analogous to money values in industrial societies. Every detail of the elaboration of etiquette, ceremony, taste, dress, manners and even conversation was an instrument in the struggle for status and power.

Privileges and prestige at court were, of course, in part a consequence of formal rank; members of the royal family, for instance, entered the bedchamber ahead of most of the mere dukes. Under Louis XIV, however, ceremony remained a very flexible instrument for signifying favour, and therefore also an instrument of power and control, for royal favour was vital to a noble's prestige standing at court, and often even to his financial solvency. The court was a hotbed of faction and intrigue, with constantly shifting alliances and rival cliques centring on the Dauphin, the Queen, the Princes of the Blood, the royal bastards and the royal mistress among others. The king did nothing to reduce the rivalry. Quite the reverse: just as in the wider state he sought to reinforce existing differences and rivalries between the estates, so at court it was to the advantage of his own power to have many factions tugging against each other. The royal mechanism worked in the smaller world of the court as well as in the larger world of the state.

At court it was therefore necessary for any player, in order to make his or her dispositions to best advantage, to know as accurately as possible the state of the game, who was intriguing with whom for what, who was going up, who down.

Every individual belongs to a 'clique', a social circle which supports him when necessary; but the groupings change. He enters alliances, if possible with people ranking high at court. But rank at court can change very quickly; he has rivals; he has open and concealed enemies. And the tactics of his struggles, as of his alliances, demand careful consideration. The degree of aloofness or familiarity with everyone must be carefully measured; each greeting, each conversation has a significance over and above what is actually said or done. (1939: ii, 271)

Thus people of the court developed an extraordinary sensitivity to the status and importance that should be attributed to a person on the basis of fine nuances of bearing, speech, manners and appearance. Observing, dealing with, relating to or avoiding people became an art in itself, and it always involved observing someone not as an individual but as a person in relation to others. And self-observation was inextricably bound up in that. 'Let a favourite observe himself very closely,' wrote La Bruyère, 'for if he keeps me waiting less than usual in his antechamber, if his face is more open, less frowning, if he listens to me more willingly or accompanies me further to the door, I shall think he is beginning to fall and I shall be right' (quoted by Elias 1969a: 104). Plainly then, great self-control was required in life at court. One had to an exceptional degree to be able to anticipate the interpretation that others would put on nuances of one's own behaviour. To sociologists reared on Erving Goffman's discussions of the arts of impression management − such as his book *The Presentation of Self in Everyday Life* (1959) − that may seem a universal characteristic of human society. In some degree it is, but Elias would argue that the *extent* to which the sensitivity was developed in court society, and its link to the peculiar form of the competitive struggle for prestige with vital interests at stake, was exceptional. A further source of pressure for self-restraint at court was that the permanence of membership of court circles meant that extreme caution was required to avoid permanent damage to what were necessarily permanent relationships.[25] Outbursts of spontaneous rage – or indeed many other strong emotions – were to be avoided at all costs:

affective outbursts are difficult to calculate. They reveal the true feelings of the person concerned to a degree that, because not calculated, can be damaging; they hand over trump cards to rivals for favour and prestige. Above all, they are a sign of weakness, and that is the position the court person fears most of all. *In this way, the competition of court life enforces a curbing of the affects in favour of calculated and finely shaded behaviour in dealing with people.* The structure of social life within this figuration left relatively little room for spontaneous expressions of feeling. (1969a: 111)

People of the court experienced pressure both from 'below' and from 'above'. Pressure from social groups below them made membership of the court an essential mark of their distinction, and competition at court increased their dependence on the king, who used its mechanisms as an instrument of control. The nobility was thus an instance of what Elias calls a 'dual-front class' or 'two-front stratum'.[26] Only the king experienced no pressure from above, yet it is mistaken to see even him as entirely free from constraints. Louis XIV and his two immediate successors preserved the nobility at a time when it was increasingly seen as a class which no longer had any function for the nation as a whole. It was in the royal interest to preserve the nobility as a counterweight to other strata. To have abolished the distance separating them from the bourgeoisie would have displaced the centre of gravity of the whole figuration of power in society and made the king far too dependent on the bourgeois stratum. The mutual dependence of the king and nobility became increasingly fixed in the course of the eighteenth century, and this too came to be reflected in the ritual of the court. By the reign of Louis XVI, the king and queen themselves were entrapped in an iron cage of etiquette (1969a: 86–7, 207). Every element became petrified in a way that Louis XIV would never have tolerated, the whole forming a 'ghostly *perpetuum mobile*'. Every element was an object of 'prestige fetishism' (analogous to the money or commodity fetishism in bourgeois society of which Marx speaks), carrying a prestige-value far removed from its intrinsic use-value. Not even the king could then change the rituals, for any change would have had adverse implications for *someone's* prestige. Thus all interests at court, as in French society as a whole immediately before the Revolution, became locked in a 'frozen clinch': no change was possible without a destructive explosion. An 'iron cage' could be constructed as well by court rationality as by the bourgeois economic rationality of which Max Weber was thinking when he used the phrase.

The final chapter of *The Court Society* is devoted to the sociogenesis of the French Revolution. After analysing the principal axes of tension between the main groups in French society, Elias attributes the final explosion to its inability towards the close of the *ancien régime* to adapt to underlying changes. With the growth of commerce and the first stirrings of industrialization, a discrepancy arose between social rank and power. The discrepancy could not be removed by gradual change, because of the frozen clinch into which all social groups had become locked.[27] No adjustment was possible without jeopardizing some group's position.

The Court Society is not confined to a sociological analysis of the life of the court, nor even to setting that within the broader figuration of power in society under the *ancien régime*. Elias also provides an interpretation of many of the distinctive *cultural* forms associated with court society, from its emergence in the sixteenth and early seventeenth centuries, through its peak under Louis XIV, to the blossoming of *salon* culture and the Enlightenment under Louis XV and Louix XVI. Through the whole period from the sixteenth century to the Revolution, Elias argues, certain threads are to be found running through the arts and intellectual life, through the successive styles of Classicism, Baroque and Rococo, all essentially associated with court society. One thread which appears early in the cultural tapestry is 'aristocratic romanticism'. This finds literary expression in the hands of generations which lived through the main phase of the courtization of the elite of nobility, their transformation from knights to courtiers, the severing of their links with the provinces and the land, and the exclusion of the provincial nobility from the central elite. Elias traces the nostalgia for a past age, the sense of uprooting or deracination, of estrangement from the land and nature as early as the poetry of Joachim Du Bellay (1522–60), Pierre Ronsard (1524–85) and other members of the Pléiade. He finds it especially in *L'Astrée*, the novel published between 1607 and 1627 by Honoré d'Urfé, a provincial nobleman from Savoy who had been on the losing side against Henri IV. Peopled with nymphs and shepherds, the novel enjoyed enormous vogue. The shepherds, representing the provincial nobility, embody a superior morality, a lack of artifice and a closeness to the natural which courtiers have lost. *L'Astrée* with its rustic cast is not unique – there were many comparable works including Sir Philip Sidney's *Arcadia* (1590) from England, where the process of deracination and courtization did not go so far nor last so long. The theme persisted through paintings such as those of Poussin (1594–1665) and Watteau (1684–1721), until towards the close of the *ancien régime* life imitated art with Marie-Antoinette and her ladies playing at being shepherdesses. More generally, Elias suggests that a mood of melancholy and a romanticization of the past is a cultural characteristic of dual-front classes experiencing pressures from both above and below. He has in mind the middle class of Wilhelmine Germany. Romantic undercurrents – as seen for example in Wagner's operas – go hand in hand, he observes, with being obedient subjects as second nature (1969a: 222–4).

The sense of the restraint imposed in courtly life is perhaps most directly evident in the French classical dramas of Corneille (1606–84) and Racine (1639–99), highly cerebral plays of declamation where the murders happen off stage, plays which formed part of the life of the court itself. Even the comedies of Molière (1622–73) contrast with the much broader comedies of Restoration England, where the direction of development of court society had already been greatly changed. Even French formal gardens embodied the impulse to control and restrain nature; Saint-Simon contrasted them unfavourably with the more 'natural' (though in fact equally man-made) English gardens (Elias 1969a: 227).

Elias also sees the imprint of courtly restraint in the major intellectual or philosophical developments of the era. We have seen how 'reflection', intervening more or less automatically between the spontaneous impulse to act and the actual performance of an action in word or deed, became a necessary part of relationships at court. Many people of the time were well aware of this element of reflection and self-constraint in their social habitus, but they tended to perceive it not as something which had developed gradually but as an eternal, timeless, immutable 'human nature' or 'human condition'. Some thinkers evaluated it positively and elevated it to 'Reason' with a capital R. Descartes (1596–1650) played a major part in establishing the tradition of philosophy which is preoccupied with a consciousness of one's own consciousness, and striving to understand one's own understanding, as a single adult mind, inside, striving to grasp by Reason the problematic world outside (1969a: 253). (Elias's objections to this tradition are the starting point of his theory of knowledge and science, to be discussed in chapters 7 and 8 below.)

The same can even be said of people like Rousseau, who put a negative value on courtly 'reflection' and inhibition of spontaneity. His mythologization of 'Nature' has something in common with the literary tradition of aristocratic romanticism, and (for all his hounding by the régime) the impact of his work – and of his dictum that 'Man is born free, but is everywhere in chains' – owed something to its resonance in court circles.

'Court society' was an historically important type of social formation which has left many traces in the modern world, yet has not been very greatly discussed by sociologists. In choosing to study specifically the French court in relation to French society under the *ancien régime*, Elias was consciously opting to analyse in detail a single '*real*-type', in contrast to Max Weber's method of building a composite (and static) *ideal*-type (such as 'patrimonialism') where a model constructed from a great many examples ends up bearing a most problematic relationship to any particular instance of social reality.[28] That does not mean that Elias treats the French case as 'unique', as if there was nothing to be learned from it in studying other countries and other periods. On the contrary, the French court selected itself as a case study because of its immense cultural influence throughout Europe.[29] More important, however, establishing clearly the axes of tension and figurational dynamics in the one case facilitates comparisons and an understanding of how other instances came to develop differently.

CYCLES OF VIOLENCE AND THEIR RESOLUTION

The process of internal pacification, and the courtization of warriors associated with it, extend as we have seen over very long periods. They can be discerned in most parts of Europe, and similar processes have taken place elsewhere, as for example in Japan. One cannot point to a specific moment at which they begin but it is possible to trace periods of accelerated advance, periods of reversal and periods of stagnation.

Though bound up in these very long-term processes, the particular significance of the royal court of France can also be seen in slightly shorter-term context as the outcome of a cycle of violence which afflicted France in the late sixteenth century. The idea of 'cycle of violence' is one used a good deal by Elias in his later work. Their resolution in a relatively pacific outcome is by no means to be taken for granted: it is not 'inevitable'.

Cycles of violence are figurations formed by two or more groups, double-bind processes which trap these groups in a position of mutual fear and distrust, each group assuming as a matter of course that its members might be harmed or even killed by another group if the latter had the opportunity and the means to do it. Such a figuration of human groups usually has a strong self-escalating impetus. It may end in a particularly virulent eruption of violence leading to victory of one side or another. It may find its conclusion in a cumulative weakening or reciprocal destruction of all the participants. (Elias, in Elias and Dunning 1986: 26)

In the case of France, the cycle of violence was brought to an end by a series of royal victories. What emerged from these struggles was that the kings and their representatives were quite clearly superior in power resources both to the landed upper classes and the urban middle classes. That was why, according to Elias (Elias and Dunning 1986: 35), the king's court became a major civilizing agency in France. In Germany, the course of development was somewhat different. The court of Prussia presented many cultural parallels to that of France; but there the courtization of the old warrior class took a very different form. Under Frederick the Great they were 'bureaucratized' in the royal administration and army. But more revealing contrasts with the way a cycle of violence was resolved in France are provided by Sicily, studied by Anton Blok in *The Mafia of a Sicilian Village, 1860–1960* (1974), and by England, about which Elias himself wrote at some length in *The Quest for Excitement* (1986).

Mafia in Sicily

Blok's book, which bears the strong impress of Elias's influence, is not a study of '*the* Mafia' of popular imagination and, to some extent, of present-day reality – the Mafia as a highly organized international crime syndicate. It is an investigation of the roots of *mafia* as a social process in rural Sicily in the nineteenth and twentieth centuries. Blok defines *mafia* in terms of the private, unlicensed use of violence as a means of control. Sicily was never pacified so fully as most parts of Western Europe, and the use of violence there is nothing new. But although it cannot be said to have a single definite starting point, to understand the emergence of *mafia* there is no need to go back in Sicilian history much before the early nineteenth century.

In the eighteenth century, Sicily was still in a stage of feudalism. Noble families ruled vast domains or *feudi*, and had bands of armed retainers.

Feudalism was legally abolished during the British occupation of Sicily in the Napoleonic Wars. The effect of this was mainly to transform feudal overlordship into private ownership, and deprive the peasantry of common rights essential to their livelihood. Many of them took to the hills and banditry became a very serious problem. Furthermore, the restoration of the Bourbon monarchy in Naples brought a government with benevolently absolutist ambitions towards land reform. In practice, the effect of their policies was to create a prosperous minority of peasants, the *gabelloti*, while doing nothing for the mass of the poor peasants. The land-owning nobility then faced a dual threat: from bandits and peasant unrest on the one hand, and from interference by the central government on the other. These were the circumstances in which they began to forge alliances with the *gabelloti* and enlist what were in effect the first *mafiosi* for the protection of their estates and to control a restive peasantry.

By the turn of this century, the tail sometimes seemed to be wagging the dog, as *mafiosi* began to escape the control of their patrons. As for the central government of what was by now the Italian state, its having the appearance of an effective presence in Sicily depended in practice on coming to terms with certain factions of *mafiosi*, the *civili. Mafia* went into eclipse during the Fascist era, because a stronger central government than before also posed no threat of social reform. The patrons withdrew their protection of the *mafiosi*, who were rounded up, only to re-emerge after the Allied invasion in 1943. It is perhaps too soon to say whether the offensive of the Italian government against *mafia* in the 1980s will finally break the endemic cycle of violence in Sicily.

Blok's book shows that *mafia* in a single village can no more be understood in separation from the chains of interdependence and balances of power tying it to other layers of Sicilian and Italian society than the French royal court can be understood out of context of the wider French society of the time. Note that he does not argue that violence flourishes merely in the *absence* of a state apparatus. In fact an imperfect pattern of state formation and civilizing process was precisely one element in the sociogenesis of *mafia.* The *mafiosi* functioned as middlemen, mediating between layers of society. Blok also demonstrates clearly that widespread resort to private use of violence as a means of control by no means represents a zero-point in civilization. The *mafiosi* by no means use violence indiscriminately: their victims are specifically those who belong to rival families or in any other way threaten the interests of *mafiosi* and their patrons. Violence in this context persists, but precisely as a relatively controlled means of control.

'Parliamentarization' in England

What happened in England could scarcely be in greater contrast with Sicily, but it is also subtly and importantly different from the French case. In England, a cycle of violence began (in so far as such a cycle can ever be said to start at a specific date) in 1641, when Charles I attempted to arrest certain members of the House of Commons. The forces of parliament and puritanism emerged victorious from the Civil Wars which followed, but subsequently suffered political defeat upon the Restoration of the monarchy in 1660. Nevertheless, the outcome of the Civil Wars and of the so-called Glorious Revolution of 1688 was a permanent shift in the central balances of power within English society. Although the position of the English nobility had never been buttressed by the legal and fiscal privileges seen in France, and though a trend towards an 'absolutist' court society is evident – much as in France – under the Tudors and early Stuarts, in the eighteenth century the English king and court were by no means so pre-eminent, nor was the English aristocracy so 'defunctionalized' as that of France. This much is widely known and discussed among historians and historical sociologists. However, there is a tendency to believe that, after the dramatic event of the 'English Revolution' of the seventeenth century, nothing much apart from the beginning of a major *economic* transformation happened in the eighteenth century – which was thus a quiet interlude before the further dramatic political changes of the nineteenth and twentieth centuries.[30]

That is, contends Elias, very far from the whole truth. What happened was something quite complex, and a relatively rarer pattern of development. The cycle of violence calmed down and conflicts of interest and belief came to be resolved in a manner that allowed the two main parties contending for government power to settle their differences entirely by non-violent means, in accordance with agreed rules observed by both sides (Elias and Dunning 1986: 26). This process, though outwardly less dramatic, lasted longer than the 'English Revolution' itself.

After any Civil War, hatred, fear and mistrust do not disappear overnight; generations need to pass. In England, the cycle of violence rolled on after 1660, though in less virulent form. Tensions between political antagonists remained high. The Stuart kings were still associated with attempts to create an absolutist regime on the French model, and with leanings towards Catholicism. After 1688, the exiled James II and the Jacobites formed a continuing focus for potential rebellion. On the other side, the defeated Puritans, now called Dissenters, were subject to various legal disabilities including exclusion from parliament, but in the eyes of many members of the upper classes they were still in the early eighteenth century also associated with rebellion and dictatorship.

Between the two – the monarchy and the largely lower- and middle-class Dissenters – stood the great balk of the country's most powerful social group, the landowners, who dominated both Houses of Parliament (Elias and Dunning 1986: 29). But they were divided amongst themselves. It was at this time that the names 'Whigs' and 'Tories' came into use for the two factions. The Whigs were led by immensely wealthy aristocratic families of quite recent descent. The Tories included a larger proportion of the untitled gentry, whose estates were generally smaller but their families older. The Whigs were firmer in their opposition to the Stuart pretenders and more lenient towards Dissenters; the Tories were more implacable towards Dissenters but had some leanings towards Jacobitism.

From the Restoration into the eighteenth century, the factional battle was often relatively ruthless. A politician who lost office would be treated vindictively by the opponents who succeeded him; several fled abroad for fear of persecution or even their lives.

Yet, in contrast with France and much of the rest of Western Europe, the principal political cleavage in England was a division between factions of land-owning groups. Their 'rivalry was not rooted in an antagonism between different social classes with a different style of life, different social aims and economic interests' (Elias and Dunning 1986: 29). Moreover, the untitled English gentry formed an intermediate group between the nobility and the urban middle classes but in a manner entirely different from that of the *noblesse de robe* in France. There was no clear line of demarcation between them and the nobility, with whom they shared the status of 'gentleman'.

These circumstances, among others, facilitated the 'parliamentarization' of political conflict. Of course, Parliament had existed for centuries, but what happened now was the transformation of the ancient estate assemblies into something much more like a parliament in the modern sense. During the eighteenth century, the factions were gradually transformed into two parties not radically dissimilar in social composition, which came to justify their political struggles in terms of rival 'principles' or 'philosophies'. They competed with each other for the support of a relatively small electorate, using bribery as well as arguments, but generally refraining from the use of violence against each other. And when one party lost its majority in Parliament, it came to hand power over peacefully to the other.

That presupposed a high level of self-restraint, as did the victors' now refraining from using their new power to humiliate or persecute the outgoing side. It also required the development of an adherence to a corpus of agreed rules for the conduct of political rivalry. It was in fact one more instance of a civilizing spurt, and one which followed a not very common pattern:

It was one of the rather rare examples of a cycle of violence, of a double-bind process tying two or more human groups in a condition of reciprocal fear of each other's violence, which resolved itself in a condition of compromise without absolute victors and absolute vanquished. As both sides gradually lost their distrust of each other and gave up relying on violence and the skills connected with it, they learned instead, and in fact they developed, the new skills and strategies required by a non-violent type of contest. Military skills gave way to the verbal skills of debate, of rhetoric and persuasion, all of which required far greater restraint all round and identified this change very clearly as a civilizing spurt. (Elias and Dunning 1986: 58)

The restraint of violence among the English upper classes in this period was, much more than among their French and German counterparts, a process of self-pacification. Restraints were imposed not by a king and his representatives but by members of a self-ruling oligarchy competing among themselves.

CONCLUSION

Perhaps any further summary of Elias's complex theory of state-formation processes would serve no purpose, but one final potential misunderstanding must be avoided. Elias, in both *The Court Society* and *The Civilizing Process*, talks a great deal about the social pressures towards self-restraint imposed in court and aristocratic circles in Europe before the French Revolution. These circles played an important part in the overall trend of the civilizing process. But he is not arguing that self-restraint was uniquely severe in these circles, nor that it is exclusively from the cultural legacy of these circles that the pattern of restraints in modern society is derived. In fact, in many asides comparing the constraints of life at court with those found in what is badly translated as 'professional-bourgeois' society,[31] Elias depicts the latter as the more compelling. For one thing, it was only towards their peers that court people need subject themselves to great constraint, and far less towards their social inferiors inside and outside the court. In bourgeois society, the occupational functions – competition for capital and wealth, the acquisition of professional skills, success in business – are far more central to social existence and esteem, and through the occupational sphere people of all classes are far more closely bonded to each other. Bourgeois people in the nineteenth century were shaped above all by the necessities of careers demanding regulated work and the subjection of the affects to routine; overall, the pressures upon them were more demanding than those upon courtiers. But the aspects of sociability once so central to the existence of the courtier – ornamentation and furnishing of a house, visiting etiquette, the rituals of eating and so on – were now relegated to 'private life' and no longer shaped so directly or intensely. They received their impress more indirectly, as a function of occupational situations and interests (1969a: 114–16). For this reason, in all that concerns social conduct, working-bourgeois society took over the ritual of courtly society without developing it further with the same intensity (1939: II, 305–7).[32]

To pursue this further, it is necessary to return to the main thread of Elias's argument about civilizing processes. We shall follow him through the final part of the second volume of *The Civilizing Process*, what he calls a 'Synopsis', where he at last draws together the enormously wide-ranging arguments found in the first volume on manners, the second volume on state-formation and, in effect, the case study of *The Court Society*.

4
Sociogenesis and Psychogenesis

One of the most remarkable things about Elias's theory of civilizing processes is the way it encompasses both the minutiae of people's behaviour and the broadest long-term processes of societies' structural development. In the jargon of the trade, it is at once and inseparably a *micro*sociological and a *macro*sociological theory. This is most unusual. Sociologists have long regarded as one of their thorniest theoretical problems the task of 'bridging the micro/macro gap'. In alternative jargon, it is also described as the problem of 'agency' and 'structure', and as the problem of explaining 'emergent properties', the features of 'social structures' apparently generated by the actions of individual people but unintended by and relatively autonomous from them. In the past there has often been little connection between the sort of theory and research which unfolds at the level of social psychology and social interaction between people face to face in small groups, organizations, communities and subcultures on the one hand, and the sort of theory and research which, on the other hand, unfolds at the level of structure and historical development of state-societies or of human society as a whole. Indeed it has been argued, for example by Dawe (1970), that not only do the 'individual-centred' and 'society-centred' approaches represent two distinct traditions in the history of sociology but that it is impossible in principle to bridge the gulf between them. Enough has already been said of the amazingly wide-ranging arguments of *The Civilizing Process* and *The Court Society* to cast doubt on that last assertion: Elias has plainly thrown a good many spans across the chasm. And he has not done so merely by constructing flimsy scaffoldings of abstract concepts in the manner of Talcott Parsons and others like him, but rather by using empirical evidence and theory like bricks and mortar.

The central concepts, here and throughout Elias's work, are 'process' and 'interdependence'; his subject-matter is always people-in-dynamic-interdependence. The notion of interdependence is superficially and deceptively similar to, but in fact vitally different from, the more usual sociological term 'interaction'. Theories of 'interaction' are about how people behave to each other face-to-face. But people are also interdependent with people with whom they never interact, never meet, and are affected by the activities of people far down a line of interdependence. These chains have become longer and the webs denser, with mainly only short-term and local reversals, through most of the history of human society. Though these webs are woven by the intermeshing of individuals' actions, they are not planned or intended for the most part by any individuals: if it is implausible to suppose, for example, that the modern French state was the outcome of the long-term game plan of some early Capetian monarch, still less is it credible that the overall civilizing process, composed of so many strands, is solely a product of human rationality.

The concept of interdependence is also inextricably bound up with power chances. People who are interdependent are not necessarily *equally* inter-dependent. Those who are less dependent on others than others are on them have more power chances than those others. Where balances of power within a web of interdependence are relatively equal, the web constrains the activities of those enmeshed in it even more, and more evenly for all. And the more extensive the web, the more probable is it that even the more powerful will be constrained by ambivalence, knowing that an uninhibited pursuit of their own desires could jeopardize the very links in the web on which they depend, bringing forth consequences which even they must fear.

How these constraints through other people from a variety of angles are converted into self-constraints is the question which links the mainly 'microscopic' concerns of volume I of *The Civilizing Process* to the mainly more 'macroscopic' concerns of volume II. In constructing this link, in showing how the regulation of the whole instinctual and affectual life by steady self-control becomes more and more all-embracing in step with the developing structure of society as a whole, Elias sketches their psychogenesis and sociogenesis.

FORESIGHT AND THE SOCIAL CONSTRAINT TOWARDS SELF-CONSTRAINT

Elias makes clear that the most fundamental and general structural process underlying the civilizing process is the progressive division of labour or, more broadly, division of social functions.[1] From very early in the history of European society, social functions have become more and more differentiated under the pressure of competition (1939: II, 232). As we have seen, competition takes many forms; the monopoly mechanism is one manifestation, competition between firms another, competitive refinement in court society a third. The more differentiated social functions become, the larger the number of people on whom the individual depends in all his actions. More, and longer, and more intertwining chains of interdependence intersect, so to speak, within every individual. To fulfil his own functions at his node in the web, every individual is constrained to take account of the effects of his own and other people's actions through a whole series of links in the social chains. And the denser becomes the web, the greater the division of social functions, and the brisker the competitive forces generated within the figuration, the more does this pressure *increase*.

In particular, more *foresight* is required. It is no accident that the division of social functions is accompanied by the growing consciousness of time and increasingly accurate means of measuring the passage of time. Timing becomes steadily more important as a means of co-ordinating social functions. For the modern businessman it is no longer enough, as it was for medieval people, to agree to meet someone 'this day week' or 'in the forenoon'; precise diaries of appointments long ahead are necessary. Or consider the discipline of time and motion on workers in a factory. The appointments diary and the minute co-ordination of work on an assembly line exemplify how a function situated at a junction of so many chains of action demands a precise allocation of time. This makes people accustomed to subordinating momentary inclinations to the overriding necessities of interdependence, argues Elias in remarks (1939: II, 247–8) which were much later to form the basis of a whole book (1984a; see pp. 210–17 below). It also trains them to eliminate irregularities from behaviour and achieve more permanent self-control.

This self-control is not, of course, a matter only of *conscious* self-regulation. It is central to Elias's argument that much deeper psychological changes occur in the long term. In the course of the civilizing process, a more complex and stable control of behaviour is increasingly instilled in individuals through training from the earliest years of childhood as an automatism or self-compulsion.

The web of actions grows so complex and extensive, the effort required to behave 'correctly' within it becomes so great, that *beside the individual's conscious self-control, an automatic, blindly functioning apparatus of self-control is firmly established*. This seeks to prevent offences to socially acceptable behaviour by a wall of deep-rooted fears . . .' (1939: II, 233; my italics)

People may strive to resist these self-compulsions, but they cannot eliminate them. Many of the 'ills' of civilization – and here Elias differs from Freud – derive from consciously trying to fight against deeply instilled *learned* controls.

To illustrate how both the web of interdependence and individuals' self-steering mechanisms differed between medieval and industrial society, Elias (1939: II, 233–4) uses a vivid image. Picture the muddy roads of a simple warrior society, with a sparse population and a mainly barter economy. There is little traffic. The few travellers along these roads are constantly on the watch, constantly alert to the risk posed to them by other people (and by wild animals: the landscape generally is far less tamed). But the risk of collision with other travellers is small. The main risk is that they will be attacked, robbed, even killed. They have to be constantly prepared to defend themselves violently from violent attack; and that means *temperamentally* as well as physically prepared. A volatile temperament, a constant readiness to fight, and free play of the emotions in defence of one's life and possessions is actually an advantage and necessity in these circumstances. On the roads of modern society, the dangers from other people are very different. The danger of physical attack is comparatively low. But the flow of cars and pedestrians in all directions is very dense. There are road signs, traffic lights and police to control the traffic. This external control, however, is founded on the assumption that every individual is regulating his or her own behaviour very exactly in accordance with the flow of traffic. Constant vigilance, foresight and self-control is needed whether driving or on foot. The chief danger people pose to each other here is through loss of self-control. An error of judgement in foreseeing some movement can kill. Even greater danger, though, comes from the frustrations of the traffic leading someone to lose control, vent his or her aggression on another driver, or in any way 'do something stupid'.[2]

This image can be used to fit together many of the characteristics of people in medieval society discussed earlier, and to understand how the people of court society or of modern industrial society differ. Look back to the hinge of the Middle Ages, when centrifugal forces had run to their fullest extent and created a cellular social structure. Free knights and their serfs lived a largely self-sufficient existence in their own small territory. Chains of interdependence were short. The threats to existence were those of violence from outside, ever-present but unpredictable. It was neither necessary nor possible for a warrior knight to anticipate the effects of his or anyone else's actions many moves ahead down several links in the chain. Foresight was never one of the greatest knightly virtues: nothing compelled it. On the contrary, impetuosity, swift wrath and uninhibited violence, the savage joys of battle with for the moment no thought ahead, no fear of death or of the torture and mutilation which could follow defeat – all these were positive advantages in a society so organized (1939: II, 236–7, 240). In some instances they persisted long after they ceased to be advantageous. Elias is fond of citing the Duc de Montmorency, perhaps one of the last of the type, who rebelled against the king in 1632 (1939: II, 279; 1969a: 195). Finding himself confronting the royal army in what should have been a strong position for him, his furious impulse to give battle could not be restrained even long enough to move his guns and troops into position. He galloped forward with a few followers, easily cut down by the royal forces, was put on trial and beheaded shortly afterwards. At this late stage in the process of courtization of warriors, foresight and self-control even in battle had become far more indispensable than in medieval times.

The medieval personality structure is also seen in its often-noted volatility and the co-existence of extremes within it. On the whole, the behaviour of the lowest, poorest and most oppressed strata was even more spontaneous and less strictly regulated than that of the upper strata, because the compulsions upon them were mainly of a direct physical kind – the threats of poverty and hunger, pain and violent death – which do not induce a stable transformation of constraints by others into self-constraints (1939: II, 251). But the characteristics were seen more or less in all strata. There were the leaps from laughter to anger, from grief to joy, with undiminished intensity and at seemingly slight cause. There was the ability to tolerate pain but also the much greater freewheeling in inflicting pain. There was extreme self-indulgence in pleasure, sexual or gluttonous, but also extreme self-denial and asceticism. Not that every form of inner self-control was entirely lacking in medieval warrior societies or other societies without a complex and stable monopoly of physical violence. Here, once more, there was no zero point. But, argues Elias (1939: II, 239–40), 'the agency of individual self-control, the super-ego, the conscience or whatever we call it' is *relatively* diffuse and unstable, and only a slight barrier to violent emotional outbursts. Like social life itself in these societies, the super-ego has 'greater contrasts and abrupt transitions'. Just as there were great contrasts in society between the self-indulgence of warriors and the self-denial and asceticism of monks, so there can be dramatic switches from one to the other within an individual lifetime: St Francis is an obvious example. 'The restraint the individual here imposes on himself, the struggle against his own flesh, is no less intense and one-sided, no less radical and passionate than its counterpart, the fight against others and the maximum enjoyment of pleasures' (1939: II, 240). More generally in medieval society, the fears securing socially 'correct' conduct were not banished nearly so far from the individual's consciousness, not nearly so much an unconscious automatic mechanism. That is why the precepts of the *courtois* manners books are seen to be only slightly consolidated into half-conscious habits, and why the books themselves were addressed equally to adults and children.

So how does the personality structure come to change over time? What precisely is the connection between the pacification of larger areas of land and the psychology of individuals?

Elias's argument (1939: II, 238–9) is that through the formation of steadily more effective monopolies of force, the threat which one person represents for another is subjected to control and becomes more *calculable*: everyday life is freer of sudden reversals of fortune, and as insecurity declines, the possibility of foresight rises. And there is something else: just like many of the 'animalic' aspects of individual behaviour, so physical violence too comes to be concealed *behind the scenes* of social life. As the monopoly of specialists, it is normally excluded from the lives of others. Physical violence, from being an everyday danger, breaks out to intrude on individual lives only infrequently, as an unusual disaster, and in times of war and social upheaval. All the same, argues Elias, the physical violence stored behind the scenes of social life exerts a *steady pressure* on individuals. The pressure is totally familiar from earliest childhood; it is so familiar that it is barely perceived at a conscious level. Yet it brings about a profound change, not only in *particular* forms of behaviour but in the overall structure of how individuals steer their behaviour as a whole. Because of its predictability and consistency, it can operate to a considerable extent through the individual's own foresight and reflection. In fact, the individual exerts the actual compulsion over him or herself. That is either the result of the individual's knowledge of the possible consequences of moves made in a game of intertwining activities: the conscious fear of the consequences if he or she fails to behave 'correctly'; or, at an unconscious or half-conscious level, it is the result of similar fears instilled from childhood training – the fear of adult displeasure or punishment which has now been repressed from consciousness.

Of course, fluctuations of temperament do not disappear entirely, but they are moderated and gravitate towards a middle line. This is the result of the steady constraints of more peaceful competition for money or prestige. When, as we have seen at length in the case of court society, giving way to spontaneous impulses and emotions is a threat to one's whole social existence, those individuals who are able to moderate their affects are at a great social advantage. This is even more true in bourgeois society, where success in the competitive struggle for wealth requires steady exertion in one's trade or profession, and the deferment of immediate gratification in favour of saving and investment for the future; foresight is particularly marked in the classic bourgeois syndrome.

Elias's argument is that people with temperaments better suited to a new pattern of social interdependencies will succeed better in the social contest. He sees a correspondence emerging between the more even agencies of social control forming with the more effective monopolization of violence by specialists, and the more even controlling agency forming within the personality. Instead of being like flames which flare up, burn intensely, are extinguished and then rekindled once more, the personality comes more to resemble a permanently smouldering fire (1939: II, 303).

The tempering of drives and affects is not produced directly by the division and increasing complexity of social functions alone. It is also the outcome of changing patterns of child training. Partly quite consciously, partly automatically through their own conduct and habits, adults induce in children the constant restraint and foresight they will need for adult functions (1939: II, 241–4). More stable and consistent mechanisms of self-control – call them 'reason' and 'conscience' or 'ego' and 'super-ego' – are formed, relaying social standards in an automatic self-supervision of drives, and part of the drives and affects of the young child are forgotten, no longer within reach of consciousness in the adolescent and adult. The more animalic impulses and inclinations in particular are hidden from consciousness, behind the scenes of *mental* life so to speak, paralleling the removal of so many animalic activities behind the scenes of *social* life (cf. 1939: I, 190). But the process of civilizing human young is never without pain, and it often leaves scars. Sometimes the inhibition of affects becomes so deeply ingrained and habituated in an individual that the adult is no longer capable of expressing or gratifying the repressed desires and affects in even the most modified form. This may be experienced as constant feelings of boredom or loneliness. It is as if particular branches of desires have been anaesthetized through childhood experience. Any expression of them by the child incurs such dangers – disapproval, embarrassment, punishment from parents for instance – that they remain deaf and unresponsive throughout a whole lifetime. In other cases, 'the heavy conflicts which the rough-hewn, affective and passionate nature of the small human being unavoidably encounters on its way to being moulded into a "civilized" being' divert energies into unwanted release through obsessions, compulsive actions, peculiar hobby-horses, eccentric aversions and other symptoms of 'maladjustment' (1939: II, 243).

Elias concedes that only a small minority of people emerge from childhood training with such symptoms of mild or acute psychological disturbance. There is also a lucky minority – lucky because no-one yet knows how to manage and steer the process for best results – who emerge as 'well-adjusted' adults, capable of leading a pleasurable life within the social constraints without any evident inner conflicts. Yet for the majority, the 'normal' majority, such inner conflicts – if in no way crippling – are by no means absent. They find expression in many ways. Life in society has become less dangerous, but also less exciting, emotional and pleasurable, and for what is lacking in everyday life a substitute is created in dreams, books and art. So, on their way to becoming courtiers, nobles read novels of chivalry, and now respectable middle-class people take pleasure in watching erotic and violent films. It is as if, writes Elias,

the battlefield is . . . moved within . . . [T]he drives, the passionate affects, that can no longer directly manifest themselves in the relationships *between* people, often struggle no less violently *within* the individual against this supervising part of himself . . . The vertical oscillations, if we may so describe them, the leaps from fear to joy, pleasure to remorse are reduced, while the horizontal fissure running right through the whole person, the tension between the 'super-ego' and 'unconscious' – the wishes and drives that cannot be remembered – increases. (1939: II, 243)

Elias uses Freudian vocabulary – ego and super-ego, drives, libido, unconscious, repression and so on – in discussing psychological changes in the course of the civilizing process. This vocabulary is more prominent in his early work than later. Yet Elias never accepted Freudian doctrines uncritically. He accused Freud of an ahistoric view of human psychology (1939: II, 285–6). Freud, having observed certain striking characteristics of the personality structure of people in his own time, jumped to the conclusion that these had always existed as parts of an unchanging human nature, true for all time. In particular, he assumed that there had always been the same quite strict division between unconscious and conscious mental functions that he could diagnose in his own contemporaries. On the contrary, Elias contended that this division was one result of the long-term civilizing process, but only gradually did 'the wall of forgetfulness separating libidinal drives and "consciousness" or "reflection" . . . become harder and more impermeable' (1939: II, 286). Freudians had tended to conceive the most important element in the whole psychological structure as an 'unconscious', an 'id' without a history. They failed to distinguish between the raw material of drives, which perhaps did change little throughout the history of mankind, and the drives as they are channelled through drive-controls which are formed through the person's relations with other people from birth onwards, controls which have become steadily firmer with the changing pattern of social relations in the course of the European civilizing process since the Middle Ages. Elias, in other words, denies that except in new-born babies we ever encounter libidinal energies in any human being in a purely raw, pre-social form. They have always already been socially processed, sociogenetically transformed. 'Id' functions can therefore in no way be separated from corresponding ego structures. What determines conduct is none of these alone, but rather the balances and conflicts between people's drives, which are malleable, and the *drive controls* which have already been built in through social experience since birth. What is important is always *the relationship* between these various sets of psychological functions, partly conflicting and partly cooperating in the way an individual steers himself. It is they, these relationships *within* man between the drives and affects controlled and the built-in controlling agencies, whose structure changes in the course of the civilizing process, in accordance with the changing structure of relationships *between* individual human beings, in society at large. (1939: II, 286)

One of the most important changes in the course of the process is, succinctly, that ' "consciousness" becomes less permeable by drives, and drives become less permeable by "consciousness" '.[3] This thesis is absolutely central to Elias's work; it is crucial, as we shall see later, to his theories of knowledge and science and his writings on involvement and detachment. The thesis is also, as again we shall see later, controversial especially among anthropologists. For it leads Elias to argue that in simpler societies elementary impulses – though in no sense 'raw' and socially unmoulded – have easier access to people's consciousness; later in a civilizing process, the compartmentalization of the conscious and unconscious components of self-steering mechanisms becomes more pronounced. The same thesis also underlies Elias's working out of important ideas about manifestations of foresight, to which we now turn.

VARIATIONS ON FORESIGHT

Elias pays particular attention to three aspects of increasing foresight: the process he calls 'psychologization'; the more familiar one of rationalization; and the advance of thresholds of shame and embarrassment.

Psychologization and increasing mutual identification

The division of social functions under the pressure of competition means, as we have seen, that individuals have constantly to attune their actions to those of more and more others. The habit of foresight over longer chains grows. And with this change also comes a change in the way of considering others. The individual's image of other people becomes 'psychologized': it becomes more permeated by observation and experience. Perception of others becomes richer in nuances, and freer from the instant response of spontaneous emotions (1939: II, 272–4).

What this means is seen more clearly in relation to the historical evidence. In a society with a lower division of social functions, where chains of interdependence were short and life was more insecure and unpredictable, other people were perceived in a simpler way. We have seen how in warrior society other people and their actions were perceived in more unqualified terms as friend or foe, good or bad; and the responses were correspondingly unrestrained and undifferentiated. With the greater complexity of society which gradually develops, however, people become accustomed to looking further down a human chain and reacting more dispassionately.

Only then is the veil which the passions draw in front of their eyes slowly lifted, and a new world comes into view – a world whose course is friendly or hostile to the individual person without being *intended* to be so, a chain of events that need to be contemplated dispassionately over long stretches if their connections are to be uncovered. (1939: II, 273)

The greater permeation of conduct by observation is seen clearly in the transition of manners in the sixteenth century. In the books of Erasmus and Della Casa, psychological insights and personal observation play a larger part than in their medieval precursors, and the reader is urged to take more conscious account of how his own behaviour will be interpreted by others. This was in Elias's view already an early sign of the accelerated courtization of the upper class and the closer integration of the various strata of society during that period. Later, when court society reached its zenith, the art of human observation was refined further. As Elias demonstrated at length in *The Court Society*, preservation of one's social position under severe competitive pressure necessitated a more 'psychological' view of people, involving precise observation of oneself and others in terms of longer series of motives and causal connections. Yet this was not quite the same as what is today called psychology. In a sense the courtly art of observation remained far closer to reality: it was never concerned with the individual in isolation, but always with individual people in relation to others in a social context. Only later – under the influence of the solipsistic strain in Western philosophy increasingly prominent from the Renaissance onwards, and also coloured by the still greater constraints and inhibitions of classic bourgeois society – did 'psychology' take on its more modern guise. One of the principal faults of that, maintains Elias, is that too often it implicitly assumes that the essential determinants of a person's behaviour come from 'inside', independent of his or her relation to others, and are related to others almost as an afterthought.

The social process of psychologization is a process of transition in mutual identification. Taking more conscious account of how one's behaviour will be interpreted by others can also be described as a higher level of identification with others; of course, in court society the boundaries within which identification was felt were quite narrow, and there remained great scope for expansion in subsequent phases of social development.

Rationalization

The sixteenth century also saw a strong spurt towards rationalization in many fields, from economic attitudes to religion and science. This has been noted by many historians and social scientists, among whom Max Weber is most celebrated by sociologists. Elias sets the trend of rationalization in broader context of the transformation of personality structure and pressure towards habitual foresight.

Here again, as always, Elias warns against looking for absolute beginnings. Just as there is no point at which human beings suddenly began to possess a 'conscience', there is none before which they did not possess 'reason', 'ratio', or 'understanding'. Still more misleading is it to think of rationality as some kind of internal organ which suddenly develops within the minds of numerous persons in isolation from each other. 'There is not actually a "ratio", there is at most "rationalization"' (1939: II, 277). Here again, what actually changes is the way people are bonded with each other in society, and in consequence the remoulding of the personality structure.

The theory of rationalization involved here is explained more clearly in *The Court Society* (1969a: 92–3) than in *The Civilizing Process*. It will be recalled that Elias discussed 'court-rationality', a form of rationality by which people and prestige – rather than economic opportunities – were made calculable as instruments of power. From the point of view of classic bourgeois-economic rationality, court-rationality could appear highly irrational – 'if he were running into debt, why did he not reduce his expenses?'. Yet *both* court-rationality and bourgeois-economic rationality are the outcome of powerful spurts of rational*ization*.

Elias's argument is that the forms of behaviour we call 'rationality' can only be produced within a social figuration in which an extensive transformation of external compulsions (*Fremdzwänge*) into internal compulsions (*Selbstzwänge*) takes place:

The complementary concepts of 'rationality' and 'irrationality' refer to the relative parts played by short-term affects and long-term conceptual models of observable reality in individual behaviour. The greater the importance of the latter in the delicate balance between affective and reality-orientated commands, the more 'rational' is behaviour . . . (1969a: 92)

Although he does not actually use the words, Elias is here thinking in terms of the struggle between what Freud called the 'Pleasure Principle' and the 'Reality Principle'. What is involved in any process of rationalization is a central component of the civilizing process, the increasingly sharp differentiation of the outward-directed, reality-oriented psychological functions. A more 'rationally' functioning consciousness is less directly coloured by drive impulses and affective fantasies (1939: II, 286), and always involves to varying degrees the deferment of short-term affects for the achievement of longer-term goals by means dictated (via conceptual schemes) by the external reality of social interdependencies.

It follows from this, however, that the type of reality-orientated conceptual model[4] involved in the control of human behaviour varies with the structure of social reality itself. That is why the 'rationality' of court people was different from that of the commercial and professional bourgeoisie. The two variants of rationality have in common the preponderance of longer-term reality-orientated considerations over momentary affects in the control of behaviour in particular social fields. But it is the calculation of gains and losses of prestige in the one case, and of financial gains and losses in the other case, which plays the dominant part in the 'rational' control of behaviour. Both forms of rationality involve the control of behaviour directed towards competing for the means of power prestige and capital being the dominant means of power in the respective societies. In court society a gain in prestige could sometimes be bought at a financial loss, while for a courtier to pursue financial advantage like a bourgeois could entail loss of prestige; therefore each form of 'rational' behaviour may appear 'irrational' from the standpoint of the other. Yet both, understood as expressions of the shifting tension balance within the personality between short-term affective impulses and longer-term considerations of social reality, represent spurts of rationalization.

Viewing rationalization processes in this way, it may be observed in passing, tends to render void Max Weber's famous distinction (1922a: I, 24–6) between *Zweckrationalität* ('purpose-rationality') and *Wertrationalität* ('value-rationality'). Weber constructed his ideal-type of *Zweckrationalität*, representing bourgeois-economic rationality, as the highest form of rationality from which other types were to be understood as deviations, lower or less well developed forms. Court rationality would for him be one form of *Wertrationalität*,[5] by which he meant the rational weighing of means against each other in pursuit of an end which is itself not questioned nor considered rationally. In this, Weber conformed to the prevalent view that the gradual transition to more 'rational' behaviour and thought was historically associated principally with the bourgeois strata.[6]

This is disputed by Elias. His study of rationalization processes within the aristocratic camp was undertaken, he says (1939: II, 289), partly as a counterbalance to the idea that the bourgeoisie were the originators or inventors of more rational thought. He hints in *The Court Society* (1969a: 92) that further investigation may show that court-rationality was an early stage and precondition of bourgeois economic rationality. But in *The Civilizing Process* he lays stress instead on the much more compelling argument that *no* class, stratum or other group can be seen as the sole originator of a process like rationalization. Changes of this kind do not begin in one class or another, 'but arise in conjunction with the tensions *between* different functional groups in a social field and *between* the competing people within them' (1939: II, 289). Thus, as we have seen, the competition *among* the court nobility themselves was fuelled by pressure on the nobility as a whole both from 'above' (the royal monopoly apparatus) and from below (the bourgeois strata). In their turn, the bourgeoisie – the classic 'middle class' – were also subject to pressure on two fronts as well as amongst themselves. These were the tensions which propelled processes of rationalization.

Shame and embarrassment

Much the same argument applies to a third facet of increasingly habitual foresight, the advance of thresholds of shame and embarrassment.

Like psychologization and rationalization, this too becomes more perceptible in the social habitus of people in Western Europe from about the sixteenth century. Elias defines the feeling of shame as 'a kind of anxiety which is automatically reproduced in the individual on certain occasions by force of habit' (1939: II, 292). On the surface it is a fear of social degradation, the fear that one's own behaviour will cause others to express disdain, withdraw their approval, or in some other way assert their superiority. It is a fear which cannot be assuaged by retaliation, for the individual inwardly acknowledges his or her own inferiority. The behaviour of which one is ashamed is not just a transgression of prevalent social opinion, but rather has brought one into conflict with a part of oneself that represents this social opinion within one. One fears the loss of love or respect of others to whom one is bonded or has been bonded in the past. Their attitudes have precipitated an attitude within one which one automatically adopts towards oneself. The feeling of shame is experienced whenever tension between emotions and emotional controls fluctuates towards the former at the expense of the latter, resulting in a transgression of internalized standards.

The mechanism of *embarrassment* is very similar. The difference is that it is caused by the action of *another person*, or even an object, outside one's self. 'Embarrassment is displeasure or anxiety which arises when another person threatens to breach, or breaches, society's prohibitions represented by one's own super-ego' (1939: ii, 296).

The fear of transgressions of social prohibitions takes on the character of shame and embarrassment, by definition, the more fully *Fremdzwang* has been converted into *Selbstzwang*. This fear is obviously related to vigilance and foresight in anticipating social dangers. That is why shame and embarrassment on the one hand and rationalization on the other represent two sides of the same coin. Both are related to the growing differentiation within the personality of drives and drive controls, between the id functions and the ego ('reason') and super-ego ('conscience') functions. (Elias is conscious of the risk these Freudian terms carry of reifying processes and reducing them to static entities, but he always uses them with caution – perhaps with greater caution than is always possible here in summary.) The ego and super-ego sector of the personality has a dual function. It serves to regulate a person's external relations with other people, and at the same time is involved in a person's striving for control – partly automatically, partly consciously – over his or her own 'inner life', affects and impulses. They simultaneously conduct a domestic policy and a foreign policy (1939: i, 294). Though these are not always in harmony, and indeed are quite often in contradiction, they stem from the same functions within the personality. And thus the reorganization of personality structure brought about by the division of social functions and the pressure towards the habituation of foresight finds dual expression in foreign policy as spurts of rationalization and in domestic policy as advances in the thresholds of shame and embarrassment during roughly the same historical periods.

For the same reason, in accordance with the sociogenetic ground rule (see p. 50 above), corresponding parallel processes can be observed today in the life of each individual child: 'the rationalization of conduct is an expression of the foreign policy of the same super-ego formation whose domestic policy is expressed in an advance of the shame threshold' (1939: ii, 294).

Yet again, it has to be emphasized that there are no zero-points in the shame threshold any more than in other aspects of the civilizing process. Shame and embarrassment are found in less stable, less uniform and less comprehensive form in less differentiated societies (1939: II, 293). But it is the *change*, the *advance* of the thresholds of shame and embarrassment that Elias seeks to explain.

The advance can be seen in many aspects of the history of manners discussed in chapter 2 above, and there is an important link with the monopoly mechanism discussed in chapter 3. For, with the more effective internal pacification of larger areas, physical fears subside from consciousness and fears like those of shame and embarrassment come to predominate. As physical violence becomes less familiar and exercised from the wings of social life, any irruption of it into people's everyday existence becomes deeply repugnant. For most people – though not all – in modern industrial society, to give way to their impulses and resort to violence brings on the deepest shame. To see it happen in others causes acute shock and embarrassment (though seeing it in a film or on television, as a fantasy, does not do so to anything like the same extent). Anything recalling violence between people is banished from view, or at least subjected to more and more precise social rules: that is how Elias explains the development of rules governing the use of the knife in eating and the decline (at least in some countries and strata) of cutting up dead animals at table (1939: II, 246, 296–7).

Perhaps the clearest illustration of the advancing thresholds of shame and embarrassment, however, is the development of standards governing nakedness in the presence of others. 'Reasons of respect', it will be recalled, were prominent in the transitional phase of the history of manners, from the sixteenth to the eighteenth centuries; they give explicit social reference for the adoption of new standards and to the experience of shame and embarrassment. Only later, by the nineteenth century especially, had this social reference receded from consciousness:

only when the walls between the estates fall away, when the functional dependence of all on all increases and all members of society become several degrees more equal, does such exposure, except in certain narrower enclaves, become an offence in the presence of *any* other person. Only then is such behaviour so profoundly associated with fear in the individual from an early age that the social character of the prohibition vanishes entirely from his consciousness, shame appearing as a command coming from within himself. (1939: II, 296, my italics)

That the social reference of the fear of shame and embarrassment has receded from consciousness, however, does not in any way negate the part played by changes in the structure of social relations in bringing about these psychological changes. The movement through the history of Western society towards 'functional democratization' is of key significance in explaining many striking characteristics of both culture and personality in the modern age.

'PRESSURE FROM BELOW' AND THE CIRCULATION OF MODELS

Why should so many facets of behaviour of the lower orders of society be embarrassing for those above? Or, what is much the same, why should they have been for so long the stock-in-trade of comedy?

It was not always so. So far as can be judged, knights in the epoch of free warriors felt no repugnance or embarrassment at the sight of the lower classes and their behaviour. What they felt was no more than *contempt*, which they expressed 'openly, untroubled by any reserve, uninhibited and unsublimated' (1939: II, 263). (Something of this can be seen in figures 1, 2 and 3 taken from the *Mittelalterliche Hausbuch* on which Elias drew in his section 'Scenes from the Life of a Knight' in volume I of *The Civilizing Process*.[7]) These free knights held their social position far more securely than their courtly successors (even if they were less secure of their lives). Since the lower orders posed little threat or competition to them, the thought of them was not disturbing. They provoked no anxiety, and therefore the warrior class felt no need to banish coarseness, vulgarity, anything recalling the lower classes, from their own lives.

The warriors at this stage, in other words, experienced little if any pressure from below. The estates of society lived in close spatial proximity and yet were socially distant from each other. The division of social functions was still so low that the ties of interdependence binding the estates to each other were still very loose. A symptom of this is that ideas and customs often spread more readily over great distances between town and town, court and court, monastery and monastery – that is, within the same social stratum – than between castle and town in the same district (1939: II, 262; I, 117).

That being said, even the earliest courts back in the age of the *Minnesänger* were significant in bringing together some members of the nobility and the bourgeoisie in an interdependence with each other that was as yet rare elsewhere (1939: II, 261, 302). Interdependence brings tensions, and it is mistaken to think that tensions between court aristocracy and bourgeoisie date only from when they broke out in acute form in the revolutions of the late eighteenth to mid-nineteenth centuries. They can be traced back much further, and it is part of Elias's thesis that the courtization of the nobility took place only in conjunction with a strong upward thrust by bourgeois elements; there was always a counterpoint of the 'bourgeoisification' of the aristocracy.

As we have seen in chapter 3, increasing social competition produced increased *inner* tensions and unconscious fears in the court nobility over time. The constant pressure from below, and the fear it induces above, are one of the strongest forces of the specifically civilized refinement by which the people of the upper class distinguish themselves from others (1939: II, 304). This is seen in their sensitivity to anything threatening hereditary privileges, in their constant elaboration and polishing of manners and, at a level deeper in the personality, in the automatic self-control which becomes second nature to them, and in their repugnance for anything which 'smells of the bourgeois'. In the age of court society, the 'circulation of models' was far faster than in the

FIGURE 3
Reproduced from *Das Mittelalterliche Hausbuch* (ed. Bossert and Storck, 1912)
by permission of Bodley's Librarian, Oxford.

Middle Ages. Standards of behaviour, of feeling, and cultural taste were constantly being more widely adopted under competitive pressure, so that models which were once 'refined' repeatedly became 'vulgar'. And new standards of even greater refinement were formed amongst the elite.

Yet the long-term trend in Western societies is in Elias's view something far more complicated than the simple mechanism which, after Fallers (1954), has been known as the 'trickle-down effect'. The persisting division of social functions has continued to bind all classes and strata to each other in steadily more equal – not equal, but more equal – interdependence. 'Pressure from below' becomes too one-sided a description of this process. Elias uses the term *functional democratization* to denote the process by which every individual is enmeshed in longer and denser webs of interdependence with more and more others, leading to greater reciprocal dependency and more multi-polar control within and among groups (see the fuller discussion in chapter 5 below). In the circulation of models, functional democratization is expressed in an overall trend towards *both diminishing contrasts and increasing varieties*.

Something more than simple trickle down is involved in Elias's conception of phases of 'colonization' (or 'assimilation') and 'repulsion', as the following important passage makes clear:

If the outline of these processes is followed over the centuries, we see a clear tendency for standards of living and of conduct to be equalized and contrasts levelled out. In each of the waves of expansion which occur when the mode of conduct of a small circle spreads to larger rising classes, two phases can be clearly distinguished: a phase of colonization or assimilation in which the lower and larger outsider class is still inferior and governed by the example of the established upper group which, intentionally or unintentionally permeates it with its own pattern of conduct, and a second phase of repulsion, differentiation or emancipation, in which the rising group gains perceptibly in social power and self-confidence, and in which the upper group is forced into increased restraint and isolation, and the contrasts and tensions in society are increased. (1939: II, 311)

Elias adds, incidentally, that both elements are present throughout; if distinct phases are perceptible it is because the balance between colonization and repulsion processes tilts first one way then the other.[8]

More importantly, however, the overall trend is not simply a trickle down through a static hierarchy but involves the relative levelling out of power balances between rungs of the hierarchy, accompanied by some measure of trickle *up*. Even as far back as the seventeenth, eighteenth or nineteenth centuries – earlier or later according to the different structures of England, France, and Germany – the standards of the nobility and bourgeoisie *interpenetrated* each other rather than one simply displacing the other (1939: II, 256; I, 110). Over time the process broadened to include other strata more closely. One of the peculiarities of Western society is that lower class characteristics are spreading to all classes. Most strikingly, almost every able-bodied person has gradually come to be expected to earn a living through work of the highly regulated type which has become normal; earlier, work was an attribute of the lower classes (1939: I, 152; II, 252). The upper classes – as well as, to some extent, working-class people – have also been imbued with the saving-for-future-profits ethos associated first with the middle classes (1969a: 67, 72). And, at the same time, what used to be distinguishing marks of the upper classes spread to society at large. Notably, the conversion of external social constraints into more or less automatic and habitual individual self-regulation of drives and affects has taken place in the West among the broad masses too. That is possible only for people who are normally protected from external, physical threat by sword or starvation; and the working classes of the West share that security partly because they are no longer entirely lower classes. With the spread of bonds of interdependence across the globe, they effectively form part of a world upper class (1939: ii, 255). Elias's use of the word 'colonization' is literal as well as figurative; it will be recalled that right at the beginning of his first volume, he spoke of colonialism as a late – if not final – phase of the civilizing process (1939: i, 50, 104; cf. ii, 308–9).

Of course, viewed from close quarters, there still seem to be very marked differences in social personality structure at various levels of society. The 'rougher' working class, from whom are drawn most of the football hooligans of the 1980s for example, may still appear as 'uncivilized barbarians' to their respectable superiors. Even among those who are not so overtly unruly,

behaviour may be coarser, but it is more uniform and in a way more of a piece. They live more vigorously in their own world without any claim to upper class prestige, and therefore with greater scope for discharge of the affects; they live more fully in accordance with their own manners and customs. (1939: ii, 313)

Nevertheless, looking at the broad sweep of the movement as a whole over the centuries, it can be seen that the sharp contrasts between the behaviour of different social groups – like the contrasts and sudden switches in the behaviour of individuals – are steadily diminishing.

Much the same can be said of differences in social habitus between the different Western nations. Historical differences in the structure of development of various countries have left their mark in curious amalgams and varieties of civilized conduct. 'In the conduct of workers in England, for example, one can still see traces of the manners of the landed gentry, and of merchants within a large trade network, in France the airs of courtiers and a bourgeoisie brought to power by Revolution' (1939: ii, 256).

The same interpenetration of models, derived in accordance with past and present power relationships between earlier and later dominant and rising classes, can be seen across the whole field of culture and the arts. Elias uses the term *Kitsch* to describe the resulting cultural amalgams (1935; 1969a: 56, 114), but in his hands the word is by no means entirely a pejorative term (any more than *civilization* is for him entirely a term of approbation). He wishes to use *Kitsch* as a technical term for a cultural style, emerging in the nineteenth and persisting in the twentieth centuries, which – unlike Classicism, Baroque and Rococo, all specifically courtly styles – is not firmly associated with any single class, but with the overall social process.[9] For instance, residues from the architecture, furniture, literature, painting and music of court society can be seen persisting to the present day, but this heritage underwent 'a peculiarly ghostly transformation' in the new mass society and was emptied of its original meaning (1969a: 113–14). One example is the tiny residual porch over the door of a humble English semi-detached, a faint echo of an aristocratic mansion. Yet major cultural achievements may also be instances of *Kitschstil* in Elias's sense; he sometimes uses the word *Edelkitsch* (noble-kitsch) to describe works such as Wagner's music dramas. The common characteristic of such products is the amalgamation of courtly forms originally motivated by court-rational considerations of delicacy and social exclusiveness with later bourgeois influences, motivated by economic-rational considerations of the market which may, for instance, introduce elements of bombast and 'vulgarity' to enhance mass appeal.

CONCLUSION

This chapter has already drawn together many of the interweaving themes of *The Civilizing Process* set out in the previous two chapters, so there is no need for a separate conclusion, except perhaps to make two points in brief.

First, several of the ideas Elias was developing in this major publication were generally in the air in the 1930s. Apart from the common heritage of German sociology, from Marx to Simmel and Max Weber among others, there was the massive impact of Freud, whose influence Elias has acknowledged[10] to have been stronger on him at the time than that of any sociologist. Some of the concerns of *The Civilizing Process* can be found in the writings of Mannheim but still more in the work of members of the Frankfurt School, notably Horkheimer and Adorno (1947) and Herbert Marcuse (1955). The point, however, is that Elias handled the idea of the civilizing of character in a very different way from them. They approached it very much in a philosophical framework. Elias, in contrast, turned the common question into issues for *social scientific* and historical investigation. His work unfolds from the start within what E. P. Thompson (1978) was to call an 'empirical idiom of discourse', meaning not that he is an 'empiricist' in the pejorative sense but that questions about 'human nature' which have traditionally been framed as timeless matters for philosophical speculation are made by Elias contingent upon empirical and historical investigation, always proceeding hand in hand with theoretical reasoning.

Second, *The Civilizing Process* had all the marks of a paradigmatic work, in T. S. Kuhn's (1962) sense of the word paradigm. That is to say, the book proposed convincing answers to several major questions, but also left open many other questions for further investigation. It was capable of much further extension. Many ideas mentioned in passing in *The Civilizing Process* were taken up later and developed much further by Elias himself, or by others. The next part of this book will outline these extensions.

PART III

Extensions

5

Established-Outsiders Relations and Functional Democratization

In the final sections of *The Civilizing Process*, Elias had begun to quarry a rich vein of ideas about the relationship between social inequalities, power chances, personality structure, and styles of life and cultural expression. Although the book as a whole was built out of historical material and delved back into the distant past, these concluding pages implied a great deal about many facets of life in European society in the twentieth century.

Discussing diminishing contrasts and increasing varieties, the interpenetration of cultural traits owing their origins to very different strata in the past, and the movements of 'colonization' and 'repulsion' which mark the tension-ridden relationships between rising and falling, more and less powerful strata, Elias was saying something much more complex and 'object-adequate' than is sometimes found in debates about 'working-class culture' and middle-class or 'bourgeois' culture. The styles of life of competing and coalescing groups were neither static nor isolated traditions, but developing over time, changing and adapting in response to each other and in accordance with changing power differentials between strata.

In all this, Elias was adopting neither the Marxist nor the Weberian approaches to these matters which have been most favoured among sociologists in the late twentieth century. Explicitly he denied that all could be reduced to questions of control over economic power resources in the Marxian way. Implicitly he also rejected conceptions of 'class', 'status' and 'party' as three 'dimensions' or 'factors' in the distribution of power chances, which in debates among followers of Weber has sometimes taken on an air of scholasticism. Rather, the mutual conditioning of processes of meaning and power was already central to Elias's thinking. For him, power was a polymorphous, figurationally generated property of all social interdependencies. He sought categories which, though simpler in themselves, would yet enable him to grapple better with the complexities of inequality actually observed within the flux of social relationships.

The eventual outcome was his theory of established-outsiders relations. Like the theory of civilizing processes, the later theory links changing power ratios between groups with the social habitus of group members. Indeed the two are essentially the same theory, though each is more elaborate than the other in certain areas of conceptualization. The point of entry to the theory of established-outsiders relations, however, is very different. The model arose out of a study of a small community near Leicester in the middle years of the twentieth century. The outcome was the book *The Established and the Outsiders: A Sociological Enquiry into Community Problems* (1965), written in collaboration with John L. Scotson. Although it was not widely read at the time,[1] the effect of this book can be seen clearly in much of the work on *present-day* social problems undertaken by sociologists under Elias's influence. The book helps to justify his claim not to be simply an 'historical sociologist' but to have developed an approach applicable to present-day problems too. This chapter will discuss Elias's own work and that of sociologists in the Netherlands and Germany; some equally relevant work by Eric Dunning and his colleagues at Leicester, which grew out of research into modern sport, will be covered in chapter 6.

ESTABLISHED-OUTSIDERS RELATIONS IN MICROCOSM: WINSTON PARVA

The community which the authors thinly disguised under the name Winston Parva is located on the suburban outskirts of Leicester. At the time of the study, from 1958 into the early 1960s, it had about 5,000 inhabitants. It was relatively self-contained, partly cut off from Leicester to the north by a railway line, and with its own factories in which many of the local people worked during a period of rising prosperity and high employment.

The study began in work for an MA thesis by John Scotson, who was a teacher in a local school and leader of a youth club in Winston Parva. His initial interest was in juvenile delinquency and why it arose disproportionately in one neighbourhood. This led him to undertake a study of the community by means of the usual methods of sociological investigation: he gathered official statistics on class, occupation and crime, and he conducted interviews with every thirtieth household on the electoral list, as well as with leaders of local voluntary associations and local officials. Elias occasionally joined in interviewing the families. The study was typical of the times: many such community studies were made by British sociologists in the 1950s and 1960s. In itself, Scotson's thesis might have been a sound but not startling contribution to this literature. What lifted it out of the ordinary when published as a joint book was the way that Elias used the research as a vehicle for the development of his own theorizing.[2]

The crucial characteristic of Winston Parva which made it suitable for Elias's purpose was that it consisted of three easily recognizable neighbourhoods, not only differing from each other but also standing in distinctive relationships with each other. Zone 1 contained mainly larger houses, occupied by businessmen and professional people, easily distinguished in occupational statistics as middle-class. Zone 1 was regarded both by its own residents and by the rest of

Winston Parva as the best, 'residential' district. Zones 2 and 3, on the other hand, were not at all easy to distinguish by means of objective indicators of social class. Both were working-class areas whose residents were very similar mixtures of skilled, semi-skilled and unskilled manual workers. Yet they were readily distinguished in other ways: people in each of these zones saw themselves as very different from the other.

Zone 2 was the largest of the three, and formed the centre of the 'village' – the people who lived there referred to themselves as 'villagers'. The factories, the churches, the cinema, the two pubs, the working men's club, and other communal facilities were in this zone, and the many voluntary associations met there. The self-styled villagers thought of their area as, above all, a 'respectable' area (the respectability of which was only enhanced by the presence there of a small minority of middle-class, non-manual residents).

The residents of both zone 1 and zone 2 regarded zone 3 as far inferior to their own areas. Referred to as 'the Estate' – and less flatteringly by labels like 'rat alley' – zone 3 was literally as well as figuratively on the wrong side of the railway tracks. The villagers said that the residents of the Estate were 'rough': they did not keep their houses clean, could not control their children, quarrelled noisily, sometimes fought each other and, it was hinted, tended to promiscuity. As a matter of fact, none of this was true of any but a tiny minority of eight or nine Estate families, who between them produced nearly all the juvenile delinquency in which Scotson had originally been interested. The rest of the Estate families differed little, *taken singly*, from those in the village. They lived in similar terraced houses which they kept clean, they controlled their children, they lived quietly and peaceably. They worked in the same factories on good terms with the people of the village, and relations at work between *individuals* from the village and the Estate were good.

Nevertheless, what did differ strikingly were the links which bonded the Estate families together – or rather the relative absence of links. This presented a strong contrast with the village. The Estate families tended to 'keep themselves to themselves'; there were no associations on the Estate to speak of, and the Estate people played little part in the numerous associations and social activities of the village. Moreover, a crucial finding was that residents of zone 3 'seemed to accept, with a kind of puzzled resignation, that they belonged to a group of less virtue and respectability' (Elias 1976: 8). They felt a sense of shame tinged with resentment at the hostile attitude of the villagers. They often aimed to move out of Winston Parva, whereas the villagers usually expressed satisfaction at living in their own area, and if they had ambitions to move it was only into the still better area of zone 1 nearby.

What explanations could be found for these relationships between the 'established' residents of zones 1 and 2 and the 'outsiders' of zone 3? Elias, of course, sought an answer not in how the community existed at a particular date, but in how it had developed over time. An important clue was the pride of so many of the 'villagers' in their standing as 'old' families – a pride more normally associated with propertied aristocratic or business families than with the manual working class. Zone 2, the 'village', was in fact the oldest part of Winston Parva, though by no means very old compared with hundreds of other English villages. The houses there had been built for rent by a businessman in the 1880s – barely eighty years before the date of the research, so there were still a few old people who could remember the earliest days of the settlement. Circumstances, including the availability of employment locally and the willingness of landlords to let houses to married offspring near their parents, had favoured quite a high stability of residence among families over two or three generations. Members of these 'old families', although they were only a minority of the population of zone 2, formed a core group, 'a central establishment guarding the special virtue and respectability of the whole "village"' (1976: 35). The families were 'mother-centred', on the model of the working-class community in Bethnal Green made famous by Young and Willmott (1957). They had intermarried, entangling into an 'old families network', a channel of both mutual aid and gossip, and – as we shall see – a powerful instrument of exclusion. Those who belonged to this network, along with a few people from the middle-class zone 1, virtually monopolized the leadership of the churches and associations in Winston Parva. Overall, zone 2 formed a highly cohesive community.

The middle-class houses of zone 1 had been built much later, in the 1920s and 1930s. Far from being resented as intruders in the 'village', the business and professional people who came to live in them were seen as raising the tone and standing of the township as a whole. There was a close identification between residents of zones 1 and 2 for all their 'class' differences, and they made common cause in their attitudes towards zone 3.

So what of zone 3? Where had its people sprung from? The Estate had been built as a speculative development on the eve of the Second World War, barely twenty years before the period of the study. At that time there had briefly been a housing glut in England, and the houses did not prove immediately easy to let. Gradually they came to be rented by newcomers, especially Northerners, moving to the relatively prosperous Midlands to seek work. Then, early in the war, there was sudden influx of more than a hundred Londoners when a military instrument factory was evacuated with all its employees from the capital to Winston Parva. This first wave of Londoners and the majority of the other early 'immigrants' were skilled or semi-skilled workers like the majority of the 'village' residents, and earned much the same wages. But the newcomers differed considerably from the older residents in their customs, their traditions, their whole way of life. For instance, the newcomers enjoyed themselves more boisterously. There was no conscious defiance of Winston Parva's established ways, nor did the older residents consciously concert efforts to exclude the newcomers, yet that came about without planning. At an early stage, the people of the Estate found themselves not warmly invited to join the circle of 'villagers' in one of the two pubs, and gradually ceased visiting it. The villagers correspondingly gradually left the other pub to the newcomers, and it soon acquired a reputation for being rough and rowdy. 'If one can judge from similar groups of Londoners', write Elias and Scotson (1965: 18), the new people of zone 3 'themselves probably would not have objected if "villagers" had joined their circle at the pub and shared their noisy enjoyment.'

That was probably what they expected: they were used to the easier camaraderie that often prevailed among the lower and middle ranks of metropolitan working-class groups whose norms and standards were less stringent than those of many groups higher up in the status hierarchy, perhaps because they had not the same need constantly to restrain themselves in order to demonstrate and to assert their status superiority over others. Moreover, compared with the 'villagers', the immigrants had relatively little cohesion among themselves. They were a fairly open and a not particularly exclusive group. (1965: 18)

The allusion made here to self-restraint as a means by which higher status groups demarcate themselves from lower ranks makes, of course, a link with the arguments of *The Civilizing Process*. Although those links are sketched in only very lightly by Elias and Scotson, possession of 'more civilized' standards became a key element in the villagers' image of themselves and how they differed from the 'cockney' intruders who seemed to threaten their traditions and community identity. The people of the Estate were excluded from office and even from membership in the local associations and other focuses of community life. And the established group developed an ideology which represented the outsiders as rough, uncouth, dirty, delinquent – in short, 'uncivilized'. In this process, gossip played a vital part. Gossip is highly selective and distorting. Through it, people compete in demonstrating their fervent adherence to their own group norms by expressing their shock and horror at the behaviour of those who do not conform. Only the items of news least flattering to the Estate ('blame gossip') were relayed – the perfectly acceptable behaviour of the great majority was not news. This produced an image of zone 3 which was 'a highly simplified presentation of social realities. It created a black and white design which left no room for the diversities to be found among the Estate people. It corresponded to the *"minority of the worst"*' (1965: 81; my italics). The 'villagers' also gossiped about themselves, which in itself was a powerful source of social control restraining potential infringements of their own norms of respectability. But, in gossiping about themselves, selectivity tended to operate in the opposite direction to gossip about the Estate. Here, 'praise-gossip' predominated. The 'we-image' of zone 2 – equally oversimplified as its 'they-image' of zone 3 – was based on a *'minority of the best'*. The one image tended towards denigration, the other towards idealization. The role of minorities in these processes is highly symptomatic. A working-class minority in the middle-class zone 1 had no significance at all for the social standing of that zone, while the middle-class minority in zone 2 tended only to reinforce the superiority its people felt over the recent immigrants. A small minority of notorious families in zone 3, however, tended to cast a shadow over that whole neighbourhood and to perpetuate its low standing in the eyes of the other residents of Winston Parva.

Drawing a general conclusion from this, Elias and Scotson write

By and large . . . the more secure the members of a group feel in their own superiority and their pride, the less great is the distortion, the gap between image and reality, likely to be; and the more threatened and insecure they feel, the more likely is it that internal pressure, and as part of it, internal competition, will drive common beliefs towards extremes of illusion and doctrinaire rigidity. (1965: 95)

The rigidity with which people in zone 2 upheld their belief in the infamy of those of zone 3 thus derived much of its strength from the two groups being 'objectively' so little different.

Why could the Estate not retaliate? In fact its resentments did find one expression in the activities of a minority of the Estate chilen who, knowing that by being noisy, destructive and offensive they could annoy those by whom they were rejected and treated as outcasts, set about behaving badly with still greater determination. But the people of the Estate in general could not retaliate directly with, for example, a flood of gossip about goings-on in the village. They could not do so because, in short, they did not have the power. They did not have the power for several related reasons. Key positions in local associations were monopolized by members of the 'old families network'. Lacking the web both of associations and intermarriage, the Estate also lacked the networks of gossip and mutual assistance to promote its own cohesion. Gossip travelled around the Estate not only more slowly, but mixed with an element of embarrassment because so much of it concerned the residents' own neighbour-hood. Thus, in addition to the organizational components of the Estate's lack of power to retaliate, there was a personal or psychological component. The majority of the Estate people could not retaliate against the rejecting gossip of the village

because, to some extent, their own conscience was on the side of the detractors. They themselves agreed with the 'village' people that it was bad not to be able to control one's children or to get drunk and noisy and violent. Even if none of these reproaches could be applied to themselves personally, they knew only too well that they did apply to some of their neighbours. They could be shamed by allusions to this bad behaviour of their neighbours because by living in the same neighbourhood the blame, the bad name attached to it, according to the rules of affective thinking, was automatically applied to them too. (1965: 101–2)

To put it another way, an unfavourable collective 'we-image' was incorporated into the individual self-image of people living on the Estate. In describing the social process by which that we-image was created – along with the correspondingly favourable we-image and we-ideal enjoyed by the 'villagers' – Elias also uses the twin terms *group charisma* and *group disgrace*: the creation of group charisma by and for a more powerful, established, group is inseparable from the imposition on and internalization of group disgrace by members of an outsider group.[3] According to Elias, the satisfaction derived from sharing in the group charisma which is a component of an established group's we-image serves as compensation for the frustration arising from the self-restraint required in conforming to the norms that signify its superior position.

Here again, though Elias and Scotson scarcely point to it, is a clear connection with discussions in *The Civilizing Process* of elite manners, of the shame mechanism and of ambivalent relationships between social groups, which have played so important a part in the longer-term development of societies on a larger scale. What they do point out emphatically (1965: 40–1) is how mistaken it is for some sociologists to represent status differences as being based on a consensually agreed ranking of positions and incompatible with conflict.[4] 'Terms like "status hierarchy" or "ranking order" are sometimes used as if they referred to normally harmonious figurations with which tensions and conflicts were connected only accidentally. In fact . . . tensions and conflicts form an intrinsic structural element of status hierarchies everywhere' (1965: 41). People accept their own low ranking because they cannot prevent it. Greater power may sometimes go with greater numbers, but it often happens that a close-knit minority may exercise power over a less closely knit, less well organized majority. The 'old families' of Winston Parva were far from forming the majority of its population. 'But the beliefs, the standards, the ranking of others current in this closely-knit elite group carried great weight with others largely because . . . their members held all the key positions in the community.' Here, Elias could equally well have been thinking once more of the nobles and bourgeois he had studied long before, or of the countless struggles between established and outsider groups that have been a feature of the present century.

ESTABLISHED-OUTSIDERS RELATIONS IN MACROCOSM

It may be tempting to interpret what was observed in Winston Parva in terms of notions like 'prejudice' and 'discrimination'. People often reach for these words, tending to think about the problem in broadly psychological fashion, as if it were all a matter of individual people who happened not to like each other as individuals. This way of thinking is usually very closely tied up with the wish to attribute blame to one side or the other. In view of Norbert Elias's life history, it would not be altogether surprising if he shared the widespread belief that blame attribution is one of the purposes of social scientific investigation.[5] But he emphatically does not. Even in his earliest published discussion of an established-outsiders relationship – his 1935 essay on the expulsion of the Huguenots from France where he makes very plain the parallels between that episode and the flight of the Jews from Hitler's Germany in which he was then participating – he is concerned to understand it as a dynamic social process rather than as simply the outcome of the motives, intentions and actions of isolated individuals.[6]

The ability of one group to pin the badge of human inferiority on another human group and make it stick, argues Elias, is a function of a specific figuration formed by the two *groups* with one another. The centrepiece of such a figuration is an uneven, tensile, balance of power. The prototype in Elias's thinking about such balances of power was the multi-polar tug-of-war in the royal mechanism (see pp. 73–8 above), but they are ubiquitous. They are uneven because one group has succeeded in monopolizing some power resource, at least for a time. That can be seen clearly in Winston Parva, but it is also a finding of general applicability, as Elias sought to demonstrate particularly in his preface (1976) to the Dutch translation of *The Established and the Outsiders.*[7] It is the decisive condition of *any effective stigmatization* of an outsider group by an established group.

Established-outsiders relations are the normal concomitants of a process in the course of which formerly more or less independent groups become more interdependent (1965: 17). Such processes have always occurred throughout human history. *The Civilizing Process* affords many illustrations, from the highly unequal and distant relations between the estates created by feudalization through to the complex web of tensions in the final stages of the *ancien régime*. In a different culture altogether, Elias (1976: 40–4) points to the origins of the pariah castes in India. There, just as in the tiny local instance of Winston Parva, an explanation has to be sought in how groups came to impinge on each other in the past, although in India it was the newcomers who came as conquerors to fill the place of the established, and the old residents who formed the outsider group. The Indian caste system is a byword for durability and resistance to change, but that is not true of all established-outsiders relations; in many cases the balance of power at their centre moves quite perceptibly over time.

Where the balance of power between established and outsiders is extremely unequal, it is very common for people to believe that the differentials of power are inherent in the very 'nature' of mankind. That is one very old way in which established groups of people justify and legitimate their own power. Aristotle said that it was quite clear 'that there are by *nature* free men and slaves, and that servitude is agreeable and just for the latter'. In the same way, in seventeenth- and eighteenth-century Europe, many writers still explained inequalities between the ranks of society in terms of inherent qualities. Still more recently, in discussions of differentials of power between men and women, it has been argued that it is inherent in the physical and mental nature of women that they be subservient to men.

Where the balance of power is very uneven, the oppressed and exploited cannot escape from their position. This is one of the conditions which makes it most likely that they will take into their own we-image what the established say about them. This process of stigmatization is a very common element in domination within such highly unequal power balances, and it is remarkable how across many varied cases the content of the stigmatization remains the same. The outsiders are always dirty, morally unreliable and lazy, among other things. That was how in the nineteenth century industrial workers were frequently seen: they were often spoken of as the 'Great Unwashed'. That was, and is, how whites often perceive blacks.

To illustrate the remarkable extent to which this stigmatization as a weapon of the established enters the minds of outsiders, Elias (1976) uses the example of the Burakumin of Japan. They are a group racially completely identical to the rest of the Japanese but hereditarily involved with leather-work, gravedigging, disposal of the dead, midwifery, and similar occupations regarded as dirty. From the early seventeenth century they gradually became an outcaste, with which other Japanese were forbidden to intermarry or have other close contact. One old Burakumin man was asked by an interviewer, 'Some Japanese tell me that the Burakumin are not human. Do you believe that you are human?' And the old man said 'I don't know; we are dirty, we are lesser people'. In other words, this feeling had entered deep into his consciousness, and it is often very difficult for outsiders to rid themselves of the opprobrium which established groups have placed upon them.

Nevertheless, there are many other instances of established-outsiders relations where the tensions created when groups are forced together into interdependence result in a shift – either slow and oscillating or sudden and dramatic – towards a more even power ratio. Elias himself, in a little-known byway of his research, provided an interesting historical illustration of such a case. It can be found in his study of the origins of the naval profession in Britain (1950). He showed how a naval officer in the days of sail had to unite in his person some of the qualities of an experienced craftsman with those of the military gentleman – apprenticeship to the arts of seamanship from early youth, combined with the command of men, mastery of foreign languages, dignified bearing, good manners and diplomatic skills. In medieval times there had been no contradiction: there was no permanent navy, and master mariners simply provided transport and floating platforms for knights and their soldiers to fight from. The two groups were not closely interdependent, and were drawn from entirely different social groups ashore. With the growth of a permanent Royal Navy in Tudor and Stuart times, however, they were forced into closer contact. For a long time two hierarchies, under the gentleman captain and the 'tarpaulin' master respectively, co-existed aboard in unresolved juxtaposition. In the French and Spanish navies, conflict between the two was suppressed by rigid rules defining the place of each group aboard ship, with the trained mariners being held in an inferior position right up to the Revolution. In the British Navy, however, the struggles continued bitterly throughout the seventeenth century, until resolved in the emergence of a single hybrid profession early in the eighteenth. The difference between the British and continental navies is largely explained by differences in the tension-balance of social forces in their parent societies ashore (see chapter 3 above). But the lower-level balance can also feed back into the development of the wider pattern of tensions; Elias points out that in British history standing land armies played a lesser and the navy a greater role than in most continental countries, and that it was crucial to the course of British history that the navy sided with Parliament in the Civil War – as it may well not have done had not 'tarpaulin' interests been already on an ascendant track.

When power ratios become less uneven, the imposed sense of inferiority is weakened. Inequalities previously taken for granted are challenged. The problem of inequalities between social groups has occupied the mind and conscience in the twentieth century perhaps more than ever before. It has seen an astonishing sequence of emancipation struggles: of workers, of colonial peoples, of blacks, of women, of homosexuals. In each case, the tension-balance of power between these outsider groups and their established counterparts has changed, not to equality certainly, but towards a somewhat less uneven balance. Even the balance of power between children and adults has become noticeably less unequal.[8] Why has all this happened?

In part it is the continuing process of functional democratization on which Elias touched towards the close of *The Civilizing Process*. Longer and more differentiated chains of interdependence mean that power differentials diminish within and among groups because incumbents of specialized roles are more interdependent and can thus exert reciprocal control over each other. The power chances of specialized groups are further increased if they manage to organize themselves in a cohesive way, since they are then able to act collectively to disrupt the wider mesh of interdependencies – in effect to withhold things that other groups need. In ways such as these, according to Elias, the increasing division of social functions and lengthening chains of interdependence lead to greater reciprocal dependency and thus to patterns of more 'multi-polar control' (or 'increasingly polyarchic' control) within and among groups. Yet that is only one side of the story. These same processes of differentiation create problems of co-ordination and are thus accompanied – with leads and lags – by processes of integration. That is to say, larger-scale organization in state and economy forces groups of people together in closer interdependence than formerly; and these new patterns create new concentrations of power resources, new inequalities. For all the diminution of inequalities, for instance between employers and employees, or between men and women, new inequalities constantly emerge: that between governments and governed is the most striking. Moreover, in the present century, cheap transport and increased mobility over longer distances have made it still more common throughout the world for displaced groups to impinge on older established groups. Wars, too, have played their part on an increasing scale. Groups of people whose skins are different colours or who have been brought up in different ways of life are increasingly thrust together and established-outsiders patterns are a characteristic result.

The concept of established-outsiders relationships is intended to be useful in grappling with all these problems of social inequalities. But sociologists already have many terms for dealing with inequality. Is there really any case for Elias seeking to introduce yet another? Why not, for instance, use the familiar term 'elite'? Elias generally avoids it because that was precisely the word used by many establishment groups in the past to justify themselves: the word elite implies that the people who form such a group are better in some sense – by nature, intellectually, or in terms of some achievement – than outsiders. He prefers 'establishment' to indicate that what fundamentally distinguishes established and outsider groups are the power resources at the disposal of one side or another. On the other hand, he also uses the established-outsiders notion to avoid some of the pitfalls he perceives in the best-known and most influential theory of social inequalities, the Marxist tradition.

Elias prefers to speak of established-outsiders relations rather than to use Marxist class terminology for two main reasons. First, he feels that the latter too often conveys a static, layer-cake image of one-sided and unchanging domination by one class over another. That may be true of the crudest kind of Marxism but it is not fair criticism of the more sophisticated sort. In any case, although Elias constantly strives to find more processual concepts for use in sociology, 'established' and 'outsiders' are perhaps not the most inherently dynamic of the terms he has introduced; they can easily lend themselves to carelessly static use.

Secondly, and more important, Elias disputes that element in the Marxist heritage which tends to represent all social inequality and conflict as being fundamentally matters of economic or material resources – elastic as those terms are. He recognizes the enormous progress in sociological understanding of social inequalities that Marx made; and he acknowledges his own debt to Marx's demonstration that the superior power chances of one group in relation to other groups are due to the *monopolization* of certain resources which another group needs. Elias would agree that this is true of all establishments. But although he agrees that to study material or economic power resources is 'in most cases quite indispensable to an understanding of established-outsiders relationships' (1976: 24), he argues (as we have already see in the context of state-formation, p. 70 above) that it does not make sense to privilege the monopolization of economic resources above all others. Interweaving with it are struggles for the control of other power resources, including the means of violence and the means of orientation; these other monopolization processes are relatively autonomous, and are not entirely determined by or reducible to the struggles for economic resources (Elias, 1976: 25–6; 1984c: 72–4; 1983b: 226–31). But in my opinion, the relation between established-outsiders theory and Marxist class theory can safely be left as an open question, if only because Marxists argue a good deal among themselves about what exactly 'class' means.[9]

Rather than pursue the issue any longer in the abstract, it is best to turn to some of the ways in which the established-outsiders model has been used in elucidating actual social processes. We shall concentrate on its application to the civilizing of the working class, the rise of the welfare state, race relations, women's emancipation, and homosexuality.[10]

Civilizing the peasants and the workers

Apart from a few remarks about how, especially in the nineteenth century, upper-class people in Europe sought to inculcate their own civilized standards into the workers and peasants, *The Civilizing Process* dwells mainly on the earlier stages when these standards were formed among the nobility and bourgeoisie. The gap is to an extraordinary extent filled by Eugen Weber's book *Peasants into Frenchmen: The Modernization of Rural France, 1870–1914* (1976). Weber demonstrates with a wealth of research how the rural provinces of France were perceived as a 'country of savages' with all the classic marks of an establishment's perception of outsider groups. He shows how, partly through the intentional use of the expanding educational system but mainly through the unplanned consequences of processes like improved communications, urban-ization, industrialization, migration and military conscription, the peasantry was integrated into the French state, and simultaneously civilized in manners, customs and beliefs. By chance – for Weber had not read Elias – *Peasants into Frenchmen* can be read as a third volume of *The Civilizing Process*.[11]

Turning from the country to the town, nowhere are the complexities of established-outsiders relations more evident than in modern cities, where people of diverse origins and styles of life have been thrust closely together. In the rapidly growing cities of the nineteenth and twentieth centuries, middle-class people found it more difficult to maintain a social and physical distance between themselves and the (as they saw it) uncouth, unclean, uncivilized working class who flocked into the towns. Their reactions and the social and political consequences have been studied in particularly rich detail by sociologists in Amsterdam, but similar stories emerge in other cities and other countries.

Middle-class people found themselves in close contact with the lower orders. The outsiders lived nearby: that meant that problems of sanitation and public health were, willy-nilly, shared problems. The different classes were inter-dependent with each other in face of the spreading microbe. The sense of pollution was socially more than biologically based, however. Even if middle-class people lived further out in the better neighbourhoods, they had to travel to work in the centre through the inferior quarters, on buses and trams shared with all and sundry. (Only the rich might escape this by riding in their own carriages.)

Responses included a variety of middle-class voluntary efforts to 'improve' and indeed to 'civilize' the working classes (De Regt 1984): efforts were made to teach women the elements of hygiene, infant care, housekeeping and cookery.[12] At least as characteristic, and more important in its long-term consequences, was the call for official intervention. The municipal archives of Amsterdam between the 1860s and 1920s contain many complaints from the bourgeoisie demanding that something be done (Van Daalen 1985a). The files of the city's tramway authority (Van Daalen 1979) were especially revealing: 'unwanted encounters' with the great unwashed in trams led to demands for segregated first- and second-class carriages. Complaints also helped lead to steadily increasing municipal activity in public hygiene (Van Daalen 1983), infant health care (Van Daalen 1985b) and housing.

Ali de Regt (1982) demonstrates how by the 1920s, municipal housing policy in Amsterdam played its part in the creation of a distinct outsiders group among the 'rougher' working class – and her findings ring true, *pari passu*, for Britain and other countries too. A rougher working class emerged as a residue from the process through which the bulk of working people were disciplined and 'civilized' into being respectable and proud of it. Irregular and casual labour was gradually replaced by regular employment in factories, and factory workers were forced to accept increasing discipline at work. More disciplined employment and rising living standards – in themselves part of a changing style of living – had a considerable influence on the emergent lifestyle of factory workers. The development of a more 'controlled' style of living was deliberately stimulated and imposed by employers and by trade unions, by teachers, philanthropists and social workers of all kinds. As time went on, this new style of living gradually debarred contact with other people who had not themselves taken part in these developments. The 'respectable' working class added their voice of complaint to the demand that something be done about the 'rough' minority – mainly drawn from those who had remained in irregular and casual employment.

Thus it came about that Amsterdam's municipal authorities in the 1920s built two special enclaves for what were called 'unacceptable' (later 'socially maladjusted' or simply 'antisocial') families. The label of unacceptability was applied to those who did not keep their houses clean and in good repair, annoyed the neighbours by quarrelling, fights and drunkenness, and did not pay their rent. The intention behind the special enclaves was rehabilitation and education. The families were kept under close supervision by a lady rent-collector-cum-social-worker and a janitor-cum-warden, and there were lots of rules. Families who kept to the rules could expect to be promoted to a tenancy in a respectable neighbourhood. Not surprisingly (though it seems to have surprised everyone at the time except the Communists), the policy failed. A large proportion of families could not stand living under these conditions, and moved back to slum quarters. Those who remained often stayed a very long time with no sign of improvement. The stigmatization of these neighbourhoods only reinforced the problems and their inhabitants' inadequacy; the main difference between Amsterdam and Winston Parva was that the outsiders enclaves were the deliberate creation of the authorities.

The welfare state and transitions in mutual identification

The work of sociologists in Amsterdam just described has focused on a stage in the rise of the Welfare State in the Netherlands since the nineteenth century, recognizably similar to what was seen in many other countries. In his book *In Care of the State* (1988) Abram de Swaan sets these studies in much broader comparative and historical context. He examines the social dynamics of public health, education and income maintenance in the Netherlands, Britain, France, Germany and the USA. His theoretical apparatus is, however, still broader in scope. It is a highly original blend of Elias's theories of civilizing processes and established-outsiders relationships with rational choice theory. He uses it to build an explanatory model of long-term transitions in identification with the deprived. To put it another way, he is concerned with general trends in attitudes towards poverty and inequality, and in people's collective ability to sympathize with each other simply as fellow human beings.

Relations between the poor and the better off change according to a long-term pattern. Where pacification was incomplete, the beggar or supplicant for alms always represented a distinct risk. Any encounter between strangers could either end in violence or proceed according to ancient Christian forms of hospitality or generosity. De Swaan compares the choice facing the better-off person in such an encounter with the 'prisoner's dilemma' of game theory. In such a relatively unpacified context, a ruler might choose to use charity towards the poor in order to transform his superior might and wealth into legitimacy. That is a well-known aspect of gift-giving, much discussed by theorists like Marcel Mauss (1924) and Peter Blau (1964); but as a course of action it may stem from expediency or fear, not in the least from charitable *sentiment*. Only when dependency relations are more stable and symmetric does a mutual sense of identification develop: thus, between relatives or neighbours networks of mutual aid may emerge, balanced in the long run and through multilateral 'clearing' of obligations. Such networks have been found in small stable settlements from the earliest times, and were still seen in Winston Parva and Bethnal Green. But in earlier centuries, vagrancy and rural banditry created a paradox of collective action for villages and towns in the absence of regional or national authorities. No single community could afford to adopt the needy: any which did would be overwhelmed by people flocking from afar. Rejected everywhere, therefore, vagrants became a common threat to harvests and food supplies. A solution which in one form or another suggested itself in each of the countries de Swaan studied was the workhouse. In principle, each parish was to place its own poor in such an institution, putting them to work to produce the means of their own support. Workhouses never were in practice self-supporting, but they paved the way for centrally regulated poor relief. Once the predicament of the poor appeared amenable to remedy, and the vagrant poor to moral regeneration, the established citizenry could afford a sense of identification with the paupers, and a symptomatic genre of moralistic literature sprang up during this phase.

A further characteristic phase of development in most of De Swaan's countries during the early stages of industrialism was that of workers' mutualism – that is, friendly societies and formal networks of mutual aid formed among working people themselves. However, the very solidarity that sustained them could only survive in small homogeneous enclaves – among workers in a single small community or single factory – and by their nature these were vulnerable to cumulative risks when an epidemic or unemployment struck many members at once. New, more encompassing modes of mutual identification grew: nationalism in the process of competitive state formation, class consciousness out of the clashes between workers and employees. Both contributed to the establishment of nation-wide social security arrangements. The calls for municipal intervention in public health, housing and so on in Amsterdam were concrete illustrations of this later phase.

The picture De Swaan paints is not, however, one of unilinear improvement. The very transition towards a broader identification with the deprived, by leading to more centralized provision, helps create larger-scale organizations within which new forms of established-outsiders relationships can arise. Both in the public and the private sector, large organizations present a paradox. On the one hand, rectilinear chains of command are no longer adequate, and management style shifts to one of negotiation and 'team-work'. At the same time, the number of tiers in organizational hierarchies increases and creates the possibility of new monopolizations of power. In consequence, informalization of relations with immediate superiors can go hand in hand with increasing alienation from remote authorities. Elias speaks of the established-outsiders relationship between government and the governed as playing a more central part in our lives in the twentieth century, both in the Eastern bloc and the West than ever before. Moreover, many other outsiders groups remain largely outside the scope of the new wider sense of identification within society: foreigners, immigrants, homosexuals, even in some senses women.

'Race' and 'ethnic' relations

The terms 'race' or 'ethic' relations, widely used in both in sociology and in society at large are, says Elias, symptomatic of an ideological avoidance action. Their use serves to single out for attention what is peripheral to these relationships (for example differences in skin colour) and to turn the eye away from what is central – differences in power chances and the exclusion of a less powerful group from positions with a higher power potential. 'Race relations' in other words are simply established-outsiders relations of a particular type (Elias 1976: 22), and 'racial' problems – so widespread throughout the world – can be studied in much the same perspective as relations within the little community of Winston Parva. Indeed, the established-outsider model has been applied by Dunning (1972, 1985, 1986) to the dynamics of relations between blacks and whites in the USA, South Africa and Great Britain, and by Hermann Korte (1984) to relations between the 'established' West Germans and their *Gastarbeiter* outsiders. I shall draw here mainly on Dunning's discussion of the USA.

An essential part of any 'race relations problem' is that members of the groups involved hold exaggerated, often wholly erroneous beliefs about each other. They also tend to believe that whatever differences there are between the groups are transmitted genetically. Neither belief is unique to 'racial problems'. Gross exaggeration was seen in the image of the Estate in Winston Parva. Many Japanese believe that the Burakumin – racially identical to themselves – carry a genetically inherited grey birth-mark under each arm. The role of spurious genetic theories in hatred of the Jews in Nazi Germany is well-known. 'Such beliefs', as Dunning (1986: 110) points out, 'tend to absolve any guilt-feelings that dominant groups might feel about their subordinates because they enable them to attribute to "nature" rather than themselves both their own advantages and the disadvantages of the subordinate group.'

In fact, the only differences *between groups* within the species *Homo sapiens* known to be transmitted genetically are features like skin colour, type of hair, and the shape of lips and nose. Differences in behaviour and even in intelligence *between groups* are learned – they are the consequences of social inheritance, not genetic transmission. That is not to deny that physical features such as skin colour, because they cannot be altered by the individual, may serve as peculiarly durable markers of social inequality. But the main weight of any explanation of 'racial' inequalities, like any other social inequalities, must rest on how the groups came to impinge on each other, the nature of their interdependence, and their relative cohesion within it.

The most serious and widespread problems of race relations in the world today have arisen between so-called 'white' and 'coloured' races simply because it was Europeans who, from the Renaissance onwards, achieved world dominance and were able to subordinate less powerful people who happened to be different in outward appearance. Wallerstein (1974, 1980) and others have shown at length how, on the basis of initially very small technical, economic and social (not, of course, biological) advantages, the Europeans were able to weave the peoples of Africa, Asia and Latin America into a web of dependence – in Elias's terms, very unequal *inter*dependence – which, over the centuries, greatly magnified the initial disparities.

In this process, the slave trade played a significant economic part; but here we can focus only on its social legacies. On the cotton plantations of the American Deep South, the slaves were in a situation of extreme powerlessness. Legally they were no more than chattels whose owner could do with them as he pleased. First-generation slaves were disorientated by the sufferings of capture and transport and by the severing of all their bonds to their own families, communities and cultures. Very often slaves on a particular plantation would not even speak the same language as each other. Even in subsequent generations the conditions of life made it impossible for slaves to communicate and so form any kind of social cohesion wider than the single plantation. As is typical where power differentials are very great, the inherent group tensions and conflicts were quiescent for long periods, punctuated by sporadic, brief and bloody local slave uprisings – a pattern not unlike the *jacqueries* or peasant uprisings of medieval and early modern Europe. Yet even in the highly unequal case of slaves and slaveowners, it is important to recognize that the two sides were locked together in a *double bind*: in spite of their huge superiority in power, the owners *needed* the slaves. They were a means of production, a form of property and wealth, and did have a function for their owners. This consideration tended to place some limits on their maltreatment. In contrast, where an outsider group has no such function for the established group, where they are – as for instance in the case of the Amerindians both in North America and parts of Latin America – simply in the way, they may be exterminated or driven out and left to die (Elias 1976: 24).

The stigmatization process can also be seen at work in the Deep South. The Negro was represented as lazy, feckless, lacking any foresight, and having a happy-go-lucky, child-like and essentially helpless nature. The image of 'Black Sambo' was used in resisting the case for emancipation. Yet it probably appeared to have some basis in fact too, for, as we have seen, established-outsiders relations have psychological effects, especially on the outsiders:

some blacks may have deliberately played the 'Sambo' role because they perceived it as what their masters wanted and because it enabled them, on the one hand, to gain limited privileges and, on the other, to avoid punishment. But probably as important was the fact that slaves had few opportunities to develop modes of behaviour thought appropriate by adult whites. Like children, they had only limited possibilities for initiating independent action. However, unlike children, their dependence was permanent and maintained by powerful sanctions. From the slaves' point of view, moreover, the plantation was a closed system, a kind of 'total institution' in which virtually the whole of their life was encapsulated. They were hardly able to broaden their experience of the world and by exposure to models different from those of their masters. (Dunning 1986: 113; cf. Elkins 1959 and Abrams 1982: 241–50)

The abolition of slavery changed little immediately in this overall figuration. Only with the movement of blacks to the northern cities of the USA on a large scale from the 1920s did the balance of power between American blacks and whites slowly begin to shift. In the towns it was possible to organize and for social cohesion to develop. Particularly important was the growth of a black bourgeoisie. This differentiation within the black population of a stratum rising in status and in economic power constituted a strand of functional democratization, and helped to blur the hitherto rigid and caste-like boundary between black and white. Moreover, the black bourgeoisie played an important role in the pursuit of civil rights. As is usually the case when highly unequal power differentials begin to shift in favour of outsiders, the inherent group tensions, hitherto quiescent or evident only sporadically, exploded openly in the 1960s and early 1970s. These were also the years of the 'black power' movements, promoting black pride ('black is beautiful') and even, for a time, separatism; these, again, are typical manifestations when differentials between established and outsiders are diminishing.

There is an old debate between sociologists about whether 'race relations' are simply a form of class and status relations. Most American sociologists, whether Marxist or functionalist, tended to accept that they were. Against these strange bedfellows, David Lockwood (1970) was one author who contended that there were limits to analysing race relations in class and stratification terms. Among other arguments, he said that class inequalities stem from the division of labour but racial inequalities do not; and that the axes of racial tension both divide classes and involve identification across class boundaries (as in the instance of bourgeois and working-class blacks in the campaign for equal rights in the USA). To apply established-outsiders theory to 'race relations' is not wholly to side with either party in this debate. On the one hand, this brief summary may have helped to show how relations between different 'racial' groups can be studied in the same way as relations between many other groups with unequal power chances. On the other hand, established-outsiders theory moves away from static distinctions between class position and status position, attempting to trace how economic roles, status rankings and power chances – together with the 'subjective' components of we-images, we-ideals, group charisma and group disgrace – are all related dynamically. In this perspective, as Dunning argues, 'the specificity of race relations is apparent rather than real, an artefact of the inadequacy of class and stratification theory in its current forms rather than of the total uniqueness of racial inequality as a form of stratification' (1986).

Men and women

Elias was interested in the changing balance of power between the sexes many years before such questions became a dominant preoccupation in sociological and women's studies circles. I have recounted (p. 25 above) how the typescript of his book on the subject, written during his Leicester years, was accidentally destroyed around 1971.

The *changing* balance of power between the sexes? The reaction is often 'what change?' (cf. Featherstone 1987: 203). But if the power differential between men and women in modern societies can by no means be said to have disappeared, that should not blind us to movements to and fro in the degree of inequality through history. It was little more than chance that the one part of his book Elias was able to reconstruct and publish years afterwards (1986b) was that dealing with ancient Rome. Yet it served his purpose, for, as so often, he used something far away to illuminate something close at hand.

The lost book opened with Elias's recollection of an elderly Indian man he used to encounter in the street in London, chatting animatedly to his wife who, however, walked not alongside him but directly behind him. The couple represented for him a living example of an uneven balance between the sexes, codified in their society of origin not only as a custom but as a habit deeply ingrained in individual people. There have been even more extreme manifestations of the inferior position of women – the immolation of Parsee widows, the binding of Chinese women's feet so that they could only hobble. But the Indian and his wife in the London street drew Elias's attention to how different was the traditional code of conduct of the European upper and middle classes. It was distinctly ambiguous. In most countries of Europe, at least up to the middle of the nineteenth century, married women had had no right to hold property. The laws had been more lenient towards male than female adultery. Many other forms of disadvantage had persisted. Yet, in contrast with many other societies, there were no stringent rules publicly demonstrating that women were men's property or socially inferior. And there were elaborate patterns of male deference towards women: opening doors for them, rising when they entered the room and so on. Explaining this ambiguity was the centrepiece of the lost book. The chapter on ancient Rome naturally leaves the explanation far from complete, but it is suggestive of Elias's approach. His impressive command of the sources shows that he had lost nothing of his classical learning dating from Breslau. In early Rome, marriage was by purchase. Women were chattels, under the absolute power of their husband (Elias points out that 'andrarchy' is a more accurate word than 'patriarchy'). As Rome rose to wealth and power, however, there were discernible shifts in the balance between the sexes within marriage. Under the terms of marriage contracts, it became increasingly common for women to remain under the legal tutelage of their father or brother rather than husband. This meant that property settled on the wife at her marriage remained under the control of her own lineage rather than passing to her husband's. Gradually – perhaps in part as a consequence of increasing wealth making fathers more blasé about what a daughter did with her endowment – women came themselves to exercise control over their property.

At the peak of the Empire, among the upper classes, men and women were relatively equal *within marriage*. Of course, in other spheres they remained very far from equal, women being still excluded from public office for example. Within marriage, however, wives could for instance enlist the authority of the courts on their side in retrieving debts from their husbands. The state also intervened to reduce the woman's disadvantage in questions of divorce. This is highly significant. Without the growth of the state apparatus – especially courts and the means of enforcing their judgements – the balance of power between husbands and wives could not have changed as much as it did.

Elias uses this point in demonstrating the inadequacy of the old argument that the subordination of women rests ultimately on their inferior average physical strength. If the balance of power between the sexes rested wholly upon that, nothing would ever change. In fact, physical strength differences were much more significant in warrior and pre-state societies. State-formation processes – internal pacification, the growth of state monopoly apparatuses including courts – have tended towards compensating women to a limited extent for their physical weakness *vis-à-vis* men. The process is far from unilinear, however: there have been many fluctuations.

Even in Rome, the momentum was not maintained. Under the later Christian emperors, some restrictions were imposed on the relative equality achieved by the first century AD, although Roman marriage never reverted entirely to the previous degree of inequality. At the fall of the Empire in the West, the Germanic tribes – pre-state societies – reintroduced older forms of marriage by purchase. Yet the developments under Rome had left their mark on the Christian church (which always insisted that a woman's consent was necessary to marriage) and on Roman law. These in turn had some effect on the balance of power between the sexes in the medieval period, highly unequal as that remained overall. Later still, as Elias shows in *The Court Society* (see above, pp. 55–6), among the courtly circles of seventeenth- and eighteenth-century Europe, relations between the sexes were relatively equal within a limited sphere of life.

On the other hand, it is generally agreed that among the bourgeoisie of nineteenth-century Europe, relations between the sexes even within marriage were highly unequal, with the wife held in a highly dependent, subordinated seclusion within the home. Whom a girl married was to a large extent determined by her parents. After marriage, the husband would monopolize all important financial and other decisions affecting the family, quite often without consulting his wife, whose sphere of activity was almost exclusively within the home. Indeed the seclusion of women seems to have increased rather than diminished through most of the nineteenth century. Etiquette books of the period and other historical sources show how limited was the freedom of a 'respectable' woman to move outside her home unescorted. In his article 'The politics of agoraphobia', Abram de Swaan offers an explanation of why this trend was especially marked among the middle classes. In the initial stages of industrialization, unemployed country folk were flocking to the rapidly growing cities, just as they do now in parts of Asia, Latin America and Africa. For the *petite bourgeoisie* there were new opportunities and new difficulties. The opportunities included new markets for artisans and shopkeepers, new forms of employment for clerks and officials. But it also became more difficult – as we have already seen above – to maintain a social and physical distance between themsèlves and the uncouth invading mass. The rich could afford servants to escort them, surround them, run their errands, but small tradesmen and functionaries found themselves in the midst of the daily rough and tumble. And for their womenfolk, their fears were still greater:

in the bourgeois mind the urban street . . . had become a threatened space, the scene of roughness, violent menace, and erotic seduction. A decent woman had no business there. In the recently emerging capitalist relationships, trade and craft were becoming men's jobs, and a woman had her work within the domestic sphere. Women appearing in the streets alone 'had to be' women who went working of necessity, women whose husbands could not provide for their families single-handedly; such women could not possibly be decent. Once this line of demarcation had become established, it also came to imply a licence for men to allow themselves impertinences towards women who appeared in public unaccompanied. Thus a woman could not afford to go out on those streets: a self-fulfilling prophecy if ever there was one. (De Swaan, 1979: 363)

It is not surprising that, living such a circumscribed, dependent and secluded way of life, many women should have taken into their we-image of themselves-as-women the views of femininity formed by men. In this respect they were no different from many other outsider groups in an inferior power position. According to De Swaan it was no coincidence that, when in the 1880s and 1890s some of the restrictions on women's appearing in public began to be relaxed, the psychological affliction of agoraphobia came to the attention of the rising profession of psychiatrists. For significant numbers of women had acquired so ingrained a sense of inadequacy, so great a reliance on men as protectors and decision makers, so child-like a sense of dependence, that they developed a neurotic fear of going outdoors unescorted.[13]

That was far from being true of those who campaigned for women's rights in many countries around the turn of the century, yet even they could not cast off the dominant we-image at a stroke. These women also have been studied by sociologists working under Elias's influence in the Netherlands (Kapteyn 1977, 1980; Coutinho-Wiggelendam 1983). What they discovered appears to be equally true of other countries too. The advocates of women's emancipation – the right to vote, the right to education, to practise medicine or other careers – had to contend not only with physiological arguments (like the allegedly lesser weight of the female brain!) but also with the view that such activities were inherently 'unfeminine'. This view was expressed by female as well as male opponents. Indeed, even the pioneers of women's emancipation themselves often argued as if certain traits were inherently feminine, and felt they had to show that the granting of equal rights would undermine neither femininity, nor the family, nor community life. Until very recently, the predominant 'figuration-ideal' of relations between the sexes was – indeed for large sections of the population in contemporary society it still is – one of *harmonious inequality*.

The phrase is used by Abram van Stolk and Cas Wouters in their book *Vrouwen in Tweestrijd* (*Women Torn Two Ways*, 1983 – see also 1987). There they use the established-outsiders theory in an entirely contemporary investigation of a facet of relations between men and women: 'battered wives' who run away from their husbands to seek safety in a women's refuge.

The women described the violence, intimidation and other humiliations they had suffered at the hands of their husbands. Their incentive to run away was easy for an interviewer to understand. Yet they themselves were deeply ambivalent: they had hesitated before running away, and most eventually returned to their husbands. Some had run away and returned more than once. They were 'torn two ways'.

Older women especially had tended to regard it as simply 'bad luck' that a husband proved to be 'a bad 'un' (as the English might put it). In the reception centre, such resigned, fatalistic attitudes began to change: the women now felt they had been wronged and maltreated, that they ought to resist, that something could and should be done to improve their lot, that they were better off at the refuge than if they had stayed at home. 'All the same', write Van Stolk and Wouters, 'most of them were still ambivalent, poised between resignation and resistance, between submission and emancipation. Although the feeling that they had been wronged was uppermost, the former idea of bad luck had not gone for good. One lifetime is usually too short for that anyway.'

That so many of the women had left home more than once shows how ambivalent they were about their own emancipation. This depended on the degree to which the woman's conscience still took the husband's side. In a way typical of outsiders in their relations with the established, *his* view remained embedded in her personality. She took more notice of him than he did of her; she was more sensitive to his wishes than he to hers. Most of the women could describe their husband's character in detail, while the men could not describe their wife's except in terms of clichés applicable to women in general. These men's self-esteem depended mainly on what other *men* thought of them, in other words on their ranking within the established group. The result was that women were forced to identify more with their men than vice versa. That meant in turn that they were better at understanding men than men were at understanding women; Van Stolk and Wouters suggest this is the basis of what is called 'feminine intuition'. But it is a general characteristic of established-outsiders relations that the outsiders identify with and 'understand' the established better than the established do the outsiders. Equally characteristic of established-outsiders relations in general was the course of the struggle between husbands and wives. When the women began to realize how unfairly they were treated, their first request was usually 'to talk about it'. Men, report Van Stolk and Wouters, found this utterly unreasonable. The women were just being a nuisance. The reaction to the first signs of rebellion was punishment, suppression, a show of force – very much like the European colonial rulers confronted with intellectual natives' first modest requests to discuss their grievances. Nowadays, Van Stolk and Wouters note wryly, 'the conscience of most Europeans, in keeping with the altered balance of power, sides with the early nationalists'. A similar gradual change in conscience-formation also occurred in men and women as the balance of power between the sexes changed. At the start of each new round in a power struggle, the outsiders bring up certain issues which the established refuse to consider. They are unwilling to negotiate. Yet as the struggle proceeds, the balance of power very gradually tilts. And in many spheres of life, there has been, in De Swaan's phrase (1979), a transition from management by command to management through negotiation.

It should never be forgotten that this process has consequences for men as well as women. In his essay 'Sport as male preserve' (in Elias and Dunning 1986: 267–83), Dunning has interpreted the manifestations of aggressive masculinity – including deprecation of women and of homosexuals – found in certain male sporting circles such as rugby clubs, as responses to the changing balance of power between the sexes. And Van Stolk and Wouters, in an essay on 'the equanimity of the welfare state' (1984), have traced the consequences for male identity of the impact of the welfare state on the same balance of power – men find themselves in a sense competing with the state, as the welfare system weakens the traditional dependence of women on men.

Homosexuals and heterosexuals

One of the most evident emancipation movements of the last two decades has been on behalf of homosexuals. The plight of homosexuals as an outsider group, as Van Stolk and De Regt (1979) and again Van Stolk and Wouters (1980) point out, is in several ways more extreme and less remediable than that of women.

Whereas the women studied by Van Stolk and Wouters (1983) had run away from their partners because an increase in self-respect made it no longer possible to tolerate how they had been treated, the homosexuals interviewed by Van Stolk and De Regt had come to a counselling centre essentially suffering from a lack of self-respect. The kernel of their problem is that homosexuals are brought up as heterosexuals.

From early childhood, partly unawares, people develop images and ideals about their own future in relation to others, and the respect it will bring them in the eyes of others. The ideal self-image always embraces elementary images of 'real men' and 'real women', and these images are never homosexual. Children do not become acquainted with images of a life and future as a homosexual. Sooner or later they are faced with a discrepancy between the ideal they have learned and the reality of their own sexual orientation. 'During puberty and adolescence, many homosexuals continue to fantasize about a heterosexual future, because they lack a suitable socially acceptable future perspective' (Van Stolk and Wouters 1980: 478). They continue to day-dream about fulfilling the expectations others seem to have of them, but any satisfaction is undermined by the gap between fantasy and reality. Acceptance of the reality threatens self-respect. Perhaps even more than other outsider groups, homosexuals have taken into their own conscience the viewpoint of the established, the heterosexuals among whom in a great many human societies the stigmatization of homosexuals has been especially strong. Like women, homosexuals understand the established viewpoint better than the established understand theirs: except as a joke they would never say 'I just don't understand these heterosexuals', whereas heterosexuals often say 'I just don't understand these homosexuals', without it even being considered insulting.

Many homosexuals are unable to accept themselves as such because the threatened loss of self-respect seems insurmountable. As they are not born to homosexual couples, they eventually have to discard their early ideals based on their parents' example. Yet, since homosexuals do not grow up among like-minded companions, they do not at first have an alternative group-identity to support self-acceptance. Many have sought that in the liberation movement, in therapy towards self-acceptance in counselling centres like that studied, and in the company of those heterosexuals who will accept them as they are. Any more general solution depends on a shift in the balance of power between the heterosexual established and the homosexual outsiders in the wider nexus of society as a whole. Although some signs of this have been evident since the 1960s – more definitely in the Netherlands and some other continental countries than in Britain and the USA – there are obstacles to such a shift that are not encountered in the struggle for equality between the sexes.

Most important, the ties of interdependence between homosexuals and heterosexuals are far less close than between men and women. Men and women need each other for emotional satisfaction and to have children; gays and straights emphatically do not need each other. In general, dramatic as they have seemed in some societies, the inequalities of power betwen men and women can never be as great as between heterosexuals and homosexuals. Homosexuals may be – have been – the object of extermination campaigns but women cannot be. Homosexuals, comment Van Stolk and Wouters, are also in a position more akin to that of Jews than of workers: they have no specific social function as a category, they are not needed as such, and cannot easily exert pressure on heterosexuals by the disruption of the nexus of social interdependences. For that reason, even the 'figuration-ideal of harmonious inequality' cannot flourish in this instance.

Homosexuals can and now do organize as groups, and social cohesiveness is an advantage in all established-outsiders struggles. Yet they still have no obvious way of exerting pressure. Their chief weapon – like that of women – is moral indignation. The success of moral indignation in tilting established-outsiders power balances is characteristic of the contemporary advanced societies – internally pacified societies with a relatively well-established violence monopoly and tightly knit network of interdependencies, democratized power centres and, connected with this, a relatively strong mutual identification and (in Goudsblom's phrase) a high level of *mutually expected self-restraint*. But, again, homosexuals are less strongly placed even within such a context than are many other outsider groups.

CONCLUSION

Elias's theory of established-outsiders relations has been rather overshadowed by his theory of the civilizing process. Yet the one is essentially an extension of the other. Both are concerned with the connections between the development of power relations and developments in personality structure, and both have proved valuable in a wide range of sociological investigations.

The methodological prescription of the established-outsiders theory runs along the following lines. In studying the relations between groups of people, look first for the ways in which they are interdependent with each other. That will lead directly to the central balance of power in the figuration the groups form together. In assessing how far power ratios are tilted towards one side or the other, how stable or how fluctuating they are, look at what goals and objectives, what human requirements are actually being pursued by each side. Ask to what extent one side is able to monopolize something the other side needs in pursuing these requirements. Then, if the balance of power is very uneven, be alert for the operation of group charisma and group disgrace, the process of stigmatization, the absorption of the established group's view of the outsiders within the very conscience and we-image of the outsiders, producing a high measure of resignation even though the tensions remain. Where the balance of power is becoming more equal, expect to find symptoms of rebellion, resistance, emancipation among the outsiders. In all this it will be relevant to look to the past, to how one group came to impinge on the other, to how the way they are bonded to each other makes them pursue the objectives and human requirements they actually do pursue. But for the purpose of ascertaining what is the prevailing balance of power, treat these objectives and assumptions as real in their consequences.

Naturally, it is also relevant for sociologists to ask how realistic are the images groups have of each other. Elias hypothesises that the more unequal the power balance, the less realistic and more fantasy-laden is the image of outsiders on the part of the established likely to be. (This applies to the established group's self-image too.) Correspondingly, after an intervening period of heightened tension and conflict, the more nearly equal is the balance of power, the more favourable are the conditions for more realistic mutual perceptions and the more likely a high degree of mutual identification.

Bringing collective fantasies into the focus of attention is one of the most important ways in which the established-outsiders theory complements the theory of civilizing processes. Thanks to Freud, we have long accepted that the emotional experiences and fantasies of *individual* people are not arbitrary. They have structure and dynamics of their own, and personal problems are mainly interpreted as resulting from the power relations and tensions in the family of origin. Yet *collective* fantasies, argues Elias, still largely slip through our conceptual net; they seem to come and go arbitrarily:

we have yet to work out a testable theoretical framework for the ordering of observations about group fantasies in connection with the development of groups. That may seem surprising, for the building up of collective praise and blame fantasies plays so obvious and so vital a part in the conduct of affairs at all levels of balance of power relationships; and no less obviously they all have a diachronic, developmental character. On the global level, there are for instance the American dream and the Russian dream. There used to be the civilizing mission of European countries, and the dream of the 'Third Reich'. . . . There is the counter-stigmatization of the former outsiders – e.g. of the African countries in search of their own dream and 'negritude' . . . (1976: 29–30)

Collective fantasies have to be understood in the context of fluctuating power relations and tensions in figurations encompassing families of origin but going way beyond them in complexity and scope. We-images and we-ideals are always compacts of emotive fantasies and realistic images. Elias suggests that – just as Freud once said the functioning of personality structure can be seen more clearly when it breaks down in neurotic or psychotic illness than when it is working normally – the workings of we-images and we-ideals stand out most sharply when fantasy and reality fall apart. He mentions the case of nation-states whose power has declined – thinking for instance of Britain and Germany.

The theory of established-outsiders relations, ostensibly derived initially from a limited study of a local community in the English Midlands around 1960, was always intended to be a step towards dealing with the problem of collective fantasies and social inequalities on the broadest scale. As we have seen, its scope has been fruitfully extended beyond Winston Parva both by Elias and others in the most diverse ways.

6

Sport and Violence

For all that Elias was a keen sportsman, he came to sport as a topic for sociological investigation relatively late in his career. He had made some passing mention in *The Civilizing Process* (1939: I, 202–3) of how the modern boxing match represented a strongly tempered form of aggressiveness compared with the bloodier spectacles often enjoyed in earlier days. As related in chapter 1, however, it seems to have been Eric Dunning's interest in pursuing the sociology of sport which spurred Elias in the same direction.[1] Rising public concern at 'football hooliganism' in the 1970s and 1980s led to this field of sociology coming to be regarded as of practical as well as academic importance. In the 1960s the sociology of sport was an unfashionable backwater but Elias was quick to recognize sport as a topic of great sociological significance.

The problem with games and sports is that they are too stubbornly familiar a part of life in contemporary societies. They are too easily taken for granted. Moreover, though enjoyed by so many people, they are often regarded as a trivial aspect of life. We have to make an effort to stand back and view them in a more detached way in order to see their peculiarities and the important sociological questions that need to be asked about them.

The common characteristic of games and sports is that they involve competition: in them, people as individuals or as teams use bodily strength or other skills in competing against each other, or perhaps – as in mountaineering – against dangerous forces of nature. Beyond that, Elias and Dunning make a three-fold distinction between 'sports', 'games' and 'sport-games'. In their usage, 'games' are activities in which the competition between players is *not physical*: games like chess and draughts for example. 'Sports', on the other hand, always involve *physical* competition but they are not games and are not exactly 'played': boxing and athletics are examples here. 'Sport-games' involve physical competition but *are* 'played': examples are soccer, rugby, baseball, and both the words 'sport' and 'game' apply to them. The authors do not adhere to this distinction consistently; nor shall we.

One peculiarity of many sports and sport-games is that there are rules constraining contestants with the aim of reducing the risk of physical injury to a minimum. In some, such as boxing or American football, violence is intrinsic to the activity, yet even here the rules are designed to keep such practices under control. In spite of this minimization of physical danger, sports are *exciting*, and across the world vast numbers of people give up part of their leisure time to sport, either as spectators or as participants themselves. What kind of society must it be, for people so much to enjoy the excitement and tensions engendered by physical contests where no blood flows and contestants do no serious harm to each other? This is the question underlying Elias's investigations into sport (Elias and Dunning 1986: 1).

An answer to this question necessitates comparisons with other kinds of society, past or present, where sports in quite this form are not found, or not to the same degree. An answer to this question, moreover, leads beyond a better understanding merely of sports themselves: Elias believes it is also a contribution towards a sociology of the emotions (1986: 59ff).[2]

THE QUEST FOR EXCITEMENT IN UNEXCITING SOCIETIES[3]

As Elias sought to show in his earlier work, people in contemporary 'advanced' societies have to be able to maintain a fairly even and stable control over their more spontaneous libidinal, affective and emotional impulses and over their fluctuating moods. Social survival and success depend on 'a reliable armour, not too strong and not too weak, of individual self-restraint' (1986: 41). This applies both to occupational roles and to many private relationships and activities. Indeed, they give satisfaction, both from the standpoint of each individual and from that of the others with whom he or she associates, only subject to such a pattern of restraints. In these societies, there is relatively little scope for showing strong feelings or strong dislikes of people, let alone 'hot anger, wild hatred, or the urge to hit someone over the head': 'People strongly agitated, in the grip of feelings they cannot control, are cases for hospital or prison. Conditions of high excitement are regarded as abnormal in a person, as a dangerous prelude to violence in a crowd' (1986: 41).

Elias and Dunning were being ironic when they spoke of 'unexciting societies'. Life in constantly changing complex modern societies is very often 'exciting' in most senses of the word. It is, for instance, intellectually stimulating. What they meant was that opportunities for a more unreflected expression of excitement are, in many spheres of social life, severely limited (1986: 71). Yet containing strong feelings and maintaining an even control of drives throughout life is likely to lead to emotional staleness in most people (the extent varies between individuals). How is this to be handled socially?

Other sociologists theorizing about leisure have often viewed it as simply providing opportunities for the *relaxation* of tensions generated in the work sphere of life. Polarizing work and leisure as opposites, they have implicitly used a scale of values in which work is rated the most important part of life, and leisure viewed in effect as a means to an end, in terms of its functions for work. Tensions are viewed as something bad, something to be got rid of (1986: 92–3).

Elias's and Dunning's view is different. In modern societies, there is an historically unparalleled variety of leisure activities and an important class of them – including sports – serve not simply to dissipate tensions generated in other spheres of life but to provide opportunities for pleasurable excitement. They meet a socially conditioned psychological need in their own right, and if they also relax the tensions arising from work, it is an indirect result of the *generation* and resolution of exciting tensions in leisure. More exactly, argue Elias and Dunning, the leisure sphere in modern societies provides an enclave within which *a controlled and enjoyable decontrolling of restraints on emotions is permitted* (1986: 65ff, 96). Leisure activities generally allow the emotions to flow more freely in a specially constructed setting in some ways reminiscent of non-leisure reality. Sports are an especially clear illustration of this: they always consist of a controlled struggle in an imaginary setting (1986: 50–1).

Apart from sports and games, many other kinds of leisure activity are also designed to appeal directly to people's feelings and arouse them in various ways, eliciting excitement resembling that produced in 'real-life' situations, but without its risks and dangers. Concerts, opera, plays, films, dancing, paintings, card games, novels, detective stories, thrillers – all these can perform a similar function. Elias and Dunning use the term *mimetic* for this class of activities. Literally, that means 'imative', and Elias explains the use of the term as follows:

If one asks how feelings are aroused and excitement elicited by leisure pursuits, one discovers that it is usually done by the creation of tensions. Imaginary danger, mimetic fear and pleasure, sadness and joy are produced and perhaps resolved by the setting of pastimes. Different moods are evoked and perhaps contrasted, such as sorrow and elation, agitation and peace of mind. Thus the feelings aroused in the imaginary situation of a human leisure activity are the siblings of those aroused in real-life situations – that is what the expression 'mimetic' means – but the latter are linked to the never-ending risks and perils of fragile human life, while the former momentarily lift the burden of risks and threats, great or small, surrounding human existence. (1986: 42)

Thus, as Aristotle first argued in the *Poetics*, a tragedy enacted in the theatre may evoke in the audience mimetic tension, feelings of fear and pity closely related to those experienced in witnessing the predicaments ensnaring people in real life – feelings lightened in the setting of a theatrical setting by music, movement, poetry and other mimetic symbols. In the concert hall, too, the music plays upon the audience's emotions, building up tensions which are finally relieved in applause.[4] In the same way, at a football match, spectators savour the mimetic excitement of a battle swaying to and fro on the field, knowing that in this battle little real harm is likely to befall either the players or themselves. Torn between hopes of success and fears of defeat, they openly manifest their feelings in the company of many other people, something which is all the more enjoyable and liberating because in society at large people are more isolated and have few opportunities for collective manifestations of strong feelings (1986: 43). For participants as opposed to spectators, however, it should not be forgotten that some sports and sport-games differ from other activities of the mimetic type in that that they do involve real, *not* imaginary, danger to life or limb.

THE SPARE-TIME SPECTRUM

To appreciate the full significance of the mimetic class of activities, it is necessary to make a thorough break with the misleading static polarity of work versus leisure. It is a mistake to imagine that there are only *two* strongly contrasted categories of activity: on the one hand 'work', socially highly subject to rigid time discipline and where the function for others or for impersonal social units is paramount; and on the other hand 'leisure', meaning everything we freely choose to do, primarily with ourselves in mind, in our pursuit of the excitement and pleasure absent in work. Not all forms of work are always entirely devoid of excitement and pleasure, and there are many other intermediate kinds of activities. Elias and Dunning conceptualize them in a 'spare-time spectrum'.[5] Many domestic activities – financial transactions, household maintenance, housework and so on – have to be performed like work whether one likes it or not, and this category of 'private work and family management' tends to take up more time as the standard of living rises. Then biological needs have to be catered for – sleeping, eating, drinking, washing and caring for one's body, making love. These needs recur, and satisfying them is pleasurable. Eating, cooking and making love shade into the pleasures of general sociability. But they also become highly routinized and not particularly pleasurable. They

can all be, and usually are, routinized up to a point, but they can also be de-routinized from time to time in a more deliberate manner than is often the case. At the same time, they all have this in common with the mimetic class of activities: they can provide heightened enjoyment provided one is able to cater for them in a non-routine manner, such as eating out for a change. (1986: 69)

Routinization recurrently afflicts leisure activities of the mimetic type too. Concerts, plays, football matches may sometimes be found unexciting and boring. The perpetual tension between routinization and deroutinization *within* leisure activities is a principal source of their dynamics; it is seen, for instance, in 'going to the brink', which Elias and Dunning see as an intrinsic feature of them.

It can thus be seen that the connections between activities across the spare-time spectrum are fairly complex. Moreover, the forms of activity in which excitement is found change in the course of social development.

Pressures and restraints have existed in all human societies, and so, it would appear, have leisure activities as a social enclave within which restraints may be loosened. The Dionysian festivals of the ancient Greeks – times of religious excitement or 'enthusiasm' – and the carnivals of medieval Christendom are examples of religious activities with functions analogous to the mimetic class of modern leisure activites. Here, as in other aspects of civilizing processes, there is no zero-point. However, argues Elias, the character of leisure pursuits changes in the course of the process, along with the balance between external constraints and learned self-restraints. Close analysis of the long-term civilizing process indicates that as restraints on people's behaviour become more all-embracing, more even, and internalized as a more or less automatically operating self-control, counter-moves appear towards a balancing loosening of social and personal restraints (1986: 66). New forms of relatively uninhibited music and dancing are symptoms, and so perhaps is the more active spectator participation in sports events seen in many countries.

At the same time, the overall trend of the long-term civilizing process is reflected in the way that, in order to provide a *pleasurable* excitement, modern leisure activities have to conform with the comparative sensitivity to physical violence which is characteristic of people's social habitus in the later stages of a civilizing process. Gladiators fighting to the death, Christians fending off hungry lions, public hangings or cat burnings would produce not enjoyment but severe revulsion in nearly all modern spectators. So the rules of modern sports always more or less curb the use of physical violence by participants against each other. At the same time the tension of the contest has to be kept up, both for players and spectators: the rules are usually adjusted in an attempt to ensure reasonable equality between, say, boxers of similar weight, between attacking and defensive functions in soccer (e.g. the offside rule) or between batsmen and bowlers in cricket (e.g. the lbw rule), in order to achieve relatively unpredictable contests.

A contest may also be *too* exciting – perhaps not so much because the rules maintain too high a tension as because of developments in society at large, for

if tensions arise in the wider society, if restraints on strong feelings become weakened there and the level of hostility and hatred between different groups rises in good earnest, the dividing line separating play and non-play, mimetic and real battles may become blurred. In such cases a defeat on the playing field may evoke the bitter feeling of a defeat in real life and a call for vengeance. A mimetic victory may call for a continuation of the triumph in a battle outside the playing field. (1986: 43)

These hypotheses arose out of, and in turn led to further testing in, comparative and developmental investigations of many particular forms of sport.

EARLIER FORMS OF GAMES

Game contests and forms of competitive physical exercise are ubiquitous in human societies. They were found in many small-scale tribal societies. They were found in the ancient world. Are not the modern Olympic Games a conscious 'revival' of those of ancient Greece? Was not football, albeit of a cruder kind, played between rival villages or rival guilds in the Middle Ages? Yes. But were they quite the same thing as what today we call 'sports'?

In the essay 'Sport as a sociological problem' (1986: 126–49; originally 1971), Elias examines in some detail the games of the ancient Greeks, especially their equivalent of boxing and a form of wrestling, called the pancration, which was among the most popular of the contests. He finds in them a much higher level of violence than that permitted today. Modes of attack forbidden in the modern forms of contest – such as head-butting, the use of legs and dangerous holds – were allowed. There were no time limits and contestants were not necessarily evenly matched in weight and strength. Deaths and permanent injuries were far from uncommon. Limbs were broken, eyes gouged out, people strangled. Elias (1986: 140) cites one instance in which a boxing match ended when one fighter struck his opponent with his outstretched and leather-armoured fingers below the ribs, penetrated his abdomen and proceeded to disembowel him. Baron Coubertin did not revive this form of contest!

These contests were not in fact totally unregulated. There was a judge, and people were not actually encouraged to gouge out each other's eyes. But these things happened in the heat of battle. Moreover, the contestant who killed or maimed his opponent went unpunished. It sometimes happened that the dead man's corpse was crowned as victor if he died especially valiantly but loss of the crown was the most the killer would suffer. There is no evidence that the spectators or participants felt the horror and repugnance that we would feel today at such 'brutalities' (as we would consider them).

In fact people today might easily find it difficult to reconcile these seemingly brutal facets of the Greeks with the much-admired literature, philosophy and art of the same people. The contradiction stems entirely from the standpoint of our own values. For them there was no contradiction. The skills, physical and temperamental, used in the game contest were closely related to skills necessary in 'real life'; the mimetic distance, so to speak, was relatively small. In Greek society, if murder was committed, it was the *duty* of the victim's kin – not of the state, for the state monopoly of violence was little developed – to exact revenge. Greek citizens also fought for their city in hoplite armies; it was not exceptional for all the males of a vanquished city to be slaughtered *en masse* and the women and children sold into slavery. Such instances of genocide did not, any more than deaths and maimings in the games, bring forth the moral revulsion they would today. Greek literature affords plentiful evidence of the pity and compassion which could be felt for the victims, but very little of feelings of horror and indignation towards the perpetrators. All this, Elias points out, is very much in line with what the theory of civilizing processes would lead one to expect. The level of physical insecurity was much higher, and both state-formation and conscience-formation were much less well advanced. The level of internalized inhibitions against physical violence was lower, and the associated feelings of shame and guilt weaker, than in the relatively developed nation-states of the twentieth century.

Unlike the Greek games, the folk football of medieval and early modern

Britain was not very directly related to any military skills, although certain other early pastimes like archery very obviously were. While the authorities sought to encourage the latter, they repeatedly issued edicts – which had little or no effect – making football illegal, because from their standpoint it was inherently riotous and destructive. The modern reader, thinking of football hooliganism, may be tempted to remark, '*plus ça change . . .*'; but in fact the game itself, in spite of the continuity in the name, was very different from its modern successor.[6]

Games with some generic resemblance to football were widespread in Britain, and indeed in Europe. They were much less highly regulated than their modern descendants, but not completely anarchic. They were governed by local custom and tradition. It was common, for instance, for a game to be played on certain holidays, such as Shrove Tuesday. The games themselves varied a good deal from place to place. According to local custom, the game could involve at one and the same time elements which to modern eyes are reminiscent of soccer, rugby, hurling, hockey, even polo (if some participants rode on horseback). Above all, however, the games were much more violent: they seem always to have involved fighting between the players, and not necessarily in the immediate vicinity of the ball! Often the struggle was pursued over several miles of terrain with an indeterminate number of participants, its very loose structure afforded plentiful opportunities to settle private scores. Such as they were, restraints were imposed not by highly elaborate formal regulations, which require a high degree of training and self-control (1986: 183), but by custom. A high level of violence was accepted by custom. Injuries were sustained, blood flowed, and the people – often with the connivance of the local gentry – persisted in playing their games in the face of sporadic attempts by ineffective authority to suppress them. If the state apparatus was insufficiently developed to enforce a ban, how much less likely was it that common national codes of detailed rules, written down and subject to criticism and revision, could be developed and observed? Such codes, now taken for granted, were then inconceivable.

Just as the violence of the Greek games seems to modern eyes at odds with Greek art and literature, so the violence of medieval and early modern folk games may be at odds with the nostalgic image of a harmonious folk society shared by many laymen and some social scientists. Elias and Dunning (1986: 179–81) take the opportunity to criticise the once-influential model of 'folk society' developed by Robert Redfield on the basis (among other things) of Tönnies's notion of *Gemeinschaft*, and of Durkheim's idea of mechanical solidarity.[7] The country people and townsfolk who took part in these semi-institutionalized fights between local groups lived for the most part in settlements that, by twentieth-century standards, were no more than villages and small towns, strong candidates for inclusion in the list of 'folk' or 'traditional' societies. It has often been said that such societies were permeated by feelings of great 'solidarity', which can easily be taken to mean that tensions and conflicts were less strong and feelings of friendship and unity greater than in the large-scale mass societies of today. 'As they intimately communicate with each other, every member claims the sympathy of the others', wrote Redfield

(1947). But the term 'solidarity' is misleading, for this social closeness may foster inescapable enmities and hatreds as well as friendships.

One can, indeed, often observe expressions of strong and spontaneous 'fellow feeling' in traditional societies. But such expressions of what we might conceptualize as 'strong solidarity' were perfectly compatible with equally strong and spontaneous enmities and hatreds. What was really characteristic, at least of the traditional peasant societies of our own Middle Ages, was the much greater fluctuation of feeling of which people were then capable and and, in connection with this, the relatively greater instability of human relationships in general. In connection with the lesser stability of internalized restraints, the strength of passions, the warmth and the spontaneity of emotional actions were greater in both directions: in the direction of kindness and readiness to help as well as in that of unkindness, callousness and readiness to hurt. (Elias and Dunning 1986: 180)

The folk games of medieval and early modern times were thus one manifestation of people in an earlier stage of the civilizing process. They were indeed physical contests. But were they *sport* contests in the modern sense? If not, how did the latter develop out of the former? The word *sport* acquired its modern meaning, and many of the activities to which it has applied took shape in England during the eighteenth century. Elias regards England as having played an especially important part in what he calls the *sportization* of leisure as we know it today.[8]

THE SIGNIFICANCE OF ENGLAND

Why is English the international language of sport, in much the same sense that French is the language of cookery and Italian of music? That was one of the questions which led Elias and Dunning to examine closely the part Britain played in the sociogenesis of so many sports which are now widely played in more or less identical ways in many parts of the world.[9] The list of sports which first assumed their modern, internationally recognizable form in England is impressive: soccer, rugby, horse-racing, wrestling, boxing, lawn tennis, fox-hunting, rowing, cricket, athletics and (from Scotland) golf. The very word *sport* is English, and though recorded as early as 1440, only in the eighteenth century did it acquire its specific modern connotations of a pleasurable pastime involving competitive physical exertion and skill, but with a relatively moderated use of violence.

Elias asks why it should have come about that 'the civilizing of game-contests and the restraint on violence to others through social rules which require a good deal of individual self-control developed first in England' (1986: 24). There is no suggestion that the need for pastimes of this kind was unique to England. The speed with which, mainly from the mid-nineteenth century onwards, other countries adopted many of the English models of sport (sometimes then further adapting them for their own tastes, as in for instance American football[10]) suggests that they corresponded to some human social requirement by then more widespread. Nevertheless, why was it that highly regulated contests requiring physical exertion and skill, and known both in performer and spectator forms as 'sport', first appear among the landed aristocracy and gentry of eighteenth-century England?

Elias's answer links 'sportization' to 'parliamentarization'. The parallel has often been noted between, on the one hand, political conflicts played out according to agreed parliamentary rules and on the other hand, sporting contests played according to the rules of the game. But this commonplace idea is only at the level of analogy. Elias gives it a specific historical context and explanatory weight.[11] As was related in chapter 3 Elias sees the parliamentarization of political conflict in eighteenth-century England as a relatively rare route out of a cycle of violence. Whigs and Tories peacefully relinquishing office to each other, the use of debating skills in place of force, and the gradually increasing level of mutual trust, depended on the two sides being essentially members of a single dominant class of landowners (see pages 90–2 above). Elias does not argue that parliamentarization *caused* sportization, still less that the sportization of pastimes caused parliamentarization of politics! Rather his explanation is that the *same people* were caught up in two aspects of a broader process of development. As always, he is concerned with *people in the round*; they are not separate political, economic and sporting beings.

It was simply that the same class of people who participated in the pacification and greater regularization of factional contests in Parliament were instrumental in the greater pacification and regularization of their pastimes . . . Sport and Parliament as they emerged in the eighteenth century were both characteristic of the same change in the power structure of England and in the social habitus of that class of people which emerged from the antecedent struggles as the ruling group. (1986: 40)

There were other respects in which social and political circumstances in eighteenth-century England favoured sportization. One was the relatively early establishment there of freedom of association. Political clubs began to be formed during the Commonwealth and Restoration periods, but it was only as the cycle of violence gradually subsided that they came to be seen as a normal and legitimate part of political life rather than as subversive; sociologists from Alexis de Tocqueville (1835–40) to Jürgen Habermas (1960) have emphasized the role of clubs (another English word which has spread internationally) in political development. Elias points out how the same social device was readily employed in the emerging organization of sport.

Another aspect of English society facilitated the involvement of the land-owning class in sports. The free English peasantry as a class had been all but broken by enclosures. Landowners no longer had any great fear of revolt by the agrarian lower classes. By and large, their employees knew their place. That made for easier relationships, and helps to explain how noblemen and gentry came to be involved in organizing both participant and spectator sports. Cricket matches were organized between retainers of two gentlemen, and younger gentlemen might join in with no fear of social derogation. The first cricket clubs were also formed in the eighteenth century. Similar involvement can be seen in other sports too. Often the customary rules of folk sports and sport-games were modified in accordance with the needs of gentlemen. Boxing is an example.

Tighter sets of rules were developed, eliminating among other things the use of the legs; later, gloves were introduced and competitors matched according to weight. The new rules both conformed with a higher sensitivity to violence *and* made for a more even and exciting contest. Gentlemen promoted contests between lower-class professional fighters, when betting enhanced their excitement as spectators, as in horse-racing and other sports. At the same time, however, boxing also became the 'gentlemanly art of self-defence', gradually used in place of the duel in settling disputes between at least younger males of the gentry class.

The involvement of members of the upper classes had one other consequence. When contests in whatever sport began to be arranged between parties at a greater distance than the neighbouring villages which had been the usual range of folk-games, purely local, widely varying, customary rules were no longer adequate. First gentlemen's clubs (for example in cricket) and the public schools and universities (in soccer and rugby) came to lay down standard sets of rules which made possible competition among individuals or clubs no matter from where they came. Later came county and national associations.

Fox-hunting

Elias sees in fox-hunting, so peculiarly English a pastime and so prominent a part of the lives of the land-owning classes in the eighteenth and nineteenth centuries, an especially clear illustration of sportization as a civilizing spurt.[12] That may seem strange. Fox-hunting is today somewhat marginal to most people's conception of 'sport', and indeed many people regard it as barbarous rather than civilized. Other subsequent civilizing spurts have intervened to change our perception of it. Nevertheless, when compared with *earlier* forms of hunting, fox-hunting as it became codified in the eighteenth century is a good example of what sportization involves.

The puzzlement of foreigners at fox-hunting is a long-standing joke. Elias relates the story of the Frenchman who heard an Englishman exclaim 'How admirable! the sport which the fox has shown in this charming run of two hours and a quarter.' The Frenchman replied: '*Ma foi*, he must be worth catching when you take so much trouble. *Est-il bon pour un fricandeau?*' (1986: 160). Elias draws attention to several other distinctive features, apart from the prey not being eaten. Why, if during their pursuit of the fox the hounds disturb some other animal – such as a hare, which *is* eatable – are they whipped away from it, back on to the scent of the fox? Why, as far as possible, do huntsmen try not to 'switch foxes', keeping the hounds on the track of the first fox detected? Why is it such a severe breach of the gentlemanly code to shoot a fox? Why, indeed, do the humans take no direct part in killing the fox? And why, above all and increasingly in the course of time, have huntsmen dwelt more on the pleasures of the chase than on the killing itself?

These things were not always so. Earlier forms of hunting imposed fewer restraints:

People enjoyed the pleasure of hunting and killing animals in whatever way they could and ate as many of them as they liked. Sometimes masses of animals were driven near the hunters so that they could enjoy the pleasures of killing without too much exertion. For the higher ranking social cadres, the excitement of hunting and killing animals had always been to some extent the peacetime equivalent of the excitement connected with killing humans in times of war. As a matter of course people used for both purposes the most suitable weapons at their disposal. After firearms had been invented, foxes were shot just like other animals. (1986: 161)

The fox was not even considered absolutely inedible, at least among the poor in times of dearth.

By the eighteenth century, however, not only did members of the nobility and gentry never eat foxes, but they even killed them by proxy, delegating the function to their hounds. 'It corresponded better to the sensitivity of civilized gentlemen to let the hounds do the killing and confine their own activity to assisting them, to the anticipatory excitement and to watching the killing' (1986: 163). Their sensitivity was lower than that of many people nowadays, but already higher than their forebears. It already represented an example of the long-term shift towards visual pleasures to which Elias referred in *The Civilizing Process* (see p. 58 above). Today, for many people – probably *most* non-hunters – there is no pleasure even in watching the kill.[13]

Furthermore, a shift from even visual pleasure in the kill towards the pleasures of the chase is evident among eighteenth-century fox-hunters, and still more in the nineteenth.[14] The emphasis is more and more on the fore-pleasure and less on the consummation. Killing foxes is actually rather easy, and if it were only a matter of protecting farmers' poultry they would certainly be shot. The various rules of hunting are all designed to make it *less* easy, at some cost in mortality among poultry, but considerable gain in the excitement, the competition, and even the danger to life and limb among the riders making up 'the field'.

Fox-hunting demonstrates a general principle in sports: rules are developed which serve to generate and prolong a tension-equilibrium that is pleasurably exciting for participants, and with a good chance of a culmination in pleasurable catharsis – release from tensions. That is why most sports, like good wines, need time to mature. Basketball is an example of a sport which was simply invented by a particular person (1986: 297n.), but this is rare. 'As a rule, sports have gone through a period of trial and error before reaching a form which secured sufficient tension for sufficient time without fostering tendencies towards stalemate' (1986: 157).

Rugby

In their book *Barbarians, Gentlemen and Players* (1979), a sociological study of the development of rugby football, Dunning and Sheard provide another demonstration of this process of development through trial and error, of the civilizing and sportization of older and more violent folk-games, and of England's peculiar role as a seed-bed of modern sports.

They show how rugby was one of the less violent codes which emerged in the nineteenth century out of the common matrix of traditionally more violent folk-games; how the bifurcation took place between rugby and soccer (a still less violent and more restrained code); how later in the century, when rugby had come to be played by many working-class men, the tension between middle-class players and their social inferiors – and, as an expression of this tension, the conflict over amateurism and incipient professionalism – led to the split between the Union and League forms of rugby; and how both codes have continued to modify their rules in order to achieve the optimum tension-equilibrium both for spectators and players.

Dunning and Sheard are especially interesting on the part played in this story by the English public schools, and how the development of the games cult there was linked to broader developments in English social structure (see also Dunning 1977b). Rugby, of course, took its name from one of those schools. Many of the public schools had their own variants on traditional folk games, and in the first quarter of the nineteenth century they seem to have been played with great ferocity: 'hacking', or kicking on the shins with iron-tipped boots was commonly an essential part of the game. Indeed some resisted eliminating this, on the grounds that anything gentler was less 'manly'.

How, nevertheless, did violence in play come to diminish? Little credence need be given to the story of how rugby was invented one day in 1823 in Rugby when an individual boy, William Webb Ellis, picked up the ball and ran with it. The process was much more gradual, though it is true that a set of rules for the game was for the first time written down and published at Rugby in 1845. Nor is it quite adequate to depict Dr Thomas Arnold, headmaster of Rugby 1828–42, as the 'inventor' of the games cult generally.

Dunning and Sheard's explanation in summary is as follows. The public schools had during the eighteenth century become extremely disorderly places. Out and out rebellions by the boys were quite frequent – sometimes they even had to be put down by soldiers. One reason seems to have been that sons of the aristocracy had come to constitute a large proportion of the pupils, and they despised the masters of social inferiors. Effective control tended to pass to the older and stronger students; bullying and 'fagging' were rife. Dr Arnold was one of several headmasters in the 1820s and 1830s who attempted to come to grips with the problem, setting out to reform and, quite literally, pacify the schools. He reached in effect a compromise settlement through the prefectorial system: the dominance of the older boys in matters outside the classroom was legitimized, the authority of the masters in class accepted. Circumstances at Rugby were especially favourable. It was not then one of the most prestigious public schools and had a relatively low percentage of aristocratic pupils.

Moreover, in the wider society, the process of embourgeoisement had by now proceeded to a point where the power ratio between the landed upper class and the commercial and industrial middle class was much more nearly even than formerly. The aristocracy was less able to treat the middle class with such unqualified contempt, while on the other hand the middle classes still deferentially sought to emulate the aristocracy.

In this context, Dr Arnold's principal direct contribution to the growth of the games cult lay in his effective suppression of *field sports* among the pupils – forbidding them to keep the guns and packs of hounds characteristic of the pastimes of the gentry. Once this had been achieved, games of the football type proved acceptable functional equivalents for enough of the boys.

Football nevertheless began to change markedly. Several innovations characteristic of rugby, notably the oval ball and the H-shaped goal posts, were made by the boys over a period of time. And various restrictions on violence were embodied in the rules, the observance of which required they be learned and internalized with a considerable measure of restraint. (For this process of the growth of rules and their internalization – in contexts besides sport too – Elias uses the term *regularization*.) These innovations possibly arose because by now the violent traditions of folk-football had lower-class connotations: to play according to those codes was ungentlemanly. In turn, when the rules of what was to become soccer were first codified, notably at Eton a few years later, the wish to differentiate a still more restrained, *gentle*manly code from the rugby code associated with relative *parvenus* seems to have played some part.

Even if circumstances there favoured the development of the game which bears its name, Rugby School was not unique. The sportization of games proceeded in several other schools.[15] And what was happening in the schools was part of a more general civilizing spurt in nineteenth-century England, now affecting many strata of society; the social historian Harold Perkin has said, somewhat colourfully, that between 1780 and 1850 'the English ceased to be one of the most aggressive, brutal, rowdy, outspoken, riotous, cruel and bloodthirsty nations in the world, and became one of the most inhibited, polite, orderly, tender-minded, prudish and hypocritical' (Perkin 1969: 280). England was not unique. Not all modern sports originated there. Ruud Stokvis (1979, 1982a) has pointed out that in Germany an ideology of 'keep fit' and gymnastics was developed, with a much more directly nationalist and military flavour, in rivalry with the English ideology of sport as more and more a non-military end in itself. But sports and games in many other countries were probably moving in the same direction as in England,[16] and, where regularization was first achieved in England, it may simply have been convenient to impose the English codes on diverse native variants in order to facilitate competition at national and international level. Thus the French variety of boxing gave way to the standardized English form as did the Italian *calcio* variant of football. England's political and economic position as a world power at the time also had some bearing on the spread of sport and, as Stokvis argues, on the ideology of amateurism.

Amateurism is originally an English phenomenon. At the end of the nineteenth century Great Britain was the most influential and powerful country in the world . . . England's worldwide prestige heightened the esteem in which her sportsmen were held. As a consequence of this the English were in a position to demand that amateur conditions be introduced in other countries also. If this was not done, the English refused to come to these countries for competitions, and sportsmen from these countries were not granted admission to competitions in England. (Stokvis 1982a)

VIOLENCE IN CONTEMPORARY SPORT: PLAYERS AND SPECTATORS

It may seem ironic to be discussing the emergence of less violent, more restrained forms of sports and games in eighteenth- and nineteenth-century England, when, in the 1970s and 1980s, it is widely considered that violence among players in some games is on the increase, and when England especially has attained international notoriety for violent hooliganism among its soccer spectators.[17] These problems have indeed provoked a great deal of social research, in which Eric Dunning and his Leicester research group have been very active.

On-field violence between players, in defiance of rules which forbid it, probably has been increasing in recent decades in many sports and many countries. It is difficult to measure, partly because an element of 'moral panic' and increased reporting of incidents in the media may have given an exaggerated impression of the scale of the increase. Nevertheless, Pilz (1982) gives some suggestive quantitative data from various sports in Germany, and Dunning and his colleagues have also concluded that 'moral panic' does not altogether explain away an underlying increase.

As we have seen, the 'gentling' of on-field play (if we may use an equestrian term) was bound up with a gentlemanly ethic of amateurism and playing 'for fun', an ethic associated with an upper class still retaining sufficient power potential to impress it in large degree on social inferiors. More recently, trends towards more intense competition, professionalization, greater achievement orientation, greater rewards and a growing seriousness of involvement have been observed in many sports. 'Seriousness' is seen in the nationalistic pursuit of rankings in Olympic medal tables, in the use of drugs to improve performance and perhaps in the increasing use of violence on field. Dunning has sought to account for this through the general process of functional democratization in which – as discussed in chapter 5 – many social power ratios have become rather more equal, and patterns of control more multipolar or polyarchic, the result of the lengthening chains of interdependence tying people together within state-societies and across the world.[18] He argues that the reciprocal pressures and controls that operate in industrial societies generally operate too in the sphere of sport. As a result, top-level sportsmen and women cannot be independent and play for fun, but have to represent wider social units – cities, counties, nations – in high seriousness. It may be less 'fun', but in compensation they receive training facilities, prestige and money.

In return, they are expected to produce a 'sports-performance' – that is, the sort of satisfactions which controllers and 'consumers' of the sport demand, namely the spectacle of an exciting contest that people are willing to pay to watch or the validation through victory of the 'image' or 'reputation' of the social unit with which the controllers and/or consumers identify. (In Elias and Dunning, 1986: 220)

In these circumstances, the rise of the 'professional foul' and its equivalents – the carefully calculated use of violence with a view to improving the chances of victory – is not surprising. But is this not a clear contradiction of the theory of the civilizing process? Certainly, at first blush it seems to run counter to Elias's argument that in Europe there has been a long-term decline in people's propensity for obtaining pleasure from directly engaging in and witnessing violent acts, that the threshold of repugnance regarding violent acts has advanced, and that people increasingly feel guilty when this taboo is broken. On the other hand, the theory also points to an increase in socially generated competitive pressure, and an increase in people's tendency to plan, to use foresight, and to use longer-term, more rational strategies for achieving their goals. The professional foul in this sense is highly civilized! It involves (in the first instance) no loss of self-control, and is committed not for pleasure but in a calculated way to achieve an end.

This paradox leads Dunning to introduce two distinctions, between 'instrumental' and 'expressive' violence,[19] and between 'segmental bonding' and 'functional bonding'.

'Expresssive' and 'instrumental' violence are not sharply polarized opposites, but rather ends of a continuum, and of course it is very easy for one to spill over into the other. The most coldly instrumental of professional fouls may spark off a general *mêlée* of the most expressive kind, whether on the field or among the spectators. Nevertheless, argues Dunning, the civilizing process generally, as well as specifically in the development of sports, has entailed a shift in the *balance* between expressive and instrumental violence. That is to say, while the central thrust of the process is towards a specific type of conscience-formation, producing feelings of guilt and repugnance with regard to any pleasurable use of violence, increasing pressures towards competition, achievement, and the demand for foresight actually facilitate the use of violence in an instrumental way. This is implicit in *The Civilizing Process*, and Elias in later work has laid more emphasis on 'counter-spurts' within the broader trend. All the same, the issue is complicated, for the growth of the state's monopoly of violence operates to deter the private use of instrumental as well as expressive violence. Dunning recognizes that the distinction has introduced a refinement with wider relation to Elias's theory than the immediate context of sport, and we shall return to this issue in chapter 10. For the moment, it is enough to accept that it helps to make sense of an apparent increase in on-field violence, in the context of the shifting power balances involved in the professionalization, 'spectacularization' and internationalization of sport in recent decades.

The distinction between expressive and instrumental violence does not in itself, however, do much to explain the incidence of 'hooliganism' among spectators which has caused so much popular concern in recent years. For 'hooligan violence' is predominantly of an expressive kind.[20] Surely that runs more clearly counter to Elias's theory? This is the problem which has been central to the work of Dunning and his colleagues in the 1980s, and it is where his second refinement, the distinction between segmental and functional bonding, becomes relevant.

It is abundantly clear from the research both of the Leicester team and others that for football hooligans the enjoyment of fighting is an important part of the satisfaction of attending a match. For some spectators – a minority of course –

the 'aggro' off the field, whether on the terraces or in the streets before and after the match, is *more* important than what happens on the field. Violence between rival gangs of supporters, and against property, has become the subject of public concern not just in Britain but in many other countries too. What explanations can be offered?

Popular explanations include excessive drinking, violence on the field of play, the 'permissive society' and unemployment as 'causes' of hooliganism (Dunning et al. 1988: 13ff).[21] None of these can be quite dismissed out of hand, but it is necessary to distinguish various levels of causality. Alcohol certainly can lower inhibitions, and tensions on the field are interconnected with tensions on the terraces. But that does not go very far. Why does heavy drinking form part of the occasion for a certain element among spectators? Why, even without drink, do some people have a relatively high propensity actively to seek fights, and others to fight when tensions rise? In fact we know from many sociological studies that, in certain kinds of working-class communities, prowess in fighting and an ability 'to hold your ale' are closely bound up with standards of masculinity. Even then, it is necessary to press the question further, and ask *why* that should be so.

Unemployment and 'permissiveness' appeal as explanations to the political left and right respectively, but are both inadequate. Unemployment in Britain was relatively low in the 1960s when soccer hooliganism began to be a serious matter of public concern. Moreover, although this upsurge of concern followed an apparent lull in the previous few decades, the Leicester group have shown that hooligan incidents among spectators have a long history antedating the age of the 'permissive society'.

In the *Roots of Football Hooliganism* (1988) the Leicester group provide the most complete account of their own and others' research on the history of football hooligan violence. Using sources such as the Football Association archives and a range of national and local newspapers, they show how common were incidents of violence and rowdyism among spectators in the late nineteenth and early twentieth centuries. After the First World War, there does seem to have been some decline in incidence in England (though not, it seems, in Scotland), lasting until the upsurge of the mid-1950s and especially the 1960s.

The specific character of incidents before the First World War may have been slightly different from those of today. More of them seem to have been directly related to the game itself: attacks on the referee or on the visiting team were relatively common, but not so much regular fights between rival gangs of supporters. Fighting between hooligan gangs of youths drawn from the rougher, less 'respectable' working class, however, appears to have been common then, but it was not yet so specifically linked to football or other sports. Reporting of violent incidents, whether at football grounds or simply in the streets when no sporting occasion was taking place, was much more restrained in tone. The hooligans were not generally described as 'animals', as became common in the 1970s and 1980s – their humanity was less called in question. Dunning and his colleagues infer from their evidence that earlier in the century it was much more taken for granted that working-class crowds would behave in a rough and disorderly manner.

Since then, the social 'incorporation' – and indeed, as discussed in chapter 5, the 'civilizing' – of the growing and more 'respectable' majority of the working class has continued in many ways (though the Leicester group express doubts as to whether this growth continued in the 1980s). Between the wars, football attracted very large crowds of both sexes, and particularly from the more respectable working class. Some incidents of hooliganism continued to occur, but probably at a lower level, and newspapers tended to celebrate the orderliness of working-class crowds compared with earlier decades (and compared particularly with Scotland).

This 'respectable' audience is the one which has declined most since the Second World War. Such people have tended to move towards more home-centred leisure pursuits. They have also probably been deterred by the increasingly alarming hooliganism among the rougher elements who have, since the mid-1960s, been attracted into attending matches in greater numbers and more regularly than before. The much more outraged, even hysterical, tone of reporting and public comment in the 1970s and 1980s suggests that for the great majority of people, sensitivity with regard to violence is higher now than it was earlier in the century. That is in line with the theory of civilizing processes. Yet it still leaves the question of why certain elements in society – the rougher working-class groups from which the football hooligan gangs are overwhelmingly drawn[22] – should have remained relatively untouched by the civilizing process in train elsewhere, and why indeed they may even show an opposite trend.

Dunning's argument[23] is that the 'rougher' working-class neighbourhoods from which football hooligans are mainly drawn are characterized more by *segmental* and less by *functional bondings*[24] than most other groups in contemporary society. The social attributes of such neighbourhoods are well-known through many sociological studies: relatively high incidence of poverty; poor education, unskilled and casual labour or unemployment; low geographical mobility; mother-centred families and kin networks; male dominance and rigidly separate family roles for the sexes; easy resort to violence including the socialization of children; low supervision of children; formation of street-corner gangs; and so on. One sentence produces a caricature. The point is, however, that these characteristics mutually reinforce each other. One outcome is norms of aggressive masculinity. Another is intense feelings of attachment to narrowly defined 'we-groups' and correspondingly intense feelings of hostility towards narrowly defined 'they-groups'.

In some ways such communities are reminiscent of communities at an earlier stage of development. Yet these modern forms of segmental bonding are not identical with, for example, medieval communities. For they are located in a society with a relatively stable and effective state, in which there exists a complex network of interdependencies – even if these communities are relatively less well interwoven into the mesh of functional bondings. 'As a result, the segmentally bonded local groups of today are subjected to civilizing pressures and controls from two main sources: (1) from the policing, educational and social work agencies of the state; and (2) from functionally bonded groups in the wider society' (Elias and Dunning 1986: 243). That is to say, segmental groups in modern society are subject to restraint from the outside (*Fremdzwänge* again) but not to anything like the same extent from within (*Selbstzwänge*).

The intense feelings of in-group attachment and hostility towards out-groups of such segmentally bonded groups mean that rivalry is virtually inevitable when their members meet. And their norms of aggressive masculinity and comparative inability to exercise self-control mean that conflict between them leads easily to fighting. (Dunning, in Elias and Dunning 1986: 243)

To describe the pattern of fighting which emerges in such a situation, Dunning and his colleagues borrowed from the American sociologist Gerald Suttles the term *ordered segmentation*. In his book *The Social Order of the Slum* (1968), Suttles described neighbourhoods in which there are many age, sex, ethnic and territorial segments relatively independent of each other but fitted together like building blocks to create a larger structure. Though relatively independent, members of these segments have a tendency to combine in the event of opposition and conflict, without any central co-ordination, and these alignments and alliances build up according to a fixed hierarchical sequence. The pattern of cleavages and alliances bears some resemblance to those described by Evans-Pritchard (1940) among the segmentary lineages of the Nuer, and patterns similar to those Suttles found in Chicago have been observed on working-class housing estates in Britain by the Leicester team and by other sociologists.

How does this pattern become entangled with football? It is not unconnected with the place of sport as an enclave where a relative decontrolling of emotional controls is permitted, nor with the commercial need of clubs to attract loyal supporters, nor with the attention now paid by the media to rivalry between teams. There is a transport system capable of moving the fans throughout the country and abroad to watch the teams they support. Growing numbers of fans, even from the poorer communities, can afford to travel to matches. Football hooliganism, which was once far more a local problem, is now national and international. The 'hooligans abroad' at international matches are the tip of a pyramidal structure of ordered segmental building blocks.

The pattern of ordered segmentation described by the Leicester group does not easily fit into a simple dichotomous model of class conflict. Much of the fighting at all levels in the pyramid takes place between rivals of similar rougher working-class origin, though that does not preclude fighting the police, who may or may not be seen as representatives of a class enemy. What the pattern does fit very closely is the theory of established-outsiders relations. The modern structure of social interdependencies has enhanced the power of young males, from decidedly outsider origins, to express norms which conflict with those of established groups.

CONCLUSION: TOWARDS A SOCIOLOGY OF THE EMOTIONS

The picture of human emotions that emerges from the work on sports and leisure by Elias, Dunning and their associates is not especially attractive to Elias's personal taste:

I have not *chosen* to discover that struggle and the enjoyable excitement produced by it provide an indispensable complement to the equally indispensable restraints of life. If I were free to choose my world, I would probably not have chosen a world where struggles between humans are found exciting and enjoyable . . . I would probably have chosen to say: avoid struggle. Let us all live in peace with each other. (1986: 59; my italics)

But as a sociologist, Elias presents the world as he finds it. He finds that, quite apart from the enjoyable excitement of sex, human beings also need other forms of enjoyable excitement, including the excitement of battle. In relatively highly pacified societies, the need has come to be met – in a quite unplanned way – by the provision of mimetic struggles, enacted in a specially constructed context with a minimum of injury to human beings.

More generally, Elias finds there is a human need not only for emotional controls but also for a controlled decontrolling of emotional controls; not only for routinization but also for deroutinization. There is a fluctuating tension-balance between emotional control and emotional stimulation:

The form in which this tension-balance manifests itself varies from society to society. In our type of society where control of the whole feeling continuum, from animalic drives to the most sublime emotions, is in part strongly internalized, the external control of emotions is relatively moderate and the emotional stimulation provided with public approval in leisure activities is by and large, equally moderate in character. Both, in short, require a considerable degree of emotional maturity. (Elias and Dunning, 1986: 115)

Even within relatively highly pacified societies, however, the tension-balance varies between social groups, as investigation of spectator violence suggests. Outsider groups relatively insulated from the multi-polar pressure prevalent elsewhere may continue to indulge in battles which offend the sensitivity levels attained in much of the rest of society.

Psychoanalysts might speak of this controlled decontrolling of controls as a 'socially permitted regression' to childhood behaviour but Elias and Dunning (1986: 116) disagree with this. It merely reveals the inadequacy of any psychological theory which assumes adult behaviour is all of a piece, the same in all activities. Which is not by any means to imply that sport and leisure are the only fields for which the tension-balance between emotional control and emotional stimulation has implications. If Elias is right about the ubiquity of this tension, then it may have considerable bearing on the very survival of the human species. For that reason we shall return to the issue in chapter 9, discussing Elias's most recent writings on humanity as a whole, and in chapter 10, which deals in more detail with situations such as Nazi Germany, where human beings appear to have passed through very serious phases of apparent 'decivilization'.

7

Involvement and Detachment:
a Theory of Knowledge and the Sciences

In 1956 Norbert Elias published in the *British Journal of Sociology* an essay on 'Problems of involvement and detachment'. This title led most sociologists to interpret the article as one more disquisition on the issues of 'objectivity' and 'value-freedom' in sociology. In part it was. But it ranged far more widely than that: 'rambling' was probably the way it was seen by the vast majority of readers unfamiliar with the still virtually unknown *Über den Prozess der Zivilisation*. What the essay in fact represented was the beginning of a major extension of the theory of civilizing processes to the level of humanity as a whole. In particular, it was Elias's first major statement of a theory of the long-term development of human knowledge and the rise of the sciences as part of it. Elias developed this theory in a long series of essays written in the 1960s and 1970s,[1] in which he was also highly critical of then dominant approaches to the philosophy of science, notably the work of Sir Karl Popper. The origins of his own point of view on these matters lay as far back as his youthful disagreement with Richard Hönigswald over the merits of Kantian philosophy. Other elements in Elias's complex web of arguments can be traced back to his early unpublished research on science in Renaissance Italy, to *The Civilizing Process*, and even to *The Established and the Outsiders* among his later works. The purpose of this chapter and the next is to attempt to unravel the main strands of this web – though remembering that the interweaving is part of the very character of Elias's argument.

INVOLVEMENT AND DETACHMENT

How far it is possible for social science to be 'objective' has been a perennial topic ever since the turn of the century, when many of the great names of German philosophy, sociology and history debated the part played by 'values' in the pursuit of knowledge in their disciplines. Especially influential among later sociologists have been the views of Max Weber (1922b). Weber conceded that a social scientist's personal commitment to certain social or political beliefs can legitimately play a part in his or her selection of topics for research, and also in evaluating the practical implications of findings when research is complete. Nevertheless, in his two celebrated essays on 'Science as a vocation' (1919a)[2] and 'Politics as a vocation' (1919b), Weber drew a very sharp contrast between the roles of the politician, who is expected to give free play to social and political ideals in the conflicts and decisions of the day, and the role of the social scientist, who is expected to strive for 'value-freedom' (*Wertfreiheit*) in the interpretation of evidence. Some later discussion has tended to represent value-freedom as a goal to be striven for by the heroic, self-denying individual scientist. Even more commonly, the discussion has been framed in terms of a static polarity between total 'objectivity' and total 'subjectivity'. As with other static polarities, Elias believes this one to be seriously misleading.

Elias looks at the issue not as a narrow question of methodology in the social sciences but in the broadest relation to human knowledge and behaviour as a whole. It is a matter not of polar contrasts but of a continuum along which blends of 'involvement' and 'detachment' are located. Figure 4 is my heuristic representation of the continuum: note that it is open at both ends, because there are no zero-points, no *absolute* involvement and detachment. Elias's emphasis on this point is in clear contrast with Talcott Parsons's notion that the distinction between *affectivity* and *affective neutrality* (one of Parsons's 'pattern variables') is a clear-cut, dichotomous, mutually-exclusive choice between opposites (Parsons 1951: 58ff; cf. Elias 1968: 226–7).

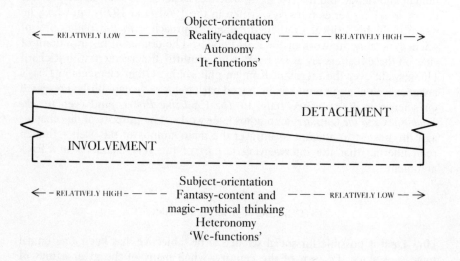

FIGURE 4

Elias explains that

One cannot say of a man's outlook in any absolute sense that it is detached or involved (or, if one prefers, 'rational' or 'irrational', 'objective' or 'subjective'). Only small babies, and among adults perhaps only insane people, become involved in whatever they experience with complete abandon to their feelings here and now; and again only insane people can remain totally unmoved by what goes on around them. (1956: 226)

Adult behaviour normally lies on a scale between these two extremes. Indeed, if standards of adult behaviour ever go too far in either direction, social life becomes impossible, for 'the very existence of ordered group life depends on the interplay in men's thought and actions of impulses in both directions, those that involve and those that detach keeping each other in check. They may clash and form alloys of many shades and kinds – however varied, it is the relation between the two which sets people's course' (1956: 226).

Nevertheless, the balance of involvement and detachment seen in normal adult behaviour varies between different human groups. Within those groups, it varies from one situation to another. It may vary greatly between different individuals in similar situations. By what criteria can people's patterns of speech, thought and activity – the data that sociologists, anthropologists, psychologists and historians in the main actually observe – be located on the continuum according to the balance of relative involvement or detachment they represent?

The criteria are neither purely 'psychological' nor purely 'social'. Elias chose the terms 'detachment' and 'involvement' – rather than more usual terms like rational and irrational, objective and subjective – precisely because 'they do not fall in line with linguistic usages which are based on the tacit assumption of the ultimate independence of the psychological and social properties of men' (1956: 227n.). At all costs, Elias wishes to avoid the mode of thinking in which psychological attributes and social attributes are conceived of as separate entities standing in some metaphysical cause-and-effect relation to each other.

Why this should be avoided is that '*The way in which individual members of a group experience whatever affects their senses, the meaning it has for them, depends on the standard forms of dealing with, and of thinking about, these phenomena*[3] *gradually evolved in their society*' (1956: 227; my italics). For example, in industrial-scientific societies people employ, as part of the knowledge they have inherited from the past and now take for granted, a very precise conceptual distinction between living and non-living things (Elias 1983d: 55). The distinction is highly 'reality-congruent' – it consistently 'works' with a high degree of certainty. Individual reactions when experiencing the forces of nature – a thunderstorm, a forest fire, even an illness – may still vary from individual to individual and situation to situation, but in scientific societies the *concepts* which all individuals now use in thinking, speaking and acting represent a relatively high degree of detachment. That is true of concepts like 'lightning', 'tree', 'disease', as well as 'electricity', 'cause', 'time', 'organism'. Today there is very little scope for lightning and fire – and only a little more for illness – to be interpreted in terms of the intentions of supernatural living beings and their meaning for the particular humans affected. In other words, the range of individual variations in detachment is limited by the public standards of detachment embodied in modes of thinking and speaking about nature (1956: 228). This is markedly less true of modes of thinking and speaking about things that happen in what we call 'society' as opposed to 'nature'.

Fantasy and reality

Any theory of scientific knowledge is inadequate, Elias stresses (1982a: 16), which does not explain how it developed out of non-scientific knowledge. Elias's own explanation of this rests on an extension of arguments first put forward in *The Civilizing Process*.

It is not an easy task to determine the structure of people's not-knowing and describe it using the words of people who already know. Members of industrial-scientific societies have great difficulties in understanding that members of societies at earlier stages of development were often unable to distinguish what they themselves distinguish easily and as a matter of course. Their assumption of a clear distinction between living and non-living things, for instance, can be so easily confirmed by testing against reality that it is hard to imagine that anyone can ever have failed to make it. Yet in fact this distinction took a very long time to develop to its present form. It did so, remarks Elias, 'as a result of the combined conceptual labour of a long line of generations in conjunction with the reality-testing of their concepts in the crucible of their experience' (1983d: 56). At some stage in the past, human beings could not yet know that a volcano or a raging sea which put their lives at risk were themselves not alive. The very phrase 'raging sea', though now only a metaphor, helps the effort of imagination needed to put oneself in the place of people who were not aware that the eruption or storm which destroyed human life did so unintentionally, and were blind physical processes.

Similarly, argues Elias (taking up a line of thought which runs back to Comte), people have not always had the wide knowledge of themselves as human beings necessary to be quite sure that a person could not transform him or herself into an animal or a tree. To be certain that that was not possible was all the more difficult because these things did happen in dreams: people could easily see themselves or other people changing, or being changed, into trees or birds or animals. Such themes now persist for us mainly in the magic and myths of folklore and children's tales: if they happen in dreams, we know they are only dreams. But how could human beings know, from the very beginning, that many things which happen in dreams could not happen in reality? Once again applying the 'sociogenetic ground rule' (see p. 50 above), Elias points out that 'For small children everywhere, the difference between fantasy and reality is blurred. They learn the distinction between fantasy and reality, like other items of knowledge, in accordance with the standard reached in their society' (1983d: 56). How distinctly the line is drawn between dreams and reality depends on public standards, which in industrial-scientific societies demand that people draw it very clearly and act accordingly. If they act out their dreams in a way not in line with the public standard their sanity may be questioned. Children have to learn this. But magical-mythical thinking, highly loaded with fantasy, is 'the primary mode of human experience' because it is part of the elementary make-up of human beings that 'their emotions, their affects and drives, are primarily attuned to other persons on whom they can fasten, rather than to lifeless things' (1983d: 63). This mode of experience does not simply cease to exist in industrial-scientific societies. As people grow up, it becomes a more or less submerged layer of the personality structure. Freud discovered it there and called it the 'unconscious' – which Elias considers a not wholly appropriate term 'for it refers to experiences which, though stored in the memory, as a result of some blockage cannot normally be remembered at will even though it continues indirectly to participate in the steering of men's conduct'. Blockages arise, and the depth of submersion increases, through learning the highly developed public standards just mentioned. But the magical-mythical mode of experience remains alive in adults in scientific societies, and is allowed relatively greater expression in some areas – cultural life and politics for example – than in the domain of the natural sciences themselves. It is also seen in the popular appeal of science fiction, astrology and parapsychology.

Science as a detour via detachment

If specific but differing balances between involvement and detachment are part of what is learned by every child in each particular society, the question is how the public standards available for learning are themselves formed and changed over time. It is here that Elias forges the link between the theory of involvement and detachment and the sociogenetic and psychogenetic theory expounded in *The Civilizing Process*: rising standards of detachment of knowledge require a similar rise over many generations in the standards of self-control that have to be learned in the course of growing up, the same transformation of personality structure. According to Elias, the 'scientification'[4] of human knowledge involves the same movement towards greater foresight seen in the social constraint towards self-constraint, 'psychologization' and rationalization (see chapter 4 above). Science, in fact, involves a species of detour behaviour – the detour via detachment. One of the results of a successful detour via detachment is greater human control of the forces – physical, biological or social – it is sought to understand.

To bring home how all these processes are connected, Elias refers to the fishermen in Edgar Allan Poe's story 'A descent into the maelstrom' (1845). It concerns three brothers whose boat is caught up in a deep whirlpool off the coast. One was swept overboard and drowned. The second clung to the boat, paralysed with fear. The third, however, though terrified enough, began to look around him and distance himself sufficiently from his immediate plight to notice that among the many circling objects being sucked down into the whirlpool, those of cylindrical shape were descending more slowly than the others. Shouting to his brother to do the same, he leapt into a barrel and threw himself overboard. His brother, incapacitated by fear, went down with their boat, but he himself survived – the whirlpool subsided before he and his barrel reached the bottom. The 'synoptic' picture he formed of regularities in the motion of objects made possible his survival. The conclusion Elias draws from Poe's story is that the fisherman who lived

began to think more coolly; and by standing back, by controlling his own fear, by seeing himself as it were from a distance, like a chessman forming a pattern with others on a board, he managed to turn his thoughts away from himself to the situation in which he found himself. It was then that he recognized the elements in the uncontrollable process which he could use in order to control its condition sufficiently for his own survival. Symbolically representing in his mind the structure and direction of the flow of events, he discovered a way of escape. In that situation, *the level of self-control and the level of process-control were, as can be seen, interdependent and complementary.* (1983d: 46; my italics)

The story of the fishermen represents what Elias refers to as a 'critical process', of a kind which can play a significant part in the growth of human knowledge. If it proves possible for people to observe the relations of elements in the process with a measure of detachment, relatively unimpeded by emotional fantasies and in a realistic manner, they may be able to form a symbolic representation – a 'theory', a 'model' – of their situation and, by means of actions based on that representation, change the situation. Of course, such 'critical processes' do not inevitably advance knowledge in this way, for at least four reasons. Sometimes the experience of imminent danger is so overwhelming that most people – like the second brother – are quite unable to control their fear and attain the measure of detachment necessary to see and seize any chances of control the situation may still offer. Sometimes the process has gone so far that such chances no longer exist – as, for example, if the boat had already gone too far down in the vortex before the fisherman drew his conclusions about cylindrical objects. Sometimes too, a cool head may not be best suited to survival in a dangerous situation; thinking once more of medieval warriors, Elias points out that to take a risk may be more realistic than a high measure of caution, to wade into battle with temper hot and courage high may be better suited to survival than sustained self-control and reflection (though, then again, in Montmorency's case, the latter would have been more advantageous). Finally, there are, needless to say, many instances where people hit upon a way of escaping from a critical situation more by accident than design (1983d: 47).

Nevertheless, detour behaviour has played a most important part in the growth of human knowledge. One of the earliest examples must have been the fashioning of stone weapons in advance of their use in hunting. Detour behaviour – a more general category than what is often referred to as 'deferred gratification' – is an essential element in what we call 'rationality', meaning the guiding of action by means of a symbolic representation of the connection between present means and future ends. Not all detour behaviour amounts to what we have come to call 'science', but all scientific knowledge involves an element of detour behaviour. In science, 'the primary tendency of man to take the short route from a strongly felt need to a precept for its satisfaction has become more or less subordinate to precepts and procedures which require a longer route' (1956: 229).

Relative autonomy and heteronomy

The scientific enterprise is thus marked by a relatively high measure of autonomy. Elias uses the expression 'relative autonomy' in several inter-related ways (1970a: 59). First, the various 'levels of integration of the universe' – by which Elias means principally the physical, biological and social levels of organization[5] – are relatively autonomous with respect to each other. In consequence, concepts and theories developed to handle forms of connectedness at each level are also relatively autonomous from and irreducible to each other. Second, scientific communities are relatively autonomous in their social *organization*. Third, scientific concepts and theories in the natural sciences embody the idea of a relatively autonomous, impersonal *order* in events; they are no longer so closely bound up with pre-scientific conceptions of the subject-matter. Fourth, by extension, the *values* which govern the pursuit of scientific knowledge are also described as relatively autonomous.

To say that the natural sciences are 'value-free' is a misuse of terms. Like other human activities, they do embody sets of values. But the values which play a key part in the natural sciences are not those directly related to promoting or impeding the interests of particular social groups, or to the personal wishes or wants of particular scientists. True, natural scientists' pursuit of their research may be influenced by personal wishes and wants: to help meet a specific need in a community to which they belong; to foster their own career; to find results in line with theories they have previously enunciated or results associated with the ideas and ideals of particular groups. In the natural sciences though, as Weber argued, these normally determine only the general direction of enquiry: they are held in check and balanced by other values which relate not to these narrower time-bound problems but to the broader, less time-bound problems defined by the theories and observations evolved by generations of investigators in each field. Natural scientists have often found that the 'direct encroachment upon their work by short-term interests or needs of specific interests or groups is liable to jeopardize the usefulness which the work may have in the end for themselves or their own group' (1956: 229). Their problems in consequence have a relatively high degree of autonomy *vis-à-vis* problems of the day. This is more obviously true of natural scientists working at the purer end of the continuum linking the 'pure' and 'applied' sciences; but truer of the natural sciences as a whole than of the social sciences, where academic endeavour is often closely linked in the social scientist's mind with the promotion of the interests of one social group or another. In the natural sciences, the question characteristic of people's involvement, 'What does it mean for me or us?', has become more subordinated to questions like 'What is it?' or 'How are these events connected with each other?'. The level of detachment represented by the latter questions has been buttressed and institutionalized as part of a scientific tradition transmitted by means of a highly specialized training, maintained by various forms of social control and socially induced emotional restraints. It has become embodied in the conceptual tools, the basic assumptions, the methods of speaking and thinking which scientists use.

This is why Elias speaks, not of the value-freedom of natural science, but of the *relative autonomy* of the values that most strongly steer scientific endeavour. He also speaks, conversely, of the intrusion of *heteronomous* evaluations, that is values related to personal or social wishes and interests from 'outside' the social institutions of science. Heteronomous values generally intrude less upon the natural sciences than on modes of speaking and thinking in the social sciences. In turn, and by definition, they play a lesser part in the social sciences than in the more involved, more emotive, modes of thinking and speaking used by people making their own way in society at large. Once again, it is necessary to repeat that there are no zero-points: knowledge is always both involved and detached, subject-related and object-related. It is the balance and blend between them that varies, which is why Elias prefers to speak in terms of relative autonomy and heteronomy rather than use more familiar expressions like 'objectivity' and 'bias'.

Double-binds in the growth of human knowledge

As the stock of knowledge has grown, concepts of the more detached, scientific type have gradually spread to people at large. In industrial societies, most people use concepts and explanations of natural events based on the idea of a course of events independent of any specific group of human observers, without being aware of the long struggle that was necessary to develop these modes of thinking. Certainly other more involved layers of experience persist alongside the more detached – as in the case of illness, where a scientific understanding of organisms may not quite drive out the question 'What have I done to deserve this?' But on the whole, for most people in industrial societies, it has come to seem that scientific methods and concepts are the obvious way of acquiring knowledge, and it is difficult for them to understand how human beings can ever not have seen something so obvious. Those who are rich in knowledge find it difficult to understand those who are poor in knowledge, just as powerful establishments usually find it difficult to understand less powerful outsider groups.

To illustrate this difficulty, Elias tells the story of a nineteenth-century French general who was ordered to march his African troops northwards to the coast as quickly as possible. After several days of rapid progress, there happened to occur an eclipse of the moon. The troops refused to continue their march. The eclipse, they said, was an omen. The prophet had given a sign to his people that they should interrupt whatever they were doing for two or three days; to defy this signal was very dangerous. Patiently, but not fully understanding their alarm, the general used stones and matchboxes to demonstrate the movements of the sun, moon and earth, and explained that an eclipse was thus a quite 'natural' event and therefore the troops need not worry. Their leaders had listened with interest and apparent understanding. So the general asked them to order the troops to resume the march. But no, they could not do that, because the prophet had given them a sign that they should interrupt what they were doing and . . . The general, now more puzzled and desperate, repeated his demonstration of the mechanics of a lunar eclipse. The troops' leaders listened again, thanked the general and assured him that he was certainly right, but the darkening of the moon was the doing of the prophet and his warning could not be disregarded . . .

The incomprehension in this case is perfectly reciprocal. The general, an innocent representative of an industrial-scientific society, thinks his own mode of experience and thinking is simply 'rational', something that can be understood by any human being to whom it is explained. The troops, on the other hand, find his explanation irrelevant, because it does not answer the question uppermost in their minds. Their question above all was not 'What are the *mechanics* of this event?' but 'What is the *meaning* of this event *for us?*' That question demands an answer in terms of a communication from one living being to another, and the traditional knowledge of their tribe provides an answer in these terms. In such a society, as in ours, it is a social stock of knowledge handed down from generation to generation that forms the basis for the orientation of living generations. Unlike most twentieth-century anthropologists, however, Elias is not satisfied to leave the matter there: it is not enough to say that some human beings see the world one way and others see it in another. He sets out to explain *why* they do.

He argues that the two modes of explanation typified by the general and his troops – usually called 'scientific' and 'animistic' – correspond to two types of personality structure which also correspond to very different social circumstances. The clue to animism lies in the higher level of involvement and emotionality of experience and thinking, and the more limited scope of knowledge, which in turn are linked to a more limited capacity for controlling dangers, which in turn again helps to maintain a high level of involvement and emotionality. This characteristic vicious circle or *double-bind* (a concept prominent in many of Elias's later writings[6]) operated to impede the growth of human knowledge for very long periods of the species' existence:

Wholly dependent on forces whose course they could neither foresee nor influence to any considerable extent, they lived in extreme insecurity, and, being most vulnerable and insecure they could not help feeling strongly about every occurrence they thought might affect their lives; they were too deeply involved to look at natural events, like distant observers, calmly. Thus, on the one hand, they had little chance of controlling their own strong feelings in relation to nature and of forming more detached concepts of natural events as long as they had little control over them; and they had, on the other hand, little chance of extending their control over their non-human surroundings as long as they could not gain greater mastery over their own strong feelings in relation to them and increase their control over themselves. (1956: 231)

The argument is, then, that extreme insecurity and hazard to life in the face of uncontrollable natural forces prevents people making the detour via detachment necessary to develop knowledge and explanations of the impersonal technical type that can be used in increasing the controllability of natural forces. Their knowledge remains innocently egocentric and emotionally involved and, as long as it does, impersonal causal explanations remain meaningless to them, because they do not meet their emotional and cognitive needs. The method

people use in acquiring knowledge is interdependent with the substance of the
knowledge they already possess and especially with their basic image of the
world. Where the world is experienced – according to a corpus of knowledge
and modes of thinking transmitted from earlier generations – as a world of
spirits and wilful acts, then the aim is to discover knowledge of hidden aims and
intentions behind events. In this context, relevant knowledge may comprise
principally tales, proverbs and practical prescriptions passed on from generation
to generation, interpreted by and expressed through priests, witches, oracles
and so on.

That for the greater part of its existence mankind has been entrapped in this
double-bind explains why knowledge in the past grew immeasurably more
slowly than in industrial-scientific societies. Much the largest part of that
existence was passed in the long ages of the palaeolithic era. In emphasizing the
force of the double-bind in the extreme insecurity which prevailed then, Elias
observes that 'Humans at that stage lived like the wild animals they hunted,
always on the alert' (1983d: 66). (This remark drew the ire of anthropologists
upon Elias – see chapter 10 below.) Even much later there was only a very
gradual changeover from animistic to causal modes of thought, the two
coexisting for long periods; Elias notes that Plutarch, for example, records both
astronomic and astrological accounts of heavenly bodies, apparently regarding
them as of equal worth and in no way conflicting. Nevertheless, though vestiges
of magical-mythical thinking persist (including in such dangerous contexts as
the rivalry of the superpowers, 1983d: 102), it has steadily lost ground as a
mode of experience during the development of industrial-scientific societies.

In every known case animistic modes of thought have preceded more
scientific, impersonal or causal modes. Elias speaks of 'earlier-stage' and 'later-
stage' structures of thought and experience – as indeed he does of earlier and
later stages of social development in general. This runs against conventional
anthropological wisdom, but Elias is defiant. He is rather scornful of Claude
Lévi-Strauss's work. Lévi-Strauss attempts to demonstrate that at a deep level
the structure of human thinking is everywhere the same, and thus limits himself
to at most a Linnean-style descriptive taxonomy of static surface differences.
Elias describes Lévi-Strauss's book *The Savage Mind* (1962) as 'a sophisticated
artefact, a riddle explained by a riddle' (1983d: 117n.). Lévi-Strauss, he argues,
deprives himself of any chance of reaching a genuine understanding of earlier-
stage human groups by his evident hostility to any developmental ordering of
evidence, even though evidence about different forms of thought can only be
brought to life in developmental terms. The reason for Lévi-Strauss's hostility
is his fear that the ordering of earlier- and later-stage people in terms of a
process of development will imply a lowering of the human dignity of the
earlier. The opposite is in fact the case, according to Elias. For only by
understanding the thought and experience of earlier-stage people in terms of
their position in a sequential order can one come to understand and explain
how later-stage forms of thinking came to develop. That is why Elias holds in
much higher regard the older work of Lucien Lévy-Bruhl (1910, 1922), who
documented very clearly the different categorial structure of thought and
experience of earlier-stage people. Unfortunately, Lévy-Bruhl used the

expression 'pre-logical' as a general description of their intellectual operations, and although he later withdrew the term, it was a mistake symptomatic of his inability actually to explain how later-stage modes of thought develop out of earlier. Lévy-Bruhl's weakness, argues Elias, was that he remained within the philosophers' tradition, 'which makes "reason" appear to be an unchanging form and knowledge a changeable content, [and] sets up an artificial barrier which prevents those brought up in that tradition from seeing clearly that human beings, at a stage when they knew less, could not help connecting events differently from groups with a larger knowledge inheritance' (1983d: 116–17nn.). Elias's own theory of involvement and detachment, and of the double-bind impediments in the growth of human knowledge, offers a clear explanation of why people who were entirely our equals in terms of biology and mental capacity nevertheless thought in specific ways different to our own.

The triad of basic controls

Elias sums up much of the argument so far about knowledge and long-term social development in the idea of the *triad of basic controls* (1970: 156–7; cf. 1956: 231–3; 1983d: 66). The stage of development attained by a society, he contends, can be identified and measured in relation to:

1 The extent of its capacity for exerting control (Elias uses the term 'control-changes') over non-human forces and events – the 'forces of nature' as they are often called).
2 The extent of its capacity for control over interpersonal relationships and events, or 'social forces'.
3 The extent to which each of the members of a society has control over him or herself as an individual.

These three kinds of control develop and function in interdependence with each other and with the development of knowledge but, Elias emphasizes, *this interdependence is not to be understood in terms of simple parallel increases* of all three in step with each other.

The first type of control, which corresponds broadly to technological development, has tended gradually to increase in the course of the overall long-term development of human societies, though there have often been setbacks. Again, in very long-term perspective, the second type of control-chances – human control over social processes has tended gradually to increase. But the connection between the two is not simple and direct.

Paradoxically, says Elias, the gradual increase in human beings' capacity for taking a more detached view of natural forces and gaining more control over them – a process which has also accelerated over the long term – has tended to *increase* the difficulties they have in extending their control over social relationships *and* over their own feelings in thinking about them. The reason for this paradox is that as humans have gradually come to understand natural forces more, fear them less and use them more effectively for human ends, this has gone hand in hand with specific changes in human relationships. More and more people have tended to become more and more interdependent with each other in longer chains and denser webs. (If this sounds rather abstract, think of the example of the early 'hydraulic civilizations' of Mesopotamia and Egypt where, as archaeologists and historians have long been aware, the harnessing of the waters for irrigation and the control of hitherto disastrous floods necessarily went hand in hand with the emergence of much more elaborate political and economic organization.) The growth of the web of social interdependence tends to outstrip people's understanding of it. The same process which diminishes dangers and feelings of insecurity in the face of natural forces tends also to increase the dangers and feelings of insecurity in face of 'social forces' – the forces stemming from people's dependence on each other for the satisfaction of their needs and for their security. Elias puts the point vividly:

It is as if first thousands, then millions, then more and more millions walked through this world with their hands and feet chained together by invisible ties. No-one is in charge. No-one stands outside. Some want to go this way, others that way. They fall upon each other and, vanquishing or defeated, still remain chained to each other. No-one can regulate the movements of the whole unless a great part of them are able to understand, to see as it were from the outside, the whole patterns they form together. And they are not able to visualize themselves as part of these larger patterns because, being hemmed in and moved uncomprehendingly hither and thither in ways which none of them intended, they cannot help being preoccupied with the urgent, narrow and parochial problems which each of them has to face . . . They are too deeply involved to look at themselves from without. Thus what is formed of nothing but human beings acts upon each of them, and *is experienced by many as an alien external force not unlike the forces of nature.* (1956: 232; my italics)

These seemingly alien forces bring about, among other things, frequent and unforeseen gains for some and losses for others, so they go hand in hand with tensions and frictions between interdependent groups. And 'tests of strength and the use of organized force serve often as costly means of adjustment to changes within this tangle of interdependencies; on many of its levels no other means of adjustment exist' (1956: 232).

The bearing of this problem on the growth of human knowledge becomes clear if the third of the triad of controls – people's differing capacity for control over themselves as individuals – is brought into the picture. Elias argues that, on the one hand, when people are in a situation of vulnerability and insecurity, it is difficult for them to control more fully their own strong feelings about events deeply affecting their lives, and to approach those events with more detachment, as long as they have little ability to control the course of events. On the other hand, it is also difficult for them to extend their understanding and control of these events so long as they cannot approach them with greater detachment and gain greater control over themselves. This double-bind can obstruct the growth of knowledge in respect of all three levels of the triad – the always interconnected levels of the 'technological', the 'social' and the 'psychological' to put it perhaps too simply – even at later stages of social development (1983d: 66). Indeed the interconnections between the three may operate not merely to impede the growth of knowledge and control but to put the process into reverse gear:

Nothing in our experience suggests that part-processes of this kind must always work in the same direction. Some of the phases in which they went into reverse are known from the past. Increasing social tensions and strife may go hand in hand with both a decrease of people's ability to control, and an increase in the fantasy-content of their ideas about, natural as well as social events. (1956: 231)

Despite all double-binds and reversals, today it is generally said that the natural sciences are 'more advanced' than the social sciences. Elias does not agree that – as is often asserted – this is because the subject-matter[7] studied by social scientists is inherently less susceptible to investigation by methods yielding a high degree of certainty. The general aim of scientific activity is the same in both fields: it is (when 'stripped of a good many philosophical encrustations') to find out in what way perceived data are connected with each other, and there is no reason to suppose social data are less accessible to human comprehension. What is different, he concedes, is the relationship between 'subjects' and 'objects', and this sometimes makes it more difficult to make the detours via detachment necessary to advance scientific understanding of society. In the social sciences, 'objects' are also 'subjects'. Investigators form part of the patterns they are investigating. They cannot help experiencing these patterns, directly or indirectly, as participants from within – indeed their own involvement is one of the conditions for comprehending the problems they are trying to solve as scientists. Yet, necessary as is their involvement, the greater the stresses and strains and the greater the level of insecurity to which they and their groups are exposed, the more difficult it is for them to perform the mental operation of detachment essential to any scientific enterprise.

This balance of involvement and detachment is never easy to achieve, and all the harder when the practical problems of one's own day are very pressing. Elias notes that the classic sociologists of the nineteenth and early twentieth century – people like Marx, Spencer, Tönnies and many others – tried to discover an inherent order in the social development of mankind, so as to put in long-term perspective the problems of their own age. Yet so involved were they in these problems that they often ended up, in spite of themselves, by in effect doing the opposite: interpreting the whole history of mankind in the light of the fears, beliefs and struggles of their own time. It is not surprising: social scientists as involved participants cannot be entirely untouched by the we-images (to use a term developed in *The Established and the Outsiders* – see above p. 119) of classes, nations or sects to which they belong. These we-images are self-justifications usually composed of an amalgam of realistic observations and collective fantasies which serve as motive forces of action. To sift out the realistic from the mythical elements is not only difficult for anyone whose group is involved in struggle with others, but to do so may weaken the group's cohesion and even its capacity to survive (1956: 236).

In the face of such difficulties, some social scientists have from time to time declined to stand aside, and argued it to be their duty to act as partisans (usually on behalf of underdog groups in contemporary struggles).[8] Elias does not agree with them. What he does argue is that, while the problem of the intrusion of heteronomous values is especially evident in the social sciences and can never be eliminated entirely, it adds perspective to recognize that the growth of natural scientific knowledge too has, in the past and even today, raised severe emotional resistance in human beings, and come into conflict with heteronomous values.

THE DEVELOPMENT OF THE NATURAL SCIENCES

Too often the history of the natural sciences is seen in purely 'intellectual' terms. Yet, says Elias, it is not just 'the intellect' but human beings in the round who are involved in the pursuit of knowledge (1983d: 67). In the case of 'natural' as much as social processes, a high fantasy-content can make knowledge emotionally much more attractive to people than knowledge that is more reality orientated. It is not a matter of a simple contest between coldly 'rational', purely intellectual arguments. The picture of the world which emerges from scientific discovery may entail a profound emotional shock.

Elias's favourite illustration is the transition from a geocentric to a heliocentric view of the universe – from the medieval, Ptolemaic view that the sun moved around the earth to the Copernican view that Earth and other planets circled the sun. It is misleading to think of the supersession of the earlier theory by the later as if it were merely a matter of which theory agreed better with measurements and calculations. Not only did the heliocentric view run counter to the unreflected evidence of people's senses – quite obviously the earth was firm under their feet, not moving, and they *saw* the sun move around the earth every day – but it also conflicted traumatically with their image of themselves and their place in the universe.

The geocentric world-image was an expression of the unreflected self-centredness which is an aspect of people's primary form of experience. For thousands of years human beings had experienced the heavenly bodies as moving around themselves and thus around the earth as the centre of the universe. As a matter of course they perceived the whole world as made for men. The severe jolt to humans' elementary self-love entailed in the assertion of learned men that the earth was moving around the sun is often forgotten today. (1983d: 68)

How, then, was it possible for people to give up a picture of the world they found emotionally highly satisfactory, and put in its place a picture which, though more realistic, relegated human beings from a central to a peripheral position and was thus emotionally less comfortable? The question is not relevant only to this one instance. Other advances in scientific knowledge have also involved comparable jolts to people's pictures of themselves. Darwin's theory of the evolution of species, including the human species, affronted the established picture of mankind's uniqueness among the animals. Freud's recognition of the part played by animalic drives in the life of human beings, even in the life of children, raised similar difficulties.[9] In each case, the new picture was accepted only after a lengthy struggle. In the case of the heliocentric theory in astronomy, the struggle lasted the best part of a century. It is well-known how Galileo, the champion of the Copernican view, was hauled before the authorities of the Church in 1633 and forced to relinquish his advocacy of it (though privately continuing to maintain that *'Eppur si muove'* – 'And yet it *does* move').

That story – and the similar opposition faced later by Darwin and Freud from religious groups and from rival groups of scientists to whom their theories were unpalatable – serves to bring power-balances back into the picture of how human knowledge grows. Yet the problem still remains why, if these new theories were emotionally difficult for many to accept and were opposed by powerful social groups, they none the less gained widespread acceptance in the end. Part of Elias's answer lies in the practical improvements in orientation and control made possible, if not directly by a theory such as the heliocentric account of heavenly bodies then by the broader stream of scientific investigation of which it was a key part: one thinks of the connection between Galileo's theoretical work and improved clocks, or between Boyle's theory of the properties of gases and the eventual development of steam engines. Elias does not pretend, however, that such an instrumental view is enough to account for the eventual triumph of ideas initially unpalatable to many people. He also argues that the admittedly arduous reception of Copernican astronomy coincided with the Reformation, when the Church's monopoly of the means of orientation was partially breaking down (and that the muzzling of Galileo occurred during the Counter Reformation attempt to reassert that monopoly). For, as Elias points out, 'the central social function of knowledge is as a means of orientation'. Therefore,

As the individual orientation of every member of a society depends on the means of orientation available there, groups of people who are able to monopolize the guardianship, transmission, and development of a society's means of orientation hold in their hands very considerable power chances, especially if the monopoly is centrally organized. (1982a: 37)

Once again, Elias is here harking back to the idea of the monopoly mechanism first described in the context of state-formation, and to the extension of it in his discussion of established-outsiders relationships: in principle any resource which people need may serve to enhance the power-chances of any group which succeeds in monopolizing control of it. The medieval Church was a large-scale organization which succeeded to a notable extent in monopolizing the basic means of orientation – revealed knowledge as opposed to theoretical-empirical knowledge – over much of Europe. The monopoly was guarded from dissenters partly by persuasion, but also by torture, fire and sword.

Any attempt to explain the rise of a scientific type of knowledge will be unsuccessful, says Elias, if it does not take account of the partial breakdown of the medieval Church's *armed* monopolization of the European fund of knowledge. Only against that background can the subsequent slow emergence of *scientific establishments* and a new form of specialization in the means of orientation be seen in perspective (1982a: 38). The formation of associations of scientists, organizationally relatively autonomous with respect to the heteronomous interests and values of political and religious authorities, eventually resulted in the scientific mode of acquiring knowledge becoming the one which is taken for granted as 'natural' and 'obvious' – as 'natural' and 'obvious' as it was in the Middle Ages to think in terms of the revealed knowledge of the scriptures.

God's laws

The transition was of course a gradual one and, while escaping from perceived religious ideas in certain critical ways, early scientists retained for some time traces of religious motivation. The break with medieval thought can be seen in Galileo's discovery of regularities in the motion of falling bodies by studying the motion of downward rolling balls.[10] By then, Elias points out (1987b: 7), Galileo could draw on a great fund of human knowledge which enabled him to be quite certain that the regularities of falling bodies that he observed at a particular time and place, and represented as a general rule through mathematical symbols, would be the same the world over. By then, concepts like 'law of nature', 'causation' and 'substance' were the common property of learned men. These concepts had not always existed. They had been only gradually developed and, because of human beings' unique capacity for transmitting an accumulating stock of knowledge from generation to generation through symbols, they had been *learned* by later generations in such a way that they were taken for granted as self-evident and 'obvious'. But a couple of centuries or so before Galileo, these concepts were not available in the stock of knowledge (the words may have existed, but the meaning was different) – they were not available in society for thinkers to use and reflect upon, and the assumption that immutable laws are the same universally was not well established. What was relatively new in the age of Galileo was the experience that it was not necessary to rely on the authority of scripture or other forms of revelation in order to discover the 'laws' that God had given to His creation, the 'universal laws of nature' (1974a: 23). We know, for example, from Robert Merton's classic sociological investigation of early scientists in seventeenth-century England (1938) and even from the writings of the great Isaac Newton himself, how strong was the religious motivation behind the pursuit of eternal laws of nature.

The assumption of immutable, universal laws proved to be reasonably well-founded in the case of many physical events, but much less so in the study of biological, social and even certain other kinds of physical processes. It is one of Elias's characteristic arguments that the notion of 'universal laws' has remained dominant in the philosophers' theories of scientific knowledge long after it has lost its unique place in the work of actual scientists. 'Laws' are not the only mode in which connections between observed events may be symbolically represented and knowledge transmitted from generation to generation. In continuing for so long to focus too exclusively on theories of the law-like type as essential features of science, the philosophers have, he says, failed to question the scale of values which had found earlier expression in theology and was taken over as seemingly self-evident by classical physics and philosophy: a scale according to which the discovery of something eternal and unchanging behind the observable changes is the highest goal in the human quest for knowledge (1974a: 23).

A 'model of models'

For a very long time, philosophers of science used classical physics, with its apparently universal and timeless general 'laws', as the unique model of what a true science should be. Social scientists especially have often suffered feelings of inferiority on behalf of their own disciplines when confronted with this – for them – unattainable, inimitable ideal. Elias, like other bolder spirits among social scientists, dismisses as erroneous the notion that all scientists must follow the archetypal model of physics (1974a: 24). That assumption rests to some extent on the *atomistic fallacy*, according to which the properties of composite units can always be explained in terms of the properties of their smallest component parts studied in isolation from each other. He spells out what that rather abstract proposition means by advancing a 'model of models', a schematic representation of how the data investigated by the various sciences differ, and how therefore the types of concepts, theories and explanations used also differ correspondingly (1956: 242–4).

The 'model of models' places the aggregate units of observation characteristic of each kind of science along a continuum. Towards one pole are those which are merely congeries, agglomerations, heaps or multitudes, whose constituents are associated with each other very loosely and temporarily, and may exist independently of each other without changing their characteristic properties.[11] Towards the other pole are units whose parts are much more highly organized and interconnected; in 1956 Elias referred to these as 'self-regulating open systems or processes', although later he assiduously avoided terms like 'system' and 'self-regulating' because of their excessively close resemblance to the terminology of Talcott Parsons and the functionalist school. Whatever one calls them, we are here concerned with complex units composed of many levels, of systems within systems, of processes within processes. The components are highly interdependent and the composite whole is highly structured; in fact 'functional interdependence' from the viewpoint of the component parts is the same thing as 'structure' viewed from the angle of the whole (1974a: 26).

Along the continuum in between the poles are many intermediary models, graded according to the degree to which their constituents are differentiated and integrated. There is no sharp dichotomy between the two extremes, and the models appropriate to the various disciplines overlap more than is often recognized.

However, says Elias, as one moves along the continuum from one pole to the other, methods of investigation developed at one level lose their usefulness, and become at most auxiliary tools. This is true, for example, of the idea of 'independent variables'. There is a view that the units studied by social scientists differ from those of the physical scientists mainly in involving the interplay of a larger number of 'variables' or 'factors' in more complicated ways, that the mathematics needed to express this interplay may also be more complicated, but that essentially the type of theory may be much the same. Elias disagrees. As one moves away from the congeries pole, it becomes steadily less useful to think of the aggregate unit under investigation as a heap of potentially independent variables, each one of which may be moved separately to observe its effects while everything else remains the same: the 'experimental method' of classical physics.

By extension, the general 'law' as a model of a scientific theoretical explanation also becomes less and less useful as we move along the continuum of models. For one of the tacit assumptions underlying the search for 'laws' is that the entities one conceptualizes, observes and manipulates are connected in a necessary and unchanging pattern, and do not change their properties irreversibly if the connections between them are broken. (In contrast with, for example, an animal – which may never be quite the same if one 'experimentally manipulates' some vital internal organ!) Regularities best suited to expression in the form of an invariant, timeless 'law' are those where the relationship between entities is impermanent although it has a permanent pattern: it can start and stop innumerable times without affecting the behaviour of other constituents of any wider nexus. Elias is thinking of such cases as Galileo rolling balls down a slope, or his discovery of the regularity in the motion of a pendulum, or Boyle's Law relating the volume and pressure of gases. 'General laws for particular cases, in short, are instruments for the solution of problems whose referential frame is conceived as a congeries' (1956: 244).[12] As we move along the continuum further away from congeries, first 'structure theories' and then various kinds of 'process theories' become more useful than law-like theories – as we shall see in a moment.

Elias's 'model of models' sheds light on a number of issues in the history of the sciences.

First, even 'those time-honoured intellectual operations known as induction and deduction' change their character to some extent as one moves along the continuum of models. Traditionally, in the context of the model associated with classical physics, induction and deduction 'are closely linked up with intellectual movements up and down between discrete and isolated universals – which may be general concepts, laws, propositions or hypotheses – and an infinite multitude of particular cases which are also conceived as capable of preserving their significant characteristics if they are studied in isolation independently of all other connections' (1956: 244). But, nearing the other pole of the model of models, where the composite units under study are much more highly organized, it is more a matter of movements up and down between models of the whole and models of its constituent parts. Elias suggests the terms 'analysis' and 'synopsis' for the operations in their new guise. Analysis means those steps in research where theoretical attention is focused on the constituent parts, with the larger unit treated more as background. Synopsis means the phases of research where attempts are made to construct a more coherent theoretical representation of the whole, bringing together more or less unconnected theoretical representations of constituent parts. The solution of theoretical problems depends in the long run on co-ordinating and balancing both analysis and synopsis. In the short run, however, synopsis may run ahead of analysis, resulting in rather speculative theories like those of many sociologists in the nineteenth century – the 'system-builders' whose models of the history of humanity as a whole outran the acquisition of detailed anthropological and archaeological knowledge available later. Or analysis may outstrip synopsis, resulting in a plethora of unconnected observational and theoretical fragments, as has been true of much twentieth-century sociology.

Reverting to the natural sciences, the model of models throws light on the historic controversy among biologists between the 'mechanists' and the 'vitalists'. The former argued that the functioning of organisms could be explained by analogy with mechanical models, the latter that it could only be explained by reference to some vital spark which marked off living from non-living matter. As Elias points out, the controversy arose because *both* sides accepted the erroneous proposition, again derived from the model of classical physics, that an explanation for the properties of a composite whole must be sought through studies of the properties of constituent parts. Nowadays it is easier to grasp that while it is true that living organisms consist of non-living chemical elements – principally carbon, oxygen and hydrogen – the chemical properties of these elements in isolation tell us nothing like the whole story: it is the way they are structured and organized that produces the characteristics of organisms. To put it another way, though living organisms consist, like everything else, of non-living chemical elements, they cannot be *reduced* to chemical properties. Thus neither the mechanists nor the vitalists were wholly correct.

A similar fallacy, says Elias, underlies discussions of the relationship between the behaviour of humans and that of other animals. Attempts have been made (notably by behaviourist psychologists like B. F. Skinner, 1953) to show that humans learn and behave according to just the same mechanisms as other animals. And, in part, they do. But the functioning and structure of entities which embody a higher level of organization and control cannot be understood entirely in terms of entities which are less highly organized. *Homo sapiens* may share descent with the other primates but, among other things, the transition to greater cortical dominance transformed the functioning of human beings overall: 'While people function partly as other animals do, as a whole they function and behave in a way no animal does' (1956: 248).

Finally, similar problems underlie discussions of 'the individual' and 'society' – of which we shall have much more to say presently.

Structure theories and process theories

Even the physical sciences began relatively soon to develop beyond 'atomism' in its simplest form towards what might be called 'structuralism' – were that not 'a term now much abused', as Elias wryly remarks (1974a: 33). In chemistry it became apparent in the course of the nineteenth century that simple quantitative or 'empirical' formulae were insufficient. It was necessary to know not just the quantities of atoms constituting a substance, but how they were connected: the *structure* of the molecule. Take the formula $C_6H_{12}O_6$ – the sugar hexose. In fact it is a formula shared by many different sugars – glucose, fructose, etc. – each with different chemical properties. There are innumerable such 'isomers' known to chemists. In order to investigate and explain these different properties, it proved necessary to build theoretical representations of the spatial arrangements of the atoms – that is, three-dimensional models. This necessity is vividly clear in the well-known story of one of the major scientific breakthroughs of our time, the discovery of the double helix structure of the DNA molecule by Crick and Watson (see Watson 1968), which Elias discusses at length (1974a: 34–8).

Though structure theories differ from law-like theories in that they do not abstract from the spatial dimensions but embody them in three-dimensional models, this too is inadequate for the investigation of certain problems in the natural sciences. For these, *process theories* are necessary. Process theories embody *four*-dimensional models; they involve both the spatial dimensions and time. They are models of *structured processes of change* over time.

One of the first process theories which proved to have a high measure of reality-congruence was the theory of evolution of species (1974a: 40–1). How such a theory – and a whole mode of research – differs from a non-processual one can be seen clearly in the work of biologists who opposed evolutionary theories. The comparative anatomists Georges Cuvier (1769–1832) and Richard Owen (1804–92) saw it as the essence of the scientist's task to discover what was unchanging behind all the variety of living things. Cuvier assumed that the different classes and types of animals were eternally set in the same mould, and then attempted through comparative studies of their anatomical features to arrive at universal laws applicable to all animals, or to particular classes of animals. For example, one of his propositions was that all animals with white blood which have a heart also have respiratory organs, and that where these exist there is also a liver; where there is no heart and no bronchi there is also no liver. Richard Owen shared the aim of discovering a law-like ideal-type behind all the variety of data; he worked out a theoretical model by means of which he was able to reduce all the huge variety of vertebrates to a single archetype representing the universals of the vertebrate skeleton.

In contrast, evolutionary biologists from Lamarck to Darwin realized that the types are not eternally fixed but are rather stages or phases in a process. It was this which provoked such opposition to theories of evolution, not just from scientists in the tradition of Cuvier and Owen but also in society at large from those who believed in the literal truth of the biblical account of creation.

The career of Georges Cuvier also provides a striking illustration of the hazards of persisting in the search for law-like one-way causal theories in a context which calls for processual ones (1982a: 29). Two schools of biologists, led respectively by Georges Cuvier and Geoffrey Saint-Hilaire, disputed for many years whether the way of life of an animal determines the structure of its organs or whether the organic structure of an animal determines its manner of life. The theory of the evolution of species, especially in Darwin's hands, showed why neither of these static positions is tenable. The Cuvier–Saint-Hilaire dispute is only one of many examples of how the reduction to static positions of what can only be understood as a continuous process of change leaves people with two polar alternatives, both equally untenable. Elias calls this *process-reduction*, and instances of it abound even today in the social sciences.

A qualification and clarification is now necessary. Elias is *not* arguing that law-like theories belong exclusively to physics, that structure theories are peculiar to chemistry, nor that process theories alone are useful in biological and social sciences and nowhere else. He is careful to say (1982a: 34) that law-like and process theories do not exclude each other; they are often complementary. He does argue, though, that their cognitive weight in relation to each other can and does shift drastically. The quest for animal universals, for instance, has not entirely lost all value (with modern molecular biology, universals are again under investigation, though at a different level from Cuvier's and Owen's work), but it did diminish greatly when Darwin published his process theory of biological evolution. In terms of his model of models, Elias contends that

Not all frames of reference of physical problems cluster around the congeries pole of the model. Not all frames of reference of biological or sociological problems have their equivalent close to the other pole. They are, in each of these fields of inquiry, more widely scattered than is often assumed. (1956: 243n.)

He points out (1982a: 34) that modern cosmology – very much a branch of physics – also involves process theories.[13] In the search for an answer to how stars, galaxies and the whole universe evolved, Newtons's laws and, even more, Einstein's law-like theories of relativity are an indispensable means of orientation. But the actual explanations offered by contemporary cosmologists are models of processes in which stars and galaxies form and decay. Process models actually embody a different kind of explanation from law-like theories. They offer 'genetic' explanations of why one thing happens after another in a long sequence of directional (though not always irreversible) events. Support for Elias's view can be found in *The Cosmic Blueprint* (1987) by the theoretical physicist Paul Davies, who argues for the limited relevance to cosmology of the old Newtonian and thermodynamic paradigms, which presented the universe 'either as a sterile machine, or in a state of degeneration and decay', and that 'self-organizing' – but blind and unplanned – processes are to be found in all branches of science.[14] In strikingly similar fashion to Davies, the biologist Richard Dawkins has argued, in *The Blind Watchmaker* (1986), that 'the evidence of evolution reveals a universe without design'.

CONCLUSION

Elias's discussion of involvement and detachment is not narrowly concerned with the problem of 'objectivity'. It raises the whole problem of the long-term development of human knowledge and the place of the sciences within it. Not many of the assumptions of the mainstream philosophy of science go unquestioned by Elias. His views stem not from any philosophical tradition but from the practical example of the three great figures he always acknowledges as pioneers of process theories: Darwin, Comte and Marx. Having dwelt particularly in this chapter on the growth of the natural sciences, we can now turn to Elias's particular concern: process theories in the social sciences.

8

The Development of the Social Sciences

If process theories in the natural sciences involve four dimensions, process theories in the social sciences go one better. They are – or ought to be, according to Elias – based on a five-dimensional image of human beings (in the plural). The fifth dimension is *experience*. That is to say, the models involve not only the directly visible 'behavioural' aspects of human activity in the four dimensions of space and time but also the 'experiential' aspects of human thinking, feeling and psychological drives. While these experiential aspects are not directly accessible to observation in the same way as bodily movements, they are nevertheless accessible to human observation through the examination of linguistic and other symbols carrying meaningful messages from one person to another (1983d: 116n.).

That the 'objects' studied by social scientists are themselves also 'subjects' certainly makes more difficult the quest for such five-dimensional process theories.

First, there is a sense in which a double self-distanciation is necessary to achieve the required degree of relative detachment. In *The Court Society* (1969a: 245–6) Elias makes an analogy with a man climbing up a spiral staircase from one floor of a tower to the next. Reaching a higher floor, not only is his perspective on the landscape outside different from what he saw from the lower floor but he can in his mind's eye (so to speak) look down to see himself on the lower floor from which he came. Moving up to a still higher floor, his view of the landscape changes once more, but now he is also able to look down and observe himself observing himself still further down. What Elias is suggesting is that the advance in 'psychologization', or in people's ability to observe themselves, which took place in early modern Europe (see pp. 101–2 above) corresponds to the first stage of climbing the spiral staircase. The growth of social science then requires a further climb, to the level where people can observe themselves as people observing themselves.[1] Phenomenologists like

Alfred Schutz, so widely influential in sociology since the 1960s, have discussed in more abstract and static terms the problems which arise from sociologists' objects also being subjects, and Anthony Giddens (1976: 162) for instance has spoken of a 'double hermeneutic' involved in sociological research.[2] But such statements differ from Elias's viewpoint in not recognizing that the growth of social scientific knowledge and the human ability to perform such a 'double hermeneutic' is itself a long-term structured process of development.

Secondly, the idea of a structured process of change which moves in a discernible direction and yet is not planned or intended by anyone is even more difficult to grasp in social life than in natural events. Long as it may have taken to overcome the idea of the forces of nature as manifestations of the intentions and whims of supernatural agents, it is even more difficult to see that many social processes are also unplanned and unintended. The inadequacy in the natural sciences of voluntaristic explanations – explanations in terms of the intentions directing a sequence of events – arise from the fact that there we are not dealing with voluntary actions at all. In contrast, social events and changes within human societies quite clearly *are* connected with people's voluntary actions and plans. It therefore seems rather obvious that voluntaristic explanations are appropriate in the social sciences. It is less obvious and more difficult to grasp that the intentional sequences of events planned and intended separately by many interdependent people interweave with each other to produce structured, directional processes of change which no-one has planned. (1977b: 131).

Third, structured processes of change with which social scientists have to deal often differ in an important respect from those studied by biologists or cosmologists. Darwin was dealing with *irreversible* processes of biological evolution, in contrast with social processes like the division of social functions, state-formation or civilizing processes which can and do go into reverse without any change at the biological level (Elias 1977b: 133). That is why Elias tries to avoid speaking of 'evolution' in a social context, preferring 'development' as more appropriate. This potential reversibility of many social processes helps to make it more difficult to discern that they are nevertheless structured.

STRUCTURED PROCESSES: ECONOMIC AND SOCIAL

If it is so difficult, how did it eventually come about that certain writers began to perceive impersonal, unplanned but structured processes unfolding in social life? Like many other sociologists (such as Nisbet 1967), Elias sees the period before and after the French Revolution as an important stage in the development of the social sciences. These sciences were not, however, just the product of a conservative political response to the excesses unleashed by the ideas of the eighteenth-century *philosophes*; just as the Revolution cannot be seen simply as the result[3] of the propagation of 'enlightened' ideas, sociology did not represent merely the outcome of an intellectual reaction against those ideas. The emergence of the discipline went hand in hand with a longer-term transformation of society itself – including, as well as industrialization, the 'functional democratization' to which we have referred before.

In the seventeenth and eighteenth centuries, argues Elias in his essay 'The sociogenesis of sociology' (1962), the writings about society of people like Hobbes, Locke, Montesquieu or Voltaire (to name only a few of the most famous among many) were beamed towards actual or potential members of governments. In absolutist states, and even in England, they were the people whose intentions and decisions seemed to count most in matters social. The tacit assumption underlying most thinking about society during the Enlightenment was that the main condition for the proper or better functioning of society was that those who governed should have the right ideas, aims and intentions. And, if one wanted to explain social events, one looked in the first place for the plans, intentions and interests of the leading men, or at the most of a few leading factions or cliques.

A growing awareness of the inadequacy of this sort of explanation was an important ingredient in the emergence of the social sciences. During and after the French Revolution, people were repeatedly confronted with social changes that were plainly not the result of the intentions of any particular person or people. Governments might plan and act in one way, yet the unforeseen outcome of their actions could be very different from what they had intended. No-one any longer seemed to be powerful enough to direct the course of change or even to see where it was going. Changes in society now seemed often to be determined not by the actions of any particular people but by anonymous forces which seemed almost akin to the forces of nature. This change was the outcome of, as much as anything, a trend towards smaller (not small but smaller) power differentials between the various sections of society, and from relatively unilateral to more multilateral or reciprocal controls. Very gradually, with increasing specialization and growing mutual interdependence of all social activities, no social stratum remained a mere passive object of the power exercised by others, devoid of any share in decision-making. And the interweaving of the intentional activities of many individuals and groups in these circumstances made it more difficult to explain the actual course of events in terms of the intentions of any *particular* individuals or groups. One result was to give increased impetus to the formation of secular political ideologies and parties (1970a: 64–7). Another was to stimulate the social sciences.

In fact, recognizably 'social scientific' discussions of relatively impersonal social processes antedate the Revolution. Arguably the first are the writings about what were to be known as 'market forces' by François Quesnay (1694–1774) and the Physiocrats in the mid-eighteenth century, on whose work Adam Smith was to build in *The Wealth of Nations* (1776), from which in turn the discipline of economics developed throughout the nineteenth century in the hands of Malthus, Ricardo, John Stuart Mill and Alfred Marshall among others. The origins of modern sociology are inextricably entangled with those of modern economics.

Especially significant in the writings of the Physiocrats was that they arose from the bringing together of the 'philosophical' writers and the practical men of affairs. The more speculative strain was tempered by the use of actual data about society – with some of which businessmen had been familiar before. Not surprisingly, given the prestige already gained by the achievements of the physicists, Quesnay and Smith spoke of economic 'laws' – as in 'the law of supply and demand' – when describing processes at work in society. The early economists, however, still found it difficult to conceptualize adequately how the properties of markets were connected to the motives and behaviour of individual people. The notion of *homo economicus* arose in this context: it was used in attempting to explain that it was individuals' apparently innately 'rational' pursuit of their own profit and advantage which was the 'cause' of market mechanisms and of longer-term processes like the division of labour. The concept of *homo economicus*, comments Elias, 'shows how difficult it was not to express primarily as properties of people what were in fact properties of configurations which people formed.' (1962: 33). The concept is not entirely without truth-content as a description of how people came to behave in the highly developed market economies of the nineteenth century; but that was not the one-sided 'cause' of the regularities of the markets. It would be just as near the truth to say that markets and their regularities pressured the behaviour of individuals involved in them into certain definite channels. The characteristic code of conduct of participants was certainly not innate, nor, in a vacuum and set quite apart from the context of established markets, could it be called simply 'rational'.[4]

It was roughly at this juncture in the development of economics that Karl Marx came upon the scene.

Base and superstructure, consciousness and society

By the mid-nineteenth century, economics had emerged as the first of the relatively autonomous social sciences. Like other scientific theories, however, those of economics did not represent *absolute* autonomy and detachment: they were also infused with elements of involvement and relatively heteronomous values. It was a short step from a theoretical demonstration of how market forces would apparently optimize the allocation of resources in a law-like way to arguing that the economy was and should be an autonomous 'sphere' of society. The 'laws' of that sphere would operate best if there was minimal interference in them from the other major 'sphere' of society, the state. The state itself was *not* seen as functioning according to impersonal, law-like regularities. This was how the nascent science of economics came to provide the intellectual foundation for liberal ideology. At the kernel of the ideology in its most extreme form was the advocacy of the 'night-watchman state'; the state, it was argued, should do no more than provide the framework of basic security within which entrepreneurs pursued their activities with minimal restrictions. Economics seemed to show that this was to the advantage of all; there is little doubt that it was to the advantage of the businessmen.

It is Elias's contention that Marx 'simply took over the basic conceptual scheme of the liberal ideology, but infused it with negative values' (1971a: 152). In his hands, a short-term economic theory was transformed into a long-term sociological theory. The liberal view that the state ought not to interfere in the autonomous play of economic forces was transmuted into the view that the economic sphere did in fact have throughout history a high degree of autonomy in relation to other spheres. And the liberal view that the state *ought* to serve the interests of entrepreneurs had its counterpart in Marx's conception of the state as a mere 'superstructure' *actually* serving the economic interests of that class.

As to how Marx really saw the relationship between 'base' and 'superstructure', it is possible to present many contradictory texts. That he placed special emphasis on economic forces in social development there is no doubt; whether he saw them as simple one-way causal determinants of everything else is much more questionable. Elias sidesteps that old issue and points to a possibly more fundamental assumption in Marx's thinking. Marx and Engels, he argues (1971a: 151) do not reach their hypothesis about the long-term importance of the economic basis from an investigation of the power of groups performing specialist economic functions in relation to the power of other groups. It comes instead from their conviction that 'laws' and 'regularities' can be discovered only in the 'economic' aspects of society. This assumption, shared with the liberal economics of the time, is mostly implicit, and needs to be teased out through careful reading. In a letter to Bloch, however, Engels made explicit that he regarded the 'economic basis' as structured, and all other aspects of social relationships as unstructured: 'as a host of accidents (that is, of things and events whose inner interconnection is so remote or so impossible to prove that we can regard it as non-existent, as negligible)' (Engels 1890: 692). If only the economic aspects of social relations were structured, they alone would be a possible subject for a science of society.

This limitation is ironic, for it was the tools of economics that enabled Marx to break away from the old philosophical modes of thought, and he extended the use of these tools far beyond the economics of his day. Yet this achievement was partly vitiated, Elias argued, by Marx's trying to conceptualize any structured, non-accidental, aspect of social relations as economic. On the one hand, as is well-known, Marx broke away from the thought of Hegel, and indeed the whole German philosophical tradition, in which concepts like 'spirit' and 'consciousness' were reified so that they seemed to refer to non-human moving forces in human history; he replaced them with concepts like 'relations of production' which much more clearly express the relationships and interdependencies of human groups (1977b: 127–8). On the other hand, he himself – perhaps unwittingly – reinforced these same reifying tendencies on a new level by introducing concepts like 'base' and 'superstructure' which also give the impression of referring to *things* quite separate from the networks of groups people form with each other. The impression is strengthened by Marx and Marxists representing the base/superstructure dichotomy as a structural characteristic of all societies, irrespective of the stage of development in each case to which economic activities have become specialized as such. (Again, here, Elias is partly thinking back to *The Civilizing Process* and the futility of arguments about whether a process such as feudalization is 'really' economic or 'really' political; see page 65 above.)

The reason for the persistence of an overly reified dualism of base and superstructure in Marx's thought seems to be that in one respect he did not break sufficiently with the philosophical tradition. Hegel had made intellectual activity, developing in an autonomous sphere of 'spirit', the primary moving force in history (1977b: 127–8). Marx instead made the production and distribution of goods for the satisfaction of the necessities of life the motive force. But, in identifying this with social 'Being' (*Sein*), and opposing it to 'Consciousness (*Bewußtsein*) identified with the non-economic 'superstructure', he gave the impression that 'economic' activities are *without* consciousness and went too far towards an equally one-sided view. That was because he never broke away from the philosophical conception of 'consciousness' as representing a high intellectual, or ideological, level of thinking and knowledge. In his theorizing, he paid insufficient regard to what would no doubt have been obvious to him: that 'consciousness' is not something inhabiting a separate sphere. Consciousness plays a part in all human social activity – in a mother's feeding her child, in a farmer's ploughing his field, in workers making cotton in a nineteenth-century mill. Knowledge is as essential to human life as food (1971a: 155; 1982a: 42). Different levels of consciousness certainly can be distinguished: the consciousness of workers carrying heavy loads is not the same as that of learned people pronouncing on the nature of society, but the differences are only degrees along a continuum. Marx's notion of consciousness is too exclusively modelled on the latter. The paradoxical result was that while Marx's work overall is (along with Comte's) one of the first great steps towards a *process* theory of social development, his base/superstructure and being/consciousness dualism led to what is essentially a circular debate:

It is not difficult to see that men are in no position to satisfy their elementary physical needs without thinking and without the knowledge to orientate themselves in their world, and that they are incapable of orientating themselves in this manner without satisfying their elementary needs. In other words, Marx's dialectical enthusiasm created a 'chicken-and-egg' problem. (Elias 1977b: 128)

In Elias's view, a theory of knowledge should deal with the development equally of both the most mundane and the most intellectual means of orientation used by human beings. So far, false dualisms and chicken-and-egg problems – the result of process-reduction and the abstraction of conceptual 'spheres' which are then placed in static opposition or causal connection with each other – have obstructed both philosophical and sociological theories of knowledge.

PHILOSOPHICAL VERSUS SOCIOLOGICAL THEORIES OF KNOWLEDGE

Sociological theories of knowledge, by tradition, pay most attention to knowledge towards the more involved pole of the involvement/detachment continuum. The tradition of philosophical epistemology, on the other hand, concentrates on knowledge towards the more detached pole. The one tradition has emphasized how knowledge of reality may be distorted, the other how undistorted knowledge of reality may be attained.

One among Marx's great intellectual achievements was to make the first paradigmatic statement of what – as developed by Karl Mannheim and many others – came to be known as the sociology of knowledge. Stripped to their essentials, the common assumptions of this tradition are simple enough. They can be condensed to the statement that 'consciousness' – meaning variously ideas, knowledge, thought, ideology or perception – is primarily determined by the position and interests of the human groups where these are produced; they are *not* determined only by the 'objects' of consciousness, nor by a 'logic' or 'reason' constituting a structure inherent in consciousness itself (Elias, 1971a: 149). Marx himself laid stress on the way in which the economic interests of a social group determined its ideas about society – as illustrated in the connection between the interests of bourgeois entrepreneurs, economic science and liberal ideology. (It would, comments Elias (1971a: 366), have been asking too much to expect Marx to have worked out an equally cogent account of how people's knowledge of society also shapes their conception of what their interests are.)

But Marx also had a theoretical model of the direction of development of society as a whole, and that enabled him to his own satisfaction to state that the ideas associated with the rising working class represented an advance over those of the bourgeoisie. They were a more 'objective' account of social reality. Marx would thus not have regarded his theory as relativistic. Subsequent writers from Mannheim to phenomenologists like Berger and Luckmann (1966), however, have abandoned any idea of structured overall change in societies, adopting instead the historians' conception of unstructured history; in consequence they have no idea of structured processes of change in knowledge (1971a: 156ff). They are left struggling with the problem of relativism. Their sociologies of knowledge, says Elias, 'lack any theoretical paradigm of the dynamics of knowledge in either direction [long-term advances or regressions] as a dimension of the dynamics of societies at large; they do not possess any appropriate conceptual tools, any yardsticks for determining these directional changes. It is for that reason that they are stuck in the relativistic trap' (1971a: 358).

Philosophical theories of knowledge, standing in a tradition far older than the *sociology* of knowledge raise contrasting problems. Philosophers have by habit concentrated their attention on forms of knowledge – especially the natural sciences – which seem to have little connection with the interests or social situation of the groups who produce it. Far from being relativists, they have been 'philosophical absolutists'. That is to say, they have by tradition sought clear-cut criteria by which knowledge may be judged true or false, right or wrong. In practice, however, scientists do not judge a new theory in such absolute terms. New knowledge is, rather, assessed in relation to the previously existing stock of knowledge. The criteria for judging that a new piece of theoretical or empirical knowledge represents an advance over older ones are not yet well conceptualized; but they are expressed in terms such as a *better* fit with the evidence, *more* adequate, *more* congruent with reality. Advances are of many kinds, from a simple addition to the stock of knowledge, to establishing more certainly something which previously rested on insecure foundations, or to relating events to each other within a more comprehensive theoretical model (Elias, 1970a: 52–3). Philosophers and historians of science have certainly begun to wrestle with these problems in recent decades. T. S. Kuhn's widely influential book *The Structure of Scientific Revolutions* (1962) is a prominent case. That book, however, also illustrates the danger: if Kuhn himself did not break away from absolutism only to fall into relativism, others have enthusiastically put that gloss on his work. The most extreme instance of a philosopher veering right over to relativism was perhaps Feyerabend's *Against Method* (1975).

Underlying both philosophical absolutism and sociological relativism, says Elias, is a shared assumption. They both reduce everything that people know to two diametrically opposite states: *either* to a state of absolute dependence of knowledge on the situation of the groups where it is used or produced, *or* to a state of absolute independence from it. To put it another way, they both subject knowledge to process-reduction, so that it can exist only in a state of total autonomy on the one hand or to total heteronomy, absolute relativity, on the other (1971a: 364).

Elias rejects this shared assumption. Most scientific knowledge, he points out, contrary to the older philosophical suppositions, has the character of 'a structured flux', and, on the other hand, modern ideologies have absorbed a good deal of factual sociological and economic knowledge compared with the ideologies of earlier ages (1971a: 364). There are no zero points of involvement and detachment – forms of knowledge have to be located along the continuum.

In short, Elias sets out to use his model of involvement and detachment to 'steer the ship between the Scylla of philosophical absolutism and the Charybdis of sociological relativism' (1971a: 358). To understand the task and the solution, it is necessary to look at Elias's critique of some central elements in Western philosophy.

Homo clausus *versus* homines aperti

A basic motif has run through Western philosophy since Plato, becoming more strongly emphasized from the Renaissance in classical philosophy from Descartes through Leibniz, Locke and Hume to Kant, and onwards to Husserl and Popper. It has stamped an almost indelible mark on sociological theorizing from Durkheim and Weber to Parsons and the many contemporary writers influenced in one way or another by phenomenology. It is the conception of the person (in the singular) as the 'subject' of knowledge; a single thinking mind inside a sealed container, from which each one looks out and struggles to fish for knowledge of the 'objects' outside in the 'external world'. Among those 'objects' are *other* minds, equally locked inside their own sealed containers, and one of the most difficult problems epistemologists (and sociologists influenced by them) pose for themselves is the question of how one thinking 'subject' inside its own container can ever know anything of what is being thought and what is known by those 'objects' – those other 'subjects' – thinking away inside their own containers in turn.

Elias labels this conception the *homo clausus* (meaning 'the closed man' or 'closed personality'). He has also spoken of it as involving an image of people as 'thinking statues' (1987a: 130) and as 'we-less I's'[5] (1987a: 266). The counterpart to this conception of the isolated ego, devoid of we-images shared with fellow humans, is the implicit notion of the 'knowledgeless group' (1984a: 26ff), devoid of symbols and concepts handed down from previous generations. To all this, Elias counterposes his own conceptual starting point of *homines aperti* ('open people') bonded together in various ways and degrees.

In his discussion of *homo clausus* (1968a: 245–63; 1970a: 119 ff; 1982a: 6–17, 27–32; 1984c: 15–16; 1987a) Elias enters into some detail about the varying manifestations of this static duality between 'subject' and 'object'. It is always associated with a doubt that the world 'outside', 'external reality', really exists or is at it seems. It was already to be seen in Plato's celebrated image of the prisoners in a cave, watching the shadows cast on the wall by the fire behind them.[6] In Descartes the perception of the individual as a thinking ego isolated in his own head is captured in the famous proposition *cogito ergo sum*; Descartes rescues him by resort to theology, bringing in God to open the cell door.[7] Alone in this tradition, Leibniz (1714) tried to set out from the image of a multiplicity of interdependent human beings, but he did so only by using a metaphysical construction to bring his own version of *homo clausus*, the windowless monads, into relation with each other (1968a: 251).[8]

It is Kant, however, who is for Elias the pivotal figure in this tradition (1982a: 7–9, 15). It will be recalled at the very start of his academic life, Elias had fallen into dispute with his doctoral supervisor Hönigswald over the fundamentals of Kantian or 'transcendental' philosophy. Kant was the very begetter of the term 'transcendental', and Elias writes that

Transcendental philosophy has led us astray. Its representatives try to persuade us that they can discover eternal and unchanging conditions or forms of whatever it is – reflection, science, or experience – while, in fact, they merely abstract selectively and, often enough in a highly arbitrary manner, law-like generalizations from a given phase in the development of human knowledge, thus adding their mite to the history of philosophy. (1982a: 8)

Basing his judgement on his early close study of *The Critique of Pure Reason* and also citing Kant's late essay on 'The progress of metaphysics since Leibniz and Wolff' (1982a: 8), Elias explains his objections to Kantianism along the following lines: Kant delved into his own consciousness and there discovered that concepts like substance, space, time and cause could not possibly be based on his experience. Therefore he concluded that they must come from a frame-of-mind set *a priori* in his own brain. In other words, the form of objects as he perceived them was founded not on the properties of the objects in themselves (the *Ding an sich*), but on the *natural* or *innate* properties of the subject. Having discovered this innate frame-of-mind in himself, Kant very cautiously said that we may conclude that other subjects also have this *a priori* frame-of-mind, *but we can never be certain* of that. Here he was very consistent, because once one has the idea that a frame-of-mind-given-by-nature determines one's thinking, so that one can never be sure that objects really correspond to one's thinking, then one can never be sure of the existence of other subjects either – because other subjects are also then *phenomena* which may possibly be corrupted by the pre-given structure of one's own reason. So Kant was quite aware that his theory of knowledge ultimately has a solipsistic grounding, solipsism being the view that the self is the only object of real knowledge or the only thing really existent.

Elias comments acidly:

A long procession of books written on these lines, a tragicomic masquerade of wasted lives, litters mankind's trail. If the world 'an sich' is unknowable, one wonders why their authors bother, often rather emphatically, to state their case. Resigned silence might be more appropriate. (1984a: 104)

He argues that this trap has continued to ensnare most philosophical epistemology since Kant. Philosophers no longer speak of a pre-given 'Reason', but they use 'logic' or 'language' in an equivalent way to denote a pre-given unchanging and eternal form behind the changing contents of knowledge with equivalent solipsistic results. There is no secure foundation for knowledge, for only the thinking mind is structured; the objects of human thinking stand on a structureless swamp, or at least it can never be proven that they have a structure of their own (1985b: 26). Elias uses the general label 'nominalism' for this assumption, which is manifested in various forms: rationalist philosophy starts from the assumption that the person's 'ratio' is ordered, if nothing else; the linguistic variant, seen in Chomsky, is that language has an unchanging 'deep structure' beneath the surface variety; the deductionist variant starts from the assumption that all human thought follows external laws of 'logic'. This conception of one unchanging logic of science, Elias remarks (1971a: 365), gives the impression that, by means of it, the theory of relativity could as easily have been discovered by Albertus Magnus as by Albert Einstein; and elsewhere (1977b: 40ff) he uses the successive world records in athletics for the men's 5,000 metres, since Paavo Nurmi won it in the 1920s, as an analogy for how scientific knowledge actually grows – by successive small advances over currently existing knowledge!

One of Elias's particular bugbears is the philosophy of Sir Karl Popper. It is easy to understand Elias's hostility, for Popper's books *The Poverty of Historicism* (1944–5) and *The Open Society and its Enemies* (1945) were very influential (in Britain at least) in reinforcing sociology's turn away from the concern with long-term processes of development Elias believes essential to the discipline.[9] But Elias's essay (1985b) on Popper, written around 1970 though not published until 1985, is not his most successful. The reason for this is that the essay is exclusively a critique of Popper's *The Logic of Scientific Discovery* (1959), the original German version of which dates from 1935. It makes a good target, for in that book Popper is clearly seeking out a single eternal 'logic' of a single 'science'. That Elias paid no attention at all to Popper's later writings such as

Objective Knowledge (1972) helped draw down upon him the wrath of the German Popperians Hans Albert (1985) and Hartmut Esser (1985). Even so, in this controversy Elias scored some palpable hits. He insisted, rightly I think, that Popper has continued to think in terms of a single eternal logic of science, a single science looking suspiciously like physics, whose explanations are always ideally of the covering-law kind and susceptible to axiomatization in formal logic. He also argues that Popper's starting point is still that of *homo clausus*, and accuses him of talking glibly of 'intersubjective testing' as if he had a theory of intersubjectivity. It does seem that Popper never rethought his position on this fundamental point, and remained wedded to nominalism and the old philosophical dualisms.

Nevertheless, if Elias had taken notice of Popper's later work, he may have had to acknowledge some superficial points of contact with his own views. The subtitle of *Objective Knowledge* is 'an evolutionary approach'; Elias would avoid the word 'evolution' in a sociological context, because of its biological connotations, and would prefer to describe his own as a 'developmental' theory of knowledge. All the same, the general thrust of Popper's later work is towards seeing scientific knowledge growing through problem solving in small increments through endless sequences of 'conjectures' and 'refutations', and by successive approximations towards 'more accurate' knowledge (Elias would say 'more reality-congruent' knowledge). There is no starting point and no final state: knowledge is always knowledge for practical purposes, and can always be thrown into doubt as new problems arise. Elias might agree with that. Yet, although in Popper's later work his earlier rigid dichotomy between science and non-science becomes a little blurred,[10] the *logic* of science remains apparently eternal, and there is no clear account of how and in what social contexts scientific knowledge develops out of pre-scientific.

Popper says that he accepts the postulate of 'commonsense realism' that an external world of objects does exist – but significantly maintains that this is a metaphysical assumption, susceptible to rational discussion but not to testing (1972: 102ff). That Popper does not make a decisive break with the old static subject/object dualism is also evident in his late theory of the three worlds. 'World 1' is the world of inner mental states, 'World 2' the external world of objects, while 'World 3' is the world of human-made symbols and theories, transmitted from generation to generation, existing in a public domain and available for critical discussion, testing and revision. 'World 3', in Popper's phrase, is 'knowledge without a knowing subject', a metaphysical way of expressing the idea. All in all, even though it could be argued that the later Popper was groping towards a developmental theory of knowledge with some resemblance to Elias's, his central notion of three worlds is crude in comparison with the theory of involvement and detachment.

The pervasive influence of *homo clausus* is detected everywhere by Elias. At an almost subliminal level it is seen in the casual way people in general have come to use the word 'phenomena' when they mean data, evidence, or just plain 'things'. The usage betrays an unconscious 'apparitionism' as Elias calls it – the feeling that things can never be as they appear. In more academic contexts, *homo clausus* appears in many guises: *homo economicus* and *homo philosophicus* (respectively already discussed explicitly and implicitly), but also the *homo psychologicus* and *homo sociologicus*[11] (1968a: 249). The last stalks the works of very diverse sociologists. He is to be found in Durkheim's notion of the 'social fact *sui generis*' beyond individuals, and in Max Weber's theoretical model (1922a: I, 24–5) of types of action (though not so much in his empirical work). He turns up in Parsons, who spoke of a process occurring 'inside that "black box", the personality of the actor' (1966: 20),[12] as well as in the writings of phenomenological sociologists, and ethnomethodologists, who 'have made the everyday concept of the "everyday" into an entirely un-everyday concept' (1978a: 22).[13]

Now why exactly does Elias pin the blame on *homo clausus* for both the highly objectivist Durkheim ('consider social facts as *things*') and the highly subjectivist phenomenologists? It is because *both* sides set up the rigid barrier between the person 'inside' the black box and the world 'outside':

In the metaphysicists' world, it seems there can be nothing really new. Though the actors change, there is little change in the roles which they play in relation to each other. There are always subjectivists and objectivists or those who try out intermediary positions and compromises. They appear in different guises – as rationalists and empiricists, as apriorists and positivists, as phenomenologists and realists, as deductionists and inductivists, . . . There is no end to it. Nothing can ever reconcile the polar views and solve the problems arising from the fictitious assumption of an existential gulf between human beings and the world they set out to discover and control – the world of which they themselves form part. This assumption is the stumbling block. Nothing new, no advances in the theory of knowledge and of sciences are possible as long as the assumption of an ontological gulf between 'subject' and 'object', explicitly or not, remains the basis of these theories. (1982a: 23–4)

Because they bow to philosophical tradition, sociologists too are condemned to endless circular arguments about 'the individual' and 'society'. They develop rival sets of concepts – microsociology and macrosociology, individual-centred and system-centred – which they never succeed in reconciling with each other. And this happens because they reduce what is actually a process to a static polarity of opposites.

There is an obvious escape route from this impasse in which transcendental philosophers have been stuck for centuries.

That way, however, is closed to them. They cannot use it without losing their identity. They are like people enclosed in a room from which they try to escape. They try to unlock the windows, but the windows resist. They climb up the chimney, but the chimney is blocked. Yet the door is not locked; it is open all the time. If only they knew it, they could easily leave the room. But they cannot open the door, because to do so would disagree with the rules of the game which they as philosophers have set themselves. They cannot open the door, because that would not be philosophical. (1982a: 15)

So what is this door of the philosophers' self-made prison? The escape from solipsism is to recognize that *no person's knowledge has its beginning in him or herself*. Each of us, with all our reflections, perceptions, intuitions and experiences, stands on the shoulders of others. In order to understand the pattern of all these intellectual activities and traits as they are today, one has to retrace the long intergenerational process in the course of which they *have become* what they are (1982a: 31). Kant, it must be remembered, like everyone else argued with a language he had learned socially. He asked 'where does my concept of "cause" come from?' He was right that it did not come from his *own* experience: he had not learned it by himself. But he *had* learned it from his teachers. The concept of cause was there in his society. Several generations earlier it had not been. It had gone through a long process of development in society, the intergenerational transmission of symbols slowly adding to the stock of knowledge and of the categories available for use in thinking by people in society.

The crux of *homo clausus*, then, is not just that it is a *single* isolated mind, but that it is also a single isolated *adult* mind. Once that is recognized and abandoned, the central problem of the theory of knowledge is no more problematic than how from birth onwards children learn and use the symbolically transmitted fund of knowledge of all kinds, and themselves *become* adult minds and personalities. It is also no *less* problematic; but somehow the great edifice of Western philosophy seems less imposing when put on a par with the humble, though highly productive and rapidly progressing, field of developmental psychology. (Elias does, incidentally, qualify his emphasis on social learning by noting that studies of new-born infants show that certain rather elementary types of perception and reaction probably are innate and therefore prior to experience – though they subsequently grow and mature hand in hand with experience. A baby's primary smile and other responses which may be elicited in reaction to an adult face are, however, a far cry from the high-level conceptual modes of reasoning Kant had in mind (1982a: 30).)

What does a sociology not based on *homo clausus* look like? The alternative image of *homines aperti* is of course precisely what underlies *The Civilizing Process*, tracing as it does changes in personality structure hand in hand with changes in the structure of human relations in societies as parts of an overall process. *The Civilizing Process* also contains one explanation for the strength of the *homo clausus* image, why it seems so self-evidently valid to people at large. For Elias never questions that this sense of the self inside its container looking out is very real as a mode of self-experience in modern societies. What he does question is whether it is universal and inevitable, found equally in all societies wherever and whenever. It is no accident that this mode of self-experience – as has been recognized at least since Burckhardt – became much more accentuated in Europe from the Renaissance; for it was precisely then that a major spurt of the civilizing process occurred there. The philosophers' *homo clausus* is an externalization of just this mode of self-experience: the sealed container in which we sense ourselves is sealed with the iron bands of the civilized self-controls forged in a long-term process.

ACADEMIC ESTABLISHMENTS AND SOCIOLOGICAL OUTSIDERS

The philosophers' establishment

Needless to say, philosophers are unlikely to accept Elias's arguments. Elias is plainly intent upon sociologizing some of the most cherished central questions of philosophical epistemology. They have always tended to dismiss 'genetic' investigations of the kind Elias advocates as 'unphilosophical' (which in one sense they are) or even as 'mere history of ideas' (which they are not). In any case, philosophers always resurrect the same old dead-end problems: in the last resort, for them a new-born infant, entering the same old timeless, ahistorical, unchanging 'world out there' will always make as good a black box as any other.

The charge of being 'unphilosophical' (1971a: 362) is highly significant. Why should that be considered a damaging criticism of a sociological theory? The question leads Elias (1982a) to sketch a theory of academic establishments, drawing on the ideas of established-outsiders relationships used in many other contexts.

Social scientists, especially sociologists, are relative latecomers to the academic community, rather as the people of the Estate came late to Winston Parva. Philosophers in contrast are among the oldest residents.

The proliferation of disciplines in modern universities is often seen simply as a process of specialization to deal with the ever-growing scope of knowledge. In part it is. Historically, the natural and social sciences may all be seen as having become differentiated out of philosophy. If, however, it were a matter only of efficient division of labour, inter-disciplinary collaboration would be much easier than it frequently is. In practice, disciplines in universities (and through their 'professional associations') often behave a little like competing states, striving to maintain clear territorial boundaries against outsiders. A disciplinary ideology and we-image is constructed, promoting a sense of belongingness. (This often includes intra-disciplinary ancestor worship of great figures from the past claimed by a particular discipline. Consider the position of Max Weber in the sociologists' pantheon; in contrast he is relatively little read by economic historians, even though for most of his career he would have described himself as one of them!) Out of this process emerge unplanned status- and power-differentials between specialized disciplines.

As one would expect from the theory of established/outsider relations, in inter-disciplinary battles and rivalries, members of a discipline pay attention chiefly to criticisms emanating from higher status, more powerful disciplines than their own. Moreover, by using them as a model they seek to gain kudos for themselves and their own discipline. In this way sociologists have often mimicked the more prestigious natural sciences by quantification and number-crunching, sometimes with valuable results but sometimes at the cost of allowing technique to dictate the questions they ask. As for philosophers, they pay less heed to sociologists than *vice versa*, and the charge of being unphilosophical is a far more effective means of stigmatism, far more damaging to the sociologists' we-image, than a charge of being unsociological would be against the philosophers. Sociologists frequently show their deference to philosophers by posing their questions in a philosophical rather than a fully sociological way. In reality, believes Elias, little is gained by this kind of mimicry. 'They inevitably fall between two stools and perpetuate the ineffectualness and lowly status of their own field' (1982a: 27).

The historians' establishment

Historians too stand higher in the academic pecking-order than sociologists and they too, like all disciplinary groups, have well-entrenched modes of approach by which they defend their territory from outsiders.[14] One attitude fairly widespread among historians is a hostility towards 'theorizing' and 'speculation'. Now it is certainly true that – as a counterpart to the renewed use of historical evidence among sociologists – in recent years it has become far more common for historians to put to use in their work concepts and hypotheses first developed by sociologists and anthropologists (see for instance the brief survey by Peter Burke 1980). It is my impression, however, that their borrowings are mainly of the least dynamic and least diachronic of sociological ideas, as if historians felt well able to supply the time dimension from their own conceptual resources: long-term developmental models remain suspect to most – not all – historians as a prime source of 'mere speculation'.

For his part, Elias asks why the shelf-life of works of historical scholarship is typically so short. Why is it that history seems to have to be written anew in every generation? Can it be *only* the continuous discovery of new historical facts? Leopold von Ranke, the founder of modern historical scholarship, was well aware of the problem. In the commonplace book he used between 1831 and 1849, von Ranke wrote:

History is always being rewritten . . . Each period takes it over and stamps it with its dominant slant of thought. Praise and blame are apportioned accordingly. All this drags on until the matter itself becomes unrecognizable. Then nothing can help except a return to the original evidence. But would we study it at all without the impulse of the present? . . . Is a completely true history possible? (Ranke 1925: 52; quoted by Elias 1969a: 4)

Ranke was pointing out that, in Elias's terms, the writing of history had been relatively deficient in autonomy from the values current when it was written, and it was this which prevented any real continuity in historical research. Ranke's own solution was to base history on the most meticulous and scholarly study of the documentary evidence. Elias is the first to admit that without the revolution in historical scholarship led by Ranke, his own studies, such as *The Court Society* and the *The Civilizing Process*, would scarcely have been possible. But Ranke's solution to the problem is not sufficient in itself. For while the methods he pioneered lead to the accumulation of well-established discrete details, they do not in themselves yield any systematic or verifiable framework of reference against which the details can be set. The details may be well-established yet the *connections between them* are often left to arbitrary interpretation and speculation.

The constraints of the tradition of historiography that allows the individual historian very great latitude for personal hermeneutics in the establishment of narrative connections between carefully researched sources finds expression among other ways, in a conscious renunciation of theory . . . Yet the proud renunciation of theory in this form of history writing leaves the door wide open for the formation of historical myths of all kinds. (1977b: 137)

It is also too easy for narrative historians – and the case for narrative as the central activity of historians is sometimes still seriously made[15] – to represent history as a jumble of 'unique' events, an unstructured sequence of the actions of particular people. Yet, says Elias, a complex of long-term, unplanned but explainable processes forms the infrastructure of any such apparently random and structureless juxtaposition of people and events. The claim that historians study unique, unrepeatable sequences of events implies that 'uniqueness' is an inherent property of the *objects* or events studied. It is not: it is a property conferred on them by the low level of abstraction of the frame of reference with which such historians choose to operate.

The claim of 'uniqueness' is linked too to the writing of history in a highly voluntaristic manner – that is, in terms of the motives and actions of apparently 'free actors'. The introduction of concepts and theory at a higher level of abstraction – especially longer-term process theories – is often seen by historians as bringing with it a quite opposite image of 'determinism'. The duality of 'freedom' and 'determinism' is one of the false polarities Elias rails against (see pp. 70–1 and 274–5n.). The need is not to establish *whether* the actions of Louis XIV or of a slave are 'free' or 'determined' but to investigate carefully *how much* scope for decision each has. There will be a big difference between the two, but in neither case are their actions absolutely free or absolutely determined. Such absolutes are metaphysical notions; in the real world, all human beings have always been interdependent with other human beings in various ways, degrees and patterns.

CONCLUSION

At the end of this lengthy exposition of Elias's theory of knowledge and the sciences, how can it be described overall? It contains elements many social scientists may find attractive, such as the idea of five-dimensional process-theories. It also contains elements with which many sociologists will feel uncomfortable: perhaps the idea of the varying fantasy-loading of knowledge, which sociologists generally do not expect to find in what they think of as 'the philosophy of science' and find troublesome even in what they think of as the separate fields of the sociology and anthropology of knowledge. What is very distinctive in Elias is how, on the foundation of the theory of involvement and detachment (itself standing on the theory of civilizing processes), he constructs what are often regarded as many different theoretical problems into a single coherent structure. His characteristic procedure is blending empirical evidence with process theory. The resulting blend is difficult to label in philosophical terms. In fact his theory of the sciences has more in common with the writings of actual practitioners of science – such as Prigogine and Stengers, Richard Dawkins and Paul Davies – than with the traditional 'philosophy of science'. Elias, indeed, believes he has thrown off the philosophical yoke, and that other social scientists should do likewise. Their deference to the philosophical establishment, however, constantly drives them to locate their own work on a philosophical map and to try to do the same to Elias.

Elias has been called an 'empiricist'.[16] That is not surprising, for Elias's use of terms like 'object-adequacy', 'reality-congruent' and the 'fitness of a theory to its objects' is provocative, and no doubt intended to be so. To a generation of social scientists brought up at best on Popper's (perfectly valid) dictum that 'all observation is theory-impregnated', and at worst on phenomenology, even to refer to reality without quotation marks or hesitation is either naïve or antediluvian. That is the psychological effect of what Elias calls apparitionism; he has also referred to 'reality-blind philosophers' (1985b). There is no doubt he lays himself open to misunderstanding by his choice of terminology. Nevertheless, he is certainly not an empiricist in the classic sense: he is no believer in what Outhwaite (1987: 28) neatly calls 'the dogma of immaculate perception'. As should be apparent from the foregoing exposition, he has a well refined notion of the relation between concepts and objects as a developmental process in the growth of human knowledge.

One of the senses in which 'positivist' has come to be used as a term of abuse among contemporary social scientists is as a near-synonym for 'crude empiricist'.[17] If Elias is not an empiricist in the classic sense, he is not a positivist either. Nevertheless, he values the contribution made to the development of sociology by Auguste Comte – the founder of philosophical positivism – far more highly than is now fashionable. The first chapter of *What is Sociology?* is devoted to showing how Comte formulated some of sociology's most fundamental questions. Comte's 'law of three stages' was one of several influences on Elias's theory of involvement and detachment, but this does not mean Elias is unaware of its weaknesses. He values Comte's pioneering effort to explain why the various branches of science have developed in a particular sequential order. And he especially values the way in which Comte – like Marx – strove to break with the myths of classical European philosophy. He sums up his assessment as follows:

Comte suggested that the classical philosophical idea of an eternal reason of an unchanging intellect that is ostensibly shared by all men in all societies independently of time and place is a reifying abstraction and therefore a fable. He tried to show that human thinking changes in the course of time, that together with the social life of humanity, it passes through a specific empirically demonstrable series of stages. His 'law' of three stages simplified the observable facts, but it showed the road along which one will have to travel in order to break with the tendency of classical European philosophy to formulate problems statically. In the work of Comte, out of an eternally unchanging antithesis between a thinking subject of knowledge and the object that is to be known a social process is made quite clear. The sequence of types of thinking is embedded in the sequence of stages of social development. (1977b: 127)

When in 1956 Elias first began to expound his developmental theory of knowledge and the sciences, the so-called 'standard view' in the philosophy of science – comprising the logical empiricism of philosophers like Hempel and Nagel, together with variants like Popper's – was overwhelmingly dominant. In relation to it, Elias's ideas must have seemed very eccentric. In the 1970s, however, a different philosophical view, often labelled 'neo-realism', became influential, and in relation to this, Elias's views may seem somewhat less heterodox. Elias himself would certainly not like to be called a realist. He polemicizes both against nominalism *and* against realism in the traditional sense; for just as categories of perception are not immanent in the human brain independent of experience, they are not inherent in objects either. 'Neo-realism', however, is not a realism in that latter sense. The philosophers involved – notably Rom Harré (1970), Mary Hesse (1974, 1980), and Roy Bhaskar (1978, 1979) – differ a good deal among themselves, but a few general points can nevertheless be made.[18]

First, a crucial step in the turn away from logical empiricism was the 'holistic turn': it was recognized that scientific statements cannot be tested in isolation, in a direct confrontation with experience (Outhwaite 1987: 15). Their meaning derives from complex networks of metaphors, models and theories in which they are embedded. The traditional philosophy of science concentrated on the logical structure of scientific theories and explanation but found great difficulty in accounting for the construction of models and use of analogies and metaphors. These were highly prevalent in scientific thinking, yet could not be assimilated into deductive theories, seeming to have the status of heuristic devices – psychologically useful in the 'context of discovery' but not logically necessary in the 'context of justification'. Neo-realism reverses this order of priority. Hesse in particular argued that 'deductivist conceptions misrepresented the structure of scientific theories, making them out to be more tightly integrated both internally and with respect to empirical evidence than they actually were, *and also misrecognized their function, as models of natural processes*' (Outhwaite 1987: 17; my italics). This is strikingly closer to the view of the role of models Elias had advanced in his 1956 'model of models'. There is also a resemblance in Bhaskar's distinction (1978) between open and closed systems, though Elias soon rejected that terminology and emphasized more clearly than Bhaskar that this is a matter of a continuum not a dichotomy.

Secondly, and by extension of the first point, realist philosophy of science, like Elias, pays far more attention than philosophers previously did to examining past and present examples of actual scientific practice. Kuhn's work in the history of science was, indeed, influential in the 'holistic turn' among philosophers.

Thirdly, by removing hypothetico-deductive nomological (i.e. 'law-like') theories from the central place in their conception of *natural* science, the neo-realist philosophers have been able to argue that the *social* sciences are sciences in exactly the same *sense* but not in exactly the same *ways* as the natural sciences. This stance is known as 'naturalism' (Bhaskar 1979). More convincingly than Popper, who wished to show a particular *logic* as the hallmark of all sciences, the neo-realists are able to accept that all the sciences consist in establishing patterns or connections between observed events, but they do so by many different methods and use different models. Again this view was clearly anticipated by Elias.

Before anyone is tempted to assimilate Elias into the world of the philosophers, however, it has to be pointed out that the neo-realists remain quite firmly within the philosophical mode of reasoning, for which Elias has scant respect. None has sought to reframe the old questions in so thoroughly a sociological way as does Elias.

In particular, Elias's remains the most radical rejection in sociology of the subject/object dualism.[19] Something resembling his attack on the central Cartesian–Kantian tradition has, however, emerged in the work of a few so-called 'anti-foundationalist' philosophers, notably Richard Rorty (1980). From that tradition was inherited the conception of philosophy as an all-encompassing discipline which legitimized, 'grounded', or provided the foundations for knowledge-claims made by all other disciplines, and indeed in culture at large. The claim to be able to expose the 'foundations' of knowledge, Rorty points out, was based on the conviction that philosophers could form a 'theory of knowledge' based on properties of the 'mind' and 'mental processes' reflecting more accurately or less adequately the objects 'outside'. Rorty does not describe these assumptions as *homo clausus*, but he does implicitly agree with Elias in tracing them all to Descartes, Locke and Kant. In a close study of three twentieth-century attempts to re-establish the foundational claims of philosophy – by Wittgenstein, Heidegger and Dewey principally – Rorty adopts as radical a stance as Elias in dismissing the whole problematic of a philosophical theory of knowledge. He arrives, for example, at the same conclusion as Elias, that reformulations of foundational claims in terms of language instead of the properties of 'mind' does not essentially change the Cartesian-Kantian problematic. And that Enlightenment problematic, he concludes, ought to seem as irrelevant to philosophy today as the problematic of the medieval scholastics seemed to the philosophers of the Enlightenment.

In the end, Elias does not like being labelled. Perhaps the only label he would happily accept is one which goes all the way back to his beloved Greeks. He is on the side of Heraclitus of Ephesus and against his contemporary Parmenides of Elea. Around 500 BC, Parmenides argued that the world we see around us is not real, because it is ever-changing; reality could be found only in pure unchangeable thought. Heraclitus, on the contrary, argued that the world around us is real; its very distinguishing characteristic is eternal change and movement.

9

Humanity as a Whole

It was close study of the history of European society and culture from which sprang the theory first advanced in *The Civilizing Process* and extended since in many directions. Yet in his later work, especially in the late 1970s and 1980s, Elias has been at pains to correct the misconception that the European civilizing process is *the* civilizing process. It is not. It is one of many specific instances of civilizing processes (cf. 1986c: 382–7). In the most general sense, civilizing processes are a human universal. Why it is possible to make that assertion will become clearer if we follow Goudsblom (1984a) in distinguishing between civilizing processes *on three levels*.

Two of the levels are familiar; we have already discussed them at some length. The first is the 'civilizing process' which every human person inevitably undergoes from birth onwards. In the social scientific literature this is more usually referred to by such terms as 'socialization', 'enculturation' and 'personality formation'. Whatever it is called, this individual lifetime learning process is closely bound up with processes of biological maturation. Furthermore, the *capacities for learning* all the human skills and modes of behaviour, thinking and feeling – from walking, sitting, talking and cooking, to the vast array of customs, manners and beliefs peculiar to particular human groups – are laid down in the biological and genetic structures of the human organism, which are the same in every society.

The second level of civilizing processes is that of the development of social standards and codes of acting, thinking and feeling in particular societies. This, of course, is principally the level at which Elias worked early in his career, through his study of the development of table manners, courtly etiquette and so many other facets of the European civilizing process. On this level too, a civilizing process is a learning process, and a process of social psychological development, but over periods of time much longer than an individual lifetime. It is highly misleading, as Elias has stressed ever since his early work, to think of the 'individual' as something quite separate from 'society', as if the social standards learned by every individual were something fixed and static, eternally given. They too develop over time and every person's lifetime learning process is also part of a longer and wider learning process of a society.

The third level is less familiar. No civilizing process in any particular society, it must always be remembered, represents an absolute beginning. It never proceeds *in vacuo*, without reference to other – earlier or contemporary – civilizing processes undergone by other human groups. It always represents an advance upon earlier standards. (*De*civilizing processes may also occur, but these too have to be understood as regressions *from earlier standards*.) Just as every individual lifetime civilizing process is a part of the longer-term development of a particular society, so also are civilizing processes in every society parts of a still longer-term civilizing process which encompasses humanity as a whole. In this even longer-term perspective, humanity as a whole has undergone a learning process in which it has acquired such distinctively human skills as speech, the use of fire, the making of tools and weapons from wood, stone and metals, and the vast and still growing stock of subsequent knowledge.

One simple reason why it is possible to think in terms of the civilizing of humanity as a whole is often overlooked. It is that biologically *Homo sapiens is one single species*.[1] All human beings, whether they be Americans, Russians, Chinese, Hottentots or Eskimos can interbreed, communicate (not, of course, without linguistic obstacles), and learn from each other. This is so familiar a fact that it is easy to ignore how remarkable it is. For in all previous phases of biological evolution, successful innovation in biological organization was accompanied by far-reaching processes of biological differentiation or speciation. That is to say, plants, insects, fishes, birds and animals all divided into a great number of species no longer able to interbreed, each exploiting its distinctive capacities in a particular environment, and thus filling all the different niches of the planet which could offer them a living. In contrast, the single human species adapted itself to vastly different conditions on earth by means not of biological but of *cultural* differentiation.

Humans filled the earth by learning from experience and by handing on knowledge from one generation to another. They adapted themselves to new surroundings with the help of a sequence of social transformations: that is, transformations in the form of social development, and without further evolutionary transformations breaking the biological unity of the species. (Elias 1987c: 343)

What had happened was that *Homo sapiens* had acquired a novel form of biological organization – 'natural' equipment which gave it the capacity to adapt to very different conditions without (except in the most superficial ways) further biological differentiation. Elias contends that insufficient attention has been paid to the distinct biological characteristics which enabled human beings to learn from experience, to transmit knowledge from one generation to another, to change their forms of group life according to new circumstances, and, along the way, to subject themselves to a process of 'self-domestication'. Or, as he sometimes phrases the question, 'Which biological characteristics of human beings make history possible?' (1970: 107).

THE HUMAN ORGANISM AND HUMAN EMOTIONS

An answer to this question is obscured, according to Elias, both by what he calls 'isolationist dualism' and 'reductionist monism'. The first is represented by the German tradition of *Geisteswissenschaften* with its rigid opposition between the natural sciences and the human sciences, and by the philosophical tradition of thinking in terms of *homo clausus* (see pp. 188–93 above). They are dualistic in two senses: they conceive of the human mind as a distinct entity encased in an organic container (the 'mind/body' dualism); and they assume human thinking, feeling and action to be quite different in character from those of the lower animals. 'Reductionist monism', in contrast, is well entrenched in academic psychology, and is represented by such schools as behaviourism, ethology and sociobiology.[2] They share the 'monistic' assumption that the human mind, behaviour and emotions work basically like those of lower animals and will ultimately be explained through experiments on animals and studies of animal behaviour.

Both traditions are misleading, argues Elias. Once again, the traditional ways of framing a question set up a false polarity. Neither the monistic nor the dualistic view is wholly valid. Dualism tends to overlook the continuities between the development of humanity and of non-human nature; in the case of monism, it is the uniqueness that is overlooked. A processual view is necessary in order to see that both continuities and unique structural characteristics are found within the overall developmental process. Human beings function in some specific respects as other animals do, Elias contends, but human beings as a whole function as no other animal does. The human organism embodies organizational innovations which make inferences from the functioning of other animals quite hazardous. That is as true of the living apes as of rats and pigeons. For the living apes represent a rather early colateral branch of the human ancestral tree. The immediate ancestors of *Homo sapiens* are all extinct. There do appear to have been other species of hominids but they disappeared long ago. Probably they were extinguished through competition with *Homo sapiens*, who represented so decisive an evolutionary breakthrough that their advantage in the elimination contest was overwhelming.

The most obvious biological manifestation of this breakthrough is the sheer size and complexity of the cortex in the human brain, and the dominance of the cortex in the functioning of the human animal. Yet Elias equally stresses that the innovatory advantages of the human organism are not to be understood in terms of the evolution of the brain – the 'mind' – alone, separate from the body. The distinction between 'physical' and 'mental' properties is unhelpful in understanding the processes of development involved. Take the human hand, with its flexible fingers and opposable thumb and forefinger, the usefulness of which in the distinctly human activity of toolmaking has often been noted. The properties of the hand are often thought of as a physical characteristic, while the co-ordination of the hands and the eyes in making tools is seen as a mental capacity.[3] This simple counterposition is an unsatisfactory conceptual device, notes Elias: 'Every co-ordination of fingers by a person who is making a tool demands a cerebral or mental activity, and the co-ordinating activity of the cerebrum would be rather useless without the existence of physical details such as fingers' (1987b: xxxiv). The development of the brain and the hand must have proceeded step by step as parts of one overall process of biological development.

But the human capacity for making tools cannot have been the outcome of a biological process alone; it emerged through the *intertwining* of a biological and a social process. It cannot be considered as a once and for all event – as if one day a human being, already equipped with all the necessary but hitherto unused capacities of brain, hand and eye, for the first time suddenly hit upon the usefulness of stones as missiles in hunting, or discovered equally abruptly that stones could be fashioned by humans to improve their usefulness. Rather, the slowness with which toolmaking advanced in the earliest stages of the development of humankind was probably due in part to biological limitations on learning capacity (as well as, then and later, to the sorts of reasons mentioned on pp. 166–8 above for the initially slow growth of the human stock of knowledge). But eventually the biological capacity for learning grew – probably in part responding to the pressure of social processes – and went on increasing far beyond the learning capacity of any other species. Ultimately, the human biological capacity for learning became so great that it could accommodate the growing – and ever more quickly growing – social fund of knowledge *without further biological changes* (1987b: xxxv).

This represented an evolutionary breakthrough, and Elias states clearly why it was so in his essay on human emotions (1987c: 344–5; cf. 1970a: 104–10). Hitherto, in all the pre-human stages of biological evolution, an unlearned, genetically transmitted repertoire of reactions remained dominant in steering the behaviour of each species. Many animals have, besides this, some capacity for learning. Even the earthworm shows some minuscule traces of learning ability. The scope of learning capacity increased gradually in the course of evolution. The apes can learn a great deal: they can remember individual experiences and modify their behaviour accordingly. Yet even in their case, the balance between learned and unlearned forms of conduct is weighted heavily in favour of the latter. Unlearned, genetically programmed behaviour is species-specific and unvarying. Even with the apes, individual behaviour and group structure show only minor local differentiation among members of the same species. Their capacity for learning is vastly superior to that of most other animals but still vastly inferior to that of *Homo sapiens*.

In humans, the balance between unlearned and learned conduct was for the first time tilted in favour of learning. The biological equipment for steering conduct mainly by means of individually learned and remembered experience conferred on humans an enormous advantage over all other species, whose behaviour remains governed largely by innate mechanisms. Innovations through the hit-and-miss process of biological evolution come about only very slowly, and thus the genetically programmed behaviour dominant in all other species can also change only very slowly. It is human beings' biological equipment for learning that has emancipated them from dependence on further biological change. Elias sometimes refers to this as *the symbol emancipation*. For it is their exceptional capacity for learning and their unique capacities for synthesis – that is, for making connections through the use of symbols – and transmitting their accumulating stock of learned knowledge in the form of symbols from generation to generation which makes possible rapid social differentiation and adaptation to new circumstances independently of biological change.

Human beings not only *can* but also *must* learn more than any other species (1987c: 345). Innate and species-specific means of orientation have virtually disappeared in the human case: a human being cannot even find food or distinguish between the edible and inedible without having acquired a large social fund of knowledge by learning from fellow humans. Nor can humans adequately communicate with each other without having learned a language from other humans. Like other species, it is true, they have a repertoire of unlearned forms of behaviour – such as smiling, groaning and crying in pain – which a new-born infant already possesses. But even these are less rigid, more malleable than in other animals, and when they persist as spontaneous reactions among adults it is often in a modified form, overlain by learned responses.

Without wishing to reopen the old and rather sterile debates about nature versus nurture and nature versus culture, Elias argues (1987c: 346) that it is necessary to reconceptualize what 'nature' means in a human context. It is misleading to think of 'nature' as applying only to human characteristics which are fixed, unmodifiable through stored and remembered experiences. These exist but there are besides them other *natural* human dispositions which cannot fully function unless awoken and moulded through relationships with other people. An obvious case is the human vocal apparatus. It is used by infants entirely for the production of unlearned pre-language sounds, which are spontaneous and fairly rigidly tied to the internal or external situation – pain, discomfort, hunger, alarm. Yet, for the development of the full, flexible, distinctively human use of the vocal apparatus, processes of biological *maturation* and of social *learning* have to intertwine with each other. If, at a specific stage of growth (roughly from the age of six months), the human infant does not have the opportunity to learn the use of language in relationship with adults, it seems that subsequently linguistic skills (in both their 'mental' and 'physical' aspects) will be severely impaired. Moreover, it is not a matter merely of learning to *produce* linguistic sounds; the process is inseparably also one of learning to understand other people's use of language. One reason why an appropriate 'love-and-learn' relationship – usually with parents in the first instance – seems to be essential to an effective learning process is that learning is always a matter of two-way traffic.

This applies to human emotions too. Every human being, by his or her whole constitution, is fundamentally directed and orientated towards others, towards emotional stimulation through other human beings.

Put a child alone for days in a room and see what happens. It 'wilts', however good the food it gets. The reason is that, this elementary need for such 'two-way' traffic of all that which we call, still very imperfectly, 'drives' or 'emotions', the need for a stimulating emotional response to one's own emotional messages is cut off. (Elias and Dunning 1986: 115)

For children, interruption of this two-way traffic can be damaging. As they grow up and pass through the individual civilizing process, they have to learn to curb and control these always very powerful needs for emotional communication with others.

Elias contends, in fact, that *no emotion of a grown-up human person is ever an entirely unlearned, genetically fixated reaction pattern* (1987c: 352). But that does not mean that it can be understood as purely learned, with no innate and biological foundation. What we call emotions have a somatic (bodily, or physiological), a behavioural, and a feeling component. (Unlike other animals, humans can verbalize their feelings, so we know far more about how humans feel than we do about the supposed feelings of lower animals.) An example is the 'alarm reaction': the response to danger, when the adrenalin flows, digestion slows, pulse rate increases, and more blood is pumped into the muscles of the limbs in preparation for 'fight or flight'.[4] This basic instinctive reaction is shared with many other animals, but in the human case the feelings and behaviour which accompany the somatic response – what is done to escape or defend oneself – though perhaps still almost automatic, are as much shaped by what one has learned.

The face and its place in communication between humans is one of Elias's favourite examples. Take the smile. It exists as an innate response – spontaneous, unlearned, rigid and undifferentiated – in infants. In the course of growing up, this wholly innate form of smile is greatly weakened, and in the case of the adult,

the core of the smiling emotion, both in its feeling and its behavioural component . . . is much more malleable than in its baby form. It can be deliberately used to convey to others a rich variety of shades of feeling. It can be a hesitant, a withdrawn, a broad, a triumphant, a supercilious and even a hostile smile. And yet in all these cases a learned and deliberate steering of conduct merges with an unlearned form of steering one's face muscles. (1987c: 359)

Because of this interplay of learned and unlearned elements, the innate infant smile, universal in all humans, is moulded in different societies into somewhat varying adult facial repertoires.

But how did the human animal acquire a face capable of all this? It is unique. Even the apes have relatively rigid, immobile faces. In contrast, the human face is extremely complex, composed of hundreds of muscles, capable not only of showing many nuances of emotion but also of being remodelled and shaped to some extent by experience. How did this come about? Elias takes it as a sign of how the evolutionary process has fashioned human beings in such a way that their 'nature' prepares them for life in groups. He speculates that facial signals emerged as a means of communication among hominids before any very elaborate language appeared. Their advantages in group life are evident: 'signals designed to probe each other's intention in anticipation of the enactment of conduct, and thus also signals such as the smiles which are capable of allaying suspicion and fear, must in the life of our ancestors have helped to temper frictions and to make a more differentiated life with each other possible' (1987c: 358).

Much of Elias's argument so far may seem common ground among social scientists. Many sociologists, notably 'symbolic interactionists' and others influenced by George Herbert Mead, have laid stress on the human ability to use symbols and, through notions like 'taking the role of the other', on human learning as two-way traffic. What has been less widely recognized, but is emphasized by Elias, is the necessity of reconceptualizing these issues in terms of process theories, dissolving such unhelpful static polarities as nature versus nurture. In Elias's thinking, even the nature of 'nature' changes over time in a human context.

Elias believes that what he has achieved by rethinking a problem in processual terms is a clarification of the *hinge* between the processes of biological evolution and of social development (or 'history'). The two processes, though connected, are quite different in kind. For one thing, biological evolution is irreversible, while social development is reversible – knowledge can be forgotten. Yet the one term 'evolution' is too often used indiscriminately for both, and this conceptual confusion encourages the monistic tradition in its attempts to represent the social process as part of a unitary biological process. In the dualistic tradition, on the other hand, no attention tends to be paid to the connection. Elias's argument is that

The biological propensity of humans for learning provides the answer. Without the changeability as well as the factual changes of what can and what has to be learned, without changes in knowledge including language changes, social development would not be possible. The *biological* dominance gained by learned forms of steering experience and conduct over unlearned forms of conduct links irreversible evolution to reversible development. Learned knowledge can be forgotten. The large human potential for forms of orientation and communication acquired through learning which is part of human nature also constitutes the hinge between nature and society, nature and culture, and in consequence between natural and social sciences. (1987c: 351)

Human beings' 'natural changeability' is a universal feature of human society (1970a: 104ff). This dissociation from biological mechanisms is directly relevant to the question of civilizing processes on each of the three levels. For all human beings have to *learn* to control their emotions, 'drives' and 'instincts'. They are not by nature 'civilized', but they are by nature civilizable. Here another misapprehension often arises: because human beings lack innate means of orientation – such as those which enable other animals to distinguish the edible from the inedible without having learned to do so – people jump to the conclusion that *Homo sapiens* as a species has only weak instincts. The philosopher Arnold Gehlen is one whom Elias (1970: 178–9n) sees as falling into this trap in his 'philosophical anthropology', where he speaks of humans 'instinctual deprivation'.[5] The greater plasticity of human instinctive behaviour implies a greater ability to control instincts, but does not imply that the instincts are weak. What humans lack is not strong instincts or drives, but innate controls over them. The controls are acquired through social learning, but that does not mean simply that drives are 'natural' and the drive-controls 'social'; on the contrary, the biological disposition to acquire the controls by social learning is itself built into the human constitution. Indeed, the unique potential which human drives and elementary impulses possess, by their very nature, for being contained, deflected and transformed in various ways has a very high survival value.

Given the fact that they lack instinctive or inborn controls, a life in groups – social life as we know it – would be impossible among human beings if they did not possess a natural disposition for learning impulse-control, and thus for civilizing themselves and each other. Nor . . . could a human being survive individually without a natural disposition for controlling, delaying, transforming, in short for patterning spontaneous impulses in a great variety of ways by means of *learned counter-impulses*. No person could acquire the essential characteristics of a human being if he or she remained, like a newborn baby, wholly at the mercy of uncontrollable urges. (Elias, in Elias and Dunning 1986: 59–60; my italics)[6]

So, as part of the individual civilizing process, learning self-control is a human universal. It follows that the conversion of external constraints into self-constraints takes place in all societies. But the degree, strength and pattern of this process vary between societies, as does the balance between external constraints and self-constraints adopted as a social standard in each society. The *special* civilizing processes – those at the level of particular societies – vary from tribe to tribe, nation to nation (Elias, 1986c: 382–7). But, at the level of humanity as a whole, the particular civilizing processes have formed parts of a much broader civilizing process following a directional track in the extremely long term. For all the major technical breakthroughs in the human past – making tools and weapons, the use of fire, the agricultural and industrial 'revolutions' – involve a civilizing process in a specific sense. That is, they all involve the control of immediate impulses in order to achieve a longer-term result. They involve what has often been called 'deferred gratification' and 'detour behaviour', or what Elias would term a detour via detachment (cf. pp. 163–4 above), an act of 'distanciation' from the immediate situation to achieve greater detachment (cf. 1987b: xxxv–vi). That is the case when a human takes time from hunting to shape a weapon that will make his next hunting expedition more productive; it is even clearer when people learn to refrain from eating all their harvest and keep seeds to sow next year. These breakthroughs all involve the use of symbols in thought, combining the memory of past experience with the symbolic anticipation of a future state of affairs. The argument is clearly illustrated in Johan Goudsblom's work on the human use of fire.

THE DOMESTICATION OF FIRE

Goudsblom is involved in a task of a kind highly unusual among present-day sociologists.[7] To use the insights of modern sociology, anthropology and psychology in interpreting *historical* evidence is common enough. To use them in assessing the evidence of archaeology, palaeo-anthropology, ethology and ecology is rarer. Yet, in seeking to trace and understand the mastery of fire and its place in human societies from the origin of species to the modern era, Goudsblom had to start his investigation in a period many millennia before the first written records.

The active use of fire is unique to humans. The use of tools and of language are often seen as distinctively human, and indeed in the degree of their development they are; but in more rudimentary forms, language and even the use of tools can be seen in other species. Control of fire, on the other hand, is exclusively a human possession. Moreover, it is not only a human monopoly but a human universal: there is no definite historical or archaeological record of any human society which lacked the active use of fire.

Myths about how humans acquired the use of fire are prominent in many cultures. Most often, as in the Prometheus myth, they represent the acquisition as a once-and-for-all single event, the achievement of a single person. That it happened in that way is extremely unlikely. Goudsblom shows (1987) that the mastery of fire must have been a far more gradual and long-term process. Of course, the evidence from early pre-history is never likely to permit anything so clear cut as final verification or falsification; though the scope for speculation must remain relatively wide, Goudsblom aims to advance an account of the process which is both plausible and not inconsistent with any of the known facts. Approaching the subject from a sociological point of view, he considers the control of fire as a function of social interdependence and of socio-cultural development.

Everywhere the use of fire and caring for it require certain social arrangements and individual adjustments. Fire exerts inexorable constraints to which people respond by developing commands and prohibitions and forms of self-restraints. The control of fire is always part of a system of social control and self-control . . . (1987: 458–9)

That is why it is possible to consider the mastery of fire as a kind of civilizing process in Elias's specific sense.

Taking into account the natural causes of fires (lightning, eruptions, and so on), together with the varying forms it takes, speeds it travels, and ecological effects it has in various environments, it is clear that hominids – like other animals – must often have encountered wildfires. A forest fire spreading rapidly is extremely alarming and no reaction but flight is possible. But in the aftermath of a fire it is known that many species of predators – hawks for instance – seek the charred remains of animals for food among the warm embers. Hominids no doubt did the same, and had advantages over most other species, for instance their more flexible hands, with which they could use sticks to probe the embers without burning themselves. Moreover, not all fires are equally dangerous:

smouldering bush fires spread relatively slowly and can be approached with less risk. It is therefore very likely that hominids discovered, probably on countlessly repeated occasions, that poking a fire with a stick could cause it to flare up again, that a fire could be prolonged by putting new wood on it, and that a stick burning at one end could be carried elsewhere with reasonable safety.

Nevertheless, fire is always dangerous to some extent: it burns skin on contact, and that has not changed throughout history. Handling it or using it in any way always necessitates caution and precaution. It is easy to overlook the control of fear which must always have played a part in handling fire. If people have gradually learned to control fire, this is due in considerable part to their also having learned to control the fears it arouses in themselves. Technical control is always bound up with a measure of self-control.

It is also easy to overlook the fact that gathering wood and feeding a fire with it are activities which people perform, not in their own immediate interests, but so to speak 'in the service of fire' (Goudsblom 1987: 465). Tending a fire was a rudimentary form of the 'detour behaviour' which was later to be required in more obvious form in herding and agricultural societies, where animals and plants had to be tended in order to reap future benefit from present work. That in turn involves the mental capacity for synthesis, of symbolically making connections between past, present and future.

The 'domestication of fire', and the transition from its passive to its active use by humans, can perhaps only be said to have actually begun when they discovered how to collect and preserve it, transporting it to and keeping it alight at a place of their choice. Again, this was probably repeated many times. Just to keep a fire burning requires social arrangements and self-discipline; probably fires often went out through rain or neglect, so that hominid groups for a time possessed fire only intermittently. For it was probably only much later that the much more elaborate skills of *making* fire (by such means as the rotating of wood of the 'fire-drill') were discovered; but these skills were mastered by at least some members of every recorded human group.

The long process of the human mastery of fire, beginning even before *Homo sapiens* had assumed its final biological form, illustrates many of the features encountered in the investigation of long-term social processes. It is impossible neatly to separate 'causes' from 'effects', or to point to a few decisive 'factors'. Rather the process is marked by spiral effects, in which the consequences of one stage of the process feed back onto the preconditions in shaping the next phase of development.

The preconditions for the mastery of fire include humans' flexible hands and erect posture. The species responsible for maintaining fires for over two hundred thousand years in a cave near Peking was indeed the appropriately named *Homo erectus*, an immediate precursor of *Homo sapiens*. But we have already just cited Elias's argument that the evolution of the hand cannot be understood separately from the evolution of the brain and the human capacity for synthesis and for learning from each other. The same applies here too: the mastery of fire involves at once technical, mental and social developments interwoven with each other.

The ability to carry fire to a chosen place and maintain it there had immense advantages. It would have enabled early humans to drive away wild animals and defend a cave, for instance, as a permanent place of residence. That in turn would facilitate the transmission of the arts of tending fires over many generations. Those arts included not just technical skills but also certain insights and emotional attitudes, all of which could be developed only by learning from others in a social context.

The control of fire implies a combination of knowledge, courage and skill. In dealing with fire it is of vital importance that people can command an appropriate balance of daring and caution, that they neither immediately panic nor grow reckless and forget how dangerous fire is. A certain measure of self-control is part and parcel of technical control – this applied to tending a fire just as much as to any other human skill. The emotional security with which people can approach fire is furthered in turn by the knowledge and dexterity which they have acquired and on the basis of which they can be confident that they are indeed able to master the fire, to let it flare up, smoulder, or go out at will. (Goudsblom 1987: 469–70)

It is easy to see how humans' use of primitive fire-arms (in a quite literal sense) tilted the power ratio between humans and wild animals decisively in humans' favour: other animals could only flee. But it is also possible that it was the greater skill of *Homo sapiens* in the use of fire which proved critical in competition with other hominids. They, indeed, may have been driven back into the forest and regressed. At any rate, they are now extinct, and the human species-monopoly of the active use of fire is and has been for a great many millennia absolute.

In the course of later human social development, the dangers associated with fire have changed: in some respects they are less, in others greater because of the changing patterns of social interdependencies. In the same way, societies may have become less conscious of the dangers and skills in fire management now taken for granted. But the full picture must await completion of Goudsblom's ambitious project.

TIME AND TIMING

Elias's own most ambitious investigation of a civilizing process at the level of humanity as a whole is his *Über die Zeit* (1984a). This is one of his most profound and important books, which he places (1984a: xliv) on a par with *The Civilizing Process* and his sociological theory of knowledge. It is, however, a very difficult book. That is partly because it was first written in four separate instalments (in English) and published during 1974 to 1975 in Dutch in issues of the journal *De Gids*. The part-work origin makes Elias's usual spiral interweaving of many complex arguments on various levels seem even more difficult to follow. That is compounded by its further expansion for publication as a book of nearly 200 pages without any division by chapters or even sub-headings.[8] The effect is more than ever to make Elias seem the James Joyce of sociologists; yet just as there is great art in Joyce's stream of consciousness, so there is substantial content in the apparent shambles of Elias's argument. But these are superficial reasons for the book's difficulty: the more important reason is that, as even Elias is forced to confess, the whole question of time and timing is inherently extremely difficult. The book rewards close study. Only a brief outline of its argument is possible here, but the book is equally relevant both to this present chapter and to the two preceding ones.

Elias's theory of time springs directly from what has already been said of the human capacity for the use of symbols and the accumulation of knowledge through intergenerational learning processes. For the perception of events which happen one after the other as a 'sequence in time' presupposes the uniquely human potential for synthesis – that is, the capacity to make connections through the use of symbols. This is, as we have seen, innate but activated and patterned through experience. The specific manifestation of the capacity which is crucial to all forms of timing is human beings' capacity for seeing in their mind's eye what happened earlier, together with what happened later and what is actually happening now, and for connecting them together in a single mental picture. Memory obviously plays a fundamental part in the process of visualizing together what does not happen together in actual fact, and experiencing them as being connected. Putting it in a nutshell 'it is meaningless to say that it is 4 o'clock now, unless one envisages at the same time that it was 2 o'clock before and will be 6 o'clock later' (1984a: 45). The very concepts 'earlier' and 'later' are manifestations of this human facility.

The capacity for synthesis in general is fundamental to human beings' means of orientation. Less than any other species are they orientated by unlearned reactions. More than any other creatures they are orientated by perceptions patterned by learning and, uniquely moreover, by the experience not of each individual but also of long chains of generations. It is this capacity for intergenerational learning processes which has led to the gradual improvement and extension of human means of orientation over many centuries. Elias's thesis is that what is today conceptualized and experienced as 'time' *is also just a human means of orientation*, evolved through experience in a long intergenerational learning process.

For all its simplicity, this proposition is quite difficult to grasp. It seems *too* simple. The word 'time' itself seems to refer to an object, a substance. It is yet another, and a particularly important and difficult instance of a process-reducing concept. If we speak of 'measuring' time, it seems as though we are dealing with something like the height of a mountain or the width of a river.[9] It helps to avoid this pitfall if, instead of using the substantial form, the noun 'time', we use the verbal forms 'to time' and 'timing'. They serve to remind us that time-measurement or synchronization is 'not merely a relationship, but a capacity for establishing relationships'. They are a human social activity with specific objectives. But who relates what to what, and why? Elias's basic answer is that the word 'time' is

a symbol of a relationship that a human group – that is, a group of beings biologically endowed with the capacity for memory and synthesis – establishes between two or more continua of changes, one of which is used by it as a frame of reference for the other (or others). (1984a: 11–12)

Habits of thought cannot be easily overturned. It remains very difficult for most people in modern societies to escape the feeling that time, though less tangible, is essentially like a river, flowing on at a certain speed and carrying them along in it whether or not they exert themselves and even if their eyes are closed. That 'time' refers to the human social activity of timing, and that our modern conception of time as a continuous flow is not the way all human beings have always conceived it, is difficult to grasp.

The social need for timing was much less acute and pervasive in earlier societies than in the more highly organized modern industrial states. As early as *The Civilizing Process* (1939: II, 247–8), Elias had noted how the increased differentiation and integration of social functions meant that in most modern societies, many long chains of interdependence intersect within the individual, requiring a constant awareness of time in the co-ordination of numerous activities (see p. 96 above). Thus the increasingly complex structure of social interdependencies has gone along with the development of a particularly complex system of self-regulation and an acute individual sensibility with regard to time. The external, social compulsion of time, represented by calendars, timetables, clocks, personal diaries and wristwatches forms a fine mesh of relatively unobtrusive, moderate, even and non-violent, *but omnipresent and inescapable* social constraints. These are precisely the characteristics which promote the formation of individual self-constraints.

Moreover, the early stage in a child's life at which the social regulation of time begins to be individualized through training contributes a good deal to the solidity and inescapability of the personal time-conscience.

The inner voice asking the time is ever-present. It is no wonder that, to people with this personality structure, the experience of all natural, social and personal sequences in terms of the regulative time symbols of their societies often appears as a feature of their own nature, and then of human nature in general. People equipped with such an ingrained, uniform and omnipresent time-conscience find it difficult to imagine that there are others who lack the ever-alert compulsion to know the time. *This individualization of social time-control therefore bears in almost paradigmatic form the features of a civilizing process.* (1984a: xxxii; my italics)

Still further difficulty arises from the very effectiveness of the symbols that have been developed for timing. So reality-congruent are they, so adequate to their purpose, that people have difficulty in distinguishing between symbol and reality. For example, the distinction is easily blurred between a sequence of events such as a person's life, on the one hand, and the relation between this sequence and that of the calendar on the other. The result is that people find it hard to resist the feeling that 'time' is passing, 'whereas in reality it is the natural sequence of their life, or perhaps the transformation of society and nature, to which the feeling of passing applies' (1984a: xxxiii). This characteristic 'fetish-quality' of time, as Elias calls it, applies at least as strongly to clocks as calendars. People in urban societies especially, he observes (1984a: 95), make and use clocks in a manner reminiscent of the making and use of masks in many pre-urban societies. People are aware that they are made by humans but they are experienced as if they represented an extra-human existence. Masks are seen as embodiments of spirits; clocks are seen as embodiments of 'time'. They 'indicate time'. But time is not a substance.

Nowhere is the fetish quality of time more evident than in the long tradition of discussions of time among philosophers and scientists. They have, says Elias (1984a: 101), indulged down the centuries in a wild goose chase, a hunt for something that does not exist, a hunt for 'time' as an immutable datum given to, and experienced by, all humans in the same way. They have again and again forced themselves into a choice between two equally untenable basic assumptions about time. Underlying *both* positions, yet again, is the unquestioned epistemological model of *homo clausus*: the unchallenged assumption of the great divide between the individual mind 'inside', looking out on and trying to make sense – alone and unassisted by others – of the 'external' world outside the self.

On the one hand there has been the view that 'time' is, like any physical object, part of the external nature existing quite independently of human beings perceiving and conceiving of it. That was Newton's view, and it largely persisted among scientists until Einstein set the seal on the discovery that time was a form of relationship, and not an objective flow, a part of Creation. Even Einstein, remarks Elias, did not entirely escape the pressure of word-fetishism and in his own way gave new sustenance to the myth of reified time, for example by maintaining that under certain circumstances time could contract or expand (1984a: 9).

On the other hand, in the mainstream Western philosophical tradition, which Elias once again traces from Descartes through Kant to more recent metaphysicians like Bergson and Heidegger, 'time' is assumed to be a universal form of human consciousness. In this view, it is an inherent quality of the human mind that it has not just a *general* capacity for synthesis, for making connections, but for making connections of *specific* kinds – according to categories such as substance, space, mechanical causality, and time. As part of their power of reasoning, humans can and must, always and everywhere, order events in the same way, in terms of 'time', without any learning or prior experience.

That view, says Elias, is the result of philosophers simply using the concepts available to them in their own society – concepts they have learned from their elders – and simply projecting them to all of mankind past, present, or future, as universals of human perception, without considering how they arose in an intergenerational learning process.

People did not always experience sequences of events in the way most common today – as an even, uniform and continuous flow of time. 'Time' in this sense is already a concept at a very high level of synthesis,[10] and it presupposes a very large social fund of knowledge about ways of measuring time-sequences and about their regularities. At earlier stages, people did not have this knowledge, not because they were less 'intelligent' but because this knowledge by its nature took a long time to develop. Among the earliest time-meters were the movements of the sun, moon and stars; and yet our most remote ancestors lacked the clear picture we now have (and have had for centuries) of how these movements are connected and regular. Or they had only a partial and fantasy-laden picture of the connections. Nor did the specific time-units such as 'day', 'month', 'year' neatly interlock according to an established calendar – let alone era time-scales for dating the years in non-recurrent sequence – always exist. In the remote past, people would use more particularizing terms, such as moon when we would say month, 'harvest' when we would say year, and so on. Without a firm yardstick for timing events, without the development of time-reckoning in social life and the close-knit grid of clocks, calendars and era scales, the conception of time as smoothly and continuously flowing is impossible.[11]

Nor has it always been necessary. Like many other social skills, timing has grown slowly over the centuries hand in hand with the growth of specific social requirements. In this instance, it is people's need to co-ordinate and synchronize their own activities with each other and with sequences of natural events such as the seasons. The basic question to which they need an answer is 'When shall we do it?'. The question, however, is not equally pressing in every kind of society. In groups of hunters and gatherers the need for actively timing and dating events is minimal. Passive timing in response to bodily urges with little or no reflection may suffice. At least where food is naturally abundant, it may be enough for people to hunt when they feel hungry and stop exerting themselves when they are full, to fall asleep when it grows dark (or when they are tired) and get up with the sun.

With the transition to agriculture, problems of active timing – and also of active social and self-control – become more pressing. It is essential to know the right time to sow one's seeds (and also probably to perform the festivals associated with securing a successful harvest). Elias gives a number of instances, especially from West African ethnography, of the role of priests in watching for and keeping count of the new moon. Even when they already knew that the movements of the sun and moon in the sky were quite regular, people in many simpler societies still could not calculate them in advance by blind reckoning. The new moon had actually to be sighted. It was often a priest's duty to call out when he saw it; interestingly, the word 'calendar' is derived indirectly from the Latin *calare*, to call out. Similarly, whatever its precise religious functions were, Stonehenge seems to have been a device for fixing the point at which the solstice occurred.

In such simpler societies, timing tends to have a 'point-like', discontinuous character (1984a: 64ff). Continuous time-keeping is neither possible nor necessary. All that is needed is to fix a few points at which vital activities must be performed. The transition towards a continuously flowing, fine mesh of timing and time-consciousness takes place very gradually in conjunction with the growth of more complex social organization and the necessity for co-ordinating and synchronizing many more elaborately interlocking activities.[12] In particular it was associated with the development of state-societies (1984a: 19ff;

181–6). The first systematic calendar began to be made in the ancient civilizations. Priests, as learned men, continued to be involved, but time-keeping (like the minting of money) often became a monopoly of the secular rulers. At the height of Rome's power Julius Caesar consulted Egyptian priests in formulating a calendar which still leaves clear marks on timing today. Only in the sixteenth century did Pope Gregory XIII reform the Julian calendar to bring it back, notably through the intercalation of leap years, into line with astronomical cycles. Only gradually was the Gregorian calendar imposed by secular rulers in the various states of Europe. It appears to have been King Charles IX of France who in 1563 fixed the New Year at the beginning of January: custom in that respect until then had varied.

Nowadays, people are mostly unconscious of the difficulties of establishing a calendar. They are probably slightly more aware of the increasing precision with which activities are co-ordinated by means of smaller recurrent time-units like minutes and seconds. The spread of railways gives a vivid demonstration of the link between the development of time-keeping and of increasingly complex webs of interdependence. Though Elias does not mention it, 'railway time' was a great source of humour in mid-nineteenth-century British magazines: puffing provincial gentlemen were depicted as missing the train which left their local station at noon Greenwich Mean Time, rather than noon by the church clock which was still set by the sun as it was observed locally. The electric telegraph, as well as the railway, was a condition for that national, and later international, synchronization. Soon the church clock would be set by the Greenwich time signal on the radio. Something that Elias does mention is the astonishment of a Latin American lady on discovering that station clocks in Germany nowadays have a second hand as well as hour and minute hands – the density and complexity of traffic movements make it essential.

More difficult even than formulating a regularly recurring annual calendar was working out era time-scales for hundreds or thousands of *non-recurring* years. Both the necessity and the possibility of such scales arose only with the development of social units such as states and churches which were long-lasting but never static and unchanging. Within these long-lasting 'continua of changes', living groups – usually the ruling groups – found it necessary for the functioning of their institutions to keep alive the memory of the continuity of these institutions in a precise and articulate manner (1984a: 24). The long-lastingness of such institutions raised not only the need but also the possibility of era-scales, for a typical early method of keeping account of the sequence of the passing years was in terms of a sequence of rulers and the sequence of years in each reign. The longest and best-known era scale of the ancient world was of this kind, counting the non-recurrent sequence of years from the reign of one Babylonian ruler. Later there were Greek and Roman era scales. That most widely employed today, counting the succeeding years before (BC) and since (AD) the (inaccurately estimated) birth of Christ, came into use in Western Europe only from the eighth century AD onwards (see Herrin 1987: 3–6). 'The emergence of long-lasting and relatively stable state-units . . . was a condition of the experience of time as a uni-directional flow' (1984a: 24).

Era time-scales had, and have, notably two uses which to modern eyes may present a contrast. On the one hand they enable the living generation to determine with accuracy their own position in the sequence of generations. In modern terms, that may seem a matter for history and the social sciences. On the other hand, time-reckoning in terms of consecutive reigns and their years also made it possible, quite early in Babylonian times, to describe the distance in time between unusual events in the sky, such as eclipses. Later, it was the Babylonian era time-scale which Ptolemy employed when constructing his model of the physical universe. In the modern view, that looks like 'natural science'. This is only one example of the intertwining of the development of social and physical time-meters. One of the recurrent themes of Elias's *Über die Zeit* is how the study of timing blurs the taken-for-granted divide between nature and society, nature and culture.

This brings us back to the question of what it is that people really do when they use slowly and painfully developed symbols of 'time'. What exactly is happening when people are timing something? They are employing not just the general human capacity for synthesis but, says Elias (1984a: 42), a specific form of intellectual synthesis which is far from simple. When they ask *when* something happens, they are aiming to pinpoint events within a continuous flow of events, to fix milestones indicating relative beginnings and endings within the flow, to mark off one stretch from another, to compare their length or 'duration', and so on. The milestones are built into such a sequence *with the aid of another sequence*. Timing arrangements always involve connecting *two or more* different sequences of continuous changes to each other, using one sequence as a timing standard for the others.

There is one set of much-used time concepts – 'past', 'present', 'future' – the meaning of which takes into account the human capacity for synthesis in a way that concepts like 'year', 'month', 'hour' do not make immediately evident. To speak of a past, present and future is to draw attention to the experience of human beings focusing on a sequence of events:

the meaning of past, present and future constantly changes, because the human beings to whom they refer and whose experience they represent also constantly change. The connection with them and their experience is included in the meaning of these terms . . . The concepts past, present and future include in their meaning the relationship of an experiencing person (or persons) to a sequence of changes. It is in relation to someone who experiences it that one moment of a continuous flow assumes the character of a present *vis-à-vis* [other moments with the character] of a past or a future . . . One might say that past, present and future, although three different words, form a single concept. (1984a: 47–8).

In fact, says Elias, the terms past, present and future are characteristic of the fifth dimension of the universe. For with the emergence of human beings, the universe takes on, in addition to the four dimensions of space and time, a fifth dimension of consciousness or experience. Everything which takes place within the purview of human beings now becomes capable of being experienced and represented by man-made symbols, and needs in this sense to be defined no longer by four co-ordinates but five (1984a: 52–3).[13] Yet this fifth dimension,

Elias attempts to demonstrate in his *Über die Zeit*, can be investigated as precisely as the aspects of timing to which scientists principally pay attention. There is no need to relegate to metaphysics what does not fall within physics.

'Time' raises the sort of puzzle with which sociologists, at least since Durkheim, have often struggled. The use of the term as if 'time' had an independent existence is certainly 'a striking example of the way in which a widely used symbol, cut loose from any observable data, can in common discourse assume a life of its own' (1984a: 98). The impression of its independent existence has a double origin. First, 'time', in common with many other social institutions, is relatively independent of any particular human beings, though not of human beings as societies or as humanity as a whole. Secondly, it is also connected with the fact that timing devices, whether or not made by humans, are self-moving physical processes. This double-layered relative independence as a social institution and as a physical movement, however, easily misleads. It is a relative independence akin to that of language. 'Just as languages can only fulfil their function as long as they are common languages of whole groups of people and would lose it if every person made up a language of his own, so clocks can fulfil their function only if the changing configuration of their moving hands – in short the 'time' they indicate - is the same for whole groups of people; they would lose their function as timing devices if every person made up a 'time' of his own (1984a: 99).[14] This is one of the sources of the compelling force 'time' has over any individual person. The individual has to attune his or her own conduct to the established 'time' of any group of which he forms part; and the denser the web of interdependencies binding people to each other, 'the stricter becomes the regimen of the clocks'.

SURVIVAL UNITS AND THE INTEGRATION OF HUMANITY

The integration of people in longer chains and denser webs of functional interdependence, especially in long-lasting state-societies, helped to raise both the need for and the possibility of more standardized timing. This process of the integration of humanity, over a longer period and on a broader canvas than he attempted in *The Civilizing Process* has itself been one of the major intellectual concerns of Elias's old age.[15]

Hobbes, attempting to form a picture of the earliest condition of human societies on the basis of the very limited factual knowledge available to him in the seventeenth century, postulated as the primal condition of humankind the war of all against all. It was not a bad guess, although in the light of the fuller knowledge available to us from archaeology and anthropology it requires significant correction. Hobbes, like most of his fellow philosophers, took the individual as his point of departure. However, though the life of early humans may well have been, in his famous phrase, 'poor, nasty, brutish and short', it was never (as Hobbes also asserted) 'solitary'. The primal condition of society is not a war of every human being against every other. It appears to be rather a condition in which human *groups* have no other protection against possible annihilation or enslavement by another stronger *group* than their own fists, weapons and *collective* fighting capacity. In other words, people always lived together in groups which Elias calls *survival units*.[16] Between members of one survival unit, the level of co-operation in finding food and other necessities, and in defence against or attacks upon other survival units, was relatively high. But at first the survival units were tiny – hunting and gathering bands of a few dozen at most – and all other survival units were to be feared as potentially each other's most dangerous enemy.[17] The level of violence customary between members of different survival units – each regarding the other as outsiders – was very high.[18]

Over the course of human development as a whole, the overall trend has been towards survival units larger and larger both in population and in geographical extent. Of course there have been many reversals. One example is the period of centrifugal feudalization in Western Europe between the decline of Rome and the reassertion of centripetal forces in processes of state formation (see chapter 3 above). The European state-formation process itself is one small instance of the overall trend towards bigger survival units incorporating more people and more territory. Elias recognizes, however, that a full study of this tendency would have to deal with the great variety of competitive figurations in different continents at different stages of the development of society. Such a study would, for instance, have to show why it was that the war-leaders of sedentary populations organized as military-agrarian state-societies were eventually able to mobilize the military and economic resources to defeat decisively recurrent invasions by migrant pre-state peoples. (Only at the stage of development which European society reached approximately in the fifteenth and sixteenth centuries did the power differentials between state- and pre-state societies become so great that the latter no longer constituted any serious military danger for the former. In Africa, the age of migrating peoples persisted very much later.) Such a study would also have to explain why military-agrarian societies generally supplanted religious-agrarian societies (Goudsblom 1988). It would have to look too at the role of military power in state-formation processes in continents and periods beyond those with which Elias dealt in the European case.[19] But the overall trend towards bigger survival units is clear.

Equally clear, too, is the persistence throughout this long-term trend of a differential use of violence within and between survival units. It is often overlooked that in volume II of *The Civilizing Process*, Elias constantly draws attention to the contrast between the taming of impulses towards the use of violence *within* state-societies and the relatively unbridled persistence of violence in relations *between* states. The size of the power-system encompassing rival survival units has grown: from the French and English kings in the Middle Ages, through the struggles of the Valois and Habsburgs, until it encompassed all of Europe by the Thirty Years War and was world-wide by the twentieth century (1939: II, 144–7).

Writing on the eve of the Second World War, Elias was highly conscious of the tensions propelling the states of the world towards a global conflict, but saw the possibility that in the long term the outcome might be something like a world government. What he wrote then was as follows:

[T]hat, in our day, just as earlier, the dynamics of increasing interdependence are impelling the figuration of state societies towards . . . conflicts, to the formation of monopolies of physical force over larger areas of the earth and thus, through all the terrors and struggles, towards their pacification, is clear enough. And . . . beyond . . . the tensions of the next stage are already emerging. One can see the first outlines of a worldwide system of tensions composed by alliances and supra-state units of various kinds, the prelude of struggles embracing the whole globe, which are the precondition for a worldwide monopoly of physical force, *for a single central political institution and thus for the pacification of the earth.* (1939: ii, 331–2; my italics)

In part, that passage still seems highly prescient, in view of the emergence after 1945 of inter-state groupings such as NATO, the European Community, the Warsaw Pact and Comecon and others. But the last vision, of a single central monopoly apparatus with the capacity to punish states which breach the peace, seems more remote than ever, as Elias himself emphasizes in his later writings such as *Humana Conditio* (1985a: 112). He rates the chances of nuclear war between the superpowers as quite high.[20] The consequences of that would be far-reaching social *dis*integration, putting an end, perhaps for a very long time, to the long-term civilizing trend. He surveys a great many instances of 'hegemonial struggles' between state-societies from antiquity onwards, and the 'hegemonial fevers' which members of competing survival units experienced in the course of their struggles with each other. There has been no case in history, he says (1985a: 68–9) where competition between great powers did not sooner or later lead to war.

From this, many people are apt to conclude that there is, innate in human beings, an 'aggressive instinct'. Elias is careful to deny this.

One has to take some care to distinguish between aspects of human beings which do not change over time because they are – or are connected with – *biological* universals, and other aspects of humans which have not changed because they are closely connected with *social* problems that have so far remained unmanageable and unsolved, though there are no reasons to think they cannot be solved. (1984a: 131; my italics)

As an example of a biological universal, Elias once again cites the 'alarm reaction', the automatic response to experienced danger which puts the organism in a higher gear, preparing for 'fight or flight'. This is a well-researched reaction pattern which in broad outline *Homo sapiens* shares with many other species. It can easily give rise to the notion of an inborn aggressiveness. In fact, Elias points out, this automatic preparation for fast and energetic action in response to danger is far less specific than the concept of 'aggressiveness' suggests. It has to be distinguished clearly from human beings' long-standing custom of settling inter-tribal or inter-state conflicts by reciprocal killings.

Elias denies, on the one hand, that there is any evidence for the suggestion that human beings are unable to solve inter-group conflicts by means other than violence. There is indeed a great deal of evidence – accumulated through his own and others' investigations of civilizing processes of various kinds – that human beings' aggressive impulses are capable of being tamed. On the other hand, Elias also denies that any solution to the *social* problem of settling inter-state disputes without major wars is yet on the horizon. In that respect he has had a longstanding, if mild, disagreement with his friend Godfried van Benthem van den Bergh.

The Taming of the Great Powers?

Van Benthem van den Bergh, one of the leading Dutch writers on international relations and nuclear weapons, has employed Elias's theory of civilizing processes and his notion of 'double-bind figuration' in arriving at a lower estimate than Elias's own of the chance that the rivalry between the superpowers will end in nuclear war. He argues in fact that nuclear weapons have unintended benefits: they force the great powers to conduct themselves in a much more prudent and restrained manner than in prenuclear times, and may come to serve, in the absence of anything yet resembling a world government, as a functional equivalent at the international level of the central monopoly of violence held by states. He has presented his case in a series of essays (Van Benthem van den Bergh 1980, 1983, 1984), culminating in a book, *The Taming of the Great Powers* (1989).

Both he and Elias (1983d: 74–115) see the risk of a nuclear holocaust arising not because any group of people with the means to do so seriously wants to bring about such a war, but because the bi-polar struggle between the superpowers has assumed the form of a double-bind figuration. The compelling force of such an unplanned social process cannot be understood simply in voluntaristic terms – that is, in terms of the perceptions, plans and intentions of one side or the other considered alone. For the perceptions, plans and intentions of each side are in considerable part formed in response to the perceptions, plans and intentions of the other. The two sides are bound together in interdependence through the danger they pose each other. Each can destroy the other. They are locked together like boxers in a 'frozen clinch' (1970a: 169), neither able to escape for fear of exposing itself to the other's blows.

Moreover, a double-bind figuration tends to be *self-escalating* for several reasons. Each side accumulates more arms in response to the other's growing arsenal. Each side has scientists who conduct research into new means of gaining a decisive advantage over the other. It also tends towards self-escalation for a reason more distinctive to Elias's thought: the reciprocal danger enhances emotive fantasy and unrealistic ideology on both sides.

In the essay 'The fishermen in the maelstrom' (1983d), Elias dazzlingly brings together his theory of involvement and detachment in human knowledge, the notions of we-images and they-images (associated with the model of established-outsiders relations), and his view of the contemporary superpower double-bind. Breaking the escalating propensities of the double-bind cannot be achieved by agreements on material weapons only. Ideological weapons have to be scrapped too, for the emotional fantasies and belief of the antagonists in relation to each other play as major a part in keeping the process going as does the competitive circularity in the development of weapons. Each side's they-image involves a distortion (based on something like the 'minority of the worst'), just as its we-image is an exaggerated picture of virtue ('minority of the best'). Relaxation of the double-bind process may just be possible because fear of the bomb may outweigh the fear and hatred of the enemy; but it can only be very slow for it requires 'a change in the mentality of both sides, a higher level of detachment and self-control in their dealings with one another'. And this is extremely difficult, because

If the danger which one group of humans represents for the other is high, the emotivity of thinking, its fantasy-content, is also likely to remain high. If the fantasy-content of thinking and knowledge is high and thus its reality-orientation low, the ability of both sides to bring the situation under control will also remain low, the danger level and the level of fear will remain high, and so on *ad infinitum*. (1983d: 99)

For Elias, the current struggle of the superpowers differs little in its symptoms from any of the hegemonial fevers he has instanced (1983d: 86–8; 1985a) in the earlier history of humanity. What *is* different, however, is the very existence of nuclear weapons since 1945. On that, Elias and Van Benthem van den Bergh are agreed, though they do not fully agree about its implications.

Van Benthem van den Bergh's argument is developed with far more attention to the precise implications of the nuclear balance and the development of superpower relations since the Second World War than Elias gives. The gist of his argument can still be summarized briefly.

The nuclear balance, based on the vulnerability of each other's societies and the invulnerability of their nuclear arsenals, has changed the nature of deterrence. Deterrence no longer means that one state through the strength of its arms and armies prevents an attack by another state. Now the opponents are deterred by the *common* danger, a *shared* risk that any use of violence between them *may* escalate into nuclear war. And nuclear war may in turn lead to the total destruction of *both* sides, with neither side's social institutions (nor those of the rest of the world's states caught up in such a holocaust) able to continue to function in any recognizable form. In contrast to all former weapons, which made the fighting and winning of wars possible, nuclear weapons only have (in Bernard Brodie's phrase) 'utility in non-use', for the prevention of war. The situation has been summed up as Mutually Assured Destruction, or MAD for short. But, says van Benthem van den Bergh, the iron embrace of the nuclear powers is not so mad at all, and certainly the least mad of all the ways of thinking about nuclear weapons and strategic situations between nuclear powers. *Nuclear weapons may thus have already begun to function as an external constraint towards self-restraint* in international relations. Drawing on Elias's work, Van Benthem van den Bergh sees an analogy with the civilizing process within states. Peaceful conduct within states is not a gift from God: it requires the ever-present threat of the state's monopoly of violence, even if that threat, at least in Western Europe, has been pushed more and more into the background.

In inter-state relations, nuclear weapons are the only conceivable alternative to a world monopoly of violence. More exactly, the particular figuration formed and perceived as such by the nuclear powers could develop into a 'global pacification regime, as the danger of escalation of any conflict anywhere in the world may bring the great powers jointly to help remove the sources of what are usually called 'regional conflicts'. Not nuclear weapons *per se*, but the MAD balance has acquired a civilizing function in international politics: it forces the political and military establishments of the great powers to restrain themselves and to act with great care and circumspection. Playing with acronyms, one could say that MAD leads to MES: Mutually Assured Destruction exerts pressures towards Mutually Expected Self-restraint. Possibly the most graphic illustration of the 'civilizing' functions of MAD is the extraordinary lengths to which both sides have gone to eliminate the possibility of accidental or unauthorized use of their own nuclear weapons. Also, since the object lesson or 'reality shock' of the Cuban missile crisis, the great powers have avoided any crisis at that level of intensity.

There is, Van Benthem van den Bergh argues, of course no certainty that the risk of global destruction and of wilful or unintended escalation in the long run will lead to a complete 'domestication of the great powers'. The process of taming faces formidable obstacles, inherent in any double-bind figuration: political conflicts first of all, but also military-bureaucratic and industrial interests, the development of military technology in mutual anticipation, and pre-nuclear strategic modes of thought. The last raises many paradoxes. MAD is widely regarded as morally repulsive, yet any attempt to undermine its stability could greatly raise the risk of uncontrollable escalation. Nuclear arsenals could be scaled down quite safely, but not abolished, for the knowledge of how to make atomic weapons is indestructible and so, if both sides agreed to scrap all their nuclear weapons, weapons would become relative again and the risk of war could increase – war in which nuclear weapons would then be sure to be used. President Reagan's Space Defence Initiative is dangerous for the same paradoxical reason in its undermining of the 'immoral' notion of MAD by offering the possibility of surviving a nuclear exchange, while in fact increasing its likelihood.

If such obstacles could gradually be overcome, Van Benthem van de Bergh considers it possible that the common interests of the nuclear oligopolists may in the long run lead them to collaborate in acting toether as 'international sheriffs' (as President Roosevelt termed it in his vision of collective security at the time of Yalta). However, this cannot become a great power condominium, jointly ruling the world. 'In terms of all other areas but the nuclear, and perhaps the military in general, in the economic, political and cultural spheres, the great powers will not derive many benefits from their oligopoly, as nuclear weapons cannot be used for positive political influence' (1983: 197–8). At first, argues Van Benthem van den Bergh (1989), the external constraint of the great powers regime will *force* other states to behave peacefully; but in the longer term, the existence of a functional equivalent for the central monopoly of the state could become a social constraint towards self-restraint, as it will change states' expectations of each other's conduct. He does not see this as likely, but as the only possible way in which a peaceful world can emerge.

Elias remains sceptical of this argument, even as far as it goes. The gist of *his* argument seems to stem from the conclusion he drew at the end of *The Civilizing Process*, that 'wars between smaller units have been, in the course of history up to now, inevitable stages and instruments in the pacification of larger ones' (1939: II, 331). (The royal mechanism operated in a similar way in the pacification of competition between social groups within states.) Elias's view is that, before the nuclear age, there have always been pressures and incentives towards integration on a higher level, because other larger survival units posed a threat from outside. Now, the integration of humanity as a whole means there is no *outside* threat: no they-threats, only we-threats. Van Bentham van den Bergh argues that nuclear weapons make development to a higher level of integration through hegemonial war impossible: a nuclear war would result in a throwback to a much lower level of integration.

Elias and Van Benthem van den Bergh do not quite agree with each other. Elias emphasizes the risk of war inherent in any inter-state double-bind figuration; Van Bentham van den Bergh does not disagree, but argues that the actual conduct of the great powers demonstrates that the nuclear balance and the ever-present risk of escalation makes them aware both of that danger and of the fact that it has become meaningless and suicidal to take risks that they would indeed have taken before MAD developed. He emphasizes the differences between the nuclear age and pre-nuclear times, Elias the continuity. Their disagreement demonstrates that Elias's kind of sociology leaves many questions open for discussion and further research, as it should.

CONCLUSION

The subjects discussed in this chapter – human emotions, the control of fire, timing, war and the nuclear arms race – seem at first glance very disparate. The connection between them is that they all involve considering civilizing processes on a third and hitherto less familiar level – the level not of the individual lifetime civilizing process, nor that of patterns of behaviour developing in particular human groups, but on the level of humanity as a whole. The very early development of the human species and human groups can be understood as resulting from the interweaving of biological and social processes. The development of humans' exceptionally powerful capacity for synthesis is to be seen in this way, and its significance is seen in both fire-control and timing considered as *very* long-term civilizing processes. Timing, it emerges, is very far from being a matter simply of technological advance alone: that intertwines with changes in social habitus. The domestication of fire, too, is seen to be bound up with self-domestication. From early in the development of humanity, fire posed dangers which humans learned to handle technically, socially and emotionally;

and their responses changed the character of the dangers, requiring new responses. At the present day, nuclear weapons pose severe dangers – humanity, now as an interdependent whole, is in an early phase of another process of learning to handle them.

PART IV
Disputes

10

Civilization and Decivilization

In the late twentieth century it is often easier to speak of *de*civilization than of civilization.

Most people, especially in the rich industrial countries, have – with much justification – become far more inhibited than their parents and grandparents about speaking of their own societies as the pinnacle of 'civilization'. This is partly because the dominant mood is more doubtful about whether the direction in which the rich countries have developed and are developing any longer represents 'progress' and the improvement of human happiness. But it is also partly because any mode of speaking and thinking which appears to rank the peoples of the world as 'higher' and 'lower', as more or less advanced, is seen as casting doubt upon the fundamentally equal worth and rights of all human beings. This is a very civilized way of viewing humans. Elias's own theories, as we have seen, give a clue to why this shift of attitude has taken place: it is connected with tilting of world balances of power, through colonial liberation movements and political and economic changes, to be somewhat less unequally against the Third World countries. But the fear of speaking in terms such as 'more civilized' and 'less civilized' is deeper than that: most people are only too conscious of the appalling atrocities committed in this century in the name of 'superior' races or belief-systems.

Yet if it is now difficult to speak unselfconsciously of 'civilization', the same does not apply to its opposite. There is a widespread readiness to speak of events in Hitler's Germany in the 1930s and 1940s, or Cambodia and the Lebanon in the 1970s and 1980s – to name just three examples – as 'a breakdown of civilization'. Even some less bloody trends in Western societies themselves are described in similar ways. The relaxation of manners, and particularly of sexual mores in the twentieth century is often viewed – by those who disapprove of it – as 'a breakdown of civilized standards'. Here the word 'civilization' is being used – albeit negatively – in popular discourse with all the connotations traced by Elias.

Translated from the plane of popular opinion to that of academic debate, however, these issues lead directly to the four major criticisms made of Elias's theory. These are what I shall call:

1 *The argument from cultural relativism.* At its most extreme, this argument calls in question whether it is valid to think in terms of developmental processes at all – civilizing, decivilizing or any other kind. Certainly the attitude that Wittfogel (1957: 7, 371) called developmental agnosticism has been widespread among twentieth-century social scientists.

2 *The argument from 'stateless civilizations'.* This is in effect a less extreme form of the first argument: it is simply that 'civilized' modes of behaviour and personality formation are found in societies where the conditions by which Elias explains their development in Europe – principally state monopolies of violence and advanced division of social functions – are absent.

3 *The 'permissive society' argument.* This is usually deployed by critics who, while prepared perhaps to accept Elias's picture of the civilizing of manners in Europe from the Middle Ages to the early twentieth century, nevertheless point to the 'permissive society' which has emerged since then, and argue that the civilizing process has gone into reverse and thus invalidated at least some aspects of Elias's theory.

4 *The 'barbarization' argument.* This could also be called 'the death camp' argument, for the Nazi period in Germany comes immediately to critics' minds. Sir Edmund Leach (1986) is typical of many in arguing that at the very time that Elias was formulating his thesis, 'Hitler was refuting the argument on the grandest scale'. In effect, this argument is yet another variant on cultural relativism: the contention is that, whatever may be true of superficial matters like table manners, fundamental qualities like the propensity to aggression and sex drives do not change much. 'Civilized' modern men and women are as capable of violence, bloodshed and cruelty as Stone Age tribal people of New Guinea.

THE ARGUMENT FROM CULTURAL RELATIVISM

Criticisms from the point of view of cultural relativism have often been levelled at Elias's work by sociologists, and especially by anthropologists who – working as they traditionally have done predominantly among non-European and pre-industrial societies – find any distinction between 'more civilized' and 'less civilized' human groups offensive. (The intimate association of anthropology with colonial rule in the past serves only to heighten anthropologists' sensitivities today.) Such critics have often seemed to have only slight acquaintance with Elias's writings. Here, however, we shall examine the version of these arguments put forward by the Dutch anthropologist Anton Blok at a conference held in Amsterdam in 1981.[1] What was remarkable about Blok's case was that not only did he have a close familiarity with all aspects of Elias's work, but that together with people like the sociologist Johan Goudsblom and the political scientist Godfried van Benthem van den Bergh he had, over the previous decade, championed Elias's cause among Dutch social scientists. We have already mentioned his use of Elias's ideas in his study of the Sicilian mafia (Blok 1974); in addition he had written an introduction to anthropology from this point of view (1978), and devoted his inaugural lecture at Nijmegen to the subject of 'Wittgenstein and Elias' (1976). It therefore caused a sensation when, at the 1981 conference, he first presented a paper distancing himself from Elias and then, in discussion, expressed his change of heart in much more emotional and emotion-arousing language. Blok moved quite suddenly, it seems, towards a viewpoint which is much closer to anthropological orthodoxy than his earlier one. His conference paper, 'Primitive and civilized', has been published in Dutch, along with other papers more or less critical of Elias, in a special issue of the journal *Sociologische Gids* (1982). The same journal later published a long critique of these papers by Goudsblom (1984). For an account of the discussion at the conference, however, it is necessary to rely on the report of it written by Nico Wilterdink (1982).

In his paper, Blok examined the conceptual opposition or dichotomy *primitive/civilized*. Now it must be said straight away that Elias himself never uses the term 'primitive' except (like Blok) in actual or implied quotation marks, and never as a crude opposite to 'civilized'. Nevertheless, the opposition undoubtedly has been used in popular thought, and indeed by an earlier generation of anthropologists. Blok came to the conclusion that these and similar concepts serve to legitimize the dominance of one group (who called themselves 'civilized') over another group (who were called 'primitive'). This, of course, is a very common pattern in established-outsiders relationships. It was, Blok said, 'the contribution of the Eliasian theory of the civilizing process to draw attention to the theme and idiom as well as the function of the notion of "civilization", not only with regard to Western Europe, but also other societies including the so-called primitive ones.'

The universal theme of all ideas of 'civilization', according to Blok, was the control of bodily functions, or in other words the repression of the 'animalic' characteristics of human beings. That is indeed, as we have seen, one element – though surely not the only or uniquely most basic one – in the civilizing process traced by Elias; and it is an element further elaborated by, among others, Blok, in his essay 'Behind the scenes' (1979). In the 1981 conference paper, however, Blok argued that different cultures handle the repression of the animalic in very different ways, and use correspondingly different scales to measure civilization. Therefore, he thought, it is impossible to develop a 'scientific' concept of civilization, a generally valid measuring rod against which the respective grades of civilization or differences between more and less civilized social formations can be read off (1982: 205–6).

This critique was not only greatly at odds with Blok's earlier work but, as Wilterdink (1982: 288) noted, also clearly derived from structuralist anthropology. This is seen not only in the discussion of primitive/civilized as a binary opposition in the style of Lévi-Strauss (a style that is anathema to Elias), but also in the way in which this apparently universal mental opposition has a purely arbitrary connection with the actual patterns of behaviour to which it is applied in one culture as against another.

In presenting his paper verbally, Blok considerably elaborated on his critique. According to Wilterdink's report, he argued that the concept of civilization is a native concept, strongly bound up with Western norms, prejudices and feelings of superiority; and this native category cannot be transformed without further development into a *sociological* category for typifying people's modes of behaviour and feeling in a scientifically based way. In *The Civilizing Process*, according to Blok, the transition from the native to a sociological category was made without any further argumentation. The consequence was that in that book, as well as in subsequent work influenced by it, 'the native and sociological categories are mixed up with one another' and that 'the assumptions and civilized norms developed in Western Europe had been used as general norms outside Europe too'. And Blok used this argument to level at Elias and his associates the charge of ethnocentrism.

A vigorous debate inevitably followed, which finally drew Blok into some intemperate remarks. He said that Elias's theory

is not only ethnocentric, it is evolutionist, it is unilinear-evolutionist, it is progressivist; and it is moreover – here we are concerned with the functions of the concept of civilization and of the theory of civilizing processes – it is moreover an aspect of a power structure, part of the apparatus of control by a powerful group, legitimizing their dominance; to put it in a less friendly way, *it is racist*; it means that other people, other cultures, can be denied an authentic humanity. (Quoted by Wilterdink 1982: 289–90; my italics)

Later, Blok repeated the epithet 'racist' with reference to Elias's remark (in his lecture on 'Pacification and violence' at the same conference) that people in unpacified African societies must have 'lived like wild animals' (cf. Elias 1983d: 66 and p. 168 above).

Some of Blok's arguments are more easily rebutted than others, but all need to be dealt with.

The charge of racism is patently absurd. The whole tenor of the *The Civilizing Process* is obviously *anti*-racist. In the 1930s, there were many people who were only too eager to interpret differences in manners, customs, mentality, personality structure and capabilities as proof of the inherent, biologically based, racial superiority of white, Western people. Elias's book demonstrated precisely that these differences were not in any sense inherent; on the contrary, they were the outcome of *social* processes capable of moulding more or less equally any human being caught up in them. As for his remark about 'living like wild animals', as Wilterdink commented (1982: 290), 'one would have to be hard of hearing not to have understood that by this Elias was referring to the *social realities* under which people in non-pacified societies have to live' – for example, the absolute necessity of being forever alert to danger with the watchfulness of the hunted.

The charge of ethnocentrism, of employing a theoretical schema entangled
with the values and prejudices of European society, falls into two parts. The
first is the more technical matter, concerning the distinction between 'native'
and 'sociological' (or 'scientific') concepts. Many attempts have been made to
draw a rigid line between the two, especially by social scientists influenced by
phenomenology and structuralism. From the 1950s onwards, cognitive
anthropologists studying native systems of taxonomy ('ethnobotany', 'ethno-
zoology', 'ethnomedicine' and so on) tried to distinguish strictly between 'emic'
and 'etic' data (from phon*emics* and phon*etics* in linguistics), by which they
referred respectively to data which are dependent for their meaning on context
and usage within a specific culture, and to data which (like population, or areas
under cultivation, or types of food eaten) can be compared cross-culturally by
reference to some standard grid or measuring rod (see Harris 1968: 568–604).
Within the discipline of sociology, similar arguments were deployed in the
1960s and 1970s by the ethnomethodological school of thought founded by
Harold Garfinkel. They criticized conventional sociology, as Blok criticized
Elias, for hopelessly entangling together the 'common sense' or 'everyday'
concepts which 'members' of a society use for practical purposes with the
'scientific' concepts of sociology itself; they alleged that sociologists tend 'to use
common sense knowledge of social structures as both a topic and resource of
inquiry' (Garfinkel 1967: 31). Their criticisms were derived from the views of
the phenomenological philosopher Alfred Schutz (1899–1959), who argued
that, out of the 'first degree constructs' or practical recipes and concepts used by
people in 'everyday' life, social scientists had to develop for their own purposes
clearer, more consistent 'constructs of the second degree'. I have argued at
length elsewhere (1975) that the ethnomethodologists went far beyond Schutz
in presuming that a rigid line of demarcation could be drawn between the two
kinds of concepts. For the present it is enough to acknowledge that the
relationship between 'native' and 'scientific' use of concepts is a general
question in the social sciences, not in any way peculiar to the notion of
'civilization'. Indeed Elias himself draws attention to the problem in emphasizing
the need for investigations in terms simultaneously of 'we-perspectives' and
'they-perspectives' (vocabulary, incidentally, which Blok continued to use at the
conference). However, Elias would emphatically deny that a sharp demarcation,
dichotomous polarity, can be drawn in a permanent, abstract, once-and-for-all,
timeless way. He argues (as we have seen) that concept-formation in the social
sciences is always a long-term *process*. All social-scientific concepts have been
gradually derived and developed out of ideas originating for more practical
purposes in so-called 'everyday' life. Only through using and refining them in
the course of whole sequences of investigations can they be made slowly more
suitable for use in a less involved, more detached way; only gradually do they
become less permeated by fantasy and heteronomous values and more 'reality-
congruent'. And Elias would claim to have made some contribution to
developing the notion of 'civilization' into forms more appropriate to social
scientific investigation.

This brings us back to the second, more substantive, part of the charge of ethnocentrism: the allegation that the theory of civilizing processes, like the 'native' use of 'civilization', serves to legitimize the dominance of the powerful. Here it is as well to recall that Elias, far from being blindly naïve about these things, actually begins *The Civilizing Process* by devoting the first forty-eight pages (see pp. 34–6 above) to showing how the very notion of civilization originated in a polemical context in Western European society, and how the concept had been used to legitimize the dominance first of certain groups in European states and then, increasingly, of European society as a whole *vis-à-vis* non-European and especially so-called primitive societies. Nevertheless, he said, with his eyes wide open to the ethnocentric use of the word by natives of Europe, 'The value judgements contained in such statements are obvious; the facts to which they relate are less so' (1968a: 222).

The facts include differences in social habitus, or the characteristic make-up of the personality, between different societies, cultures and periods. Few anthropologists object in principle to looking at how typical personality varies from society to society. One major speciality within American anthropology in particular from the late 1920s onwards was just such an investigation of 'Culture and Personality'.[2] Elias, however, is not interested only in comparing differences in social personality structure between societies synchronically; he is emphatically interested in diachronic changes, and in plotting the changes over time on an ordinal scale (not a ratio scale, of course – as he never tires of repeating, there are no zero points in any of these matters).

For this reason, among all Anton Blok's criticisms of Elias's theory of the civilizing process, by far the most crucial is that there is, and can be, no standard measuring rod against which to plot such changes. Against this, Elias's defenders at the 1981 Amsterdam conference proposed several related potential measuring rods. Cas Wouters observed that one important criterion in the degree of civilizing undergone was the distance between the emotional condition of adults and young children. Eddy Szirmai said that in his moralistic critique, Blok had skated over the question of 'whether members of so-called primitive societies might be proven to be "less civilized" in a technical sense if one employed a scientifically tenable theory, such as the level of development of the superego' (reported by Wilterdink 1982: 289, 296).

In fact Elias's theory of civilizing processes requires two measuring rods, for he is interested in the relationship between two sequential orders, broadly the sociogenetic and the psychogenetic. With some misgivings – for Elias does not see them as 'independent variables' – one might picture these as two axes of a graph. One scale or axis would concern the structure of development of social interdependencies, including the division of social functions and state formation. The second scale or axis would relate to the civilizing of behaviour and changes in personality structure,[3] also conceived of as a sequential order, in which development takes place in a discernible *direction*. One test of his theory may be thought of as involving the plotting of changes of personality structure and changes in social structures against each other on the relevant scales. Each plot would be dated, and the more closely a regression line could be fitted, and the more consistently were later dates more distant from the origin than earlier ones, the better would it be for Elias's hypothesis. A random scatter of date plots would negate the theory.

Some care is required, however, in using this heuristic image of a graph. What Elias does in *The Civilizing Process*, figuratively if not literally, is to draw a graph of development within a single cultural area. In this case the imaginary graph represents the track of development over time in European society. (Several different tracks would really be needed to cope with differences between regions and between strata.) Even in his later work on civilizing processes at the level of humanity as a whole, where the span of time is still greater, he is concerned with a *sequence of changes* within a given social unit.

Something logically very different would be involved if, while remaining on the level of civilizing processes in particular societies (Goudsblom's second level), an attempt were made to plot all the *different* cultures known to anthropologists – tribal societies, ancient civilizations, contemporary nation-states – on a single graph. Each of the plots of personality structure against social structural complexity and integration would then represent a single static snapshot of one society at one point in time. Bearing in mind the precise initial conditions Elias specifies for the process and how many variations he sees within the overall trend in Europe alone, it would be a very remarkable result indeed if an imaginary regression line fitted the plots for so many varied cultures snatched out of context in time as closely as those for Europe *through* history. Some of the plots would come from societies the circumstances of whose original development was in most respects very different from Western Europe, some from societies changing slowly and therefore in a short-term perspective not discernibly undergoing an actual civilizing process as societies,[4] and still others from societies changing rapidly but under the modern world-wide impact of European-type societies. If such a regression line did emerge, it would represent not the track which a particular society had followed over time but evidence of a more generally valid and 'unilinear' track of general social development.

For the moment, however, let us concentrate on the question of what is required in order for changes in social behaviour and personality structure to be represented on an ordinal scale, as a sequential order, as 'earlier' and 'later' stages of development. The first essential is that one can point to 'things once allowed' that 'are now reproved' – forms of behaviour earlier regarded as normal which are later regarded as impolite or repugnant. To a determined relativist, that is not conclusive evidence of an advance in repugnance. Elsewhere (Mennell 1985: 294) I have spoken of 'the quantum theory of taboo' dominant among anthropologists. It is that all societies pretty well equally use avoidances to demarcate boundaries of various sorts. The actual patterns differ but the principle of patterning is the same. If one pattern of behaviour previously allowed is now avoided, then probably there are others which were once avoided but are now allowed. People in all types of societies have similar capacities for repugnance, and changes in the patterning of repugnance are not to be interpreted as advances or movements in any particular direction. The quantum theory is impossible to refute: the particle of repugnance jumps unpredictably, and no matter how much evidence one accumulates for advances in repugnance it can always be argued that somewhere in the society there must be other not yet observed movements in other directions. But precisely because the quantum theory is thus untestable, a theory based on actual evidence of changes in behaviour is to be preferred over it.

Nevertheless, for Elias, this is only the beginning. Having deployed evidence of a directional change in social behaviour, he also seeks to show that over time there are related psychogenetic changes: a changing balance between external and self-constraints, with controls operating more evenly over a person's behaviour as a whole and among all members of society in general. It is this which raises the possibility of cross-cultural comparisons of civilizing processes. For one could not expect the details of, say, table manners to follow precisely the same sequence in Europe, China, India or among the Eskimos; but in principle, psychological characteristics could form a common denominator for purposes of comparison.

This, however, is particularly controversial: the idea of there being 'earlier' and 'later' stages of *psychological* development across whole societies[5] causes alarm, because it is hard to avoid the association with 'lower/higher', 'worse/ better', 'inferior/superior', even if the connection is not a logical one. If one then goes one step further and looks for similarities between, say, the medieval European personality structure and that found in less complex, relatively unpacified and preliterate societies which exist or have existed in the twentieth century, one almost inevitably offends against the ostensibly egalitarian cultural and moral relativism which is something of an article of faith among anthropologists.

The charge of 'unilinear evolutionism'

At this point, the question of whether Elias is or is not a 'unilinear evolutionist' can no longer be postponed.

Why should being a 'unilinear evolutionist' be such a serious accusation as it is among most anthropologists? A brief explanation is necessary. On the whole, most anthropologists have always agreed that more complex forms of social organization have developed out of less complex. Since the early twentieth century, however, they have rejected any notion of a universal sequence of stages of development with labels like 'savagery', 'barbarism' and 'civilization' (Morgan 1877), and by extension there has been debate about whether contemporary tribal societies are at all like the earlier stages of development of what are now 'advanced societies'. There is great sensitivity about the idea of 'backwardness'.

The rejection of social evolutionism in favour of cultural relativism is associated particularly with the long-dominant American school of cultural anthropology whose founding father was Franz Boas (1858–1942). The general stance of Boas and his followers may be described as 'historical particularism' (Harris 1968: 250ff). Boas had no objection to seeking evidence, where it might exist, of the sequential pattern of development over time *within* a particular culture area. That indeed was his preferred mode of explanation for why a culture was as it was. But he rejected all the general, universal evolutionist schemata of a fixed ladder of stages, up which all human societies had climbed further or less far. And he particularly scorned the Social Darwinist outgrowth of evolutionism, which had increasingly sought to explain cultural differences between 'modern' and 'primitive' societies in terms of supposed differences in the inherent biological and mental endowment of their members. One of Boas's greatest contributions throughout his long life was the rebuttal of such racist ideas by demonstrating, through the painstakingly detailed mapping out of cultural traits, that there was no correlation whatsoever between the distribution of these traits and that of 'racial' differences. This standpoint established by Boasian anthropology came to be shared by other major schools such as British social anthropology and French structuralism, and – apart from the periodic efforts of a few wayward psychologists to revive the old nature/nurture controversy – has stood the test of time among serious social scientists.

Most of this is in line with Elias's views too. Yet he believes that the anthropologists have thrown out the developmental baby with the evolutionary bath water. As we have already mentioned, he himself avoids the term 'evolution' in a social context; its association with biology makes it treacherous. Biological evolution and social development are very different in crucial ways. Human societies develop through *cultural*, not biological, differentiation, by means of the inter-generational transmission of symbols.[6] This has at least two important implications. One is that social development, unlike biological evolution, is reversible. Another is that there is no equivalent in social development to the process of *speciation* in biological evolution. That is to say, there is no equivalent to the phylogenetic process by which organisms became differentiated into separate species incapable of interbreeding with each other. In contrast, human beings have remained one species, capable of communication with and learning from each other, so that social characteristics can pass from one society to another at very different stages of development; it is (as someone vividly remarked) as if pigeons and elephants could mate.

Those few anthropologists who have tried to rescue the evolutionary perspective, notably White (1959), Steward (1955) and Sahlins and Service (1960), while recognizing these differences between biological evolution and social development, have tended still to make comparisons between the social and biological processes frequently enough to attract continuing criticism.[7] Nevertheless, Sahlins's distinction between specific and general evolution (Sahlins and Service 1960: 12–44) may be helpful – despite the word evolution – in elucidating Elias's objectives.

To study 'specific' evolution, in Sahlins's terms, is to take a multilinear 'phylogenetic' perspective on how cultures diverged and differentiated, how traits diffused from one to the other, and so on. This is quite compatible with Boasian orthodoxy and with cultural relativism. 'General' evolution is not. The perspective of general evolution involves comparing whole classes of cultures or societies as more or less advanced, and for this, *general* criteria are necessary. It is this perspective which attracts the label 'unilinear', although since more than one criterion may be used, the word is potentially misleading.

In the end the difference between unilinear and multilinear conceptions of development is simply a matter of levels of abstraction. Taking the 'multilinear' view one may choose to look at societies at a low level of abstraction, emphasizing every small difference of detail, and pushed to its extreme, this becomes indistinguishable from the historical particularism of the Boasians. As Dunning (1977a) points out, a very low level of abstraction is also essential to Popper's rejection of developmental theories in the social sciences. At the other extreme, if one adopts an extremely high level of abstraction – if in Lévi-Strauss's phrase one takes 'the view from afar' to a sufficient degree – all human societies can look alike and there seems to be no social development.

But it is a form of naïve egalitarianism to deny the developmental differences which, at a lower but sociologically more meaningful level, exist among them. In short, the possibility of a scientific approach to problems of social development is dependent on the achievement of a level of abstraction which is neither too low – as in the case of Popper – nor too high, as in the case of Lévi-Strauss. (Dunning 1977: 347)

Elias himself has always tried to follow just such a middle course. One might say that in his early work on the European civilizing process, the balance of his concerns was slightly more towards the 'multilinear' and particularizing side, and that later, in his writings on civilizing processes at the level of humanity as a whole, it tilted slightly the other way. But he *always* stressed that social development involves simultaneously differentiating or diverging movements *and* movements which represent regressions and progressions ('progressions', not 'progress', he maintains).

To study progressions and regressions, however, demands the formulation of general criteria or measuring rods. This he does in many places in his work. In *The Court Society* (1969a: 221) he lists four criteria in need of refinement and more accurate calibration to facilitate such comparisons. They are:

1 The number of routine contacts that people of different classes, ages and sex have at one stage of social development compared with another.
2 The number, length, density and strength of chains of interdependence which individual people form within a time–space continuum at one stage of development compared with another.
3 The central balance of tensions in society: the number of power centres increases with a growing differentiation of functions, and inequality in the distribution of power decreases (without disappearing) – but Elias specifically notes that this criterion needs to be better calibrated than at present.
4 The level of controls over (a) extra-human nature, (b) of people over each other, and (c) of each individual over him or herself. These too, says Elias, change in a characteristic way from stage to stage of social development, 'though certainly not by a simple increase or decrease'.

This last criterion, the 'triad of basic controls' and especially the latter two components of it, is distinctively Eliasian and was discussed in chapter 7. The first and second criteria are a sympathetic nod in the direction of the development of models of social networks undertaken by mathematically inclined sociologists and anthropologists. The third criterion, while plainly much connected with state-formation processes, is actually framed in a more general way.

The appeal of cultural relativism rests partly on the fear that any developmental perspective will make the people of pre-industrial cultures seem either 'backward' or simply 'quaint' from the ethnocentric viewpoint of people in industrial societies. Elias avoids that through his stress on studying the actual patterns of interdependence binding people together. He explains this most clearly when justifying the study of the people of court society, who may certainly seem just as quaint and irrelevant to modern society as any group studied by anthropologists.

We saw that the people forming this society were bound together in different ways – formed different figurations – from those of industrial society, and that they therefore developed and behaved in many respects differently from people forming industrial societies. We saw that this 'differentness' of people in other societies is treated by the study of figurations neither – relativistically – as something peculiar and quaint, nor is it reduced – absolutistically – to an 'eternal human essence'. As was shown, the tracing of interdependences makes it possible to preserve the uniqueness and differentness of people in other societies, while recognizing them as people whose situation and experience we can share, with whom we are bound by an ultimate identification as human beings. (1969a: 212)

Testing the theory of civilizing processes involves plotting the psychogenetic thread of the process against the sociogenetic thread, but they are closely entangled with each other. The best test – urgently needed – of whether the specific pattern of development first sketched for Western Europe represents a more generally valid model would be to investigate other historic civilizations – India, China, Japan for instance. Superficial differences in etiquette would of course be observed – developments in table manners towards the use of chopsticks rather than knives, forks and spoons, or the persistence of eating with the fingers, would not in themselves undermine Elias's thesis. It would, however, be necessary to show that the basic shift in the balance between external constraints and self-constraints in the social habitus of individuals was correlated with the social web becoming more extensive and complex. This correlation is what is disputed by the second major criticism of Elias – the argument from 'stateless civilizations'.

THE ARGUMENT FROM 'STATELESS CIVILIZATIONS'

Proponents of this argument do not deny that it is possible to distinguish between groups, societies and cultures in terms of their degree of civilization more or less in Elias's sense. What they deny is that such standards are at all closely correlated with the formation of a state apparatus, or more generally with levels of social complexity.

A principal exponent of this view is the Dutch anthropologist H.U.E. Thoden van Velzen who, at the same 1981 conference in Amsterdam, presented a paper on the 'civilization' of a non-complex society, the Maroons of Surinam, also known as the Aukaner, the Djuka, or Bush-negroes (Thoden van Velzen 1982). The argument received support from two other papers published in the same issue of *Sociologische Gids*, Wim Rasing's essay (1982) on conflict management among the nomadic Inuit Eskimos, and, in a rather different way, René Jagers's discussion (1982) of violence within tribal societies.

Thoden van Velzen argued, in opposition to Anton Blok, that the concept of civilization was usable and that it did permit distinctions to be drawn between more and less civilized societies. But, contrary to what might be expected from Elias's writings on the civilizing process in Europe, an extraordinarily high level of civilization could be observed in many small-scale, isolated, non-European, stateless societies. The Maroons were one such case; they had no state apparatus but did have a highly developed form of etiquette and put marked value on self-restraint. Their manners were exceptionally polite, prudent and self-controlled and the level of openly displayed aggressiveness was very low, especially among men. Self-control, indeed, was the prescribed norm. How had that arisen, in the absence of a state apparatus monopolizing the means of violence, and of other extensive webs of social interdependence? Thoden van Velzen sought an alternative sociogenetic explanation for these modes of self-control. He found it inside the structure of Maroon society itself. The society was uxorilocal: when he married, a man went to live in his wife's home village. Nevertheless, he retained close contacts with his own village of origin and visited it frequently. He had, so to speak, no home port and had to exercise considerable diplomatic skills to make his way successfully in both villages. Moreover, uxorilocality meant that the male members of a particular lineage had divergent interests in many other villages rather than forming, as they often do in a patrilocal system, 'fraternal interest groups' in their own village. Such interest groups, strongholds of agnates, create a climate in which people do not have to pay much attention to the opinions of others and, according to Thoden van Velzen, the use of force is endemic in such societies. In contrast, in the Maroon uxorilocal system, the priorities of close male relatives no longer coincided, which removed an important incentive to co-ordinated action and left the individual male to a much greater extent dependent on cultivating the good opinion of others. It was this that had contributed to the remarkable level of 'civilization'.

Rasing's article on the management of conflict among the Inuit Eskimos raised the possibility of yet another sociogenetic route to an apparently high degree of 'civilization'. The Inuit were nomads inhabiting the central Canadian Arctic. Their small-scale communities lacked any external control of force and their own impulses and liberty from interference by others. Self-control and physical conditions of life created strong interdependencies: everyone must contribute to survival. A sharp social control resulted. On the other hand, outside the role requirements with which people were expected to conform, very high value was placed on individuals' freedom of action, ability to control their own impulses and liberty from interference by others. Self-control and social control were both emphasized, the first being the ideal form of the latter. This found expression in the way violence was handled. Ways of managing conflict included simply withdrawal and avoidance but also, more interestingly, ritualized singing and butting contests. Even murder conformed to the pattern: most of the known instances were committed in a controlled, rational way. When violence was used, according to Rasing, it was done in a way that, *pace* Elias, could not be called 'passionate'.

Jagers's essay had a more complicated and – in the end – rather blurred bearing on Elias's thesis in so far as that concerns violence. Examining anthropological accounts of a number of hunting and pastoral societies, Jagers suggests that the use of physical force among them is mainly *intra*-tribal – that is, it is used mainly between members of the same tribe rather than between neighbouring tribes. He contends that violent conflict with neighbouring tribes may be limited by a recognition that escalating cycles of retaliation could lead to total annihilation – a recognition which entails a measure of foresight, of course. Within tribes, on the other hand, violence is a means of creating order and distinction within relationships. The fragmentation of the means of violence, the small differences in physical force and the constant shifts in these differences entail a carefully calculated and restrained use of violence. Something similar, it will be recalled, had emerged in Blok's study of *mafia* in Sicily (see pp. 89–90 above), but there Blok had explained the functioning of violence in relation to the historic weakness of the state apparatus in Sicily. Jagers, like Rasing, is pointing out that, even in stateless societies, violence is often a highly controlled, calculated, pragmatic and rational form of behaviour, involving foresight, the weighing of risks, and therefore a considerable measure of self-constraint – in contrast to violence as a strongly affect-laden, more or less spontaneous expression of aggressive impulses. Much the same argument was also applied to knightly combat in the Middle Ages by de Jong (1982) and Maso (1982).

These papers certainly raise interesting and important questions, but they are marred by the tendency, so widespread among social scientists, to pose the issues in terms of static polar opposites. Jagers, Rasing and Thoden van Velzen do not throw much light on civilizing *processes*; they tend to use 'civilization' as a substantive, a quality which societies either have or have not. Thoden van Velzen, for example, uses the word virtually as a synonym for 'courtly culture', finding superficial resemblances between the manners of the Maroons and those of eighteenth-century European courtiers.[8] None of the three authors pays much attention to the wider figurational context within which the observed patterns have developed and continue to change. Goudsblom (1984b) argues in particular that all three neglect the effect of colonial and post-colonial regimes on the tribal societies they are discussing. Jagers's cases were drawn from contexts where the colonial powers had acted to suppress inter-tribal warfare, more effectively and directly than they controlled inter-personal violence within tribes. Among Rasing's Inuit, bloodshed appeared to have declined during the twentieth century, and the Canadian authorities had probably played a significant part in that. Thoden van Velzen's Maroons too now live within the framework of a state-society (Surinam). Thoden van Velzen countered this point by arguing that there was some evidence that these groups had already achieved a high level of 'civilization' in the eighteenth century, when it was scarcely possible to speak of pacification having taken place within a state. But Goudsblom pointed out that from the outset Maroon society had been formed by ex-slaves in the margins of a colonial society marked by extreme inequalities of power. Goudsblom warned especially against accepting at face value eighteenth- and nineteenth-century accounts of Maroons 'not showing their feelings'. It is one of the clichés of colonial societies (and of established-outsiders relations more generally), a direct consequence of the extreme inequalities of power, that to the colonialists the natives seem 'inscrutable'.

Moreover, the Djuka always lived in a remote area where the level of external danger was low. Putting aside the question of whether the ethnographic description is adequate, it is possible that the *isolation* of such a society might be the key to what was observed, along with its small scale, which would not promote strong internal stratification. An absence of strong, internally generated conflict, together with an absence of regular fighting with external enemies could be conducive to the apparent 'politeness' and restraint in Djuka manners. Thoden van Velzen says nothing by way of explanation of how the uxorilocal pattern developed. It is at least possible that a higher level of danger would have steered Djuka society more towards patrilocality, fraternal interest groups and a higher propensity to the use of force. There is no need to make uxorilocality a mere dependent variable, however: what is needed is a more processual investigation of the developmental connections between the kinship system, manners and levels of danger and violence.

That foresight serves to inhibit violence between and within tribal societies need be no surprise. Elias would argue that no human society can ever have been devoid of all foresight; the capacity for foresight is one aspect of the exceptional capacity for synthesis possessed by *Homo sapiens*'. Therefore it is extremely unlikely that there has ever been a society where people did not sometimes use violence in a calculated, instrumental way, bearing in mind the likely consequences (or, equally, refrain from doing so on the same grounds). Elias does of course argue that where a state monopoly of the means of violence is well established, the consequences of resorting to private use of violence are likely to be severe, and this helps to inhibit violence. Thus far in the argument, the increasingly severe probable costs of resorting to violence represent only stronger forms of external constraint produced by closer interdependence with more people. It is extremely likely that in different societies and circumstances, a similar increase in constraint could be produced by functional alternatives or equivalents (to use Robert Merton's terms (1968: 106)). In other words, it is entirely plausible, and not at all at odds with Elias's theory, that the physical context in which Eskimos (or Bushmen) exist will produce very strong interdependencies, and an awareness of how violent conflict would jeopardize survival. Conceptually, the strength of external constraints may vary from one society to another. But the thrust of Elias's theory is about processes of *change*:

the argument is, to recapitulate, that the *increasing* webs of interdependence spun by state-formation and the division of social functions exerts pressures towards *increasing* foresight and a change in the balance of controls; the *relative* weight of self-constraint over the impulsive resort to violence (among other things) increases, and becomes 'more even and all-round'; and people experience *greater* inner guilt and remorse if the self-constraints fail. Now, again, this shift in the balance of controls *may* be produced by functional alternatives to state formation and division of functions – it may arise by different routes. But anthropological evidence, because it is nearly always couched in the form of static contrasts (and because of the relativistic taboos of anthropologists), is rarely precise enough to throw much light on the question.

THE 'PERMISSIVE SOCIETY' ARGUMENT

In the 1960s and 1970s there emerged in many countries the various tendencies collectively labelled 'the permissive society'. There was an apparent relaxation of controls, even a 'loosening of morals' as many saw it, and a pervasive *informalization* of social behaviour. Does this mean that the civilizing process has gone into reverse? And since the increasing complexity of the web of social interdependencies in which people are caught up has manifestly *not* gone into reverse, does the emergence of the 'permissive society' disprove Elias's theory?

Many people who have read *The Civilizing Process* since its belated publication in English have asked these questions in a casual way. Serious argument about them has, however, taken place more among sociologists strongly influenced by Elias than among his opponents. Extensive research into the precise character of contemporary trends has been carried out particularly by Cas Wouters (1976, 1977, 1986, 1987, 1988), Christien Brinkgreve (1980, Brinkgreve and Korzec 1976a, 1978, 1979), Paul Kapteyn (1980, 1985a, 1985b) and Bram de Swaan (1979). That these names are Dutch is appropriate, for the social transformations of the 1960s and 1970s were perhaps more dramatic in the Netherlands than in most Western societies.

It must not be forgotten, however, that the wave of informalization that took place in the 1960s and 1970s was not the first. People perceived the periods of the *fin de siècle* and then again the 'Roaring Twenties' in much the same way. Generally speaking there was then in most of the Western world a subsequent period of consolidation or even retreat of informality and 'permissiveness' until the rather dramatic wave of the 1960s. In the 1980s, another period of reformalization appears to have set in (Wouters 1986, 1987). Behind the ebb and flow, it would nevertheless be generally agreed that manners have become less 'stiff' and attitudes to many aspects of social relationships more 'permissive' than in the Victorian period (the period of the last manners books on which Elias drew in detail in *The Civilizing Process*).[9]

Elias was well aware of this when he was writing the book in the 1930s. He discussed the apparent 'relaxation of morals' which had taken place since the

First World War (1939: I, 186–7; cf. II, 324), though without using the word informalization, and without fully incorporating the process into his theory. Reversing Caxton's dictum that 'Things once allowed are now reproved', he observed that 'Many things forbidden earlier are now permitted'. On this trend he offered two comments which are not at first glance entirely compatible with each other. It was not, he pointed out, the first time such apparent reversals of the civilizing process had occurred. In very long-term perspective, the overall trend was clear, especially among the upper classes, but on closer examination there had always been criss-cross movements, shifts and spurts in various directions. The informalization of the inter-war years was probably just another such fluctuation.

On the other hand, he also pointed out that some of the symptoms of an apparent relaxation of the constraints imposed on the individual by social life actually took place within the framework of very high social standards of self-constraint, standards possibly higher even than formerly. He gave the example of bathing costumes and the relatively greater exposure of the body – especially the female body – in many modern sports. In the nineteenth century it would have meant social ostracism for a woman to wear in public a bathing costume as relatively scanty as those worn between the wars. The bikinis and the topless bathing of the decades after the Second World War were, of course, still over the horizon. This development, Elias had already argued in 1939, could only take place 'in a society in which a high degree of restraint is taken for granted, and in which women are, like men, absolutely sure that each individual is curbed by self-control and a strict code of etiquette' (1939: I, 187). This second observation, while not yet fully reconciled with the first, was to prove highly significant in the discussion of informalization in the 1970s.

Elias continued to think about these issues over many years, and in 1967, in the essay 'The quest for excitement' (in Elias and Dunning 1986: 44), used the phrase 'a highly controlled decontrolling of emotional controls', to summarize the kind of development that years before he had mentioned in connection with bathing costumes. He used the phrase again when teaching in Amsterdam in 1970, at the height of the 'student revolt', the hippie movement and diverse experiments with alternative lifestyles, all of them adding up to a very dramatic informalization of many aspects of social life.[10] It was then seized upon and developed especially by one of his students, Cas Wouters (1970: 51).

The first systematic research into informalization processes to be published, however, was Brinkgreve and Korzec's study (1976a; 1978) of the changing contents of the advice columns in the leading Dutch women's magazine *Margriet* between 1938 and 1978.[11] Some of the trends, such as the far more open discussion of problems of sexuality, had often been noted before. Brinkgreve and Korzec, however, were interested in what the changing forms of advice revealed about changing social relationships, particularly the balances of power between parents and children and between men and women. They found that the expectation that teenagers submit unprotestingly to their parents' wishes, or wives to their husbands', diminished dramatically between the 1950s and the 1970s, in consequence of more equal balances of power. For instance, when women did not have jobs of their own, their lack of financial leeway made them utterly dependent on their husbands and limited their alternatives. As this dependence diminished, the ideal of marriage came to be expressed less in terms of complete unity and harmony; the relationship was seen more in terms of competing interests, in which negotiations played a more decisive part than fixed roles. Blanket rules were no longer given for what was right and what was wrong.

Brinkgreve and Korzec summed up the changes as a shift from 'moralizing' to 'psychologizing'. It was less a matter of judging and censuring, and more one of considering a situation from all angles. All kinds of psychological questions were posed, to enable people to see the roles they were playing in their problematic relations with other people. In the past people had been seen as possessing good and evil inclinations, and the evil ones had to be forcibly repressed. By the 1970s, however, desires had to be kept in check not because they were evil in themselves, but more because giving in to them could lead to so many problems.

The rules of conduct, argued Brinkgreve and Korzec, had become less and less rigid. More emotions could now be expressed and, moreover, there had in Elias's phrase been a trend towards 'increasing varieties' in permissible behaviour: couples living together 'out of wedlock', extra-marital affairs, voluntary childlessness and homosexuality had once all been frowned upon but were now far more widely accepted. What interpretation was to be put on this increasing appeal to one's own conscience and not to pay so much attention to other people? At first, Brinkgreve and Korzec were inclined to interpret informalization as an actual reversal in the trend of the civilizing process. Wouters (1976) strongly disagreed, arguing that 'a highly controlled decontrolling of emotional controls' was at the kernel of the informalization process, which represented a still further shift of the balance from constraint by others (*Fremdzwänge*) towards self-constraints (*Selbstzwänge*), and therefore a continuation of the main thrust of the civilizing process. In response, Brinkgreve and Korzec (1976b) accused Wouters of seeking to immunize Elias's theory from being falsified by contrary evidence. This in turn spurred Wouters to try to establish clear criteria for deciding between the rival interpretations, and in a later article Brinkgreve and Korzec (1979: 139–40n.) expressed much more sympathy with Wouters's argument.

Wouters (1977) catalogued the pervasiveness of informalization processes. He mentioned such manifestations of informalization as the increased use of the familiar second person (*tutoyer, duzen* and so on in European languages other than English), the increasing use of Christian names (for example by subordinates to superiors in offices, and by children to their parents), the decreasing insistence upon titles, the less formal regulation of the written and spoken languages, of clothing, hairstyles, forms of music and dancing. Mourning customs and attitudes to death, too, were less formally defined than before (Wouters and ten Kroode 1980). All this was in addition to the changes in the key fields of marriage, divorce and sexual relationships, and to the protest movements (whether rebellious or retreatist) which abounded in the 1960s and 1970s.

Modern etiquette books are a good source of evidence on many of these trends, serving as lineal successors to the 'manners' books used by Elias. Significantly, Wouters (1987) found that in the Netherlands there had been a gap in the publication of such books between 1966 and 1979; their place was taken by a glut of what he calls books about 'liberation and self-realization', which put the emphasis on the individual's right and duty to fulfil his or her own personality rather than conforming to social standards.

This is revealing. For, on the face of it, these examples of informalization represent a relaxation of social standards and self-controls, and that was how young people at the time understood the difference between their own mode of conduct and their parents'. Often they did not simply 'reject their parents' social code of conduct, but would argue that they themselves do not follow *any* social code and, furthermore, that people ought not to follow any code imposed by society. They should conduct their behaviour in accordance with their own individuality and in accordance with what they sense that others as individuals want or need' (Wouters 1977: 440). Underlying such a claim is a very specific mode of self-experience underlying such otherwise dissimilar protest movements as hippies and militant marxists, and fundamentally related to the image of *homo clausus*, in terms of the freedom of the individual and the oppressiveness of a society which denies this freedom.

Yet appearances – even the experience of one's own self – can be deceptive. In fact, as Brinkgreve (1980) points out, strengthening Wouters's argument, the 'commandments of the new freedom' are rather demanding. New style 'open marriages' make very high emotional demands, and indeed Brinkgreve is plainly sceptical about whether many people are capable of taking a happy, open and encouraging interest in their partner's liaisons with third parties. The 'new divorce', in which former partners remain friends and continue to move with equanimity in the same social circles, is also quite demanding. The level of 'mutually expected self-restraint' (Goudsblom's phrase used by Wouters 1987) has risen.

In personal relationships more generally, people are told to be guided by their own feelings, yet 'the *self* which must weigh and decide everything is often a capricious compass to sail by' (Brinkgreve 1980). In choosing between her husband and her lover a woman is advised by *Margriet* to consider her feelings in relation to eighteen separate questions forcing her to look at the situation and its consequences from the angle of everyone involved. She has to make eighteen honest answers 'before she is *permitted* to make a choice'.

This is not simply 'individualization' but something far more subtle. Wouters's central argument is that while a lessening of power inequalities is conducive to greater informality,

Contrary to the superficial impression, greater informality in the relationships of interdependent people induces and requires more deeply built-in self-restraints than relationships of a more formal nature, characteristic of greater and more overt status and power inequalities and more authoritarian behaviour by social superiors. (Wouters 1977: 447)

By way of illustration, Wouters points out that giving children more freedom imposes more self-restraints on parents. Permitting children more leeway to do things on impulse at possibly inconvenient times, or tolerating infantile masturbation for example, require parents to have their own emotions under firm control. In turn, more permissive attitudes by parents eventually induce greater self-control in children. A child beaten for every transgression will avoid transgressions as long as they cannot be concealed from the parents but will not itself learn to control the impulses leading to the transgressions. Controlled more by fear than by feelings of guilt, it will be unable to control itself in the absence of external authorities of which it is afraid. If, on the other hand, parents try to restrain their own anger at a child's behaviour and try to induce the child, perhaps through a slight withdrawal of affection, to control this type of behaviour on its own or, in other words, to civilize itself, it will develop a more stable and deep-rooted self-control than a child who is ruled by the stick (Wouters, 1977: 446). This of course is a direct extension to modern child-rearing of Elias's argument about the relationship between pacification and the balance between external and self-constraints. So too is Wouters's observation that children raised in a relatively authoritarian way tend to veer between excessive deference and running amok, whereas those raised on a looser rein are able to vary their behaviour in a more graded way according to circumstances.

Another extrapolation from Elias is Wouters's argument about the psychological side of social informalization processes. The process creates not just a different pattern of self-constraints but also a different, more conscious, *level* of controls. There is evidence, from even the most private of diaries for example, that in the nineteenth century many young, especially middle-class, girls repressed all thought of sex, except in the unguarded context of dreams.[12] Today, young people learn to express their sexuality in a controlled and socially acceptable way, not totally without inhibition but within a more lenient and differentiated social standard. Thus, argues Wouters (1977: 448), young people's self-control in regard to sexuality has so much increased that they are *able to think about* expressing or repressing sexual urges or emotions. This heightened consciousness enables them far more than their parents and grandparents *both* to restrain *and* to express their impulses and emotions according to circumstances.

Does this discussion and the research it prompted clarify the theoretical problems involved in interpreting informalization processes? Is it now possible to say whether the 'permissive society' represents a reversal or a continuation of the civilizing process, and whether it undermines or strengthens Elias's theory? Yes – but only if some careful distinctions are drawn. Informalization is at once a sociogenetic and a psychogenetic process, and some of its social manifestations can lead to misleading simplistic inferences about what is happening to personality structure.

Elias frequently stresses that the civilizing process is not a matter simply of 'more' self-control. He speaks in terms of the changing *balance* between external and self-constraints, and of the changing *pattern* of controls. In particular, he speaks of controls becoming 'more even', 'more automatic' and 'more all-round', as well as of a movement towards 'diminishing contrasts and increasing varieties'. In English translation especially, the distinctions between the first three terms are not always obvious. By 'more even' and 'more automatic' self-constraints, Elias means 'psychological' changes: individuals' oscillations of mood become less extreme and the controls over emotional expression become more reliable or calculable. 'More all-round' – 'more all-embracing' might be a better English term – refers to a decline in the differences between various 'spheres' of life, such as contrasts between what is allowed in public and in private, between conduct in relation to one category of people as against another, or between 'normal' behaviour and that permissible on special occasions like carnival which are seen as exceptions to the rules. Finally, 'diminishing contrasts, increasing varieties' refers to social contrasts – reduced inequalities between social groups but a wider choice of permissible models of behaviour.

Bearing these distinctions in mind, it can be seen that the informalization processes in general represent a definite continuation of the latter two components: diminishing contrasts, increasing varieties, and more 'all-roundedness'. What is more ambiguous is whether they also represent a movement towards more evenness and greater automaticity. Because they involve a less tyrannical form of conscience-formation and more conscious deliberation, it is easy to overlook how far the new, more liberal, standards presuppose an extremely reliable capacity for controlling one's impulses and a still greater level of mutual identification. They do not, in general, appear to involve a switch backwards in the balance from *Selbstzwänge* towards *Fremdszwänge*. Such actual reversals of the civilizing process can occur; the shift back towards *Fremdzwänge* would be detected in the spread of the attitude which Wouters once memorably encapsulated as 'Fuck the rules, watch the traffic' – following one's impulses, subject only to avoiding actual danger. The difference between these 'true decivilizing processes' and the informalization processes is clear in principle, although in practice it may involve careful and sensitive study of the evidence from instance to instance. Moreover, the picture is further complicated by the interweaving of informalizing and formalizing threads; according to Wouters's latest thinking (1987, 1988) in relation to current reformalizing trends in the 1980s, there is in the short term a wave-like succession of periods in which informalization and formalization are dominant in turn, parts of the advances of informalizing periods in this century being incorporated subsequently into more formal codes.

THE 'BARBARIZATION' ARGUMENT

Violence and its controls are, as we have seen, central to the theory of civilizing processes. So nothing undermines the plausibility of the thesis more than the widespread intuitive perception that we are now living in a world which is 'more violent' than ever before. It is not just that people feel that it is more dangerous to walk the streets of their cities than they believe it was a generation or two ago. There is also the looming threat of mass extermination through nuclear, biological or chemical warfare. Though that has not happened yet, wars across the globe are never out of the news, nor is the latest terrorist outrage. Above all, people know of the mass murders on a vast scale which have occurred in the present century. Millions of people have died in far away countries of which we used to know little: Uganda, Cambodia, China under Mao, Russia under Stalin. The last alone killed considerably more people than died in the extermination camps of Hitler's Germany but it is probably the 'Holocaust' which looms largest in the European mind. For that was too close to home. And was not Germany – along with France – at the heart of the European civilizing . process studied by Elias?

Let us deal first with the perception that 'law and order' is breaking down in the cities of the Western world, and that the level of danger in everyday life there is rising. The perception cannot be taken at face value. In the case of Britain, for example, Pearson (1983) has shown how, for hundreds of years, successive generations have voiced similar fears of escalating violence, moral decline, and the destruction of 'the British way of life'. At the same time, the perception cannot be dismissed out of hand. Certainly there seem to be short-term fluctuations in violence, in response to rising and falling tensions, often connected with migration and other established-outsiders relationships. Yet there is very little hard historical evidence for a rising curve of violence over terms longer than one or two generations. Admittedly, trends are difficult to study even in the short-term, since a rise in officially recorded or publicly reported incidents of violence may at least partly reflect an increase in the effectiveness of the police or indeed a diminished tolerance of minor violence. However, such evidence as we have of long-term trends in violent crime over many generations, notably the quantitative studies of Gurr (1981) and Stone (1983), appears to support Elias's case rather than otherwise.

Over a shorter time-scale, and once more in the specific case of Britain, Dunning and his Leicester colleagues are investigating trends in violent disorders between 1900 and 1975. In a preliminary account of their work (1987) they classify reported incidents of violence into four categories: disorders connected with politics, with industrial disputes, with sports and leisure, and with the 'community' in general – the last serving as a catch-all for episodes of street fighting not clearly belonging in the other categories. Except in the sports-related category (on which see chapter 6 above), the trend over the period as a whole was downwards. On the other hand, the graphs do show an upward turn in the 1960s and 1970s. It is not easy to say whether this represents simply a minor short-term fluctuation or a more definite reversal of a long-term trend, but the latter possibility has led Dunning (Dunning and Sheard 1979: 288–9; Dunning, Murphy and Williams 1988: 242–5) to speculate that Britain is experiencing an actual 'decivilizing' upsurge in violence. The explanation he tentatively offers for this introduces an interesting qualification into the theory of civilizing processes. He suggests that functional democratization, as one of the central components of the civilizing process, produces consequences which are, on balance, 'civilizing' in its early stages, but that when a certain level has been reached it produces effects which are decivilizing and promote disruptive conflict. Functional democratization has perhaps proceeded far enough for the demands of outsider groups to be expressed strongly, but not far enough, in Britain at least, to break down rigidities which prevent their demands being met fully. At any rate, Dunning and his colleagues admit that 'we do not fully understand the periodicity and ups and downs, . . . the conditions under which a society moves, on balance, in a "civilizing" direction and the conditions under which a civilizing process moves, as it were, on balance into "reverse gear"' (1988: 243). That is one of the key problems in the theory of civilizing processes to be clarified by further research.

What of the appalling mass murders of the present century? Elias published *The Civilizing Process* before the 'final solution' had taken final form, but something of the character of the Nazi regime was already clear. In fact, he explained in the preface, 'the issues raised by the book have their origins less in scholarly tradition, in the narrower sense of the word, than in the experiences in whose shadow we all live, experiences of the crisis and transformation of Western civilization as it has existed hitherto' (1939: I, xvii). While he, like virtually everyone else, no doubt failed to foresee the extent of the killings, a sense of foreboding is occasionally evident. For example, explaining that the control of dangers gradually established in society was a precondition for the 'civilized' standard of conduct, he added that

The armour of civilized conduct would crumble very rapidly if, through a change in society, the degree of insecurity that existed earlier were to break in upon us again, and if danger became as incalculable as once it was. Corresponding fears would burst the limits set to them today. (1939: I, 307n.)

In other words, civilized conduct takes a long time to construct but can be destroyed rather quickly. Of course, *The Civilizing Process* does not explain why such extreme decivilizing processes occur, but some threads of the work have a bearing on what happened in Nazi Germany.

Historically speaking there is nothing unusual about the mass murder of defeated enemies, or about pogroms of outsider groups. They were long taken for granted. Perhaps only two things are really distinctive about such modern episodes as the Nazis' attempted extermination of the Jews. One is the scale of the revulsion felt when all became known, and this was symptomatic of the extent to which most modern people are now capable of identification with the sufferings of their fellow human beings, simply *as* fellow human beings. The growth of mutual identification is, as we have seen, one of the components of the civilizing process as Elias depicts it.

The second distinctive feature is the sheer scale of the killings themselves. For modern social organization has vastly multiplied the technical capacity to kill. The very long chains of interdependence and 'division of social functions' which play such a part in the civilizing process were also essential to implementing the 'final solution'. And paradoxically, as Elias argues, 'civilized' controls in turn play their part in making possible those long chains of organized and co-ordinated activities.

Certain right-wing 'revisionist' historians, who wish to deny the existence of the extermination camps, argue that the killing of Jews and other victims was mainly the result of massacres in the aftermath of battle by soldiers of the *Wehrmacht* and SS carried away by what in 1939 Elias had termed *Angriffslust* (literally, 'pleasure in attacking'). If that had indeed been the case, *far fewer Jews would have been killed than actually were.* That the camps were able to slaughter on such a huge scale depended on a vast social organization, most people involved in which squeezed no triggers, turned no taps, perhaps saw no camps and set eyes upon few victims. They sat, like Adolf Eichmann (see Arendt 1963) in a highly controlled manner at desks, working out railway timetables.

The Jews had, of course, always been an outsider group; there had always been anti-semitism in Germany, although, as Elias's recollections of his own childhood and youth remind us, it is easy with hindsight to exaggerate its extent. It is striking how hard the Nazi regime had to strive to diminish the identification which many Germans felt with their fellow-Germans, the Jews. It was not merely a matter of propaganda, whipping up a sense of danger. The Jews were first removed ('behind the scenes') to ghettos, breaking their personal contacts with their non-Jewish neighbours. Then, under the official pretext of 'resettlement in the east', they were removed to transit camps, labour camps, and finally extermination camps. Significantly, all the *extermination* camps were outside Germany itself: the regime remained apprehensive of German public opinion even at this stage.[13]

In the end it seems there was no shortage of people – even if they were only a minority – who did derive pleasure, or failed to experience displeasure, from the actual killing in the camps, or from aggression towards the victims before they reached there. This is what, looking back, 'civilized' people find most difficult to comprehend. Some are tempted to believe that there must lurk within *Homo sapiens* an 'aggressive instinct'. *The Civilizing Process* indeed deals with the taming of *Angriffslust* – that is, with the increasing control of expressive violence and the growth of repugnance towards committing or witnessing acts of violence. But, as we saw in chapter 9, Elias, unlike sociobiologists, ethologists and some psychoanalysts, does *not* believe that there is in human beings an unlearned aggressive drive or instinct. His explanation of the aggressiveness of medieval warriors rests not on any assumption of an in-built instinct but on a close examination of the competitive social figuration which produced it.[14] What he does believe is that there is certainly no inbuilt mechanism which, unlike in many animals, instinctively controls and limits aggression. The very variability in the forms taken by aggressiveness historically and cross-culturally show clearly that, whatever physiological roots it may have, it is patterned according to many different social standards and, moreover, is partly dependent upon the learned controls. Elias always emphasized that while the permissible expression of violence between members of a state-society may have tended to decline, that customary between members of different survival units has always remained high. Even *within* modern societies, there is considerable variance in the cultural patterning of aggressiveness and violence.

For people with a particular type of conscience and/or when there is a legitimating ideology, (connected, for example, with a notion of occupational or national 'duty' or 'loyalty' to a community), certain forms of violence and aggressive behaviour can be positively sanctioned and enjoyable. There is no need to postulate an 'aggressive instinct' in order to account for such satisfactions. People are sometimes trained to behave aggressively and rewarded on that account: soldiers, policemen and professionals in certain sports are examples. (Some people are attracted to occupations of this kind because of the opportunities they allow for aggressiveness.) In such cases, apart from the prestige and financial rewards that can accrue, the pleasure and enjoyment derived from acting aggressively are, in part, a form of self-reward for 'a job well done'. . . (Dunning, Murphy and Williams 1988: 192)

CONCLUSION

In the past, discussions of the theory of civilizing processes often seem to have been guided by what Goudsblom once called the 'shooting-gallery' conception of scientific progress: one apparently contrary instance falsified the theory completely, after which no further serious discussion or investigation was necessary. Of the four main lines of debate about the theory sketched in this chapter, only the argument from cultural relativism is of that sort. It raises what are perhaps the most complicated 'theoretical' issues for social scientists, but in effect seeks to block off further investigation of the issues the theory raises, which can only be pursued by actual empirical-theoretical research. The arguments about 'stateless societies', 'informalization', and 'barbarization', in contrast, open up new and interesting lines of research. The theory leaves open many issues for further discussion: that is as it should be.

11
Some Principles of Process Sociology

Although Norbert Elias remains most famous for *The Civilizing Process*, it should now be clear that his writings extend far beyond that. His work as a whole is intended to offer solutions to major problems of sociology and the social sciences more generally.

Elias has often been accused of wanting to attract sociological 'disciples' and to form a 'theoretical school' in sociology. He always denies the charge. For he is at once both less ambitious and more ambitious than the charge suggests. Less, because he has no wish to lay down a fixed set of doctrines of the type, often based on some philosophical stance, which underlie most theoretical 'perspectives' in sociology. He wants rather to encourage people to pursue through further research some of the problems of humans' life together to which he has drawn attention; in this modest ambition of initiating a research tradition he has, as we have seen, had some belated success. On the other hand, he also has a far greater ambition. He believes he has diagnosed many of the faults which have beset the social sciences throughout his long lifetime, and he would like his insights to find acceptance by social scientists in general. To establish a mere 'school' would not assist, and would very likely frustrate, the attainment of that objective.

That is why, by the late 1980s, Elias had become irritated by the term 'figurational sociology', applied to his own work and that of others influenced by him. Elias himself had introduced the word 'figuration', especially in *What is Sociology?* (1970a).[1] Not a word in common use, according to the *Oxford English Dictionary* it means 'the action or process of giving shape' to something. Elias employed 'figuration' as a more processual and dynamic term, in contrast with expressions like 'social system' and 'social structure' which in common sociological usage are not only very static but also give the impression of referring to something separate from, beyond and outside individuals. Figurations were rather to be thought of, in Van Benthem van den Bergh's succinct phrase, as 'networks of interdependent human beings, with shifting asymmetrical power balances' (1971: 19). Probably because the word is so distinctive, opponents of Elias's kind of sociology began to speak of it as 'figurational sociology', and his associates then adopted the label for themselves.[2] This certainly proved a mistake, not only because it facilitated their being parcelled up as just one more 'school', but also because a new word is never enough in itself to solve intellectual problems or change habits of thought.[3] 'Figuration' can easily lose its force and be used in just as static and reifying a way as 'social system'. For this reason, Elias came to prefer to speak of 'process sociology'. Because 'process' is such an ordinary word, it is less susceptible to use as a *cordon sanitaire* with which to quarantine his ideas.

Elias is also irritated by programmatic statements in sociology. Most of his own work is at once 'theoretical-empirical', as he believes all sociology should be. His writing abounds in 'theoretical' and 'methodological' comments, but theory and method are almost always developed hand in hand with the investigation of substantive problems of human society. He believes his work should speak for itself, without need for formulation in more 'abstract' form. When seen as a whole, I think his work does speak for itself, and that is why in this book I have tried to look at it in the round *before* turning to the kernel of his thinking about sociology and its subject-matter as a discipline. Much of that should now be clear, at least by implication. Yet, in spite of his mistrust of programmatic statements, he did write *What is Sociology?* as something between a demanding introductory text and a statement of his own general view of the subject. It was not wholly successful, perhaps partly because it was heavily abbreviated and partly because it did not engage in detail with the main landmarks of post-war sociology familiar to most sociologists. That detailed engagement is rather to be found in Johan Goudsblom's *Sociology in the Balance* (1977a), an important, elegant and judicious critique of contemporary sociology. Unfortunately, Goudsblom's book did not attract the attention it deserved, most probably because, like *What is Sociology?*, it appeared before Elias's main works were published in English, so that the foundation upon which the critique rested was then still rather unfamiliar.

THE PRIMACY OF PROCESS

Goudsblom (1977a: 6, 105) takes as his points of departure four principles drawn from Elias's work. They are:

1 That sociology is about *people* in the plural – human beings who are interdependent with each other in a variety of ways, and whose lives evolve in and are significantly shaped by the social figurations they form together.
2 That these figurations are continually in flux, undergoing changes of many kinds – some rapid and ephemeral, others slower but perhaps more lasting.
3 That the long-term developments taking place in human figurations have been and continue to be largely unplanned and unforeseen.
4 That the development of human knowledge takes place within human figurations, and is one important aspect of their overall development.

These principles – all related to each other – are deceptively simple. Most sociologists would agree with them. Yet they are often not followed in sociological research and thinking. Almost everyone now acknowledges that in the heyday of Talcott Parsons's static conceptual schemes, sociologists handled 'social change' inadequately.[4] Handling it more adequately, however, is not simply a question of ceasing to think in terms of 'functions' and 'systems' in the old manner. Inappropriate habits of thought run much deeper, and Elias (1970a: 111ff) argues that new means of speaking and thinking about the kinds of interconnectedness encountered in human society are urgently needed. But tools of thought cannot be changed overnight. Because they are also tools of social communication, they are very durable, and if one seeks to change them all at once, words and ideas swiftly lose their communicability.

Nevertheless, Elias believes that new means of speaking and thinking would actually simplify the work of sociologists:

The complexity of many modern sociological theories is due not to the complexity of the field of investigation which they seek to elucidate, but to the kind of concepts employed. These may be concepts which either have proved their worth in other (usually physical) sciences, or are treated as self-evident in everyday usage, but which are not at all appropriate to the investigation of specifically social functional nexuses. (1970a: 111)

At the heart of Elias's critique of sociological categories and conceptualization is his notion of 'process-reduction',[5] by which he means the pervasive tendency to reduce processes conceptually to states. It is seen as much in everyday language as in the specialized discourses of the sciences. 'We say, "The wind is blowing", as if the wind were actually a thing at rest which, at a given point in time, begins to move and blow. We speak as if the wind were separate from its blowing, as if a wind could exist which did not blow' (1970a: 112). This tendency is very widespread in the languages Benjamin Lee Whorf (1956) called 'Standard Average European', which most commonly assimilate the experience of change and process through sentences made up of a noun or substantive, apparently referring to a thing at rest, plus a verb to indicate that it then moves or changes. This tendency was already hardening in antiquity, and was reinforced by Aristotelian logicians and grammarians. Grammatical pressure makes it difficult to escape this mode of thinking, whether in everyday speech or in the sciences. Whorf argues, however, that there are other, non-European languages which assimilate the experience of process in ways that do not linguistically reduce it to a state.[6] That does not alter the fact that the languages of modern science are European.

Whatever force process-reduction may derive from grammatical forms, it is also reinforced, according to Elias, by a widespread but largely unacknowledged evaluation in Western culture of that which is eternal and immutable over the changing and changeable. We have already in chapter 7 mentioned the theological influence on the pursuit of eternal laws of nature in classical physics. What is changeless is constantly interpreted as what is most real and significant.

In sociology, the pressure towards process-reduction is seen in taken-for-granted conceptual distinctions between the 'actor' and his activity, between structures and processes, between objects and relationships. This is a special handicap when studying figurations of interdependent people. We too often speak and think as if the 'objects' of our thought – including people – were both static and uninvolved in relationships. Concepts of this kind abound in the sociology textbooks: norms, values, roles, social stucture, social class. They appear to refer to separate, motionless objects; but on closer scrutiny they actually refer to *people* in the plural, who are now or were in the past constantly in movement and constantly relating to other people. Above all, at the very centre of problems of sociological thinking, the concepts of the 'individual' and of 'society' have this same quality of seeming to refer to static and isolated objects.

Consequently we always feel impelled to make quite senseless conceptual distinctions, like 'the individual *and* society', which makes it seem that 'the individual' and 'society' were two separate things, like tables and chairs or pots and pans. One can find oneself caught up in long discussions of the nature of the relationship between these two apparently separate objects. Yet on another level of awareness one may know perfectly well that societies are composed of individuals, and that individuals can only possess specifically human characteristics such as their abilities to speak, think, and live, in and through their relationships with other people – 'in society'. (1970a: 113)

One result of this deeply ingrained but erroneous way of thinking about 'the individual' and 'society' has been to trap sociologists in an endless series of futile arguments about which of the two is the more 'real', and which should come first as point of departure in sociological investigation. Such arguments are circular: they have the same endless possibilities as debating which came first, the chicken or the egg. The misconception – in the most literal sense of that word – is reinforced by the widespread tendency to speak not of people in the plural, but of 'man' (or nowadays, the 'person') and 'the individual' in the singular.[7] Needless to say, 'the individual' is normally thought of as an *adult* person, already fully equipped with the skills necessary for living among his fellow humans; that he has undergone a process called 'socialization', through relationships with other 'individuals', is usually mentioned as an afterthought. (The tendency, prevalent until quite recently, to speak of 'he' also helped to reinforce the dominant conceptualization, since to mention men *and* women is instantly a reminder of the ineluctable interdependence of human beings.) Altogether, the outcome is the 'egocentric' model of society, in which the isolated, static 'me' or 'Ego' stands at the centre of a series of concentric circles, the first labelled 'my family', with 'my workplace', 'my town', 'my country' in a succession of ever-wider zones beyond (see Elias 1970a: 14). Collectively, they may even be referred to as 'the individual' and his 'environment'. Very few sociologists have attempted with real determination to break away from this egocentric conception – which is another variant of *homo clausus*.

It is often asserted that particular 'individuals' are what we can actually *see*, that they are 'real'. 'Society', it is said in contrast, cannot be seen directly; it is not real, but a sort of intellectual construct (Elias 1987a: 130). The superficial plausibility of this assertion is based on an unconscious overemphasis on the corporeal, material aspect of human beings which, while certainly not irrelevant to sociology, as Elias has often demonstrated, is by no means what mainly counts in the forms of interconnectedness which sociologists chiefly study. This 'methodological individualism' and 'nominalism' has ensnared several of the best minds in the history of sociology. George Simmel, for instance, grappled with the problem in a sophisticated way, and yet felt compelled to write that 'Society is merely the name for a number of individuals, connected by interaction . . . Groping for the tangible, we find only individuals; and between them, only a vacuum, as it were' (Simmel, 1908a: 10–11). Much more influential in later sociology than Simmel has been Max Weber, whose methodological views were similar. In his handling of comparative and historical evidence Weber is unrivalled, and nothing can detract from his towering achievement. But when it came to formalizing a conceptual scheme in the posthumous *magnum opus*, *Economy and Society* (1922a), Weber was beset by severe methodological inhibitions. Although, like Simmel, fully aware that 'individuals' were steeped in the social, he nevertheless 'axiomatically believed in the "absolute individual" . . . as the true social reality' (Elias 1970: 117). Concepts like 'state', 'family', 'army' or 'class' therefore seemed to him to 'signify no more and no less than a particular pattern of individual people's social action'. This led him to formulate, in the opening sections of *Economy and Society*, a typology of social action – what would later be called a 'social action theory' – in which prime attention is given to the motives of individuals' actions. It led him into such absurdities as arguing that private prayer, an accidental collision between cyclists, or many people simultaneously putting up umbrellas when it rains are not instances of social action – as if praying or riding a bicycle or using an umbrella were activities that could be understood independently from the social development of religion and technology (Goudsblom 1977a: 120; Elias 1970a: 120).

Later, Talcott Parsons's 'voluntaristic theory of action', in its various transmogrifications, shows the same difficulties. In approaching the problem of 'individual and society', Parsons typically began from the model of interaction between just two people, usually referred to as 'Ego' and 'Alter' (Parsons and Shils, 1951). It is highly significant that in this famous dyadic model, not only 'Ego' but also 'Alter' – the 'other person' – is conceptualized as a single, isolated entity, rather than as a multiplicity of other people, directly or indirectly interdependent with 'Ego' and with each other. Perhaps no-one now takes this aspect of Parsons's work very seriously, but a similar undifferentiated dyadic model *implicitly* underlies most other, more fashionable action and interaction theories.

The great counterbalancing influence in sociology to methodological individualism and nominalism is Emile Durkheim. It is well known that for him the subject-matter of sociology was 'social facts', existing outside any particular individual and his 'inner' consciousness. Realizing that a sociology based on the study of the psychology and motives of individuals could not do justice to the extent to which individuals are social products, Durkheim tended to make 'society' appear as something existing over and above individuals, enveloping, surrounding and 'penetrating' them. But still there is the assumption of 'society' and 'individuals' as two separate things standing in causal relation to each other. Durkheim in fact struggled valiantly with the chicken-and-egg problems raised by *homo clausus* assumptions, as the varying formulations over the course of his career reveal, but he never escaped from them any more than Weber did.

The escape route, according to Elias, is to recognize *ab initio* that the bondings between people are as real as the 'individuals' themselves. And, conversely, it is equally true that 'individuals' are as much conceptual constructs as are social bonds and social entities. This is especially clear when Elias emphasizes that people are bonded together in a 'continuum of changes' through time, as well as at any particular moment:

in many processes of change the unity is not due to any substance which remains unchanged throughout the process, but to the continuity with which one change emerges from another in an unbroken sequence. Take the example of a specific society, the Netherlands in the fifteenth and twentieth centuries – what links them to each other is not so much any core which remains unchanged but the continuity of changes with which the twentieth century society emerged from that of the fifteenth century, reinforced by the fact that it is a remembered continuity. Take a human being: Hume once confessed that he could not understand in what sense the grown-up person he was now was 'the same' as the little child he used to be. Again, the answer is that the identity is not so much one of substance, but rather that of the continuity of changes leading from one stage to another, and in this case too it is a remembered continuity. (1984a: 191n.)

Elias recognizes the need for a far more dynamic mode of conceptualization in sociology. Something, but not much, can be achieved by choosing process-words like social*ization*, individual*ization*, civil*ization*, scientific*ation*, or Elias's neologism court*ization*. Such words easily lose their processual character if simply embedded in more general process-reducing modes of thought. The problem of sociological concepts is really much more difficult. In order not to fall into the trap of process-reduction, Elias follows a strategy which has been described as 'concept avoidance' (Gleichmann 1979b: 176; cf. Blumer 1930). What this provocative phrase means can best be explained in relation to a nominalist and methodological individualist like Max Weber, who took an exactly contrary view. Weber's opinion was that there was an unbridgeable gulf between the actual social world, elusive and unknowable in its complexity, and the social world as depicted by sociologists. Weber, as Goudsblom (1977a: 85–6) shows, was keenly aware of what A. N. Whitehead (1926: 75ff) was to call the fallacy of misplaced concreteness; that is, the tendency to assume that every concept which has been abstracted from reality for special purposes of thought corresponds to some actual object existing in reality. Precisely because of this lack of congruency between 'concepts' and 'reality', Weber argued that '*sharp* distinction is often impossible in reality; clear *concepts* are therefore even more necessary' (1922a: I, 158). His theoretical models therefore took the form of 'ideal types' that were to be regarded as no more than mental constructs, logically coherent, but 'against the concrete reality of the historical relatively *empty* of content' (1922a: I, 4). According to the nominalist view, in other words, social structures must always elude us, and all we can do is build models of actors and their assumptions. Ideal-type conceptualization, moreover, is peculiarly prone – unlike Weber's substantive historical and comparative work – to process reduction.[8]

What then is the alternative? Elias denies that unless concepts are defined in a highly formalized way for eternity they are 'unscientific' and unusable in sociological research. Anton Blok (1976) draws on the writings of Wittgenstein to support Elias's view. Wittgenstein's theory of family likeness may help release sociologists from their obsession with formal logic. Wittgenstein demonstrates that it may be impossible to give an adequate definition of a word, even though its meaning is perfectly clear. So it is not a defect if we cannot define a term: 'To think it is would be like saying that the light of my reading lamp is no real light at all because it has no sharp boundary' (Wittgenstein 1958: 27).

Elias's view is not unlike that of Herbert Blumer, who in a well-known paper (1954) argued that concepts were not to be defined as a preliminary to research but employed as 'sensitizing concepts' in guiding investigation. This is particularly relevant to the task – more typical of Elias's work than Blumer's – of handling historical evidence in building process theories of long-term social development. Goudsblom quotes Nietzsche's remark to the effect that 'only that which has no history is definable', and we have seen many examples of that in earlier chapters of this book. What is signified by the concept 'bourgeoisie' changes very markedly with the development of a social stratum over a period of several centuries (see pp. 78–9 above); what it means in the nineteenth century is something very different from what it means in the eleventh, yet the two meanings are linked by a long continuum of changes and, used with care, the concept has a clear meaning in context throughout the social process of development. Much the same goes for other concepts like 'sport', 'nobility', or 'concept'. Elias is well aware of this, and therefore avoids the use of ideal-types; he sees greater value in the dealed investigation of a single '*real*-type' or case study, such as he undertook in *The Court Society* (see p. 88 above). A study of that kind does not seek to define the universal features of the concept 'court', but is certainly not 'empty of content' against the concrete reality of history, and invites further comparative and developmental investigations.

In the end, the problem of concept formation in sociology cannot be solved by talking about it in the abstract. What is needed are concepts better attuned to the study of figurations as 'networks of interdependent human beings, with shifting asymmetrical power balances'. For that, we need to start from the connections, the relationships between people and work from them to the elements involved in them (Elias 1970a: 116). Obviously, the painstaking mapping out of social interconnections between individual people becomes impractical if the object of interest is a wider society of hundreds, thousands or millions of members. Sociologists cannot dispense with imprecise concepts like 'organization', 'institution' and 'community'. But the image of a complex network can usefully be borne in mind. The many kinds of collective social units of which sociologists speak, such as families, villages, towns, factories, schools, bureaucracies and classes, can be thought of as various kinds of knots and tangles, more or less highly connected networks strung together through more dispersed networks. These networks within which people are caught up in alliances, conflicts and fluctuating balances of power, have dynamics of their own, the character of which is not always easy to grasp, either by sociologists or by the people actually entangled in them. The interweaving of people's actions leads to the emergence of patternings and processes ('emergent social properties' in sociological jargon) seemingly independent of any individual's actions and beyond his or her control. Elias's most imagination-reorientating demonstration of why this is so is the series of models of the interweaving process presented in *What is Sociology?* (1970a: 71–103).

THE GAME MODELS[9]

The idea of unintended or unanticipated consequences of social action is a commonplace among sociologists. In an early article, Robert Merton (1936) demonstrated that the notion has a long ancestry in the writings of many earlier sociologists and philosophers (for example in Hegel's discussion of the 'Cunning of Reason'), and Merton's own subsequent work has done much to popularize it. Merton's most extended and explicit discussion of unintended consequences (1949: 475–90) has, however, led to too narrow an interpretation of their sociological significance.

Starting from W. I. Thomas's dictum that 'if men define situations as real, they are real in their consequences', Merton proceeds to focus merely on an oddity, the 'self-fulfilling prophecy', with passing mention of the converse 'self-contradicting' or 'suicidal prophecy'. The self-fulfilling prophecy occurs where people's actions are based on a false perception or 'definition' of a social situation but have consequences which subsequently make that definition accurate – as for example in a panic run on a bank. Such situations are a fascinating but fundamentally a trivial diversion, because they are only a rather unusual and special case of something far more common and of far greater theoretical significance.

Much more clearly than Merton, Norbert Elias recognizes that people's knowledge of the figurations in which they are caught up is virtually always imperfect, incomplete and inaccurate. The strategies of action which they base on this inadequate knowledge therefore more often than not have consequences which they do not foresee. So unanticipated consequences are not a curious footnote to sociology but nearly universal in social life. For Merton, the self-fulfilling prophecy is like a boomerang: the consequences of men's actions rebound upon their initiators. For Elias, the analogy is much less exotic and much more commonplace: like the effect of a stone dropped into a pool, the consequences of people's actions ripple outwards through society until they are lost from sight. Their effects are felt, not at random but according to the structure of the figuration in which they are enmeshed, by people who may well be quite unknown to each other and unaware of their mutual interdependence.

Moreover, more clearly than Merton, Elias emphasizes that separate, adult, purposively acting individuals are not the beginning of the story. 'Unintentional human interdependencies', he writes (1970a: 94–5), 'lie at the root of every intentional interaction.' People's 'definitions of the situation' do not come from nowhere: they, and the purposes people pursue on the basis of them, *and indeed the people themselves*, are shaped over time in figurations of interdependent people. The full force of how their actions interweave to produce 'compelling trends' which no one has planned or intended, and which then constitute and constrain the perceptions, purposes and actions of people, can only be fully understood in developmental perspective. 'In the development of human societies, yesterday's unintended social consequences are today's unintended social conditions of "intentional human actions"' (Goudsblom 1977a: 149).

In Elias's game models, the actions and responses of interdependent people are viewed as moves in games. He uses the models as greatly simplified analogies to real social processes, but because real games are themselves social processes the analogy is a good deal less dangerous than the physical and biological analogies so frequently encountered in sociology.

The one great danger is that, because real games are played according to rules, the game models may help to give credence to the assumption that rules are essential, the *sine qua non* of any patterning or structure in social life. Rules are certainly an ingredient in probably the greater proportion of social relationships; it is important not to give credence to the myth that people enter interaction as *tabulae rasae*, untouched by upbringing and previous social relationships. But to emphasize that his game models are very different from Parsons's consensual model of dyadic interaction, Elias prefaces them with what he calls the Primal Contest, which is anything but a game. He uses this model as a reminder that social relationships can settle down to a stable pattern without any moral component in expectations, a pattern based entirely on expectations in the probabilistic sense.

Consider two tribes, both hunters and gatherers, who repeatedly encounter each other as they search for food in a tract of land. Food is scarce, and for reasons beyond their control and understanding – drought for instance – it is becoming scarcer. Conflict breaks out and deepens between the two tribes pursuing the same scarce resources; one tribe raids the other and kills a few of its members, and shortly afterwards a similar retaliatory raid takes place. Each tribe makes such arrangements as it can to defend its camps but the war drags on. It may go on until both tribes are wiped out, until only one remains, or until both are so diminished in numbers as to make food supplies adequate once more. Or none of these things happen and the war just goes on and on. The tribes are clearly ecologically interdependent. Their interdependence stems from material circumstances, not from shared cognitions, norms or values. Nor do they acquire such shared orientations. They may not even speak each other's languages. None the less, it is impossible to understand the actions, plans, goals or general ways of life of either tribe except by its interdependence with the other. This may be a limiting or rare case, but examples are not unknown. The possibility should be borne in mind as a safeguard against the too ready assumption that relationships tend inevitably towards co-operation, harmony and equilibration.

After this prefatory warning, the game models themselves do assume that games are played according to rules. But they illustrate more emphatically that games are also *contests*, and this is no contradiction. The game models are all based on trials of strength. Strength or 'power' in the game is not an absolute quantity, a substance of which each player has a store, but rather a quality of the relationship in question. In chess, skill is very obviously a relative thing even at the very highest levels.

The first game models involve only two players, and resemble real games like chess; as more players are introduced, team games like football are called to mind; but the last group of game models are too complex for real games and are actually based on Elias's studies of state-formation processes.

Imagine a game played by two people, one of whom is a much stronger player than the other. The stronger player has a great deal of control over the weaker, and can actually force him to make certain moves. Yet, at the same time, the weaker player has some degree of control over the stronger, to the extent that in planning his own moves the stronger player has at least to take the weaker's into account. Both players must have *some* strength or there would be no game. Nevertheless, because one player's strength or skill so considerably exceeds the other's, he can to a large extent control *the course of the game itself* – not only winning, but virtually dictating how he will win and how long it will take.

However, even when only two players are involved, a rather different situation emerges if, for whatever reason, their strengths in the game gradually become more equal. Two things diminish: the stronger player's ability to use his own moves to force the weaker to make particular moves, and his ability to determine the course of the game. The weaker player's chances of control over the stronger increase correspondingly. But, as the disparity between the players' strengths is reduced, the course of the game increasingly passes beyond the control of either. As Elias explains:

Both players will have correspondingly less chance to control the changing figuration of the game; and the less dependent will be the changing figuration of the game on the aims and plans for the course of the game which each player has formed by himself. The stronger, conversely, becomes the dependence of each of the two players' overall plans and of each of their moves on the changing figuration of the game – on the game process. The more the game comes to resemble a social process, the less it comes to resemble the implementation of an individual plan. In other words, to the extent that the inequality in the strengths of the two players diminishes, there will result from the interweaving of moves of two individual people a game process *which neither of them has planned*. (1970a: 82)

Predicting the state of even a two-person game like chess, say twelve moves ahead, is extremely difficult. There are numerous possible outcomes with differing degrees of likelihood. What is more, the probabilities change with each successive move. That is not to say that the development and figuration of past games cannot be studied, analysed and explained.

The introduction of increasing numbers of players into the game models makes possible infinitely more complicated figurations. Elias first postulates a contest in which a very strong player simultaneously plays separate games against a number of less skilled opponents. The weaker players do not co-operate with each other. The stronger player's advantage in each separate game is very great, but his superiority might be undermined as the number of separate games increases; there is a limit to the number of separate relationships which can effectively be carried on at the same time by one person.

The next possibility is that the weaker players form a coalition against the stronger. The balance of power is then much more indeterminate. If the coalition is unified and harmonious, its members' degree of control over their opponent's moves may be enhanced. If it is beset by inner tensions and disagreements, however, that is likely to reduce the advantages of the coalition and might conceivably put the opponent at a greater disadvantage than he was prior to the coalition.

More interesting still, though, are games in which two groups of roughly equal strength play against each other. With many players, there is a flurry of move and countermove. Neither side can quite determine either the other side's tactics or the course of the game. The moves of one player can be understood neither alone nor solely in relation to those of fellow team members but only with respect to the whole game. Episodes acquire a certain fleeting structure of their own, and – as one can actually see in most sports – a distinct vocabulary comes to be used to describe these patterns and phases in the game.

In the third group of game models, the number of players is larger still, and it is difficult to think of counterparts among real-life sports; we are now concerned with rather elaborate social processes. It becomes more and more difficult for any single player to put together a mental picture of the state and process of the game in which he is involved. That is very confusing, for every player needs such a picture in order to anticipate what will happen next and plan his next move accordingly. If the web of interdependencies becomes too far-flung and enravelled, the individual can no longer make sense of the game nor formulate his strategy.

If the number of interdependent players grows, the figuration, development and direction of the game will become more and more opaque to the individual players. However strong he may be, he will become less and less able to control them. From the point of view of the individual player, therefore, an intertwining network of more and more players functions increasingly as though it had a life of its own. (1970a: 85)

As in previous models, this is no more than a game played by many individuals. The difference is that, as the number of players grows and the chains of interdependence lengthen, the individual becomes gradually more *conscious* of the figuration's opacity and of his inability to understand and control it.

If players can no longer map out what is happening overall and plan their moves accordingly, the game is likely to become disorganized, and pressure builds up for the players to reorganize themselves. They may segment into several small independent groups; or the large group may remain interdependent, but assume a more elaborate figuration with two or more tiers. In a multi-tier game, not all the players any longer play directly with each other. Opposing sides still play against each other and test their relative strengths. But the moves are made by specialized functionaries on an upper tier – leaders, delegates, representatives, negotiators, committees, elites, governments. Yet these are not independent of lower-level players, and they are in fact involved in subsidiary game contests with the lower tiers.

When there is a comparatively small circle of upper-tier players, and they are very much stronger than the lower tiers, the game is an oligarchic one. Each player on the upper level is once more able to picture the figuration of players and the development of the game, and to plan a coherent strategy through it for himself. As Elias remarks, the Duc de St Simon believed he knew exactly the mechanisms of courtly society at Versailles. Yet though the figurational process may appear relatively transparent, it is in fact much more complex than anything observed in the earlier models; it is far more difficult for one player to steer the game in the direction he desires. For several different balances of power have to be taken into account; between the top-tier players; between top-tier players and lower-tier players; between lower-tier groupings.

If power differentials between upper and lower tiers diminish, the balances of power and the course of the game become even more indeterminate, fluid and beyond the control of any single individual or group. This, of course, has happened over the last two centuries as first the bourgeoisie and then workers have come to occupy more and more strategic positions in the webs of interdependence within modern societies. In an oligarchic game, lower-level players may seem to be entirely controlled by the upper tier. But as the ties of interdependence between the tiers increase, the opposite may seem closer to the truth. The upper-tier players become, more overtly, spokesmen for the lower groups. For each spokesman, his strategy with respect to the lower-tier groups becomes as important as strategy towards others on the upper tier. The course of the game becomes still less susceptible to control and direction from any quarter, and more than ever people find themselves subjected to 'compelling social forces'. This is reflected, though not very lucidly, in people's consciousness, in the way they think about themselves and 'society'.

Instead of players believing that the game takes its shape from the individual moves of individual people, there is a slowly growing tendency for impersonal concepts to be developed to master their experience of the game. These impersonal concepts take into account the relative autonomy of the game process from the intentions of individual players. A long and laborious process is involved, working out communicable means of thought which will correspond to the character of the game as something not immediately controllable, even by the players themselves. Metaphors are used which oscillate constantly between the idea that the course of the game can be reduced to the actions of individual players and the other idea that it is of a supra-personal nature. (1970a: 91)

It is at first difficult and even repugnant, argues Elias, for people to come to terms with the idea that the society of which they themselves are part largely follows a 'blind' course, relatively autonomous of the objectives of its members.

Similar obstacles to understanding that *natural* phenomena are blind, purposeless sequences of events impeded the rise of the natural sciences. The obstacles to social science are all the greater. The opacity of social networks to those caught up in them is characteristic of all stages of social development, 'but only in a particular phase of this development could people become aware of this opacity and also, therefore, of uncertainty about themselves as a society' (1970a: 68). Sociology had its beginnings in the eighteenth and nineteenth centuries, when increasing specialization, growing differentiation and lengthening chains of interdependence were making social processes still more opaque, and transforming society with a rapidity which made it imperative to try to understand them.

The game models, along with the primal contest model, distil many aspects of Elias's work. The implicit allusions are obvious, not just to his studies of sports but also to the elimination contest between territorial magnates, to the oligarchic court society, to his theory of the development of the social sciences, above all to the interweaving of the long-term, unplanned civilizing and state formation processes. Indeed, in *The Civilizing Process* Elias was already fully aware of the interweaving process through which unplanned, blind compelling trends are shaped (see for instance the passage quoted on p. 72 above). The game models are, however, framed in a more general way to stimulate the sociological imagination. Here we shall first mention two general points which they raise.

The first is raised by the emerging of *non-intended structuredness*, illustrated by the models. There is a long tradition of academic thought which associates 'structure' with 'order' in the sense of 'logic'. As Artur Bogner has written

Since 'order' and 'structure' are symbols which, as such, at least in scientific discourse, exhibit an immanent relationship to logical order – as do all symbols employed by scientists – this tendency is further strengthened. The problem is even more acute for social scientists since 'social structures' are concerned with people who form and use symbols and, in so doing, can use those rules which we term 'logical order'. Furthermore, by means of the transformative capacities of human beings, they create *planned* structures, forms of connections of social or natural events which correspond to, although they are not *identical* with, 'order' in the sense of meaningful relations between symbols. The result is an overwhelming tendency to identify 'structure' or 'regularity' in general with logical order. (1986: 387)

The tendency is reinforced by the philosophical tradition so often attacked by Elias, which draws a distinction between the unchanging form and the changing content of knowledge, and identifies the form with an eternal 'logic' rooted in immutable *a priori* rules of human 'reasoning'. Thus when 'structure' is identified with 'logical order' in this way, it acquires a peculiarly static connotation, and comes to be associated with the search for something fixed and unchanging *behind* the flux of surface appearances. Phrases like 'the structure of social action' (Parsons 1937) come tripping off the tongues even of sociologists quite aware of the 'unintended consequences of social action'. The structuredness of social processes, observes Bogner, 'is of a very different kind to the *logical* order of intentions and symbols'. One theme of Elias's work is to lead sociologists to think in terms not of 'change of structures' or 'structure *and* process', but rather in terms of 'structures of change' and 'the structure of processes'.

A second point to emerge strongly from the game models is that the concept of 'function' and the concept of 'power' are closely connected with each other, and both are concepts *of relationship*. This indeed is only to draw attention once more to something prominent in Elias's work from the earliest days. When he uses the term 'function', it is not used as an expression for a task performed by a section within a harmonious 'whole'. 'We can only speak of social functions', says Elias, 'when referring to interdependencies which constrain people to a greater or lesser extent'. In other words,

when one person (or group of persons) lacks something which another person or group has the power to withhold, the latter has a function for the former. Thus men have a function for women and women for men, parents for children and children for parents. Enemies have a function for each other, because once they have become interdependent they have power to withhold from each other such elementary requirements as that of preserving their physical and social integrity, and ultimately of survival. (1970a: 78)

The potential of people or groups for withholding from each other what they require is usually uneven, so that one side has greater power to constrain than the other. But such unevenness is not always accepted unquestioningly. Balances of power are usually labile, and fluctuate to a greater or lesser degree. Changes in the overall nexus of social interdependencies – changes in the structure of society – may trigger trials of strength, in the form of acute and violent conflicts, or in the form of smouldering conflicts inherent in the structure of a society at a certain stage of development. Such trials of strength are characteristic of the interdependent functions of workers and entrepreneurs in a modern capitalist society, as they once were between kings, nobles and citizens in medieval and early modern Europe.

PERSONAL PRONOUNS AS A FIGURATIONAL MODEL

The concept of function is a simple example of the multi-perspectival character of social relationships. Even at a simple dyadic level, the relationship between A and B always comprises two distinguishable relationships – the relationship AB as seen from A's perspective, and the relationship BA as seen from B's perspective. In the game models – even the one-level models – there are more complicated multiple perspectives, just as there are multiple balances of power. For every player there are relationships with each of his or her own team-members, who are thought and spoken of as 'you' or 'he' or 'she', and collectively as 'we'. The other team are 'they', but from *their* perspective, of course, 'they' become 'we' and 'we' become 'they'.

Elias (1968, 1970a: 122–8) suggests the personal pronouns can be used as a model of a less reifying mode of sociological concept-formation, and as a corrective to the naïvely egocentric image of society and the image of persons as what he was later (1987a) to call 'We-less Egos'. Every person can refer to him- or herself as 'I' and to other people as 'you', 'he', 'she', 'we' or 'they'. The pronouns are relational and functional – they express a position relative either to the speaker at a certain moment, or relative to the whole intercommunicating group. The function of the pronoun 'I' can only be understood in the context of all the other positions to which 'you', 'he', 'she', 'we' and 'they' refer, and a child's coming to understand this set of relationships is basic to its acquiring a conception of itself as a separate person related to other separate persons. There is no-one who is not or was not interwoven into a network of people, and the experience of this is thought of and spoken about by means of the pronouns and related concepts.

One's sense of personal identity is closely connected with the 'we' and 'they' relationships of one's group, and with one's position within those units of which one speaks as 'we' and 'they'. Yet the pronouns do not always refer to the same people. The figurations to which they currently refer can change in the course of a lifetime, just as any person does himself. This is true not only of all people considered separately, but of all groups and even of all societies. Their members universally say 'we' of themselves and 'they' of other people; but they may say 'we' and 'they' of different people as time goes by. (1970a: 128)

All this is implicit in the theory of civilizing processes,[10] as well as the related theory of established-outsiders relations. But it reminds us especially that people – that is persons – are processes too. Their I-, we-, and they-images change over a lifetime. They change, moreover, over periods longer than a single lifetime. For, when Elias uses expressions like 'lengthening chains of interdependence' he is, as Eve (1982) puts it, 'not talking just of changing patterns of "relationships between" but changing structures *of* people, changing constitutions – and not least, changes in the boundaries of "I", "we", and "they"'. Indeed, Elias has encompassed the long-term changing balance between external constraints and self-constraints in the idea of 'changes in the We–I Balance' (1987a: 207–315).

Another use of the pronoun model is in connection with 'function' as a concept of relationship. In old-fashioned functionalism, the word was used in linking the activities of individual people to their consequences for the 'social system'. In analysing an interweaving process, Elias contends, there is no need to posit any such over-arching system. But, in looking at interweaving actions from the point of view of the various participants in turn, it is useful to draw distinctions between I-functions, you-functions, we-functions and they-functions.[11] That is to say, it will usually be found that people are engaged in activities through which they are serving partly their own interests (I-functions) and partly common interests (we-functions). The same activities may have 'they-functions' too – serving the interests of other people thought of as 'they' – but if the they-functions of an activity predominate, it must by definition be performed because 'they' have the capacity to withhold something 'we' or 'I' require. There are also 'it-functions': social actions are often performed and justified in the service of a symbolic 'it' – a creed, a flag, the honour of a family, the glory of a nation. In the end, 'it-functions' also refer back to people, but the force of the appeal of such symbols should not be discounted. Which kind of these various perspectival functions is dominant will vary according to how power ratios between people and groups vary.

The classic example in Elias's own work of what we may call 'pronoun-functional analysis' is found in *The Court Society*. Why were the activities of the royal court so dominated by ceremony and etiquette? Not because of the 'needs' or requirements of some overall 'system'. But, given the distribution of power chances in France as a whole, the 'I-functions' of etiquette for the King took precedence over we- or they-functions: it was principally a means of dominating the nobles. For the nobles, rituals had I-functions in calibrating each noble's standing among his fellows, and we-functions for the nobles as a group in exhibiting their superiority over the bourgeoisie. Then, as power ratios in the wider society shifted, king and nobles both became entrapped in the figuration they had, in a sense, blindly created.

The idea is capable of general application.[12] To give just one other example, Elias remarks (1970a: 126) that as a result of functional democratization, the functions of government posts for state-society (we-functions, or it-functions) come to take precedence over their functions for those who occupy them (I-functions), *although the latter do not vanish altogether*. The train of thought can be pursued without using the word 'function' at all, if it is too reminiscent of 'functionalism', though as a word it is convenient. The point is, however, that activities interweave within figurations which are in flux, have no fixed boundaries and lack any ulterior 'goal' from which all functions can be explained.

Max Weber struggled with just these problems in his discussions of *Verstehen* or 'interpretative understanding', and in urging social scientists to seek to grasp the 'subjectively intended meanings' which the various participants in a social process attached to their actions. Yet sociologists continue to make pretty heavy weather of what *Verstehen* involves.[13] One reason why it continues to seem so mysterious – even though every human being continually employs *Verstehen* in coping with the everyday problems of social existence – is probably that

most methodological attempts at explaining it are made in terms of a singular 'I'-perspective. The gist of the problem then is: how can I, as one single individual, understand the utterances of other people, of so many other 'I's? Stated in these terms, the problem may indeed be insoluble: the longer one ponders over it, the more enigmatic it becomes. It is not very realistic, however, to conceive of oneself as a wholly isolated 'I'. The very fact that we are capable of saying 'I', and of understanding others when they say 'I', indicates that as talking human beings, as *homines sapientes*, we take part in a universe in which we can also significantly speak of ourselves as 'we'. The key to understanding what is involved in *Verstehen* seems to lie in the recognition that *Verstehen* is not just a matter of 'I'- but also of 'we'-perspectives. (Goudsblom 1977a: 186)

Verstehen, and grasping 'subjectively intended meanings', are in any case not enough in themselves. Are sociologists to be condemned to recording only an infinite series of separate 'subjective' points of view? The pronoun model can also be used as a non-metaphysical way of posing the old problem of 'objectivity' versus 'subjectivity', usually posed in an epistemological and therefore ultimately solipsistic way. The game models have been used to show how people's perspectives intermesh to form a process unintended, unplanned and uncontrolled by anyone. They help to show, therefore, why it is not enough *only* to study 'subjectively intended meanings', indispensable though that may be. Even if one were to grasp fully the perspective of every last participant in an interweaving complex game, that would not yield a wholly adequate explanation of the course of the game, among other reasons because allowance has to be made for ignorance and self-deception. Sociology, in consequence, has to take account both of the first-person and third-person perspectives; it has, indeed, to form third-person perspectives of its own. That involves an effort of detachment, but increasing detachment itself, as we have seen in chapters 7 and 8, is not the achievement of individual people alone but also of long-term social processes.

IMPROVING MEANS OF ORIENTATION AS A PRIMARY TASK OF THE SOCIAL SCIENCES

The human animal is more dependent than any other for its survival and escape from dangers on the learned means of orientation developed and transmitted from generation to generation. This is true not just of learning which foods are poisonous, but also of the dangers posed to fellow humans by each other in the trials of strength which are characteristic of all human figurations. Indeed the means of orientation are one of the sources of power chances which have repeatedly been subject to monopolization by social groups (such as priests) as the basis of their dominance in many phases of history (see Elias 1983b). That is the context of Elias's belief that a primary task of sociology 'is finally to make people in every kind of association better able to understand themselves and others' (1969a: 210).

In the most general sense, the central task of social scientific research is to discover previously unknown connections, and the resulting theories in some ways serve people like maps.

If one stands at point A, where three roads meet, one cannot 'see' directly where these roads lead . . . So one uses a map . . . Like maps, theoretical models show the connections between events which are already known. Like maps of unknown regions, they show blank spaces where the connections are not yet known. Like maps, they can be shown by further investigation to be false, and they can be corrected. (Elias 1970a: 160)

This sets a far more ambitious objective than the pursuit of law-like, 'nomothetic-deductive' theories on the model of the natural sciences which many sociologists accept as their ideal. Elias is careful not to rule out the possibility of achieving such theories in certain areas of social investigation, but it would limit the scope of sociology too narrowly if they were taken as the exclusive ideal. Indeed, to return to the issues of chapters 7 and 8, the notion of scientific 'laws' originally emerged as one expression of the more general concern with improving the human means of orientation, and indeed with improving the human ability to control natural forces. But it is far more difficult to find domains of the social world where relations are as fixed and unchanging as among the events of nature. Sir Karl Popper, a major advocate of the assumption that laws are the only conceivable form of scientific explanation, argues that 'it is an important postulate of scientific method that we should search for laws with an unlimited realm of validity. If we were to admit laws that are themselves subject to change, change could never be explained by laws' (Popper 1944–5: 103). As van Benthem van den Bergh points out (1980: 187), this argument is manifestly circular and, moreover, does not take sufficient account of the fact that to search for laws implies an assumption of recurrence. The natural milieu appears constant because its tempo of change is so slow. That is why the assumption of recurrence has been so eminently useful in the natural sciences. But there is no reason to assume that it is as useful in theorizing about societies, since it would radically restrict the scope of investigation to recurrent features, usually part-processes which recur – often as minor elements – within larger, *non*-recurrent overall processes.[14]

The pursuit of timeless, law-like generalizations by many sociologists is reflected in their methods of research. Perhaps the questionnaire, which treats the respondent as an isolated individual, a recurrent atom, is the best symptom of this. Questionnaires are useful and necessary tools in many contexts. Yet the problem of opacity in social figurations is such that, even if questionnaires yielded full evidence of all individuals' perceptions of the figuration into which they are woven, that evidence would not necessarily simply add up to produce an adequate understanding of the dynamics of the figuration. If sociologists are to unravel social processes, they have to spot the consequences of people's interweaving actions which participants do not perceive, and this involves finding the factual links – from a they-perspective – missing from participants' pictures of their social figurations. As a matter of fact, questionnaires very often *are* useful in revealing unperceived structures of processes – as in the case of research into social mobility (e.g. J. H. Goldthorpe et al. 1982) – but this does not resolve in principle the limitations imposed on such data by its origins.

Underlying all Elias's writings is a belief that to understand the compelling nature of blind social processes is to increase the *chances* of controlling them.[15] He describes sociologists as 'destroyers of myths' (1970a: 50–70). By factual observation they endeavour to replace myths, religious and metaphysical speculations, and all unproven images of social processes, with theories testable and correctable by factual observation. This task will never be finally accomplished. For one thing, scientific theories are always being turned into belief systems and used in ways for which they were not intended. Sociology in particular has from its origins been inextricably entangled with the development of the modern social ideologies.[16] If one result of an awakening consciousness of the relative opacity of social processes has been an effort to investigate them by means analogous to those of the older sciences, another result has been that people tend to orientate themselves to relatively opaque social situations with the aid of relatively impersonal but emotionally charged social belief systems and ideals. These are all the more satisfying because they usually promise immediate relief for all social ills and sufferings, or even a complete cure in the near future . . .

The development of human society still remains opaque and is still beyond our powers of control. Sooner or later we shall consciously have to decide which of the two types of orientation, the scientific type or that based on preconceived social beliefs, is the more likely to succeed in elucidating it and making it more susceptible to control. (1970a: 69–70)

Of course, to help people to foresee the hitherto unforeseen consequences of their actions precipitates no automatic amelioration of the problems of social life. Examples abound of people unwilling to change a pattern of behaviour merely because its factual origins and consequences are revealed to them. George Orwell once pointed out (1970: IV, 274–5) that although everyone knew that deaths and injuries result on a large scale from the use of motor-cars, the very low speeds necessary to avoid the evil would be quite unacceptable (cf. Elias 1986d). When it is a case, as so often, of an escalating cycle of fears and threats between two or more sides, emotional and unrealistic beliefs about the other side are often actually strengthened, and the cycle is difficult to break merely by the propagation of more realistic knowledge. Nevertheless, it is a tenet of Elias's work, which few sociologists would wish to dispute, that social science can only improve the human lot by clearing through some of the fog which obscures our understanding of social forces.

'ONLY CONNECT': ELIAS'S ACHIEVEMENT

'The work of a significant thinker', Ernest Gellner has written, 'can never be simply a list of atomized, isolable ideas. What makes a thinker significant, amongst other things, is that his work possesses some measure of unity, and that it contains some central ideas, which pervade and inspire the corpus as a whole' (1985: 14). I hope that I have shown in this book that Norbert Elias is beyond doubt just such a significant thinker.

Elias has spoken of human beings' great capacity for synthesis. In a more specific sense, he himself has that capacity to an exceptional degree. No-one else has so coherently drawn the connections between manners and morals, power and violence, states, war and peace through human history. These are issues of acute interest and concern to humankind in general, not just to the narrow circle of professional social scientists and historians. Such matters were the common property of the intellectual milieu from which Elias came, but to dwell on the points of departure he shared with others is to miss the essential character of the uniquely powerful synthesis at which he has arrived.

For much of Elias's lifetime, sociologists turned their faces away from broad questions of the development of human society. They fashioned very sophisticated tools of *analysis*, but these outstripped their powers of *synthesis*, of relating their findings to the continuing development of wider human figurations. Elias has opposed the excesses of both the number crunching and the concept munching[17] forms of trivialization in sociology. Statistical and mathematical techniques, of course, represent a great advance, so long as technique does not narrow down the focus to exclude questions of wider human relevance. Elias's harshest words, however, are reserved for the social theorists who, from Parsons to the present generation, have flown off into deep conceptual space.

Not understanding the long ascent to a higher level of synthesis and its conditions, people often get so used to communicating with each other in terms of one of its manifestations, what they themselves call 'abstractions', at a very high level, that they lose sight of the symbolic representations of sensory details to which all high-level abstractions are related . . . [C]ircles of learned people who communicate with each other in a language full of ritualized high level abstractions which no-one outside that circle can understand. Within the circle these ritualized abstractions are used with a halo of associations which are never explicitly stated . . . Non-initiated people, assuming that the inquiries of the select must have results that have cognitive value and relevance for everybody, are often at a loss when they are exposed to a hail of abstractions of this kind. They . . . look in vain for any connection of these abstractions with symbols of anything tangible, with a conceptual synthesis representative of observable details. Without recognizable links with the latter, symbols of high-level syntheses are often no more than empty words. Getting lost in a maze of symbols of this type is one of the permanent pitfalls of life in societies with a fund of knowledge rich in symbols of high level syntheses. (1984a: 166–7)

Elias has invented some new terms himself. Though they may initially be unfamiliar, they are not 'abstract'. When new terminology is necessary, he strives to find modes of expression that are not remote from actual people; they always refer back to the experience of people, in the round and in the plural. That is as true of terms referring to macroscopic social processes as to microscopic, face-to-face processes; these are not two separate levels – they are always bound up with each other.

Above all, Elias believes it is 'dangerous for the wheels to grind without corn'. Concepts and theories take shape most fruitfully when, as in his own work, they are developed while grappling with evidence of actual social processes. 'Theory' cannot usefully be a separate speciality divorced from research.

Today there are many signs that historians and social scientists are turning their attention back towards the once deeply unfashionable questions Elias has steadfastly posed. There is renewed interest in longer-term trends in sexuality, violence, manners and morals. There is an efflorescence of writing about state-formation, a subject touched by few sociologists between the 1920s and the 1980s.[18] There is a return to questions of the globalization of human society and global history.[19] Nowadays, Elias has many fellow travellers. No-one in the current generation, however, rivals him in the scope of his interests nor brings so much together so coherently. I believe we have much still to quarry from his work. It offers many insights and some answers, yet has the protean quality of provoking more questions, opening up innumerable further lines of investigation.

Notes

CHAPTER 1   NORBERT ELIAS: A DETERMINED LIFE IN UNCERTAIN TIMES

1 See 'De Geschiednis van Norbert Elias', the transcript of a long conversation between Elias, A. J. Heerma van Voss and Abram van Stolk, published in the colour supplement to *Vrij Nederland*, 1 December 1984 (Elias, 1984a). (This was edited in book form by Van Stolk to mark Elias's 90th birthday in 1987.) The biographical information in the present chapter is drawn mainly from that source, from Elias's only published essay in intellectual autobiography (1984b), and from recollections of some of my own conversations with Elias and his friends.

2 The phrase is from Bryan Wilson's 1977 article in *New Society*, marking the publication on Elias's birthday of a *Festschrift* in his honour (Gleichmann, Goudsblom and Korte, eds, 1977); as late as this, Elias was still virtually unknown among anglophone sociologists outside the limited circle of his personal acquaintance.

3 However, Bershady (1973) demonstrates quite convincingly the Kantian foundations of Parsons's project, and indeed Parsons himself hints on this in his essay in intellectual autobiography (1970).

4 Talcott Parsons was in Heidelberg at around the same time as Elias, and also frequented the Weber circle, yet Elias cannot recall having met him then. Elias taught German to foreign students, and often wondered subsequently whether Parsons could have been one of them.

5 The idea of the 'free-floating intelligentsia' seems to have originated with Alfred Weber.

6 Conversation in Amsterdam, 2 July 1986.

7 Hermann Korte (1988) has also failed to solve this problem of chronology.

8 By strange coincidence, the first book published by the firm was Richard Hönigswald's *Philosophie und Sprache* (1937). Fritz Karger relates the story of the ill-fated first edition in his essay 'Fata Libelli' (1977).

9 Thomas Mann, *Tagebücher 1937–1939* (1980: 440, 443, 445, 446, 447): 'Elias's book more valuable than I thought, especially the picture of the late Middle Ages and the decline of the knightly age'.

10 When, in 1959 and 1960, Elias returned for the first time since the war to Germany, it was to lecture by invitation on the distinctive character of public opinion in England (Elias, 1959, 1960).

11 See S. H. Foulkes: *Therapeutic Group Analysis* (1964), especially pp. 269–78; 'Group analytic dynamics with special reference to psychoanalytic concepts' (1957); and Foulkes and Prince, eds., *Psychiatry in a Changing Society* (1969).

12 For a good account of the long-running dispute between Melanie Klein, Anna Freud and their respective partisans, see Phyllis Grosskurth, *Melanie Klein: Her World and Her Work* (1986).

13 When asked about his earlier publications Elias apparently said vaguely that he had written 'something about manners'; Dunning had to ask Neustadt for the details and for the loan of a copy of the first edition.

14 A reasonable impression of the content of Cohen's lectures can be obtained from the book *Modern Social Theory* which he published in 1968.

15 Personal conversation with Francis Carsten in Amsterdam on the occasion of Elias's ninetieth birthday, 22 June 1987. Carsten had got to know Gordon-Walker when guiding him through the Berlin underground resistance in about 1934, and he was, I believe, the link between Elias and the future Foreign Secretary.

CHAPTER 2   MANNERS

1 On Elias's relation to Huizinga, as well as Weber and Freud, see Goudsblom (1984).

2 Still worse, the second volume appeared under two different titles: *State-Formation and Civilization* in the British edition, *Power and Civility* in the American.

3 For a study of the history of the word *civilisation* in French see Febvre (1930). Cf. Elias 1939: I, 3–50.

4 The socially demarcating, delimiting function of the word *Kultur* has carried over into the modern anthropological use of the term *culture*; on this, see especially Z. A. Bauman, *Culture as Praxis* (1973). For a famous discussion of the meanings of 'culture' in English, see Raymond Williams, *Culture and Society 1780–1950* (1958). On the problematic spatial image of 'above' and 'below' too often taken for granted by sociologists, see Johan Goudsblom's essay 'On the high and low in society and sociology' (1986b).

5 On how these trends were related to the changing layout of dwellings and to housing patterns, see Gleichmann (1977, 1979a).

6   It adds perspective to Elias's remarks on the peculiarity of the history of spitting in Western Europe to recall that in China spitting is still today very uninhibited, even though many other aspects of behaviour and feeling have been subject to a very long civilizing process. Nor is the process of inhibition equally complete throughout Europe itself; spitting is still very unrestrained in Portugal for example.

7 Elias's account of meat consumption remains, I think, broadly true, even though it is now known that meat became more plentiful for all social ranks after the Black Death. For more detailed discussion of this, see Mennell, *All Manners of Food* (1985, chs 2 and 3).

8 Elias relegates to an extended note (1939: I, 305–7n.) a discussion on cleanliness, washing and bathing; this should not be overlooked.

9 Giddens (1984: 129) wrongly asserts, without any precise reference, that Elias does make such a claim. See Dunning's (1987) forceful rebuttal of Giddens in his article discussing Elias's use of the *Mittelalterliche Hausbuch* drawings.

10 For evidence of the brevity and abruptness of sexual encounters in early modern Europe, see Shorter 1982: 9–10.

11 On the deprecation of love within marriage in the teaching of the Church and attitudes of the laity in medieval and early modern Europe, see Flandrin 1976: 161–73, and Duby 1981: 27.

12 Cf. Peter Laslett's conclusion from more recent research 'that Christian doctrine . . . failed almost entirely to control western sexual expression' (Foreword to Ariès and Béjin, (eds) 1985: ix).

13 There is an interesting parallel here between Elias and Philippe Ariès, who in his celebrated book *Centuries of Childhood* (1960) was to speak of the 'discovery' of childhood. Elias and Ariès even draw independently on some of the same sources, such as the account of the childhood of Louis XIII given by the court doctor Héroard in the early seventeenth century (Elias 1939; ɪ, 189; Ariès 1960; 50ff). Ariès certainly demonstrates in more detail than Elias how the boundary between childhood and adulthood gradually became less fluid and more firmly defined, and the 'privatization' of family and sexuality. His *explanation* of these changes, however, seems to me to rest more on adults coming to *view* children in a more sentimental way, no longer requiring so early an attainment of adult standards. He offers no explanation of why the adult standard itself advances; the changes in adult standards are themselves given as an explanation of the changing view of childhood. Ariès provides a good example of the history of ideas approach to the question.

14 Elias points out that this could in a sense be rationally justified in an age when feeding and containing prisoners could be beyond the capacity of existing social organization, yet when merely to release them uninjured would be to return them to reinforce the opponent's army (cf. Contamine 1980: 35); however, whatever the coldly rational justification, we are here concerned rather with mutilation carried out by soldiers in the heat of battle and exultation of victory, not as the result of cold calculation.

15 Cf. Robert Darnton, *The Great Cat Massacre* (1984).

16 It is documented, independently of Elias, by historians such as Huizinga (1924), Mandrou (1961), and Le Goff (1964).

17 Cf. Keith Thomas, *Man and the Natural World* (1983); Mennell, *All Manners of Food* (1985, ch. 11).

CHAPTER 3   STATES AND COURTS

1 *Carolingians*: the line of kings descended from Charlemagne. In AD 987, the last of them was succeeded by Hugh *Capet*, whose descendants are known as Capetians.

2 Elias emphasizes that it was a shift in the *balance* between barter and money economies. Long-distance trade in certain goods (especially luxuries) never entirely disappeared from Europe; the money economy and urban life persisted more strongly in Italy and Provence than further north (cf. Bloch, 1939–40: ɪɪ, 299). Elias's discussion of all these matters is much more nuanced than an inaccurate reading such as that of Robinson (1987) represents it.

3 I have changed the tense of this quotation from the published translation. The historic present works better in German and French than in English, where it can convey an air either of naïveté or of over-generalization. I have occasionally made other minor corrections when quoting published texts elsewhere in this book.

4 The details and the timing vary between parts of Europe, as Elias constantly asserts.

In particular, the Conquest made England a special case, and its kings were generally unusually strong – in comparison with their contemporary French and German counterparts – in the next few centuries. (The extent to which *The Civilizing Process* as a whole is, among so many other themes, a comparative historical sociology of France, Germany and England has often been overlooked.)

5 See Van Benthem van den Bergh (1977) for a comparison of Elias with a variety of Marxist writings on the state.

6 For a Marxist view which explicitly rejects this 'percentage' approach, see Wickham (1984), a fine article which also serves as a useful up-to-date survey of the debate about the transition from antiquity to feudalism.

7 The US citizen's constitutional 'right to bear arms' is not really an exception to this. It was the Founding Fathers' fear of standing armies as a threat to civil liberties which led to this right being enshrined in the Constitution, but they would not have foreseen the interpretation of the phrase by the National Rifle Association as guaranteeing individuals the right to carry guns in order to kill each other at whim. Nevertheless, the widespread ownership of handguns in the USA, even by many pacific citizens, often shocks Europeans (not to mention many other Americans) who see it as, in a sense, 'uncivilized'.

8 *Apanage*: the provision made for the maintenance of the younger children of kings or princes; in this context, it means a province to be governed as a dependent territory by a younger brother of a king.

9 The question of whether a sequence of social development can ever be said to be 'inevitable' has tended to become entangled with the philosophers' metaphysical antithesis of 'determinism' and individual 'free will'. The muddle is then further compounded when 'free will' is linked to 'freedom' in the sense of political and social liberty, and 'determinism' to lack of liberty. This link is false; as Elias points out, '*it is usually forgotten that there are always simultaneously many mutually dependent individuals, whose interdependence to a greater or lesser extent limits each one's scope for action*' (1970a: 167). That simple sentence of Elias's, in my opinion, pithily cuts across centuries of metaphysical debate.

In *The Civilizing Process*, Elias demonstrates the inadequacy of the static polarity between 'inevitability' and 'indeterminancy' as it applies to social processes in his subtle handling of historical evidence. In his later work, he often returns to the problem in more 'theoretical' terms. Models of developmental processes, or 'process theories' as we shall call them in chs 7 and 8, are *not* theories conforming to the 'covering law' model of explanation. He explains their character briefly as follows:

Terms such as 'growth' or 'development' refer to a specific way in which events are connected with each other. It is a type of connectedness different from that with which classical physics was concerned. Every datum forming part of such an order presupposes an antecedent datum as its necessary (though not necessarily its sufficient) condition and may in turn become a necessary (though not necessarily a sufficient) condition for a further stage within that process of growth or development. I use as conceptual badges for this type of order terms such as '*sequential order*'; or 'serial order'. (1972: 121; my italics)

He also uses the alternative term 'genealogical order' (1970a: 162–3).

More subtle and reality-orientated modes of thinking are necessary to come to grips with the issue of prediction and 'inevitability' in sequences of social development. Elias proposes that we think of such development as a continuum of changes, or figurational flow. Within the flow, we can identify a sequence of figurations, which we can label A, B, C, D; these are not static, discontinuous *stages* of development, but points inserted in a flow – various figurations of people, each figuration flowing from the previous one as the development takes its course from A to D. The kernel of Elias's argument is then as follows:

Retrospective study will often clearly show not only that the figuration is a *necessary* precondition for D, and likewise B for C and A for B, but also why this is so. Yet, looking into the future, from whatever point in the figurational flow, we are usually able to establish only that the figuration at B is *one possible* transformation of A, and similarly C of B and D of C. In other words, in studying the flow of figurations there are two possible perspectives on the connection between one figuration chosen from the continuing flow and another, later figuration. From the viewpoint of the earlier figuration, the later is – in most if not all cases – only one of several possibilities for change. From the viewpoint of the later figuration, the earlier one is usually a necessary condition for the formation of the later. (1970a: 160)

There is, then, an asymmetry in the two time-perspectives. The reason is that figurations vary greatly in their pliability, plasticity, potential for change (or, conversely, in their rigidity). Retrospective investigation will usually show that the possible outcomes have to be thought of in terms of probabilities; moreover, as a particular figuration changes into another, and a scatter of possible outcomes narrows down to a single one, another range of possible outcomes, once more with differing probabilities, hoves into view in the next phase of development.

Elias's later discussions of the issue ought always to be read in conjunction with his earlier handling of empirical material.

10 In another place, however, while still speaking of 'a higher degree of probability', he makes the following incautious remark: 'In the language of exact science this observation would perhaps be called a "law". Strictly speaking, what we have here is a relatively precise formulation of a quite simple social mechanism which, once set in motion, proceeds like clockwork' (1939: ii, 99). This comment offered a hostage to fortune; it played into the hands of readers determined to misunderstand Elias's argument, such as the historian Geoffrey Barraclough, who in a review (1982) headed 'Clockwork history', accused Elias of having a mechanistic, deterministic, conception of the course of history. Such a reading is obtuse, for Elias constantly makes contrary comments such as 'the course of events in reality is usually far more complicated than in this schematic pattern, and full of variations' (1939: ii, 107). What I think Elias probably meant was *not* that the monopoly mechanism was like the inexorable steady progress of a timepiece (since that clearly contradicts what he constantly says about it being a matter of probabilities), but that it *was* a bit like a clockwork toy which, once wound up, runs forward in a straight line across the carpet, *unless it hits some obstacle, in which case it is halted or deflected*. But it was an incautious remark, which he would have been unlikely to make later in his career, when he became very much aware of the deficiencies of language available for grasping the dynamics of social progresses. By the 1960s, he thought 'mechanism' as misleading as 'law' – see chs 7 and 8 below. Elias's actual view of the monopoly mechanism is much more subtle than the word 'mechanism' (let alone 'clockwork') suggests.

11 See the discussion of game models in ch. 11 below.

12 The way in which social scientists have tended to skate over this problem is illustrated in the following excerpt concerning the absolutist monarchy of Louis XIV, from a book which covers similar ground to the first part of the second volume of *The Civilizing Process*:

Rule now rested solely with the monarch, who had gathered all effective (as against formal) public prerogatives to himself. To exercise it, he first had to increase his own prominence, had to magnify and project the majesty of his powers by greatly enlarging the court and intensifying its glamour . . . It . . . appeared to outsiders (and foreigners) to be a lofty plateau, an exalted stage at the centre of which the ruler stood in a position of unchallengeable superiority. (Poggi 1978: 69)

As Elias notes, Louis XIV himself was not a man of exceptional personal ability, let alone of 'charisma'.

13 Readers interested in tracing the antecedents of ideas used by Elias may see in 'the royal mechanism' an echo of Georg Simmel's famous discussion of triadic relationships, and especially of the principle of *tertius gaudens* (Simmel 1908a). Elias probably had read Simmel, but Simmel's discussion (which, after all, is only a development of still older ideas) remains at the formal level, while Elias develops the principle in processual terms and shows how it fits specific historical evidence in a context immeasurably more complex than three-person groups.

14 See, for example, Berelson et al. 1954. Again, Simmel's earlier essays on 'Conflict' and 'The web of group affiliations' (1908b) tended in the same direction. It should be noted that Elias's idea of ambivalence rests not so much on actual cross-cutting group *memberships* as on the ambivalence of *interests* resulting from *mutual dependence* of individuals and groups.

15 The various regional *parlements*, including the one in Paris, did continue to exist until the Revolution, but in spite of the name were essentially courts of law rather than parliaments in the English sense. Nevertheless, they did have certain powers which resemble 'parliamentary' ones, and there were conflicts between them and the kings.

16 Max Weber touched on the courts of *ancien régime* Europe in many places, but mainly from the point of view of administration. A clear distinction between private and official revenues was of course one of the defining characteristics of *rational-legal* bureaucracy in Weber's celebrated ideal-type (1922a; II, 956–69). See also Elias's extended discussion of Weber's contrast between patrimonial and charismatic rulers (1969a: 121–6).

17 See Poggi (1978: 79–95) for a further discussion of how towards the close of the age of absolutism, 'an increasingly significant section of the European bourgeoisie – the capitalist entrepreneurs – had been redefining their social identity as that of a *class*, no longer that of an *estate*'.

18 *Courtization*: the original German word is *Verhöflichung*. In English Elias frequently uses the expression 'courtization' (as in 'the courtization of warriors') – to the sheer awfulness of which word I find it hard to reconcile myself, preferring to use the neologism 'curialization' invented by Elias's French translator. Nevertheless, with a heavy heart, I use 'courtization' henceforth, in order to avoid confusion in relation to the published texts.

19 On the struggles of priests and warriors, see also Goudsblom (1984: 157ff; 1988).

20 See for example the *Chanson de Roland* (see under Anon. *c.*1100 in Bibliography), laisses 93–102 *et passim*. Benjo Maso (1982) suggests that one of the chronicles cited by Elias to illustrate the cruelty of knights might better be interpreted as 'war propaganda'. There may be an element of that in some of the sources, but the picture as a whole still seems to me to support Elias's interpretation overall. See Contamine 1980: 250–9.

21 Elias, writing in 1939, strongly emphasizes the economic forces undermining the power of the French nobility (as well as the subordination of their military potential to the royal monopoly). He presents the argument in more detail in *The Court Society* (1969a: 151ff), probably on the basis of research conducted *before* he wrote *The Civilizing Process*. For a more recent discussion on this point, see Salmon 1974: 37–47.

22 Elias also drew on *The Court Society*, then unpublished, in writing *The Civilizing Process*, and there is a summary of some of the main points especially in vol. II: 258ff.
23 This is implied by Elias, but explained much more clearly in Mark Girouard's *Life in the English Country House* (1978: 144–8).
24 In the end, some of the greatest families, whose rank was beyond question, did break the taboo on participation in industrial enterprises – strictly large-scale ones, for small enterprise remained degrading (Elias 1969a: 73; see also Richard 1974).
25 To a limited extent, the court could be argued to have had some of the characteristics of what Goffman (1961) labelled 'total institutions': the people of court society 'did not stand for ten or twelve hours a day in the glare of public life and then withdraw to a more private sphere' (Elias 1969a: 115). Elias could have read Goffman's essay by the time he was revising *Die Höfische Gesellschaft*, though he makes no reference to it. Goffman, on the other hand, in *Asylums* (1961: 304) and *Behaviour in Public Places* (1963), does footnote the original 1939 edition of *Über den Prozess der Zivilisation*; that is remarkable, considering the obscurity of Elias's work at that date. (See also Kuzmics 1986, for a comparison of Goffman and Elias.)
26 Georg Simmel (1908c: 734) uses the expression *Zwei-Fronten-Position* in relation to the nobility.
27 Some anticipation of the idea of a frozen clinch in the same historical context can be seen in Alexis de Tocqueville's (1856) discussion of the French, who 'were split up into small, isolated, self-regarding groups' (*The Ancien Régime*, pt 2, chs 9 and 10); see the introduction to Stone and Mennell (eds), *Alexis de Tocqueville on Democracy, Revolution and Society* (1980).
28 For more discussion of this point, see ch. 11, pp. 256–7 below.
29 The influence of the French court on the courts of Russia, Sweden, Germany and even the Netherlands in the eighteenth century is traced by Baudrillart in his *Histoire de Luxe* (1878–80: IV, ch. 8).
30 For an example of this tendency, see Corrigan and Sayer, *The Great Arch* (1985); this is less true of Barrington Moore (1967: 3–39), whose remarks on 'the contributions of violence to gradualism' make an interesting comparison with Elias here.
31 'Professional', with its rather narrow connotations in English of the liberal professions like medicine and the law, is plainly a bad translation, though sanctioned by Elias. The German word is *beruflich*, having broader the sense of pertaining to 'calling', 'career', or 'occupation'. By 'professional-bourgeois', Elias means a society dominated by a *working* middle class.
32 Paradoxically, in view of the development of a full court society on the continental model having been aborted in England in the seventeenth century, by the late nineteenth century it was in England that aristocratic social forms remained longest and most vigorously alive (1939: II, 306–7). For a fuller discussion of why this was so, see Davidoff (1973).

CHAPTER 4   SOCIOGENESIS AND PSYCHOGENESIS

1 Adam Smith's *The Wealth of Nations* (1776), often seen as the starting point of modern economics, probably influenced social scientists' thinking about the division of labour more than any other book. Sociologists, however, tend to make more frequent reference to Emile Durkheim's *De la division du travail social* (1893). Durkheim's book is more or less a polemic against Herbert Spencer who, in line of descent from Smith, explained the process in terms of individuals' pursuit of their own advantage in competitive interdependence. In *The Division of Labour* Durkheim,

by contrast, emphasized the necessity of trust, order and consensus *before* people felt able to put themselves in others' hands by dividing their labour – 'all that is in the contract is not contractual'. In stressing competitive forces, Elias may appear at first glance to be on the Smith/Spencer side of the dispute, until one remembers that his spiral view of the process (pacification facilitating trade, trade facilitating pacification, to put it crudely – see p. 70 above) constitutes a rejection of both Durkheim's and Spencer's views as one-sided, as a false and static polarity. Durkheim's book also encourages static thinking in setting up the polarity between 'mechanical' and 'organic solidarity'; it encourages sociologists to lose sight of the fact that the *division* of labour is a *process*, not a matter of static contrast between 'high' and 'low'.

2 Elias returned to develop this traffic image much later in his essay 'Technization and civilization' (1986d).
3 This trend may be reversed in phases of informalization, such as that of the 1960s and 1970s with, in Cas Wouters's phrase, 'its voyages of discovery into the land of drives *and* consciousness'; see ch. 10, pp. 241–6.
4 On the idea of increasing reality-orientation and the problem of the correspondence between an external reality and conceptual schemes, see the discussion of Elias's theory of knowledge and science in chs 7 and 8 below.
5 That seems to me to be the case even though elsewhere (1922a; II, 926–38) Weber discussed status-chances as an important power resource in certain social formations.
6 In a similar way, Max Horkheimer and Theodor Adorno in *The Dialectic of Enlightenment* (1947) were also, as Artur Bogner (1987: 267) points out, 'too quick to identify instrumental reason, whose realization according to their theory has been a goal pursued by the human species *since prehistoric times*, with the rationality of commodity exchange'.
7 The *Mittelalterliche Hausbuch* dates from the fifteenth century, which at the princely courts was already the age of the 'courtly knight' rather than of free knights. But the book comes from a region which was then something of a backwater where earlier ways persisted.
8 For Elias's most detailed remarks on 'pendulum swings' in social life, see his Adorno Prize address (1977a).
9 Elias's scattered discussions of problems of art and style were a major influence on Bram Kempers's important book *Painting, Power and Patronage* (1987), a study of the development of the profession of painter in late medieval and Renaissance Italy, in which Kempers recasts the traditional art historians' stylistic sequence from Gothic to Mannerism in terms related to changing power ratios in society, especially between artists and patrons.
10 In a letter quoted by Goudsblom (1977b).

CHAPTER 5 ESTABLISHED-OUTSIDERS RELATIONS AND
FUNCTIONAL DEMOCRATIZATION

1 *The Established and the Outsiders* seems almost to have shared the fate of *The Civilizing Process*. For some obscure reason, the publisher seems to have made negligible attempts to sell it, not even sending out copies for review, and allowing it soon to go out of print. It was the first in a series under the title 'New Sociology Library', edited by Norbert Elias, which went on to include titles by Giddens, Dunning, Bell and Newby.

2 Elias's imprint can be seen throughout the book, but especially in ch. 7 ('Observations on gossip') and in the first and last chapters where he raises issues of general significance to sociology, anticipating his lengthier discussion of similar matters a few years later in *What is Sociology?* (1970a). These issues are covered mainly in ch. 11. Special note should be made here, however, of three appendices to *The Established and the Outsiders* which stand over Elias's initials alone:

1 'Sociological aspects of identification', dealing with Freud, Mead and the problem of 'sociological inheritance' (as opposed to biological).

2 'A note on the concepts "social structure" and "anomie"', criticizing Merton for seeing these concepts as opposites. (Elias himself uses the word 'anomie' in a sense that does not coincide with the usage of most sociologists.)

3 'On the relationship of "family" and "community"', criticizing the well-known studies by Young and Willmott and by Elizabeth Bott for tending too readily to take family structure as an 'independent variable' and working 'outwards' to community networks as part of an 'environment'; he argues that they must be seen as mutually shaping each other within a figuration. This is an early version of Elias's attack on 'egocentric' modes of thinking in sociology, written up at greater length in *What is Sociology?* (In their later work, notably *The Symmetrical Family* (1973), with its greater historical depth, Young and Willmott seem to me to have in effect responded to this criticism, though probably without having read what Elias wrote.)

3 Elias first spelled out the general implications of these ideas in his unpublished paper 'Group charisma and group disgrace' read at the Max Weber Centenary conference in Heidelberg in 1964.

4 For a clear statement of the position Elias is criticizing, see for example Shils's essay 'Deference' (1968). Elias would have in his gunsights the whole tradition of the 'functionalist theory of stratification' associated with names like Talcott Parsons, Davis and Moore, as well as Shils. But his strictures about associating status-ranking with consensus apply to some extent to certain sociologists – not all – writing under the influence of Weber, who associate 'class' with conflict but 'status' with stability and consensus.

5 See. Van Benthem van den Bergh's essay 'Attribution of blame as a means of orientation' (1980: 7–46).

6 One of Elias's poems, 'Die ballade von Armen Jakob,' (1987e: 97–8) written in the internment camp on the Isle of Man in 1940, reveals his attitude even then:

> Er erzählte von Feinden und wie sie zu bekämpfen, denn so ist unsere Erde
> aber ohne Bitterkeit
> und daß auch sie Getriebene sind wie wir alle
> und im Grunde ohne Schuld . . .
>
> Warum können wir uns nicht vertragen?
> Wir haben nichts als uns.

7 In the following discussion I have also drawn on the talk on 'Established-Outsiders relationships' given by Elias at the University of Leeds, 18 January 1980. I am grateful to Richard Kilminster for supplying the tape-recording of this talk for me to transcribe. I have in addition drawn on an unpublished manuscript on 'The figurational dynamics of racial stratification' by Eric Dunning, to whom I am indebted here as elsewhere.

8 On the balance of power between children and adults, see Paul Kapteyn (1980,

1985a, 1985b). On a similar problem of generations, see Wouters, 'On youth and student protest' (1970).

9 See for example G. E. M. Ste Croix's excellent book *The Class Struggle in the Ancient Greek World* (1981), in which the author devotes several pages to controversy on this point with fellow Marxists such as M. I. Finley.

10 I was unable to find room in the text to discuss several other interesting and diverse uses of the established-outsiders model. They include Herman Roodenburg's article on 'Predestination and group charisma' (1981), concerning conflicts between Calvinists and other believers in the early Dutch Republic (a contribution from an Eliasian viewpoint to the huge sociological literature on Weber and the Protestant Ethic), and Mart Bax's extensive writings on religious conflicts, state-formation and pillarization in the Roman Catholic southern Netherlands (see for example Bax and Nieuwenhuis 1982; Bax 1983). These authors discuss the process of the monopolization of the means of orientation as a power resource. A completely different topic is Evenhuis, Klos and van Lingen's study of 'Outsiders in their own home: patients on the ward of a nursing home' (1980). Anneke van Otterloo (1986) has drawn on the model in discussing the food eaten by native Dutch and immigrants in the Netherlands. And Gillisen and Lissenberg (1985) in their study of *Women in a Male Bulwark* – women students of two generations in a College of Technology – have modified the established-outsiders model to include the third pole of 'marginals'; that was necessary because the women were such a small minority and posed so little threat to established male norms at the college that the male–female power balance was far from central.

11 Weber's book has been controversial among historians. Much of their debate (sketched in Magraw 1983) has, however, centred on the question of the dates between which the civilizing of the peasantry took place. Elias, and probably Weber, would regard such debate as futile, recognizing that such processes have no precise beginning or end.

12 On cookery lessons in the Netherlands, see Van Otterloo, 1985; for similar movements in Britain, see Mennell 1985: 184–6, 225–8.

13 In a critique of De Swaan's paper, Wouters (1979) argues that agoraphobia had more to do with women's fears of *rising* rather than falling, and that similar fears are not uncommon among rising groups when power ratios between established and outsiders are becoming less unequal.

CHAPTER 6   SPORT AND VIOLENCE

1 Elias's work in this field, both his own and in collaboration with Dunning, dates mainly from the 1960s. The essays were written in English, and for a time Elias was probably better known among anglophone academics as a sociologist of sport and leisure than for any of his other work. Together with some of Dunning's later essays and an important new introduction by Elias, the essays were collected in the book *Quest for Excitement* (1986). It includes full versions of some essays first published in abbreviated form, as well as some which, though dating from the 1960s, had not previously been published. For simplicity's sake, therefore, in this chapter references are made throughout to *Quest for Excitement*, ignoring for once the original dates of publication.

   During the 1970s and 1980s, Dunning continued research at Leicester with other collaborators, culminating in the establishment there in 1986 of the Sir Norman

Chester Centre for Football Research with Dunning as Director. Apart from numerous essays, Dunning's later books include *Barbarians, Gentlemen and Players* (1979), a study of the development of rugby football written with Kenneth Sheard, and *Hooligans Abroad* (1984) and *The Roots of Football Hooliganism* (1988), both with John Williams and Patrick Murphy. Among Dunning's former students, Christopher Brookes has written *English Cricket* (1978) and Chris Rojek written a survey of sociological theories of leisure, *Capitalism and Leisure Theory* (1985), which includes a chapter on the Elias/Dunning approach.

Elias's influence can also be seen in the research on sport by Ruud Stokvis in the Netherlands (1982a, 1982b) and Gunter Pilz in Germany (1982, 1983, 1984, 1985).

2 'Sociology of the emotions' may be an unfamiliar term, though it is a possible label for one thread running through Elias's work from the beginning. The term has recently crept into American sociology – the American Sociological Association has a specialist section under that title. See Hochschild (1983), Wouters (forthcoming 1989), and the special issue of *Symbolic Interactionism* (1985).

3 This was the original title of the paper published as 'The quest for excitement in leisure'. The irony in the expression 'unexciting societies' is explained below.

4 Elias observes how today applause is postponed until after the final movement of a symphony, concerto or quartet, instead of after each movement as in the time of most of the classical composers. The delay can be an uncomfortable experience, and Elias speculates that it may itself be the outcome of a self-escalating civilizing process (1986: 49–50).

5 Elias and Dunning provide two versions of the spare-time spectrum in *Quest for Excitement* at pp. 68–9 and 96–8. The former is a preliminary draft from which after some experiment, the latter 'more precise and comprehensive' version emerged. Elias and Dunning stress that the scheme is subject to revision in the light of its usefulness in research.

6 On this subject, see both Elias and Dunning's essay 'Folk football in medieval and early modern Britain' (1986: 175–90, originally 1971) and Dunning and Sheard (1979: 21–45).

7 See also Elias's essay 'Towards a theory of communities' (1974b).

8 Elias apologizes (1986: 287n.) for the neologism, and I can only associate myself with the apology.

9 That question was, at any rate, the way in which Elias broached the issue with me in one of our earliest meetings in the early 1970s.

10 Not all English sports diffused as widely as soccer; cricket for instance is little played outside the British Commonwealth. Moreover, the USA is an anomaly in that specifically American forms like baseball and the 'gridiron' form of football developed there while cricket and soccer have not caught on.

11 In his review of *Quest for Excitement*, Sir Edmund Leach (1986) castigated Elias for no more than reiterating the analogy, apparently having quite overlooked the theoretical elaboration Elias provides.

12 Elias's essay on fox-hunting is somewhat opaquely entitled 'An essay on sport and violence' (Elias and Dunning 1986: 150–74).

13 Elias does not mention it, but a ritual persists of 'blooding' initiates with the blood of the fox at their first kill; this practice now excites widespread revulsion among the general public.

14 See the novels of R. S. Surtees and Anthony Trollope, where the kill is little dwelt upon.

15 This is one point stressed by Stokvis in his critique, also from a 'figurational' point of

view, of *Barbarians Gentlemen and Players*. See Stokvis (1981a, 1981b) and Dunning's reply (1981). Stokvis's review of *Quest for Excitement* (1987) is also relevant to this dispute.

16 Even the Spanish bull-fight, now regarded by many people as still less civilized – in the colloquial sense – than fox-hunting, has shown long-term civilizing tendencies, according to Henk Driessen (1982). Driessen is not uncritical of Elias's theory (his article was published in the 1982 special issue of *Sociologische Gids* devoted to critique of Elias), and argues that the cultural mechanism of ritualization also played a part. Nevertheless, he says that since the eighteenth century bullfighting has developed increasingly towards professionalization, specialization, differentiation, sequestration in permanent bullrings, and regularization. All of these developments, he says, can be interpreted as part of the civilizing and state-formation processes. The present stylized form in which the bull-fighter allows the bull's horns to pass close to his almost motionless body demands very great self-control.

17 This new slant on 'the significance of England' in popular perception is not entirely justified. In *Hooligans Abroad* (1984), Williams et al. produce copious evidence that the problem of sport-related hooliganism has never been confined to Britain, nor indeed to soccer.

18 Dunning developed and refined his argument in many publications from *Barbarians, Gentlemen and Players* onwards. He contrasts his own views with those of the historian Johan Huizinga and the sociologists Gregory Stone (a symbolic inter-actionist) and Bero Rigauer (a Marxist). For a clear brief statement, see his essay 'The dynamics of modern sport' (in Elias and Dunning 1986: 205–23).

19 Alternative terms are 'rational' and 'affective'; Dunning (in Elias and Dunning 1986: 226) says explicitly that he is using a modification of some aspects of Weber's typology of action.

20 Dunning points out, however, that in their battle with the authorities, the hooligans have been led to be more instrumental in planning opportunities for engaging in expressive violence (personal communication.)

21 Dunning et al. (1988: 18–31) criticize not only popular explanations of football hooliganism but also academic explanations, notably the work of Marsh, Rosser and Harré (1978) who write under the influence of ethological theories of aggression in non-human species, and Taylor (1971, 1982) who writes from a Marxist perspective. Space precludes giving this debate the attention it deserves.

22 Dunning and his colleague are careful to point also to the minority of middle-class males they have discovered among hooligans. Dunning also emphasizes that the masculinity norms of the core hooligans (whether working or middle class) are variants of the dominant masculinity norms of our society, 'a fact which provides testimony to how relatively uncivilized we remain' (personal communication). See also his essay 'Sport as a male preserve' (in Elias and Dunning 1986: 267–83).

23 The argument is a good deal more complicated than it appears in summary: see Dunning's essays 'Social bonding and violence in sport' and (with Murphy and Williams) 'Spectator violence at football matches', both in Elias and Dunning (1986: 224–66).

24 When he speaks of 'bonding', Dunning is not using the word in the sense associated with ethology and sociobiology, which hypothesize some genetic basis for human social bonds. He is using it – as I have used it in this book – in Elias's sense of *observably socially produced* forms of relationship (Elias and Dunning 1986: 225). The distinction between segmental and functional bonding is related to Durkheim's

familiar concepts of mechanical and organic solidarity (Dunning, in Elias and Dunning 1986: 232), though faults in Durkheim's conceptualization make it advisable to use different terminology.

CHAPTER 7   INVOLVEMENT AND DETACHMENT: A THEORY OF KNOWLEDGE
AND THE SCIENCES

1 The original essay, 'Problems of involvement and detachment', was apparently truncated by the then editor of the *British Journal of Sociology*. Elias continued to work (again in English) on the unpublished part, which took final shape around 1980 as the long essay 'The fishermen in the maelstrom' (1983d). In many respects the matter of this 'sequel' is logically prior to that of the original essay; at any rate, they need to be read together. Along with a couple of important fragments (entitled 'Reflections on the great evolution'), they were published in book form, first in German translation (*Engagement und Distanzierung* 1983) and then in English (*Involvement and Detachment* 1987b). The Introduction to the English edition is new, and had not been previously published in German.

There are plans to publish a second volume (probably under the title *The Image of Man*) containing some, but probably not all, of Elias's essays on knowledge and the sciences. Those of most relevance to the present chapter and the next include: 'On the sociogenesis of sociology' (originally 1962, published 1984); 'Sociology of knowledge: new perspectives' (1971); 'Towards a theory of social processes' (published in German translation, 1977); 'Scientific establishments' (1982); 'Über die Natur' (1986).

Elias's critique of Popper's *The Logic of Scientific Discovery* is in 'The creed of a nominalist' (1985b), a paper read at a staff seminar in Leicester in 1969 or 1970 but not finally published until 1985, when it appeared under the German title 'Das Credo eines *Metaphysikers*' (note the difference of terminology). This drew responses in defence of Popper from Hans Albert and Hartmut Esser, and a counterblast from Elias, the title of which in English translation is 'Science or sciences? Contribution to a discussion with reality-blind philosophers' (1985c).

Also relevant are the Preface (1968a) to the second impression of *The Civilizing Process*, the Introduction on 'Sociology and history' to *The Court Society* (1969a), and much of *What is Sociology?* (1970a). Finally, Elias's essays on utopias (1982a, 1982b) should also be mentioned.

2 The German title of this essay is 'Wissenschaft als Beruf'; *Wissenschaft* has a wider meaning than 'science', and the title could perhaps better be rendered as 'Academic life as a vocation'.

3 Later, Elias would have written 'data' rather than 'phenomena', expressly regretting using the word 'phenomenon' in some of his earlier writings. He became more and more conscious of its philosophical overtones which cast doubt on the reality of appearances. He refers to these philosophical connotations as 'apparitionism'. The attentive reader ought not to be distracted too much by minor inconsistencies of phrasing, especially in a chapter like the present one where passages are quoted from writings widely separated in time. It must be emphasized that the substance of Elias's point of view has remained remarkably consistent ever since *The Civilizing Process* but the terminology he uses has changed in minor ways.

4 Sociologists writing in English have terrible difficulties with the word *Verwissenschaftlichung* so often used by German sociologists as shorthand for 'the process of

becoming more scientific'. I prefer 'scientification' as a slightly less ugly rendering than 'scientization', used by Habermas's translators among others.

5 This aspect of Elias's thinking reflects the unfashionably high regard in which he holds Auguste Comte (see Elias 1970a: 33–49) who, although 'very likely a little mad', produced insights still of relevance today. The phrase 'level of the universe' is easily misunderstood. It does not mean that Elias believes in an *ontogenetic* barrier between inanimate and living things, or between the human and the non-human. Quite the opposite. Humans are part of a 'unitary universe' (1970a: 105; 1971a: 163; 1987b: xxxvi), of which they have striven to achieve conceptual mastery by means of knowledge slowly developed over many generations.

6 In the 1956 essay, Elias speaks of 'the principle of increasing facilitation', meaning that each successive step towards greater detachment makes the next step easier. In later writings, although the essential argument remains the same, he uses the term 'double-bind' to reverse the emphasis. That is, he stresses instead the extreme difficulty of the *first* steps out of the double-bind trap.

7 The English term 'subject-matter' is highly confusing. German and other European languages permit a clear distinction between *objects* (that which is studied) and *subjects* (humans who do the studying). Elias, following German usage, often writes of the 'object' of sociology, but this can also be confusing in English, since he does *not* mean the *goal* or *aim* of sociology. Perhaps it would be best to reform the language by introducing the term 'object-matter'.

8 See for instance the debate between Alvin Gouldner (1962, 1968) and Howard S. Becker (1967). For a discussion of the issue from a point of view strongly influenced by Elias, see Godfried van Benthem van den Bergh's essay 'Attribution of blame as a means of orientation' (1980: 7–46).

9 Elias is here following Freud, who on more than one occasion compared the jolt given to the 'naïve self-love' of humans by Copernicus and Darwin with the impact he foresaw his own work having. See *The Standard Edition of the Complete Works of Sigmund Freud* (1958–64), vol. 16, pp. 284–5; cf. vol. 17, pp. 140–1; vol. 19, p. 221.

10 Elias's fullest discussion of Galileo, reflecting an interest dating at least from his research visit to Italy in the 1920s (see p. 11 above), can be found in his *Über die Zeit* (1984a: 81–92).

11 The word 'congeries' is used in a similar context by Sorokin (1943). It is instructive to compare Sorokin and Elias on this. Sorokin's models of integration are seen as much more discontinuous and mutually exclusive, and in consequence he develops the idea in a far less subtle way. Sorokin, of course, also remained firmly attached to functionalist modes of thought, and indeed claimed to have anticipated all the main ideas of Talcott Parsons and his school.

12 Even Boyle's Law is only an approximately valid universal law. Some gases, even, are more structured than others, and the law fits best those which are least structured (Elias 1974a: 29).

13 For Elias's most technical discussion of cosmology since the Herzsprung-Russell Diagram and the Hubble Constant, see the second of the two fragments published under the title 'Reflections on the great evolution' in *Involvement and Detachment* (1987: 141–5).

14 Davies's book shows the imprint of the chemists Prigogine and Stengers's influential book *Order out of Chaos* (1984). Like Davies, Prigogine and Stengers can be read as giving general support to the view of science advocated by Elias.

CHAPTER 8 THE DEVELOPMENT OF THE SOCIAL SCIENCES

1 Elias also uses this image of the spiral staircase of consciousness in the *Über die Zeit* (1984a: xlvi–xlvii).
2 The term 'double hermeneutic' is an oversimplification - 'multiple hermeneutic' would be better, because people in 'everyday' life may already be involved in double or still more complex hermeneutics. '*Double* hermeneutic' over-privileges the social scientist.
3 On Elias's views on the sociogenesis of the French Revolution, see pp. 86–7 above.
4 Once again, see the discussion of the rationality of 'court-rationality' in its own specific context – pp. 83, 103–4 above.
5 The German is more striking: *wirlosen Iche*.
6 See Plato, *The Republic*, Book 7.
7 Descartes, *Discourse on Method*, 1637.
8 G. W. von Leibniz, *The Monadology* (1714); for a very clear brief discussion, see Russell (1946: 604–19).
9 Eric Dunning (1977a) has critically scrutinized Popper's arguments against a developmental sociology, measuring them against the views of both Comte and Elias.
10 For a discussion of Popper's later writings in relation to his earlier ones, see Gellner (1985).
11 Ralf Dahrendorf's discussion in his book of that title (1965) is relevant here.
12 In Parsons, notes Elias (1968a: 250), 'the static image of the ego, the individual actor, the adult abstracted from the process of growing up, coexists unmediated with the psychoanalytical ideas he has taken over in his theory – ideas which relate not the state of adulthood but to the process of becoming an adult, to the individual as an open process in indissoluble interdependence with other individuals.'
13 For an extreme statement of the ethnomethodological position and a statement of the *homo clausus* assumptions which would have been considered a caricature if Elias had attributed such views to them, see Pollner (1987). Pollner argues that the basic assumptions sociology and 'common-sense' share – that the outside world exists independently of the knower and that it is accessible to the competent perceiver – are in fact historically emergent, culturally contingent and situationally accomplished.
14 Elias presents his views on this topic in the Introduction to *The Court Society* (1969a), in *Über die Zeit* (1984a: 175–8), and in scattered remarks elsewhere.
15 See Lawrence Stone's article 'The revival of narrative' (1979), and Eric Hobsbawm's reply (1980); Abrams (1982: 300ff) discusses this dispute very clearly.
16 See for example Layder (1986). Although Layder does Elias at least the honour of calling him a 'sophisticated' empiricist, his limited and superficial study of Elias's writings results in a grotesque misreading of Elias's position. See the crushing refutation by Bogner and Dunning (forthcoming, 1989).
17 For a careful analysis of the various ways in which the term 'positivism' is used, see Bryant, *Positivism in Social Theory and Research* (1985). Paradoxically, as Elias shows in *What is Sociology?*, Comte was not a positivist in many of the later senses.
18 See Stockman, *Antipositivist Theories of the Sciences* (1983) and Outhwaite, *New Philosophies of Social Science* (1987).
19 That is not to say that Elias was the *first* sociologist to reject it. Layder (1986) quotes passing remarks of C. H. Cooley as one anticipation; but it could scarcely be argued

that Cooley or others in what later came to be known as 'social behaviourism' or 'symbolic interactionism' carried through their insight as radically as Elias.

CHAPTER 9 HUMANITY AS A WHOLE

1 Strictly speaking, according to the latest biological thinking, one should say *Homo sapiens sapiens*. Neanderthal man was already *Homo sapiens*, but not until the time of Cro-Magnon man is the present form of *Homo sapiens sapiens* attained.

2 For classic representatives of these three traditions, see respectively B. F. Skinner (1953), K. Lorenz (1963) and E. O. Wilson (1975). For critical comments by Elias on the work of Konrad Lorenz, see *What is Sociology?* (1970: 177–8n.) and *Über die Zeit* (1984a: 134–6). Though recognizing the care shown by Lorenz in his studies of animal behaviour, Elias castigates him for the carelessness of his inferences from there to human behaviour.

3 Cf. Talcott Parsons's discussion of the evolution of the human hand and brain (1964).

4 The classic discussion of the alarm reaction is by the biologist W. B. Cannon in *Bodily Changes in Pain, Hunger, Fear and Rage* (1915); Cannon later summarized these findings in his book *The Wisdom of the Body* (1932: 227–9), which influenced Talcott Parsons as well as Elias and many other sociologists of that generation.

5 Though he does not give the references, Elias must have had in mind Gehlen's *Der Mensch, seine Natur und seine Stellung in der Welt* (1940) and *Urmensch und Spätkultur* (1956). A brief discussion in English of Gehlen's work is Berger and Kellner (1965).

6 This idea of learned counter-impulses was employed as early as *The Civilizing Process*: see p. 59 above.

7 At the time of writing, the task is not complete. Goudsblom's essay, 'The domestication of fire as a civilizing process' (1987) is the first report on the work published in English, but deals only with fire in the earliest origins of humankind. I have had access to later chapters in draft form, dealing notably with the role of fire in the transition to agriculture.

8 In book form, the essay on time appeared first in German (*Über die Zeit* 1984) and then in Dutch (1985); an English edition is expected in 1989. Numbered sections 30–46 were written in English in the early 1980s, together with a long new introduction written in German, both being included in the German edition, making the book twice as long as the original four parts published in *De Gids*. The English edition will contain a translation of the German introduction as well as the English *Urtext*. (The publishing history of this book thus takes the prize for complexity even among Elias's *opera*.)

9 In the use of any time-meter, Elias points out, a more complicated synthesis is involved than in the use of any space-meter. Einstein was right when he showed that any change in time was also a change in space, and any change in space was also a change in time. But that, and the practice of modern science, is to blur an important distinction between time-meters and space-meters. In using space-meters, people can legitimately abstract from the flow of events: they can legitimately (for once) indulge in process-reduction. In using a time-meter, they cannot. For his more detailed argument, see Elias 1984a: 72–6.

10 It would be more common to speak of concepts at a high level of 'abstraction', and to say that in earlier societies people made do with more 'concrete' concepts. But, as

Elias notes (1984a: 4–5; 191n.), properly speaking no *concept* can be 'concrete' ('more particularizing' would be an acceptable alternative), while on the other hand it is by no means clear what the concept of time is 'abstracted' *from*.

11 Without era scales, it is difficult for a person even to have an accurate knowledge of how old he or she is – something which has often astonished European visitors to remote tribal societies.

12 An interesting comparison can be made of Elias's essay on time with Edmund Leach's two well-known essays on the symbolic representation of time (1961: 124–36). Leach discusses the symbolization of time as oscillation in contrast to continuous flow. However, his developmental agnosticism – in line with anthropological orthodoxy – makes him evade, rather than deny, the connection between the conceptualization of time and the development of social organization. Very different is Joseph Needham's valuable *Time and Eastern Man* (1965), in which he attacks the view that the sense of linear continuous time was a peculiar trait of European culture, and disposes of the myth of the 'timeless orient'. China too had a linear, continuous conception of time. Although Needham's main preoccupation is with demonstrating that it could not have been differences in the conception of time which explained why modern science and technology arose in Europe but not in China, he incidentally provides a great deal of evidence to suport Elias's contention that advances in timing are connected with needs for co-ordination of interlocking social activities in a complex empire such as China was. On the advantages which none the less accrued to Europe as it established a technological lead in the making of clocks, see David Landes, *Revolution in Time* (1983).

13 Elias draws from this the valid but at first glance surprising conclusion that strictly it is only possible to use 'past', 'present' and 'future' in speaking of physical processes – for example, 'the future of the sun' – in a figurative way by anthropomorphic identification (1984a: 50–1).

14 Contrast this passage with Haferkamp's summary (1987) of Elias's thesis (in the course of attempting to assimilate Elias with phenomenological sociologists among others) in the words 'time is only what actors consider it to be'. See also my own comment on Haferkamp (1987b).

15 See, for instance, the discussions in 'The retreat of sociologists into the present' (1983b) and in *Die Gesellschaft der Individuen* (1987a: 218–26).

16 He came to prefer this more general term over 'attack-and-defence-units', which he had used in *What is Sociology?* (1970a).

17 The degree to which this was true probably varied according to the pressure of human populations competing for scarce food; see Elias 1970a: 76–80 and pp. 259ff. below.

18 Elias dwells on the torture of prisoners among American Indians in *Über die Zeit* (1984a: 133–44) (where it has rather limited relevance problems of timing).

19 Two ambitious recent books relevant to this problem are William H. McNeill's *The Pursuit of Power* (1982) and Michael Mann's *The Sources of Social Power* (1986).

20 Elias has written about this in some unexpected places, such as in *Über die Zeit* (1984a), 'The fisherman in the maelstrom' (1983d), and the new introduction to the English edition of *Involvement and Detachment* (1987b). The subject arises in a more predictable way in *What is Sociology?* (1970a) and *Humana Conditio* (1985a).

CHAPTER 10   CIVILIZATION AND DECIVILIZATION

1 I had just completed the text of this book when the German anthropologist Hans Peter Duerr's book *Nacktheit und Scham* (1988) was published. In it Duerr presents a critique of what he calls 'the myth of the civilizing process', with particular reference to nakedness. Although it appeared too late to be discussed fully here, the arguments of Duerr's book are very similar to those advanced by Blok (1982) and others. What is most striking is that the anthropological critics of Elias pay little or no attention to the *second* volume of *The Civilizing Process*, and by thus neglecting the connection between psychogenetic and sociogenetic processes, they largely miss the essential point of Elias's thesis. Duerr, however, promises a second volume of his own book.

2 Even in America, where the connection between 'culture' and typical personality traits was once an important focus of research, anthropologists in the 1970s and 1980s seem to have lost interest in these issues, turning especially towards synchronic symbolic analysis.

   Space precludes the detailed comparison I had intended to make between Elias and the culture and personality school. The school originated as a particular line of research within the Boasian historical particularist approach. Personality traits were studied *comparatively* between cultures, but not placed in developmental sequence even when the influence of Freud became paramount. The concepts 'shame culture' and 'guilt culture', used by Benedict in *The Chrysanthemum and the Sword* (1946: 156–9) and by Margaret Mead and others, reveal both the similar interests they shared with Elias and marked differences of approach. The two concepts are used to refer to differences in the make-up of the personality which Elias would conceptualize as a balance tilting towards a preponderance of external constraints and towards self-constraints respectively. Elias never uses 'shame' and 'guilt' as antonyms; still less would he allow himself to imply that feelings of guilt *and* shame were not found in every society. By not looking at these matters developmentally, and in terms of polar contrasts rather than subtle changes of balance, the culture and personality theorists rather discredited their approach, introducing the appearance of caricature into the comparisons they made between, for example, Japanese and American character.

   Several other writers did use the notions of shame and guilt cultures in a more developmental way, notably the classicist E. R. Dodds in *The Greeks and the Irrational* (1951), and Barbu (1960) on English national character since the Renaissance; David Riesman's celebrated study of American social character, *The Lonely Crowd* (1950) was also strongly influenced by Benedict.

3 Of course, this involves oversimplification. As Cas Wouters points out (personal communication), Elias's work would lead one to distinguish changes in the We–I balance, in the involvement/detachment balance, in the balance of external and self-constraints, in the degree of mutually expected self-restraint, of rationalization, psychologization, standards of shame and repugnance, trends in social contrasts and varieties, social distance and hierarchical strictness, behavioural and emotional alternatives, modes of conscience formation and sublimation, and so on.

4 Even in that context, individuals' lifetime civilizing processes would be occurring.

5 Of course, it is not controversial to speak of 'earlier' and 'later' stages of psychological development in *individuals*.

6 Rom Harré, in *Social Being* (1980: 364ff), argues that in consequence social development is more like evolution on the Lamarckian (inheritance of acquired

characteristics) model than the Darwinian, *and that it has become more so in the course of the development of human society* because in the course of integration processes a relatively uncoupled adaptive mechanism linking organism and environment has gradually given way to a highly coupled one. Striking as the thought is, it is really only an analogical translation of a social process into biological terms, and thus retains the hazards of biological analogies.

7 For a recent statement of the mainstream orthodoxy against evolutionary theory in the social sciences, see Giddens (1984: 227–80). Much of Giddens's argument is directed towards demonstrating differences between biological and social processes that have long been recognized; but this highlights the need to avoid the word 'evolution' in a social context.

8 Thoden van Velzen blatantly overlooks the stress Elias puts on the fact that among these courtiers controls were relatively low in 'all-roundness' – their restraint and consideration were not all-embracing and did not, for instance, apply in their dealings with outsiders beyond the established courtly circle. Court society was certainly no pinnacle for all time in the civilizing process.

9 For Germany, Horst-Volker Krumrey has comprehensively studied the evidence of the manners books published between 1870 and 1970 in his *Entwicklungsstrukturen von Verhaltensstandarden* (1984).

10 Elias took part in a student discussion group under the title (highly symptomatic of the times) of 'Revolt – personal and social'. I am grateful to Cas Wouters for letting me see the notes he and Willem Kranendonk made of these discussions.

11 *Margriet* is roughly the equivalent of *Woman* or *Woman's Own* in Britain. While doing my own research on cookery columns in *Woman's Own* (1985: 238–61), I took the opportunity to glance at the advice columns too, and can confirm (albeit on an impressionistic basis) that the trends described by Brinkgreve and Korzec for the Netherlands were closely reproduced in Britain.

12 There is no space to discuss the now extensive literature on Victorian sexuality. In spite of instances of the most enthusiastic expression of sexuality, documented for instance by Gay (1984, 1986), I am inclined to think Wouters's inference remains sound.

13 On all this, see Noakes and Pridham, (eds), *Nazism 1919–1945*, vol. III, *Foreign Policy, War and Racial Extermination* (1988), pp. 1049–208.

14 Benjo Maso (1982) charged Elias with resting his account of medieval warriors on a belief in an in-built aggressive drive. See Goudsblom's rebuttal of Maso's argument (1984).

CHAPTER 11   SOME PRINCIPLES OF PROCESS SOCIOLOGY

1 'Figuration' was introduced after some experimentation earlier in the 1960s with the more familiar English word 'configuration', used in *The Established and the Outsiders* and early versions of some of the essays on sport.

2 Thus a 'Figurational Sociology Section' was set up within the Dutch Sociological and Anthropological Association.

3 For example, it is not true that Elias and his associates believed (as Laeyendecker, forthcoming 1989, appears to suggest) that they could bridge the gap between 'macrolevel' and 'microlevel' sociology simply by introducing the new concept of 'figuration'. Their solution to that problem rests on a whole approach to

conceptualization and theorizing, in which the word 'figuration' plays a useful but not essential part.

4 For a contrary view, see Robert Nisbet's essay 'Developmentalism: A critical analysis' (1970).

5 The German word is *Zustandsreduktion* – literally 'state-reduction'. In consultation with Elias, I translated it in *What is Sociology?* as 'process-reduction', because it is not states which are reduced, but processes that are reduced to states.

6 Readers of *What is Sociology?* should not overlook Elias's elaboration of his remarks on Whorf, linked to a criticism of Lévi-Strauss, which he relegates to a note, printed at pp. 179–80.

7 It is interesting that in the nineteenth and early twentieth centuries, it was very common especially for Europeans who had visited the colonies to speak of 'the native' in the singular, as in 'The Hottentot is a simple and happy fellow . . .', as if all the natives were the same and could be spoken of as a collective substance like a pound of butter. This usage now sounds condescending and racist to our ears, and is less common. Yet something equally distorting is involved in the conceptualization of 'the individual *and* society' among sociologists.

8 Elias's most detailed critique of Weber's methodology is in the unpublished Leicester staff seminar paper 'Reflections on personal pronouns' (1968b), but see also his essay in intellectual autobiography (1984c: 70–1).

9 This section is based largely on my discussion of the game models in my contribution to the Elias *Festschrift* (1977), and in an earlier book (2nd edn, 1980).

10 The earliest reference to the pronouns in this sense appears to be in *Die Gesellschaft der Individuen* (1987a: 92–3) – i.e., in the part written in 1939.

11 Elias uses the idea in *The Court Society* (1969a: 59–60, 210–11), and he discusses it, not very clearly, in *What is Sociology?* (1970a: 126) – possibly this section was a casualty of the pruning the typescript underwent for publication in German. A much clearer account is given by Goudsblom (1977a: 177–80).

12 Goudsblom (1977a: 179) notes that this approach has affinities with the argument of Gouldner's well-known paper 'Reciprocity and autonomy in functional theory' (1959).

13. For a good survey, see Outhwaite, *Understanding Social Life: The Method Called Verstehen* (1975).

14 Van Benthem van den Bergh also comments that the examples Popper gives (1944–5: 62) of social scientific laws analogous to those of the natural sciences are not very persuasive. Take, for example, 'You cannot introduce agricultural tariffs and at the same time reduce the cost of living'. The validity of that generalization would depend on who 'you' was, and would not apply equally to all governments within the highly specialized network of the modern world economy: some are more equal than others.

15 In *The Civilizing Process*, in a passage which might just conceivably have been prompted by the dogmatically anti-planning views of F. A. von Hayek (who was at the London School of Economics at that period), or more likely by awareness of Mannheim's growing interest in social planning, Elias wrote:

it is precisely in connection with the civilizing process that the blind dynamics of men intertwining in their deeds and aims gradually leads towards greater scope for planned intervention into both the social and individual structures – intervention based on a growing knowledge of the unplanned dynamics of these structures. (1939: II, 232)

This suggestion of trend towards the increasing possibility of social planning is qualified, many years later, by the implication of the game models that figurations marked by increasingly more equal balances of power become more difficult to steer according to players' plans and intentions. There is no inconsistency here – it is simply that the two tendencies are in tension with each other.

16 A particularly lucid discussion of the links between sociological 'perspectives' and the ideologies of conservatism, liberalism and socialism can be found in Goudsblom (1977a: 153–73).

17 I am pleased to acknowledge the contribution of my friend Don Handelman, of the Hebrew University, Jerusalem, in the creation over lunch at NIAS of the notion of concept munching as the counterpart to the more familiar number crunching.

18 For a selection of recent work, see J. A. Hall (ed.), *States in History* (1987).

19 I am thinking of, among many others, the work of Wallerstein (1974, 1980), Jones (1981), McNeill (1964, 1976, 1982), and Mann (1986).

Bibliography

As far as possible, reference dates in the text are to the date of first publication. When use has been made of an edition other than the first, or of a translation, the original date of publication is given in this bibliography in square brackets, followed by details of the actual edition from which page references or quotations are taken.

The first section contains as nearly complete as possible a list of Norbert Elias's works published up to 1988, whether or not they are actually cited in this book. However, where an English translation is available of an item first published in German (or, occasionally, in Dutch), only the date of the original publication is given. As explained in chapter 1 above, the date at which Elias first drafted a manuscript was often many years earlier than the date of eventual publication.

WORKS OF NORBERT ELIAS 1924–87

1924   *Idee und Individuum: Ein Beitrag zur Philosophie der Geschichte. Dr.phil.* thesis, Universität Breslau (Unpublished).

1929   Contributions to discussion, in *Verhandlungen des Sechsten Deutschen Soziologentages von 17 zu 19 September 1928 in Zürich*. Tübingen, J. C. B. Mohr. (a) Comment on Karl Mannheim, Die Bedeutung der Konkurrenz im Gebiete des Geistigen: 110–11 (reprinted in Volker Meja and Nico Stehr (eds), *Der Streit um die Wissenssoziologie*, vol. I, Frankfurt, Suhrkamp, 1981, pp. 388–90); (b) Comment on Richard Thurnwald, Die Anfänge der Kunst: 281–4.

1935a   Kitschstil und Kitschzeitalter. *Die Sammlung*, 2 (5): 252–63.

1935b   Die Vertreibung der Hugenotten aus Frankreich. *Der Ausweg*, 1 (12): 369–76.

[1939]   *The Civilizing Process.* Vol. I: *The History of Manners.* Oxford, Basil Blackwell, 1978. vol. II: *State Formation and Civilization* (title of US edition is *Power and Civility*). Oxford, Basil Blackwell, 1982.

1950   Studies in the genesis of the naval profession. *British Journal of Sociology*, 1 (4): 291–309.

1956   Problems of involvement and detachment, *British Journal of Sociology*, 7 (3): 226–52.

1959   *Die öffentliche Meinung in England.* Bad Homburg vor der Höhe, Verlag Dr Max Gehlen (pamphlet, 15 pp.)

1960   *Nationale Eigentümlichkeiten der englischen öffentlichen Meinung.* Bad Homburg vor der Höhe, Verlag Dr Max Gehlen (pamphlet, 23 pp.)

[1962]   On the sociogenesis of sociology. *Sociologisch Tijdschrift*, 11 (1) 1984: 14–52.

1964   Group charisma and group disgrace. Unpublished paper presented at the 15th German Sociological Congress, Heidelberg, in commemoration of the centenary of Max Weber's birth.

[1968a]   Introduction to the second impression of *Über den Prozess der Zivilisation*, in *The Civilizing Process*, vol. I, Oxford, Basil Blackwell, 1978: 221–63.

1968b   Reflections on personal pronouns. Unpublished paper presented at Staff Seminar, Department of Sociology, University of Leicester.

1969a   *The Court Society.* Oxford, Basil Blackwell.

1969b   Sociology and psychiatry. In S. H. Foulkes and G. Steward Prince (eds), *Psychiatry in a Changing Society*, London, Tavistock Publications: 117–44.

1970a   *What is Sociology?* London, Hutchinson, 1978.

1970b   The genesis of sport as a sociological problem. In Eric Dunning (ed.), *The Sociology of Sport*, London, Frank Cass: 88–115. Reprinted in *Quest for Excitement*: 126–49.

1970c   *African Art from the Collection of Norbert Elias.* Exhibition Catalogue, City of Leicester Art Gallery, Leicester, 1970.

1970d   Processes of state formation and nation-building. In *Transactions of the 7th World Congress of Sociology*. Varna, 1970, vol. III, Sofia, International Sociological Association, 1972: 274–84.

1970e   Dynamics of consciousness within that of societies. *Transactions of the 7th World Congress of Sociology*, Varna, 1970, vol. IV. Sofia, International Sociological Association, pp. 375–83.

1970f   Interview met Norbert Elias, door J. Goudsblom. *Sociologische Gids*, 17 (2) 1970: 133–40.

1971a   Sociology of knowledge: new perspectives. *Sociology*, 5 (2): 149–68 and (3): 355–70.

1971b   Foreword, in Eric Dunning (ed.), *The Sociology of Sport: A Selection of Readings*. London, Frank Cass: xi–xiii.

1972   Theory of science and history of science: comments on a recent discussion. *Economy and Society*, 1 (2): 117–33.

1974a   The sciences: towards a theory. In R. Whitley (ed.), *Social Processes of Scientific Development*, London, Routledge and Kegan Paul: 21–42.

1974b   Towards a theory of communities. Foreword to Colin Bell and H. Newby (eds), *The Sociology of Community: A Selection of Readings*, London, Frank Cass: ix–xi.

1976   Een theoretisch essay over gevestigden en buitenstaanders. Introduction to *De Gevestigden en de Buitenstaanders*, Utrecht, Het Spectrum (Dutch translation of *The Established and the Outsiders*): 7–46.

1977a   Adorno-Rede: Respekt und Kritik. In N. Elias and W. Lepenies, *Zwei Reden anläßlich der Verleihung des Theodor W. Adorno-Preises, 1977*, Frankfurt, Suhrkamp, 1977.

1977b   Zur Grundlegung einer Theorie sozialer Prozess. *Zeitschrift für Soziologie*, 6 (2): 127–49.

1977c   Drake en Doughty: de ontwikkeling van een conflict (Drake and Doughty:
             the development of a conflict). *De Gids*, 140 (5–6): 223–37.
1978a   Zum Begriff des Alltags. *Kölner Zeitschrift für Soziologie und Sozialpsychologie*,
             30 (Sonderheft): 22–9.
1978b   On transformations of aggressiveness. *Theory and Society*, 5 (2): 227–53.
             (Based on a translation of pp. 263–83 of the Suhrkamp edition of *Über den
             Prozess*, but revised by Elias to reflect his later thinking).
1979   Über die Einsamkeit der Sterbenden in unseren Tagen, *Werk und Zeit*, 3:
             4–16.
1980a   Die Zivilisierung der Eltern. In Linda Burkhardt (ed.), . . . *und wie wohnst
             Du?* Berlin, Internationales Design Zentrum: 11–28.
[1980b]   Civilization and Violence. *Telos*, 64, Winter 1982/3: 134–54. (Corrupt
             translation of talk to 1980 Deutsche Soziologentage prepared from tape.
             Approved German text is 'Zivilisation und Gewalt: Über das Staatsmonopol
             der Körperlichen Gewalt und seine Durchbrechungen', in J. Matthes (ed.),
             *Lebenswelt und soziale Probleme: Verhandlungen des 20. Deutschen Soziologen-
             tages zu Bremen, 1980*, Frankfurt, Campus: 98–122; reprinted in 'Zivilis-
             ation und Gewalt', *Ästhetic und Kommunikation*, 10, 1981: 5–12.)
1980c   Renate Rubinstein. In Elisabeth Borchers and H-U. Müller-Schwefe (eds),
             Im Jahrhundert der Frau, Frankfurt, Suhrkamp: 168–70.
1980d   Soziale Prozeßmodelle auf mehreren Ebenen (abstract of talk at 20th
             Deutsche Soziologentag, Bremen). In W. Schulte (ed.), *Soziologie in der
             Gesellschaft* vol. iii, Bremen, Universität Bremen: 764–67.
1981a   Gedichte. *Merkur*, 35 (401): 1143–5.
1981b   Vier Gedichte. In B. Scheller, H. Pfütze and R. Wolff (eds), *Schau unter jeden
             Stein: Merkwürdiges aus Kultur und Gesellschaft: Dieter Claessens zum 60 Ge-
             burtstag*, Frankfurt, Roter Stern: 41–4.
1982a   Scientific Establishments. In N. Elias, R. Whitley, and H. G. Martins (eds),
             Scientific Establishments and Hierarchies, Dordrecht, Reidel: 3–69.
1982b   Thomas Morus' Staatskritik: Mit Uberlegungen zur Bestimmung des
             Begriffs Utopie. In W. Vosskamp (ed.), *Utopieforschung: Interdisziplinäre
             Studien zur neuzeitlichen Utopie*, vol. ii, Stuttgart, Metzler: 101–50.
1983a   What is the role of scientific and literary utopias for the future? In *Limits to
             the Future*, Wassenaar, NIAS: 60–80.
[1983b]   The retreat of sociologists into the present. *Theory, Culture and Society*,
             4 (2–3), 1987: 223–47.
[1983c]   Reflections on the great evolution: two fragments. In *Involvement and Detach-
             ment*, Oxford, Basil Blackwell, 1987: 119–78.
[1983d]   The fishermen in the maelstrom. In *Involvement and Detachment*, Oxford,
             Basil Blackwell, 1987: 45–118.
1984a   *Über die Zeit.* Frankfurt, Suhrkamp, 1984.
[1984b]   *The Loneliness of the Dying.* Oxford, Basil Blackwell, 1985.
1984c   Notizen zum Lebenslauf. In P. R. Gleichmann et al. (eds), *Macht und Zivili-
             sation*, Frankfurt, Suhrkamp: 9–82.
1984d   De geschiedenis van Norbert Elias. *Vrij Nederland*, 1 December, 1984.
             (Interview with A. J. Heerma van Voss and A. van Stolk.) Reprinted in *De
             Geschiedenis van Norbert Elias*, Amsterdam, Meulenhoff, 1987: 11–87.
1984e   Interview with Aafke Steenhuis, *De Groene Amsterdammer*, 16 May 1984: 10–11.
1984f   Knowledge and power: an interview by Peter Ludes. In Nico Stehr and
             Volker Meja (eds), *Society and Knowledge*, London, Transaction Books: 251–91.

1985a   *Humana Conditio: Beobachtungen zur Entwicklung der Menschheit am 40. Jahrestag eines Kriegsendes (8 Mai 1985)*. Frankfurt, Suhrkamp.

1985b   Das Credo eines Metaphysikers: Kommentare zu Poppers *Logik der Forschung*. *Zeitschrift für Soziologie*, 14 (2): 93–114.

1985c   Wissenschaft oder Wissenschaften? Beitrag zu einer Diskussion mit wirklichkeitsblinden Philosophen *Zeitschrift für Soziologie*, 14 (4): 268–81.

1985d   Gedanken über die Bundesrepublik. *Merkur*, 39 (9–10): 733–550.

1985e   Ageing and dying: some sociological problems. In *The Loneliness of the Dying*: 68–91. (Not included in original German edition.)

1986a   Über die Natur. *Merkur*, 4 (6), June 1986: 469–81.

[1986b]   The changing balance of power between the sexes in the history of civilization. *Theory, Culture and Society*, 4 (2–3), 1987: 287–316. (The English text is the original, although a German translation was published earlier.)

1986c   Figuration (pp. 88–91), Prozesse, soziale (pp. 234–41), Zivilisation (pp. 382–7). In B. Schäfers (ed.), *Grundbegriffe der Soziologie*, Leverkusen, Leske and Budrich.

1986d   Technisierung und Zivilisation. Lecture at Deutsche Soziologen Tage, Hamburg (Unpublished.)

1987a   *Die Gesellschaft der Individuen*. Frankfurt, Suhrkamp. (Contains: Die Gesellschaft der Individuen (1939); Probleme des Selbstbewußtseins und des Menschenbildes (1940s–50s); Wandlungen der Wir-Ich-Balance (1987).)

1987b   *Involvement and Detachment*. Oxford, Basil Blackwell, 1987. (Contrary to the impression given by the title page, only pp. 121–78 are translated from the German.)

1987c   On human beings and their emotions: a process-sociological essay. *Theory, Culture and Society*, 4 (2–3), 1987: 339–61.

1987d   *De Geschiedenis van Norbert Elias*. Amsterdam, Meulenhoff, 1987.

1987e   *Los der Menschen: Gedichte/Nachdichtungen*. Frankfurt, Suhrkamp.

Joint works

With Eric Dunning

1966   Dynamics of sport groups with special reference to football. *British Journal of Sociology*, 17 (4): 388–402. Reprinted in *Quest for Excitement*: 191–204.

1969   The quest for excitement in leisure. *Society and Leisure*, 2: 50–85. Reprinted in *Quest for Excitement*: 63–90.

1971a   Folk football in medieval and early modern Britain. In Eric Dunning (ed.), *The Sociology of Sport*, London, Frank Cass: 116–32. Reprinted in *Quest for Excitement*: 175–90.

[1971b]   Leisure in the spare-time spectrum'. In *Quest for Excitement*: 91–125.

1986   *Quest for Excitement: Sport and Leisure in the Civilizing Process*. Oxford, Basil Blackwell.

With John L. Scotson

1965   *The Established and the Outsiders: A Sociological Enquiry into Community Problems*. London, Frank Cass.

OTHER WORKS CITED

Abrams, Philip 1982: *Historical Sociology*. Shepton Mallet, Open Books.
Adorno, T. W. et al. 1976: *The Positivist Dispute in German Sociology*. London, Heinemann.
Althusser, L. and Balibar, E. [1966]: *Reading Capital*. London, New Left Books, 1979.
Albert, Hans 1985: Mißverständnisse eines Kommentators. *Zeitschrift für Soziologie*, 14 (4): 265–7.
Anderson, Perry 1974a: *Passages from Antiquity to Feudalism*. London, New Left Books.
—— 1974b: *Lineages of the Absolutist State*. London, New Left Books.
Anon. [*c*.1100]: *The Song of Roland*. Harmondsworth, Penguin, 1957.
Arendt, Hannah 1963: *Eichmann in Jerusalem: A Report on the Banality of Evil*. London, Faber and Faber.
Ariès, Philippe [1960]: *Centuries of Childhood*. Harmondsworth, Penguin, 1973.
—— 1974: *Western Attitudes to Death: From the Middle Ages to the Present*. Baltimore, Johns Hopkins University Press.
—— [1975]: *The Hour of our Death*. New York, Arnold Knopf, 1981.
Ariès, P. and Béjin, A. (eds) [1982]: *Western Sexuality: Practice and Precept in Past and Present Times*. Oxford, Basil Blackwell, 1985.
Barbu, Zevedei 1960: *Problems of Historical Psychology*. London, Routledge and Kegan Paul.
Barraclough, Geoffrey 1982: Clockwork history (review of vol. II of *The Civilizing Process*). *New York Review of Books*, 21 October 1982: 36–8.
Baudrillart, Henri 1878–80: *Histoire de Luxe privé et publique depuis l'Antiquité jusqu'à nos jours*. 4 vols, Paris, Hachette.
Bauman, Zygmunt A. 1973: *Culture as Praxis*. London, Routledge and Kegan Paul.
Bax, Mart 1983: 'Us' Catholics and 'them' Catholics in Dutch Brabant: the dialectics of a religious factional process. *Anthropological Quarterly*, 56 (4), 167–78.
—— 1987: Religious regimes and state formation: towards a research perspective. *Anthropological Quarterly*, 60 (1): 1–13.
Bax, M. and Nieuwenhuis, A. 1982: Peasant emancipation in the Roman Catholic south of the Netherlands: the shattering of a tableau-vivant. *Netherlands Journal of Sociology*, 18 (1): 25–45.
Becker, Howard S. 1967: Whose side are we on? *Social Problems*, 14 (3): 239–47.
Benedict, Ruth [1946] *The Chrysanthemum and the Sword*. London, Routledge and Kegan Paul, 1967.
Benthem van den Bergh, Godfried van 1971 *The Structure of Development: An Invitation to the Sociology of Norbert Elias*. The Hague, Institute of Social Studies, occasional paper no.13.
—— 1977: Is a Marxist theory of the state possible? In P. R. Gleichmann et al. (eds), *Human Figurations*, Amsterdam, Stichting Amsterdams Sociologisch Tijdschrift: 157–78.
—— 1980: *De Staat van Geweld en andere essays*. Amsterdam, Meulenhoff.
—— 1983: Two scorpions in a bottle: the unintended benefits of nuclear weapons. In William Page (ed.), *The Future of Politics*, London, Frances Pinter: 191–9.
—— 1984: Dynamik von Rüstung und Staatenbildungsprozessen. In P. R. Gleichmann, et al. (eds), *Macht und Zivilisation*, Frankfurt, Suhrkamp: 217–41.
—— 1989: (forthcoming) *The Taming of the Great Powers*. Oxford, Basil Blackwell.
Berelson, B., Lazarsfeld, P. F. E. and McPhee, W. F. 1954: *Voting*. Chicago, University of Chicago Press.

Berger, P. and Kellner, M. 1965: Arnold Gehlen and the theory of institutions. *Social Research*, 32 (1): 110–15.

Berger, P. and Luckmann, T. 1966: *The Social Construction of Reality*. Garden City, NY, Doubleday.

Bershady, Harold J. 1973: *Ideology and Social Knowledge*. Oxford, Basil Blackwell.

Bhaskar, Roy 1978: *A Realist Theory of Science*. Brighton, Harvester Press.

—— 1979: *The Possibility of Naturalism*. Brighton, Harvester Press.

Blau, Peter M. 1964: *Exchange and Power in Social Life*. New York, John Wiley.

Bloch, Marc [1939–40]: *Feudal Society*. 2 vols, London, Routledge and Kegan Paul, 1961.

Blok, Anton 1974: *The Mafia of a Sicilian Village, 1860–1960*. Oxford, Basil Blackwell.

—— 1976: *Wittgenstein en Elias*. Amsterdam, Polak and Van Gennep.

—— 1978: *Antropologische Perspectieven*. Muiderberg, Coutinho.

—— 1979: Hinter Kulissen. In P. R. Gleichmann et al. (eds), *Materialien zu Norbert Elias' Zivilisationstheorie*, Frankfurt, Suhrkamp: 170–93.

—— 1982: Primitief en geciviliseerd. *Sociologisch Gids*, 29 (3–4): 197–209.

Blumer, Herbert [1930]: Science without concepts. In H. Blumer, *Symbolic Interactionism: Perspective and Method*. Englewood Cliffs, NJ, Prentice-Hall, 1969: 153–70.

—— [1954]: What is wrong with social theory? In *Symbolic Interactionism: Perspective and Method*, Englewood Cliffs, NJ, Prentice-Hall, 1969: 140–52.

Bogner, Artur 1986: The structure of social processes: a commentary on the sociology of Norbert Elias. *Theory, Culture and Society*, 20 (3): 387–411.

—— 1987: Elias and the Frankfurt School. *Theory, Culture and Society*, 4 (2–3): 249–85.

Bogner, A. and Dunning, E. G. 1989: Transcending Elias: an appraisal of two recent critiques of figurational sociology. *Theory, Culture and Society* (forthcoming).

Bossert, H. T. and Stock, W. F. (eds) 1912: *Das Mittelalterliche Hausbuch*. Leipzig, E. A. Seemann.

Bott, Elizabeth 1957: *Family and Social Network*. London, Tavistock.

Bourdieu, Pierre [1979]: *Distinction: A Social Critique of the Judgement of Taste*. London, Routledge and Kegan Paul, 1984.

Brinkgreve, Christien [1980]: On modern relationships: the commandments of the new freedom. *Netherlands Journal of Sociology*, 18 (1) 1982: 47–56.

Brinkgreve, C. and Korzec, M. 1976a: *Margriet* weet raad: Gevoel, gedrag, moraal 1954–1974. *Amsterdams Sociologisch Tijdschrift*, 3 (1): 17–32.

—— 1976b: Kan het civilisatieproces van richting veranderen? (Can the civilising process change direction?). *Amsterdams Sociologisch Tijdschrift*, 3 (3): 361–4.

—— 1978: *Margriet Weet Raad*. Utrecht, Spectrum.

—— 1979: 'Feelings, behaviour, morals in the Netherlands, 1938–78: analysis and interpretation of an advice column. *Netherlands Journal of Sociology*, 15 (2): 123–40.

Brookes, Christopher 1978: *English Cricket*. London, Weidenfeld and Nicolson.

Brown, Richard 1987: Norbert Elias in Leicester: some recollections. *Theory, Culture and Society*, 4 (2–3): 533–9.

Bryant, Christopher G. A. 1985: *Positivism in Social Theory and Research*. London, Macmillan.

Burke, Peter 1980: *Sociology and History*. London, Allen and Unwin.

Cannon, W. B. 1915: *Bodily Changes in Pain, Hunger, Fear and Rage*. New York, Appleton.

—— 1932: *The Wisdom of the Body*. New York, W. W. Norton.

Carsten, Francis L. 1977: Some personal recollections. In P. R. Gleichmann et al. (eds),

1977: *Human Figurations: Essays for Norbert Elias*, Amsterdam, *Amsterdams Sociologisch Tijdschrift*: 25–7.

Chamberlin, E. H. 1933: *The Theory of Monopolistic Competition*. Cambridge, Mass, Harvard University Press.

Cohen, Percy 1968: *Modern Social Theory*. London, Heinemann.

Contamine, Philippe [1980] *War in the Middle Ages*. Oxford, Basil Blackwell, 1984.

Corrigan, P. and Sayer, D. 1985: *The Great Arch*. Oxford, Basil Blackwell.

Coutinho-Wiggelendam, Anneke 1983: Women's emancipation around the turn of the century and the opposition to it. *Netherlands Journal of Sociology*, 19 (2): 113–31.

Daalen, Rineke van, 1979: Ongewenste ontmoetingen in de Amsterdamse tram: Klachten aan de Gemeente Tram Amsterdam in het begin van de twintigste eeuw (Unwanted encounters in the Amsterdam tram: complaints to Amsterdam Municipal Tramways at the beginning of the twentieth century). *Amsterdams Sociologisch Tijdschrift*, 6 (3): 449–73.

—— 1983: Openbare hygiëne en privé-problemen: het ontstaan van de Amsterdamse gezondheidszorg (Public health and private problems: the beginnings of health services in Amsterdam). *Amsterdams Sociologisch Tijdschrift*, 9 (4): 568–606.

—— [1985a]: Nauwbehuisd en dichtbevolkt: Gemeentelijke voorzieningen en klachten uit de burgerij, Amsterdam 1865–1920 (Cramped together and densely populated: municipal provision and complaints from the bourgeoisie). *Sociologisch Tijdschrift*, 12 (2) 1985: 274–308.

—— [1985b]: The start of infant health care in Amsterdam: medicalization and the role of the state. *Netherlands Journal of Sociology*, 21 (2) 1985: 126–39.

Dahrendorf, Ralf [1965]: *Homo Sociologicus*. London, Routledge and Kegan Paul, 1973.

Darnton, Robert 1984: *The Great Cat Massacre and Other Episodes in French Cultural History*. London, Allen Lane.

Davidoff, Leonore 1973: *The Best Circles: Society, Etiquette and the Season*. London, Croom Helm.

Davies, Paul 1987: *The Cosmic Blueprint*. London, Heinemann.

Dawe, Alan, 1970: The two sociologies. *British Journal of Sociology*, 21 (2): 207–18.

Dawkins, Richard 1986: *The Blind Watchmaker: Why the Evidence of Evolution Reveals a Universe without Design*. New York, W. W. Norton.

Descartes, René [1637]: *Discourse on Method*. London, J. M. Dent, 1953.

Dodds, E. R. 1951: *The Greeks and the Irrational*. Berkeley, University of California Press.

Driessen, Henk 1982: Civiliseringstendensen in het Spaanse stiergevecht (Civilizing tendencies in the Spanish bull-fight). *Sociologische Gids*, 29 (3–4): 326–41.

Duby, Georges [1981]: *The Knight, the Lady and the Priest: The Making of Modern Marriage in Medieval France*. New York, Pantheon, 1983.

Duerr, Hans Peter 1988: *Nacktheit und Scham: Der Mythos vom Zivilizationsprozess*, vol. I, Frankfurt, Suhrkamp.

Dunning, Eric 1972: Dynamics of racial stratification: some preliminary observations. *Race*, 13 (4): 415ff.

—— 1977a: In defence of developmental sociology: a critique of Popper's *Poverty of Historicism* with special reference to the theory of Auguste Comte. *Amsterdams Sociologisch Tijdschrift*, 4 (3): 327–49.

—— 1977b: Power and authority in the public schools: a case study and conceptual discussion. In P. R. Gleichmann et al. (eds), *Human Figurations: Essays for Norbert Elias*, Amsterdam, *Stichting Amsterdams Sociologisch Tijdschrift*: 225–57.

—— 1981: The figurational analysis of the development of Rugby Football: a reply to

Ruud Stokvis. *Amsterdams Sociologisch Tijdschrift*, 7 (4): 533–45.

—— 1985: The figurational dynamics of racial stratification: a conceptual discussion and developmental analysis of black-white relations in the United States. (Unpublished manuscript.)

—— 1986: Race relations. In G. Hurd (ed.), *Human Societies*, London, Routledge and Kegan Paul, 2nd edn: 110–33.

—— 1987: Comments on Elias's 'Scenes from the life of a knight'. *Theory, Culture and Society*, 4 (2–3): 366–71.

Dunning, E. G. and Mennell, S. J. 1979: 'Figurational sociology': some critical comments on Zygmunt Bauman's 'The phenomenon of Norbert Elias'. *Sociology*, 13 (3): 497–501.

Dunning, E. G., Murphy, P., Newburn, T. and Waddington, I. 1987: Violent disorders in twentieth-century Britain. In G. Gaskell and R. Benewick (eds), *The Crowd in Contemporary Britain*, London, Sage: 19–75.

Dunning, E. G., Murphy, P. and Williams, J., 1988: *The Roots of Football Hooliganism: An Historical and Sociological Study*, London, Routledge and Kegan Paul.

Dunning, E. G. and K. Sheard 1979: *Barbarians, Gentlemen and Players*. Oxford, Martin Robertson.

Durkheim, Emile [1893]: *The Division of Labour in Society*, London, Macmillan, 1984.

Elkins, Stanley 1959: *Slavery*, Chicago, University of Chicago Press.

Engels, Friedrich 1890: Letter to Josef Bloc in Königsberg, London, 21 September. In *Marx–Engels Selected Works*. London, Lawrence and Wishart, 1968, pp. 692–3.

Esser, Hans 1985: Logik oder Metaphysik der Forschung? *Zeitschrift für Soziologie*, 14 (4): 257–64.

Evans-Pritchard, E. E. 1937: *Witchcraft, Oracles and Magic among the Azande*. Oxford, Clarendon Press.

—— 1940: *The Nuer*. Oxford, Oxford University Press.

Eve, Michael 1982: What is the social? On the methodological work of Norbert Elias. *Quaderni di sociologia*, 1: 22–48.

Evenhuis, J., Klos, W., and Lingen, B. van 1980: Buitenstaanders in eigen huis: patiënten van een verpleeghuisafdeling (Outsiders in their own home: patients in a nursing home). *Gerontologie*, 11 (2): 147–55.

Fallers, Lloyd A. 1954: A note on the trickle effect. *Public Opinion Quarterly* 18 (3): 314–21.

Featherstone, Mike 1987: Norbert Elias and Figurational Sociology, Preface. Special issue of *Theory, Culture and Society*, 4 (2–3): 197–211.

Febvre, Lucien [1930]: *Civilisation*: evolution of a word and a group of ideas. In Peter Burke (ed.), *A New Kind of History*, London, Routledge and Kegan Paul, 1973: 219–57.

—— [1938]: History and psychology. In Peter Burke (ed.), *A New Kind of History*, London, Routledge and Kegan Paul, 1973: 1–11.

—— [1941]: Sensibility and history: how to reconstitute the emotional life of the past. In Peter Burke (ed.), *A New Kind of History*, London, Routledge and Kegan Paul, 1973: 12–26.

Feyerabend, Paul K. 1975: *Against Method: Outline of an Anarchistic Theory of Knowledge*. London, New Left Books.

Flandrin, Jean-Louis [1976]: *Families in Former Times: Kinship, Household and Sexuality*. Cambridge, Cambridge University Press, 1979.

Forster, R. [1960]: *The Nobility of Toulouse in the Eighteenth Century: a social and economic study*. New York, Octagon Books, 1971.

Foucault, Michel [1975]: *Discipline and Punish: The Birth of the Prison*. New York, Pantheon, 1977.

Foulkes, S. H. 1957: Group analytic dynamics with specific references to psychoanalytic concepts. *International Journal of Group Psychotherapy*, 7: 40–52.

—— 1964: *Therapeutic Group Analysis*. London, Allen and Unwin.

Foulkes, S. H. and Prince, G. S. (eds), 1969: *Psychiatry in a Changing Society*. London, Tavistock.

Freud, Sigmund [1930]: *Civilization and Its Discontents*. New York, W. W. Norton, 1962.

—— [1933]: *New Introductory Lectures on Psychoanalysis*. New York, W. W. Norton, 1964.

—— 1935: *An Autobiographical Study*. London, Hogarth Press.

—— [1953–64]: *The Standard Edition of the Complete Works of Sigmund Freud*. London, Hogarth Press.

Freund, Gisèle 1936: *La photographie en France au 19ᵉ siècle: Etude de sociologie et d'esthétique*. Paris, La Maison des Amis des Livres A. Monnier.

—— 1977: Norbert Elias als Lehrer. In P. R. Gleichmann et al. (eds), *Human Figurations: Essays for Norbert Elias*. Amsterdam: Stichting Amsterdams Sociologisch Tijdschrift, 12–14.

Garfinkel, Harold 1967: *Studies in Ethnomethodology*. Englewood Cliffs, NJ, Prentice-Hall.

Gay, Peter 1984–6: *The Bourgeois Experience: Victoria to Freud*, vols I and II. Oxford, Oxford University Press.

Gehlen, Arnold, [1940]: *Der Mensch, seine Natur und seine Stellung in der Welt*. Rev. edn. Bonn, Athenäum, 1950.

—— 1956: *Urmensch und Spätkultur*. Bonn, Athenäum.

Gellner, Ernest 1985: Positivism against Hegelianism. In E. Gellner, *Relativism and the Social Sciences*, Cambridge, Cambridge University Press: 4–67.

Giddens, Anthony 1976: *New Rules of Sociological Method*. London, Hutchinson.

—— 1984: *The Constitution of Society*. Oxford, Polity Press.

Gillissen, N. and Lissenberg, A. 1985: *Vrouwen in een Mannenbulwerk*. Amsterdam, Publikatiereeks Sociologisch Instituut, Universiteit van Amsterdam.

Girouard, Mark 1978: *Life in the English Country House*. New Haven, Yale University Press.

Gleichmann, Peter R. 1977: Wandel der Wohnverhältniße: Verhäuslichung der Vitalfunctionen, Verstädterung und siedlungsräumliche Gestaltungsmacht in der Bundesrepublik Deutschland. In P. R. Gleichmann et al. (eds), *Human Figurations: Essays for Norbert Elias*, Amsterdam, Stichting Amsterdams Sociologisch Tijdschrift: 259–70.

—— 1979a: Die Verhäuslichung körperlicher Verrichtungen. In P. R. Gleichmann et al. (eds), *Materialien zu Norbert Elias' Zivilizationstheorie*, Frankfurt, Suhrkamp: 254–78.

—— 1979b: Zur zivilisationssoziologischen Begriffsbildung. In J. Diederich et al. (eds), *Sozialer Wandel in Westeuropa*, Berlin, Universitätsbibliothek der Technischen Universität Berlin.

—— 1980: Einige soziale Wandlungen des Schlafens. *Zeitschrift für Soziologie* 9 (3): 236–50.

Gleichmann, P. R., Goudsblom J. and Korte, H. (eds) 1977: *Human Figurations: Essays for Norbert Elias*. Amsterdam, Stichting Amsterdams Sociologisch Tijdschrift.

—— 1979: *Materialien zu Norbert Elias' Zivilisationstheorie*. Frankfurt, Suhrkamp.

—— 1984: *Macht und Zivilisation: Materialien zu Norbert Elias' Zivilisationstheorie 2*. Frankfurt, Suhrkamp.

Goffman, Erving [1959]: *The Presentation of Self in Everyday Life*. Harmondsworth: Penguin, 1971.

—— 1961: *Asylums*. Garden City, NY, Doubleday Anchor.

—— [1963]: *Behaviour in Public Places*. New York, Free Press.

Goldthorpe, J. H. et al. 1982: *Social Mobility and Class Structure in Modern Britain*. Oxford, Oxford University Press.

Gordon-Walker, Patrick 1951: *A Restatement of Liberty*. London, Hutchinson.

Goudsblom, Johan, 1977a: *Sociology in the Balance*. Oxford, Basil Blackwell.

—— 1977b: Responses to Norbert Elias's work in England, Germany, the Netherlands and France. In P. R. Gleichmann et al. (eds), *Human Figurations: Essays for Norbert Elias*. Amsterdam, Amsterdams Sociologisch Tijdschrift, 37–97.

—— 1979: Zivilisation, Ansteckungsangst und Hygiene. In P. R. Gleichmann et al. (eds), *Materialien zu Norbert Elias' Zivilisationstheorie*. Frankfurt, Suhrkamp: 215–53.

—— 1980: Zum Hintergrund der Zivilisationstheorie von Norbert Elias: ihr Verhältnis zu Huizinga, Weber und Freud. In P. R. Gleichmann et al. (eds), *Macht und Zivilisation: Materialien zu Norbert Elias' Zivilisationstheorie 2*. Frankfurt, Suhrkamp: 129–47.

—— 1984a: Die Erforschung von Zivilisationsprozessen. In P. R. Gleichmann et al. (eds), *Macht und Zivilisation: Materialien zu Norbert Elias' Zivilisationstheorie 2*. Frankfurt, Suhrkamp: 83–104.

—— 1984b: De civilisatietheorie in het geding: repliek en commentaar op beschaving en geweld (The theory of civilizing processes under discussion: reply and commentary on civilization and violence). *Sociologische Gids*, 31 (2): 138–63.

—— 1986a: Public health and the civilising process. *The Millbank Quarterly*, 64 (2): 161–88.

—— 1986b: On high and low in society and in sociology: a semantic approach to social stratification. *Sociologisch Tijdschrift*, 13 (1): 3–17.

—— 1987: The domestication of fire as a civilising process. *Theory, Culture and Society* 4 (2–3): 457–76.

—— 1988: Priesters en Krijgers. In *Taal en Sociale Werkelijkheid*, Amsterdam, Meulenhoff: 104–31.

Gouldner, Alvin W. 1959: Reciprocity and autonomy in functional theory. In L. Gross (ed.), *Symposium on Sociological Theory*, Evanston, Ill., Row Peterson: 241–70.

—— 1962: Anti-Minotaur: the myth of a value-free sociology. *Social Problems*, 9: 199–213.

—— 1968: The sociologist as partisan. *American Sociologist*, 3 (2): 103–16.

Grosskurth, Phyllis 1986: *Melanie Klein: Her World and Her Work*. London, Hodder and Stoughton.

Gurr, Ted Robert 1981: Historical trends in violent crime: a critical review of the evidence. *Crime and Justice: An Annual Review of Research*, 3, 295–353.

Habermas, Jürgen 1960: *Strukturwandel der Öffentlichkeit*. Neuwied, Luchterhand.

—— 1972: *Knowledge and Human Interests*. London, Heinemann.

Haferkamp, Hans 1987: From the intra-state to the inter-state civilizing process. *Theory, Culture and Society*, 4 (2–3): 545–57.

Hall, John A. (ed.) 1987: *States in History*. Oxford, Basil Blackwell.

Harré, Rom 1970: *The Principles of Scientific Thinking*. London, Macmillan.

—— 1980: *Social Being*. Oxford, Basil Blackwell.

Harris, Marvin 1968: *The Rise of Anthropological Theory*. London, Routledge and Kegan Paul.

Herrin, Judith 1987: *The Formation of Christendom*. Oxford, Basil Blackwell.

Hesse, Mary B. 1974: *The Structure of Scientific Inference*. London, Macmillan.

—— 1980: *Revolutions and Reconstructions in the Philosophy of Science*. Brighton, Harvester Press.

Hindess, B. and Hirst, P. Q. 1975: *Pre-Capitalist Modes of Production*. London, Routledge and Kegan Paul.

Hobsbawm, E. J. 1980: The revival of narrative: some comments. *Past and Present*, 86: 3–8.

Hochschild, Arlie Russell 1983: *The Managed Heart*. Berkeley, University of California Press.

Hönigswald, Richard 1937: *Philosophie und Sprache*. Basle, Haus zum Falken.

Horkheimer, M. and Adorno, T. W. [1947]: *Dialectic of Enlightenment*. London, New Left Review Editions, 1979.

Huizinga, Johan [1924]: *The Waning of the Middle Ages*. Harmondsworth, Penguin, 1972.

Hurd, Geoffrey (ed.) 1973: *Human Societies*. London, Routledge and Kegan Paul (2nd edn 1986).

Jagers, René 1982: Geweld in tribale samenlevingen (Violence in tribal societies). *Sociologische Gids*, 29 (3–4): 210–24.

Jay, Martin 1973: *The Dialectical Imagination: A History of the Frankfurt School and the Institute for Social Research*. London, Heinemann.

Jones, Eric 1981: *The European Miracle*. Cambridge, Cambridge University Press.

Jong, Mayke de 1982: Monniken, ridders en geweld in elfde-eeuws Vlaanderen (Monks, Knights and Violence in Eleventh-Century Flanders). *Sociologische Gids*, 29 (3–4): 279–95.

Kant, Immanuel [1781]: *The Critique of Pure Reason*. London, Macmillan, 1933.

—— [1784]: Idea of a Universal History from the Point of View of a Citizen of the World. In *Kant's Political Writings*, Cambridge, Cambridge University Press, 1970: 521–53.

—— [1791]: Über die von der königlichen Akademie der Wissenschaften zu Berlin für das Jahr 1791 ausgesetze Preisfrage: Welches sind die Fortschritte die die Metaphysik seit Leibnizens und Wolffs Zeiten in Deutschland gemacht hat? In *Immanuel Kants Werke*, vol. VIII, Cassirer, Berlin, 1922.

Kapteyn, Paul 1977: Aletta Jacobs and female emancipation in the Netherlands. In P. R. Gleichmann et al. (eds), *Human Figurations: Essays for Norbert Elias*, Amsterdam, Stichting Amsterdams Sociologisch Tijdschrift: 284–92.

—— 1980: *Taboe, Macht en Moraal in Nederland* (*Taboo, Power and Morality in the Netherlands*). Amsterdam, De Arbeiderspers.

—— 1985a: *In de Speeltuin Nederland* (*In the Playground of the Netherlands*). Amsterdam, De Arbeiderspers.

—— [1985b]: Even a good education gives rise to problems: the changes in authority between parents and children. *Concilium*, 5: 19–33.

Karger, Fritz 1977: Fata Libelli. In P. R. Gleichmann et al. (eds), *Human Figurations: Essays for Norbert Elias*, Amsterdam, Stichting Amsterdams Sociologisch Tijdschrift: 23–4.

Kempers, Bram 1982: Die civilisatietheorie van Elias en civilisatie-processen in Italië, 1300–1550. Over de beschaafde strijd tussen generalisten en specialisten. *Amsterdams Sociologisch Tijdshrift*, 8 (4): 591–611.

—— 1987: *Kunst, Macht en Mecenaat: Het beroep van schilder in sociale verhoudingen 1250–*

1600. Amsterdam, De Arbeiderspers. (Translation forthcoming: *Painting, Power and Patronage*, Harmondsworth, Penguin.)

Koenigsberger, H. G. 1977: *Dominium regale* or *dominium politicium et regale?* Monarchies and parliaments in early modern Europe. In P. R. Gleichmann et al. (eds), *Human Figurations: Essays for Norbert Elias*. Amsterdam, Stichting Amsterdams Sociologisch Tijdschrift: 293–318.

Korte, Hermann 1984: Die etablierten Deutschen und ihre ausländischen Außenseiter. In P. R. Gleichmann et al. (eds), *Macht und Zivilisation: Materialien zu Norbert Elias' Zivilisationstheorie 2*, Frankfurt, Suhrkamp: 261–79.

—— 1988: *Über Norbert Elias: Vom Werden eines Menschenwissenschaftlers*. Frankfurt, Suhrkamp.

Krumrey, Horst-Volker 1984: *Entwicklungsstrukturen von Verhaltensstandarden*. Frankfurt, Suhrkamp.

Kuhn, Thomas S. 1962: *The Structure of Scientific Revolutions*. Chicago, University of Chicago Press.

Kuzmics, Helmut 1986: Verlegenheit und Zivilisation: Zu einigen Gemeinsamkeiten und Unterschieden im Werk von E. Goffman und N. Elias. *Soziale Welt*, 37 (4): 467–86.

Laeyendecker, Leo 1989: What Dutch sociology has achieved. In C. G. A. Bryant and H. Becker (eds), *What has Sociology Achieved?* London, Macmillan, forthcoming.

Landes, David S. 1983: *Revolution in Time: Clocks and the Making of the Modern World*. Cambridge, MA, Harvard University Press.

Layder, Derek 1986: Social reality as figuration: a critique of Elias's conception of sociological analysis. *Sociology*, 20 (3) 367–86.

Leach, E. R. 1961: *Rethinking Anthropology*. London, Athlone Press.

—— 1986: Violence. *London Review of Books*, 23 October.

Lee, Vera 1975: *The Reign of Women in Eighteenth-Century France*. New York, Schenkman.

Le Goff, Jacques 1964: *La civilisation de l'occident médiéval*. Paris, Arthaud.

Leibniz, G. W. von [1714]: *Monadology*. Oxford, Clarendon Press, 1898.

Lepenies, Wolf [1977]: Norbert Elias: an outsider full of unprejudiced insight. *New German Critique*, 57–80.

Lévi-Strauss, Claude [1962]: *The Savage Mind*. London, Weidenfeld and Nicolson, 1968.

Lévy-Bruhl, Lucien [1910]: *How Natives Think*. London, Allen and Unwin, 1926.

—— [1922]: *Primitive Mentality*. London, Allen and Unwin, 1923.

Lockwood, David 1970: Race, conflict and plural society. In S. Zubaida (ed), *Race and Racialism*, London, Tavistock: 57–72.

Lorenz, Konrad [1963]: *On Aggression*. London, Methuen, 1966.

Lowie, Robert H. 1929: *Are We Civilized?* London, G. Routledge.

McNeill, William 1964: *The Rise of the West*. Chicago: University of Chicago Press.

—— [1976]: *Plagues and Peoples*. Harmondsworth, Penguin, 1979.

—— 1982: *The Pursuit of Power: Technology, Armed Force and Society since AD 1000*. Oxford, Basil Blackwell, 1983.

Magraw, Roger 1983: *France 1815–1914: The Bourgeois Century*. London, Fontana.

Mandrou, Robert [1961]: *Introduction to Modern France, 1500–1600*. London, Matthew Arnold, 1975.

Mann, Michael 1986: *The Sources of Social Power*. vol. I, Cambridge, Cambridge University Press.

Mann, Thomas [1918]: *Betrachtungen eines Unpolitischen*. In *Aufsätze, Reden, Essays*, vol. II, *1914–1918*, Berlin, Aufbau-Verlag, 1983: 164–256.

—— [1937–9]: *Tagebücher 1937–39*. Frankfurt, S. Fischer Verlag, 1980.

Mannheim, Karl [1927]: Conservative thought. In K. Mannheim, *Essays on Sociology and Social Psychology*, London, Routledge and Kegan Paul, 1953: 74–164.

—— [1929a]: *Ideology and Utopia*. London, Routledge and Kegan Paul.

—— [1929b]: Competition as a cultural phenomenon. In K. Mannheim, *Essays on the Sociology of Knowledge*, London, Routledge and Kegan Paul, 1952: 191–229.

Marcuse, Herbert [1955]: *Eros and Civilisation*. London, Sphere, 1969.

Marsh, P., Rosser, E. and Harré, R. 1978: *The Rules of Disorder*. London, Routledge and Kegan Paul.

Marx, Karl [1852]: *The Eighteenth Brumaire of Louis Napoleon Bonaparte*, In *Marx–Engels Selected Works*, London, Lawrence and Wishart 1968: 97–108.

Marx, K. and Engels, F. [1848]: *Manifesto of the Communist Party*. In *Marx–Engels Selected Works*, London, Lawrence and Wishart, 1968: 35–63.

Maso, Benjo 1982: Riddereer en riddermoed – ontwikkelingen van de aanvalslust in de late middeleeuwen (Knightly honour and knightly courage: on changes in fighting spirit in the late Middle Ages). *Sociologische Gids* 29 (3–4): 296–325.

Mauss, Marcel [1924]: *The Gift*. London, Cohen and West, 1954.

Mennell, Stephen 1975: Ethnomethodology and the new *Methodenstreit*. *Acta Sociologica*, 18 (4): 287–302.

—— 1977: 'Individual' action and its 'social' consequences in the work of Norbert Elias. In P. R. Gleichmann et al. (eds), *Human Figurations: Essays for Norbert Elias*, Amsterdam, Stichting Amsterdams Sociologisch Tijdschrift: 99–109.

—— 1980: *Sociological Theory: Uses and Unities*. 2nd edn, Walton-on-Thames, Nelson.

—— 1985: *All Manners of Food: Eating and Taste in England and France from the Middle Ages to the Present*. Oxford, Basil Blackwell.

—— 1987a: On the civilizing of appetite. *Theory, Culture and Society*, 4 (2–3): 373–403.

—— 1987b: Comment on Haferkamp. *Theory, Culture and Society*, 4 (2–3): 559–61.

Merton, Robert K. 1936: The unanticipated consequences of purposive social action. *American Sociological Review*, 1 (6): 894–904.

—— [1938]: *Science, Technology and Society in Seventeenth-Century England*. New York, Humanities Press, 1978.

—— [1949]: *Social Theory and Social Structure*. New York, Free Press, 1968.

Montagu, M. F. Ashley (ed.) [1968]: *Man and Aggression*. New York, Oxford University Press, 2nd edn, 1973.

Moore, Barrington Jr [1967]: *The Social Origins of Dictatorship and Democracy*. Harmondsworth, Penguin, 1969.

Morgan, Lewis H. 1877: *Ancient Society*. New York, World Publishing.

Needham, Joseph 1965: *Time and Eastern Man*. London, Royal Anthropological Institute, Occasional Paper no. 21.

Nicolson, Harold 1955: *Good Behaviour*. London, Constable.

Nisbet, Robert A. 1967: *The Sociological Tradition*. New York, Basic Books.

—— 1970: Developmentalism: a critical analysis. In J. C. McKinney and E. A. Tiryakian (eds), *Theoretical Sociology: Perspectives and Developments*. New York, Appleton-Century-Crofts: 167–204.

Noakes, J. and Pridham, G. (eds) 1988: *Nazism 1919–1945*. Vol. III, *Foreign Policy, War and Racial Extermination*. Exeter, University of Exeter.

Orwell, George 1970: *The Collected Essays, Journalism and Letters of George Orwell*. 4 vols, Harmondsworth, Penguin.

Otterloo, Anneke van 1985: Voedzaam, smakelijk en gezond: Kookleraressen en pogingen tot verbetring van eetgewoonten tussen 1880 en 1940 (Nutritious, tasty and healthy: cookery teachers and attempts to improve eating habits between 1880 and 1940). *Sociologisch Tijdschrift*, 12 (3) 1985: 495–542.

—— [1986]: Foreign immigrants and the Dutch at table, 1945–88 – bridging or widening the gap? *Netherlands Journal of Sociology*, 23 (2) 1987: 126–43.

Outhwaite, William 1975: *Understanding Social Life: The Method Called Verstehen*. London, Allen and Unwin.

—— 1987: *New Philosophies of Social Science: Realism, Hermeneutics and Critical Theory*. London, Macmillan.

Parsons, Talcott 1937: *The Structure of Social Action*. New York, McGraw Hill.

—— 1951: *The Social System*. New York, Free Press.

—— 1964: Evolutionary universals in society. *American Sociological Review*, 29 (3): 339–57.

—— 1966: *Societies: Evolutionary and Comparative Perspectives*. Englewood Cliffs NJ: Prentice-Hall.

—— 1970: On building social system theory: a personal history. *Daedalus* 99 (4): 826–81.

Parsons, T. and Shils, E. A. 1951: Values, motives and systems of action. In *Towards a General Theory of Action*, Cambridge, MA: Harvard University Press, 47–243.

Pearson, G. 1983: *Hooliganism: A History of Respectable Fears*. London, Macmillan.

Perkin, Harold 1969: *The Origins of Modern English Society, 1780–1880*. London, Routledge and Kegan Paul.

Piaget, Jean 1932: *The Moral Judgment of the Child*. London, Kegan Paul.

Pilz, Gunter A. 1982: Changes in violence in sport. *International Review of Sport Sociology*, 17 (4): 47–71.

—— 1983: Fußballsport und körperliche Gewalt. In R. Lindner (ed.), *Der Satz 'Der Ball ist rund' hat eine gewiße philosophische Tiefe*, Berlin, Transit: 81–102.

—— 1984: Zur gesellschaftlichen Bedingtheit von Sport und Gewalt. In H. Kaeber and B. Tripp (eds), *Gesellschaftliche Funktionen des Sports*, Bonn, Bundeszentrale für politische Bildung: 147–70.

—— 1985: Sport im Spannungsverhältnis von Friedfertigkeit und Gewalt – Eine Entwicklungssoziologische Studie auf der Folie der Eliasschen Zivilisationstheorie. In Deutsche Vereinigung für Sportwissenschaft, *Sport im Spannungsfeld von Krieg und Frieden*. Clausthal-Zellerfeld, DVS: 210–30.

Pirenne, Henri [1937]: *Mohammed and Charlemagne*. London, Allen and Unwin, 1939.

Poe, Edgar Allan [1845]: A descent into the maelstrom. In *Selected Writings*, Harmondsworth, Penguin, 1967: 225–42.

Poggi, Gianfranco 1978: *The Development of the Modern State: A Sociological Introduction*, London, Hutchinson.

Pollner, Melvin 1987: *Mundane Reason: Reality in Everyday and Sociological Discourse*. Cambridge, Cambridge University Press.

Popper, Karl R. [1944–5]: *The Poverty of Historicism*. London, Routledge and Kegan Paul, 1957.

—— 1945: *The Open Society and its Enemies*. 2 vols, London, Routledge and Kegan Paul.

—— 1959: *The Logic of Scientific Discovery*. London, Hutchinson.

—— 1972: *Objective Knowledge: An Evolutionary Approach*. Oxford, Oxford University Press.

Prigogine, I. and Stengers, I. 1984: *Order out of Chaos: Man's New Dialogue with Nature*. London, Heinemann.

Ranke, Leopold von 1925: *Das Politische Gespräch und andere Schriften zur Wissenschafts-lehre*. Halle, Max Niemeyer Verlag.

Rasing, Wim 1982: Over conflictreguliering bij de nomadische Inuit (On conflict regulation among the nomadic Inuit). *Sociologische Gids*, 29 (3–4): 225–42.

Redfield, Robert 1947: The folk society. *American Journal of Sociology*, 52 (4): 292–308.
Regt, Ali de 1982: Unacceptable families: on the origins of social maladjustment. *Netherlands Journal of Sociology*, 18 (2): 139–56.
—— 1984: *Arbeidersgezinnen en Beschavingsarbeid: Ontwikkelingen in Nederland 1870–1940* (Working-class families and the civilizing of workers: developments in the Netherlands, 1870–1940). Meppel, Boom.
Richard, Guy 1974: *Noblesse d'affaires au XVIIIᵉ siècle*. Paris, Colin.
Riesman, David 1950: *The Lonely Crowd*. New Haven, Yale University Press.
Robinson, R. J. 1987: The civilizing process: some remarks on Elias's social history. *Sociology*, 21 (1): 1–17.
Robinson, Joan 1933: *The Economics of Imperfect Competition*. London, Macmillan.
Rojek, Chris 1985: *Capitalism and Leisure Theory*. London, Tavistock.
Roodenburg, Herman 1981: Predestinatie en groepcharisma: Een sociologische verkenning van de conflicten tussen Calvinisten en andere gelovingen in de Republiek, c.1580–1650 (Predestination and group charisma: a sociological exploration of the conflicts between Calvinists and other believers in the Republic, c.1580–1650). *Amsterdams Sociologisch Tijdschrift*, 7 (2): 254–84.
Rorty, Richard 1980: *Philosophy and the Mirror of Nature*. Oxford, Basil Blackwell.
Russell, Bertrand 1946: *A History of Western Philosophy*. London, Allen and Unwin.
Ste Croix, G. E. M. 1981: *The Class Struggle in the Ancient Greek World*. Ithaca, Cornell University Press.
Sahlins, M. and Service, E. R. (eds), 1960: *Evolution and Culture*. Ann Arbor, University of Michigan Press.
Salmon, J. H. M. 1974: *Society in Crisis: France in the Sixteenth Century*. London, Benn.
Schröter, Michael 1985: *Wo Zwei Zusammenkommen in Rechter Ehe*. Frankfurt, Suhrkamp.
—— 1987: Marriage. *Theory, Culture and Society*, 4 (2–3): 317–22.
Seglow, Ilse 1977: Work at a research programme. In P. R. Gleichmann et al. (eds), *Human Figurations: Essays for Norbert Elias*. Amsterdam, Stichting Amsterdams Sociologisch Tijdschrift: 16–21.
Shils, Edward A. 1968: Deference. In J. A. Jackson (ed.), *Social Stratification*. Cambridge, Cambridge University Press: 104–32.
Shorter, Edward 1976: *The Making of the Modern Family*. London, Collins.
—— [1982]: *A History of Women's Bodies*. Harmondsworth, Penguin, 1984.
Sidney, Philip [1590]: *The Countess of Pembroke's Arcadia*. Oxford, Clarendon Press, 1987.
Simmel, Georg [1902–3]: The metropolis and mental life. In K. H. Wolff (ed.), *The Sociology of Georg Simmel*. Glencoe, Free Press: 409–24.
—— [1908a]: *The Sociology of Georg Simmel*. Glencoe, Free Press.
—— [1908b]: *'Conflict' and 'The Web of Group Affiliations'*. Glencoe, Free Press.
—— [1908c]: *Soziologie*. Leipzig, Duncker and Humblot.
Skinner, B. F. 1953: *Science and Human Behaviour*. New York, Macmillan.
Smith, Adam [1776]: *The Wealth of Nations*. Harmondsworth, Penguin, 1970.
Sombart, Werner [1913]: *Luxury and Capitalism*. Ann Arbor, University of Michigan Press, 1967.
Sorokin, Pitirim A. 1943: *Sociocultural Causality, Space, Time*. Durham, NC, Duke University Press.
Spierenburg, Pieter 1984: *The Spectacle of Suffering: Executions and the Evolution of Repression*. Cambridge, Cambridge University Press.
Steward, Julian 1955: *Theory of Culture Change*. Urbana, University of Illinois Press.

Stockman, Norman 1983: *Antipositivist Theories of the Sciences*. Dordrecht, Reidel.

Stokvis, Ruud 1979: *Strijd over Sport: Organisatorische en Ideologische Ontwikkelingen* (Debates on Sport: Organizational and Ideological Developments). Deventer, Van Loghum Slaterus.

—— 1981a: Rugby en Beschaving (critique of Dunning and Sheard, *Barbarians, Gentlemen and Players*). *Amsterdams Sociologisch Tijdschrift*, 6 (3): 494–504.

—— 1981b: Figuraties en argumentaties: een antwoord aan Eric Dunning (Figurations and arguments: a reply to Eric Dunning). *Amsterdams Sociologisch Tijdschrift*, 7 (4): 545–8.

—— 1982a: Debates on sport: organizational and ideological developments. *Netherlands Journal of Sociology*, 18 (1) 1982: 95–8.

—— 1982b: Conservative and progressive alternatives in the organization of sport. *International Social Science Journal*, 34 (2): 197–208.

—— 1987: Elias en Sport (Review of *Quest for Excitement*). *Sociologisch Tijdschrift* 14 (2) 316–21.

Stolk, A. van and de Regt, J. 1979: Zelfaanvaarding van homoseksuelen (Self-acceptance of homosexuals). *Maandblad Geestelijke Volksgezondheid*, 34 (1): 3–17.

Stolk, A. van and Wouters, C. [1980]: Power changes and self-respect: a comparison of two cases of established-outsiders relations. *Theory, Culture and Society*, 4 (2–3) 1987: 477–88.

—— 1983: *Vrouwen in Tweestrijd (Women Torn Two Ways)*. Deventer, Van Loghum Slaterus.

—— 1984: Die Gemütsruhe des Wohlfahrtsstaates. In P. R. Gleichmann et al. (eds), *Macht und Zivilisation: Materialien zu Norbert Elias' Zivilisationstheorie 2*. Frankfurt: Suhrkamp: 242–60.

Stone, J. and Mennell, S. J. (eds) 1980: *Alexis de Tocqueville on Democracy, Revolution and Society*. Chicago, University of Chicago Press.

Stone, Lawrence 1979: The revival of narrative. *Past and Present*, 85: 3–24.

—— 1983: Interpersonal violence in English society, 1300–1980. *Past and Present*, 101: 22–33.

Suttles, Gerald 1968: *The Social Order of the Slum*. Chicago, University of Chicago Press.

Swaan, Abram de [1979]: The politics of agoraphobia. *Theory and Society*, 10 (3) 1981: 359–85.

—— 1988: *In Care of the State: The Social Dynamics of Public Health, Education and Income Maintenance in Western Europe and the United States*. Oxford, Polity Press.

—— 1985: Special issue on 'The sociology of emotions', *Symbolic Interaction* 8 (2): 161–328.

Taylor, Ian 1971: Football mad: a speculative sociology of football hooliganism. In E. G. Dunning (ed.), *The Sociology of Sport*, London, Frank Cass: 352–77.

—— 1982: On the sports violence question: soccer hooliganism revisited. In J. Hargreaves (ed.), *Sport, Culture and Ideology*. London, Routledge and Kegan Paul: 152–96.

Thoden van Velzen, H. U. E. [1982]: The Djuka civilization. *Netherlands Journal of Sociology*, 20 (2) 1984: 85–97.

Thomas, Keith 1983: *Man and the Natural World*. London, Allen Lane.

Thompson, E. P. 1978: *The Poverty of Theory and Other Essays*. London, Merlin Press.

Tocqueville, Alexis de [1835–40]: *Democracy in America*. London, Oxford University Press, 1946.

—— [1856]: *The Old Regime and the French Revolution*. Garden City, NY, Doubleday, 1955.

Tönnies, Ferdinand 1887: *Fundamental Concepts of Sociology (Gemeinschaft und Gesellschaft)*. London, Routledge and Kegan Paul.

Veblen, Thorstein 1899: *The Theory of the Leisure Class*. New York, Macmillan.

Wallerstein, Immanuel 1974, 1980: *The Modern World-System*, vols I and II. New York, Academic Press.

Watson, James B. 1968: *The Double Helix*. New York, Athenaeum.

Weber, Alfred 1935: *Kulturgeschichte als Kultursoziologie*. Leiden, Sijthoff.

Weber, Eugen 1976: *Peasants into Frenchmen: The Modernization of Rural France, 1870–1914*. Stanford, Stanford University Press.

Weber, Max [1904–5]: *The Protestant Ethic and the Spirit of Capitalism*. London, Allen and Unwin, 1930.

—— [1919a]: Science as a vocation. In H. H. Gerth and C. W. Mills (eds), *From Max Weber*, New York, Oxford University Press, 1946: 129–56.

—— [1919b]: Politics as a Vocation. In H. H. Gerth and C. W. Mills (eds), *From Max Weber*, New York, Oxford University Press, 1946: 77–128.

—— [1922a]: *Economy and Society*. 2 vols, Berkeley, University of California Press, 1978.

—— [1922b]: *Max Weber on the Methodology of the Social Sciences*. Glencoe, Free Press, 1949.

White, Leslie A. 1959: *The Evolution of Culture*. New York, McGraw Hill.

Whitehead, Alfred North 1926: *Science and the Modern World*. Cambridge, Cambridge University Press.

Whorf, Benjamin Lee 1956: *Language, Thought and Reality*. Cambridge, MA: MIT Press.

Wickham, Chris 1984: The other transition: from the ancient world to feudalism. *Past and Present*, 103: 3–36.

Williams, J., Dunning, E. G. and Murphy, P. 1984: *Hooligans Abroad: The Behaviour and Control of English Fans in Continental Europe*. London, Routledge and Kegan Paul.

Williams, Raymond 1958: *Culture and Society 1780–1950*. London, Chatto and Windus.

Wilson, Bryan 1977: A tribute to Elias. *New Society*, 7 July: 15–16.

Wilson, Edward O. 1975: *Sociobiology*. Cambridge, MA, Harvard University Press.

Wilterdink, Nico [1982]: Die Zivilisationstheorie im Kreuzfeuer der Diskussion: Ein Bericht vom Kongress über Zivilisationsprozesse in Amsterdam. In P. R. Gleichmann et al. (eds), *Macht und Zivilisation: Materialien zu Norbert Elias' Zivilisationstheorie 2*. Frankfurt, Suhrkamp: 280–304,

Wirth, Lewis 1938: Urbanism as a way of life. *American Journal of Sociology*, 44 (1): 1–24.

Wittfogel, Karl A. 1957: *Oriental Despotism: A Comparative Study of Total Power*. New Haven, Yale University Press.

Wittgenstein, Ludwig 1958: *The Blue and Brown Books*. Oxford, Basil Blackwell.

Wolandt, Gerd 1977: Norbert Elias und Richard Hönigswald. In P. R. Gleichmann et al. (eds), *Human Figurations: Essays for Norbert Elias*. Amsterdam, Stichting Amsterdams Sociologisch Tijdschrift: 127–32.

Wolf, Eric R. 1977: Encounter with Norbert Elias. In P. R. Gleichmann et al. (eds), *Human Figurations: Essays for Norbert Elias*. Amsterdam: Stichting Amsterdams Sociologisch Tijdschrift: 28–35.

Wouters, Cas 1970: Over enkele aspekten van ontwikkelingen in de betrekkingen tussen mannen en vrouwen, ouders en kinderen, volwassenen en jongeren: een voorstudie (On certain aspects of developments in the relations between men and women, parents and children, adults and young people: a preliminary study). Doctoraalskriptie, University of Amsterdam (unpublished).

—— 1972: On youth and student protest. *Transactions of the Seventh World Congress of Sociology, Varna, 1970*, vol. III, Sofia, ISA: 197–205.

—— 1976: Is het civilisatieproces van richting veranderd? (Is the civilizing process changing direction?) *Amsterdams Sociologisch Tijdschrift*, 3 (3): 336–7.

—— 1977: Informalization and the civilizing process. P. R. Gleichmann et al. (eds), *Human Figurations: Essays for Norbert Elias*, Amsterdam, Stichting Amsterdams Sociologisch Tijdschrift: 437–53.

—— 1979: Onderhandelen met De Swaan (Negotiating with de Swaan). *De Gids*, 142 (8): 510–21.

—— 1986: Formalization and informalization: changing tension balances in civilizing Processes. *Theory, Culture and Society* 3 (2) 1986: 1–18.

—— 1987: Developments in behavioural codes between the sexes: formalization of informalization in the Netherlands, 1930–85. *Theory, Culture and Society*, 4 (2–3): 405–27.

—— 1988: Flight attendants and the sociology of emotions: Hochschild's *Managed Heart. Theory, Culture and Society* (forthcoming).

Wouters, C. and ten Kroode, H. 1980: Informalisering in het rouwen en in de omgang met doden op de snijzaal (Informalization in mourning and in dealing with the dead in the dissecting room). *De Gids* 143 (7): 481–96.

Young, M. and Willmott, P. 1957: *Family and Kinship in East London*. London, Routledge and Kegan Paul.

—— 1973: *The Symmetrical Family*. London, Routledge and Kegan Paul.

Index